T0270962

The Poverty of Strategy

At least since the ancient Greeks, strategists have sought to direct and distinguish organized activity through planned, rational decision-making, through the imaginative creation of vision, or through the assertion of will. In all cases, argue Holt and Zundel, strategy impoverishes, not because it only ever offers limited view of organized life, but because it is dedicated to concealing these limits behind grand generalities. The situation is exacerbated when machines and algorithms, not humans, organize. Holt and Zundel draw on philosophy, literature, media theory, art, mathematics, computing and military thinking in an attempt to rescue strategy by isolating what, they argue, remains its essence: strategy is a continual organizational struggle towards authenticity. This, too, is a condition of poverty, but one that sets in place an unhomely condition of questionability as opposed to one of distinctive settlement. It is, argue Holt and Zundel, the sole gift of strategy to thoughtfully refuse rather than impose, organizational imperatives.

Robin Holt is Professor of Strategy and Aesthetics at the University of Bristol Business School.

Mike Zundel is Professor in Organization Studies at the University of Liverpool Management School.

The Poverty of Strategy

Organization in the Shadows of Technology

Robin Holt

University of Bristol Business School

Mike Zundel

University of Liverpool Management School

CAMBRIDGE
UNIVERSITY PRESS

Shaftesbury Road, Cambridge CB2 8EA, United Kingdom

One Liberty Plaza, 20th Floor, New York, NY 10006, USA

477 Williamstown Road, Port Melbourne, VIC 3207, Australia

314–321, 3rd Floor, Plot 3, Splendor Forum, Jasola District Centre,
New Delhi – 110025, India

103 Penang Road, #05–06/07, Visioncrest Commercial, Singapore 238467

Cambridge University Press is part of Cambridge University Press & Assessment,
a department of the University of Cambridge.

We share the University's mission to contribute to society through the pursuit of
education, learning and research at the highest international levels of excellence.

www.cambridge.org
Information on this title: www.cambridge.org/9781107150324

DOI: 10.1017/9781316577141

First published 2023

A catalogue record for this publication is available from the British Library.

Library of Congress Cataloging-in-Publication Data
Names: Holt, Robin, 1966– author. | Zundel, Mike, 1974– author.
Title: The poverty of strategy : organization in the shadows of technology /
Robin Holt, Copenhagen Business School, Mike Zundel, University of Liverpool.
Description: Cambridge, United Kingdom ; New York, NY : Cambridge University
Press, 2023. | Includes bibliographical references and index.
Identifiers: LCCN 2022032027 | ISBN 9781107150324 (hardback) |
ISBN 9781316577141 (ebook)
Subjects: LCSH: Strategic planning. | Organizational sociology. |
Authenticity (Philosophy) – Social aspects.
Classification: LCC HD30.28 .H6734 2023 | DDC 658.4/012–dc23/eng/20221125
LC record available at https://lccn.loc.gov/2022032027

ISBN 978-1-107-15032-4 Hardback
ISBN 978-1-316-60471-7 Paperback

For Jeni – MZ
For Iris and Peter – RH

Man hath weav'd out a net, and this net throwne
Upon the Heavens, and now they are his owne.
Loth to goe up the hill, or labour thus
To goe to heaven, we make heaven come to us.
We spur, we reine the starres, and in their race
They're diversly content t'obey our pace.
But keepes the earth her round proportion still?

—John Donne[1]

That fall, all that the Mission talked about was control: arms control, information control, resources control, psycho-political control, population control, control of the almost supernatural inflation, control of terrain through the Strategy of the Periphery. But when the talk had passed, the only thing left standing up that looked true was your sense of how out of control things really were. Year after year, season after season, wet and dry, using up options faster than rounds on a machine gun belt, we called it right and righteous, viable and even almost won, and it still only went on the way it went on.

—Michael Herr[2]

[1] An Anatomy of the World. In *The Poems of John Donne*. Edited by Herbert Grierson. Oxford: Clarendon Press, 1912, 280.
[2] *Dispatches*. New York: Vintage Books, 1977, 47.

Contents

vii

Part III   The Open

Figures

Table

Acknowledgements

Thinking through the condition of poverty has been immeasurably enriched by provocation and guidance from our friends and colleagues at our workplaces and conferences during the writing of the book. Between us, we have benefitted from institutional support from the Centre for Digital Cultures at Leuphana University Lüneburg, the Swedish Collegium for Advanced Study at Uppsala University, the Japan Society for the Promotion of Science and the Otto Mønsted Foundation at Copenhagen Business School. In particular, we have received invitations to talk and study, and critical advice from: Armin Beverungen, Timon Beyes, Norah Campbell, Rasha Goumaa, Matthew Hancocks, Christian Garmann Johnsen, Peter Lenney, Renate Meyer, Claus Pias, Paul Spee, Annika Skoglund, Morten Thaning, Hari Tsoukas and Yutaka Yamauchi. We were extremely happy that Simon Denny allowed us to use the iconic image of the worker cage for the cover. Finally, we must thank everyone at Cambridge University Press for guiding us through the often delicate demands of getting the book into print.

Introduction: Strategy as the Basic Question of Organization?

The practice of strategy has been animated by a question of correlation: how to organize the world into conforming (and hence comforting) forms and rhythms through the continual application of human design. John Donne equates such design to the putting out of nets. Unwilling to travel and roam in the open heavens, humans have, instead, sought to snare the great reaches of the unknown in nets of knowledge and to haul things in, to the point where everything of the world comes ready made by human proportion. Occurrence abides by human time scales and belongs to human spaces. Donne's metaphor of a net is apt, conveying a scene of order and entrapment in which things are taken out of their raw, natural and sometimes awe inducing element and then curtailed in holding patterns, there to await their fate as things to be used by the human, living, spider-like, at the centre. Leonardo da Vinci depicts this centrality as Vitruvian Man (see Figure 0.1) using its inventiveness – especially mathematics and geometry – to reveal the harmony, perspective and beauty by which the cosmos coheres as a meaningful unity.

Keeping to the centre of things does not come easily. To cast nets demands self-control, it is an effort of will epitomized in Donne's rich monosyllable 'spur'. It is far from fatalist, far from meandering speculation, and far from fortuity. It is directed, urgent and feeds off two related forms of knowledge: habituated, practical action and theoretical understanding. The former is a sedimented awareness of how things can be made to work in accord with the agreed interests not just of the species, but of a particular subset happening to enjoy a temporary ascendancy. The latter is enquiry into the patterns of occurrence by which all life is being ordered. Together they filter and distinguish occurrence in basic temporal and spatial order: 'this', then 'that', or 'this', not 'that'. Elaborating on these basic patterns, knowledge becomes a synonym for certainty and the world becomes a synonym for its interest-bearing organization, and nothing more.

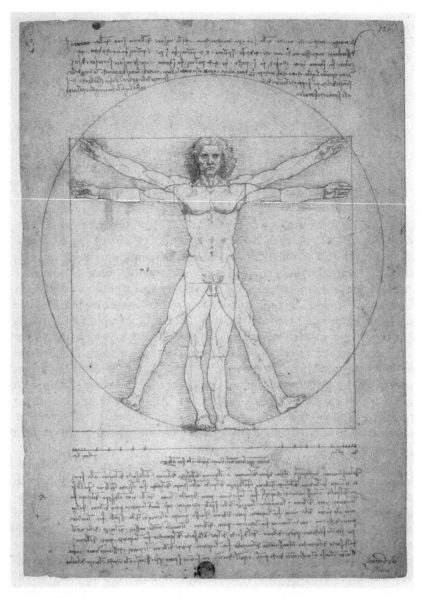

Figure 0.1 Leonardo da Vinci, Vitruvian Man, c. 1487. Wikimedia commons

When Donne was writing *An Anatomy of the World*, this human ambition seemed reasonable, exciting even. Now though, the question arises whether the effort has been worth it. Donne himself was equivocal, ending his observation with an extending question: amid all this casting of nets, can the world keep its own form, indeed does it have any form beyond the one imposed on it from within the 'reigning' mind, and is form itself nothing more than a human convention? These are important questions because there is something mechanical and thoughtless about this casting of nets to rein things in (including reigning over other human beings), and one might ask whether there is another way of organizing, another way of relating to things than attempting to consign the world to the subaltern role of a mute resource being set aside to service a specific set of human interests. Moreover, despite (or even because of) all this knowledgeable reining in and the impressive organizational edifices that have emerged from the effort, the world still seems to slip away, sometimes imperceptibly and slyly, sometimes indifferently, and at other times in lurching, barbaric shocks.

The question for strategists is whether the desired for correlation between the world and human design is even possible? Why not let strategy idle a while, barely ticking over, or just turn it off and enjoin fate? One might respond that to do so would be to relinquish what it is that makes human life distinct: it is life being organized according to a conscious, if sometimes habituated, practical direction and purpose. It is, though, an increasingly dubious response. Dubious because, as Michael Herr mordantly notes, it is largely talk: the detailed and ambitious talk of control, which carries on in its right and righteous way, regardless of events on the rough ground of everyday experience. It is the smoothing talk transcribed into maps and diagrams drawn up as isolating summaries of the past and assertive projections of the future. It is talk of world-class distinction and distinctiveness tainted by unreal ambition. Irrespective of its authority and panache, the world still refuses such strategy talk. The strategic organization of territorial, institutional and market positions has become ever more fleeting and insubstantial and their occupation ever more questionable; and the reputations and commitments by which organizations claim themselves both distinct and admirable have become ever more precarious. And, for the strategists performing strategy, the hierarchies of commitments and entitlements emerging from seasoned reasoning and practical self-control are no longer offering the source of security and confidence they maybe once did when strategy, or at least corporate strategy, was maturing after its first flush. Other more emotional, emergent, ad-hoc and partial ways of apprehending and enlisting the world are enjoying strategic ascendency: rules of thumb, micro incursions, tactical withdrawals, indirectness, avoidance, partial organization, redundancy or just plain smash and grab. There is now no obvious priority for the considered, iterative, means-end rationality by which practical and theoretical knowledge claimed their pre-eminence in strategy practice. Relatedly, it appears as if the human is losing its once unassailable (if self-appointed) position at the centre of things. It is forging alliances with machinery, notably electronic computing, at a dizzying and bewildering pace, to the point where strategists are increasingly being side-lined by the machinery designed to aid their decision making. The strategists may still sit in the boardroom chair, but only because machines are tireless, and they need no seats. And beyond the technology itself, if such a beyond is now even imaginable, disequilibria are appearing that gainsay the conceits of organization. These imbalances and perturbations are being configured as 'grand challenges', but this is old language trying to wrestle with new disturbances to which there are no edges, no predictability, no preferable alternatives, no overviews. The fires, floods, migrations, market collapses, nervous disorders, computer and biological viruses and factual disorders can spring up anywhere and spread everywhere: they no longer carry the character of an isolated problem to which recovering enquiry can be devoted.

It is within such a condition that we consider the prospects for strategy. We persist throughout in our claim that in asking: 'Who am I?', strategy poses the most basic and yet difficult question for an organization, one which is, at the same time, its most important one. Strategy opens the enquiry into the question and hence questionability of organizational form. Asking who or what one 'is' entails an enquiry into how one presents oneself, both to oneself and to others. It is only in becoming conscious of self-presentation that one can take an active role in the development of the self, a process giving rise to reflection on aims, needs and intentional force, and to what *I am* or *it is* in relation to what *I am not* or *it is not*. Engaging in strategy – that is, asking the question 'What is it, that is existing?' – requires the organizational self to experience itself as both reflecting on itself, and as being reflected upon. In both humans and organizations alike, this mirror play induces a pause whilst this 'doubling' attempts to coincide and cohere. The enquiry cannot yield a definite or settling answer; rather it institutes a relational struggle between the self that 'is' and the self that sees itself 'being' what it is; between the self's own conception of itself and how others see it; and between the self's sense of memorized past and anticipated future, all of which are being brought together in multiple correlations, again and again.

In aligning strategy with this basic enquiry into existence we are both prompted by, and yet run somewhat askance from, much of the literature and thinking on strategic practice.[1] Indeed, so much of strategic practice and thinking about strategy, at least as it appears to us, has been about finding moments and places of certainty from which the difficult questions of existence abate. As a search for repose, strategy has been engaged in busying questions of organizational settlement. How to produce, align, occupy, exit, corral, dispense and distribute in ways that

---

[1] Though often concealed, the question of organizational form is germane to much of the literature on 'strategic management'. Once called 'business policy', strategic management conceptualizes the work of managers in relation to an enterprise in its totality (Dan Schendel and Kenneth Hatten Business policy or strategic management: A broader view for an emerging discipline. *Academy of Management Proceedings*, 2017, November). Strategic management expanded the scope of managerial decision making to include environmental analysis (in particular, how market structures determine firm performance) and the formulation, evaluation, implementation and control of organizational direction or evolution. In studying this activity, academic scholarship has ranged from agency and transaction cost theories to studies of routines, resources, capabilities and firm relations across boundaries, and much more. Strategic management has also become a lucrative hunting ground for consultancies (Paul L. Drnevich1, Joseph T. Mahoney and Dan Schendel Has strategic management research lost its way? *Strategic Management Review*, 2020, 1: 35–73); and a corporate label justifying exalted hierarchical positions and matching salaries (e.g., David Knights and Glenn Morgan Corporate strategy, organizations and subjectivity: A critique. *Organization Studies*, 1991, 12(2): 251–73), and with so much going on, recurrent questions occur concerning the possible integration of strategic management into a specific 'paradigm', research programme, or even dedicated sets of concern. Here, some detect a danger of 'anything goes' fragmentation (e.g., Rudolphe Durand, Robert Grant and Tammy Madsen The expanding domain of strategic management research and the quest for integration. *Strategic Management Journal*, 2017, 38: 4–19). For others, strategic management has never been about a unified practice, but an attempt to provide practical, interdisciplinary answers for foundational problems, aimed at aiding the effectiveness and efficiency of organizations (e.g., Richard P. Rumelt, Dan Schendel and David J. Teece. *Fundamental Issues in Strategy: A Research Agenda*. Boston, MA: Harvard Business School Press, 1994). Returning to its origins we find strategy scholars concerend with more 'canonical' problems, often expressed in form of simple, clear and profound questions about organizational form. For example, Ronald Coase asked why firms exist; Alfred D. Chandler asked what comes first, strategy or structure; Edith Penrose posed the question of why firms stop growing; Oliver Williamson probed the challenges of vertical integration; and Igor Ansoff asked what firm patterns of behaviour are suited to turbulent environments and what practically useful sets of concepts and procedures a manager can use to manage (Michael J. Leiblein and Jeffrey J. Reuer Foundations and futures of strategic management. *Strategic Management Review*, 2020, 1 (1): 1–33; Paul L. Drnevich, Joseph T. Mahoney and Dan Schendel Has strategic management research lost its way?; David Knights and Glenn Morgan Corporate strategy). Since then, however, the bulk of strategic management publications has been concerned with increasingly tightly defined questions and carefully delineated theoretical approaches, often drawing on advanced mathematical models, and so become subject to criticism not just for losing the practical focus of early strategic management approaches but the concern for fundamental issues about organizational form that drove the early and seminal contributions to the field (Dan Schendel Introduction to the special issue – 'Strategy: Search for New Paradigms' *Strategic Management Journal*, 1994, 15(Summer): 1–4). It is the concern for the nature of organizational form that we seek to advance in this book, and we do so not in relation to commerce alone, but to ethics and aesthetics, to politics, international relations and policy, and above all, to the mediation of technology.

afford the organization a firm sense of historical and environmental settlement. Entangled in these operational questions of resource allocation and logistics, and with the management of daily affairs, the basic question of existence – of 'Who?' or 'What?' – has given way to an overriding concern with measured correlation. Academics speak of 'institutionalization' to explain why so many organizations align in endless cycles of comparing, imitating, competing, innovating, divesting or expanding, followed by more comparing, imitating, competing. There is neither the reason nor respite for the pause through which the questions 'Who am I?' or 'What is it?' can arise.

If they arise at all, they do so as a negative formulation through experiences of alienation, estrangement and boredom in the context of 'being organized'. And with the apparent demise of the unity called 'the organization' whose boundaries are being loosened by the technological encroachment of global logistics and information networks, this negativity has persisted, because organization still persists, only now more as a process, and with this restless machination has come a precariousness to human settlement. Questions of existence arise as an oblivion of being (*Seinsvergessenheit*), expressed by the insecurity, bemusement and impotence felt when encountering technologies whose own form of life is both ever present and yet utterly foreign to human 'users'.

In this book we argue for the explicit restoration of the basic question regarding strategy: how does organization realize form distinct from the forces continually shaping it? We do so not in opposition to technology, but in thinking from within its shadows. The shadows of technology are not just cast by large industrial-military complexes (and the ruins created by their inevitable transformation) but the algorithmic apparatuses that follow, mimic and ultimately reproduce human activities in their own form by automatically receiving, storing and processing the vast sums of data that structure and direct nearly all decision-making processes. Once artificial intelligence, machine learning and robotics have come to supplement, supplant and structure human thought and action it is not just that the future being promised by technology has arrived, but that all possible futures have, now, already been organized. Predictive algorithms calculate insurance premiums, stock market interactions, battle movements, consumer behaviour, or innovation patterns; and social media sites vacuum user data, compiling these into commercially relevant recommender systems telling us where to travel, what to buy, which product to invest in, or which customer segment to target. More subtly even, clicks, glances, gestures, steps, access events and all manner of micro engagements now augment human cognition with real-time calculations that seamlessly map, calculate, store, and retrieve information at speeds and volumes far above or below perceptive thresholds. What goes on in these vast networked circuits is largely only accessible through interfaces generating pre-structured user menus made approachable by often quaint skeuomorphic symbols, comforting us with reminders of a now-lost world, and projecting information in a way that humans can read and understand; but which in no way re-present any of the machine's workings. Even experts cannot know what machine learning algorithms do once they are set loose, and for most others, including those of us working in and charged with the running of organizations, a profound process of replacement is underway in which the coordinates of the human world (maps, postcodes and streets, product names, histories, emotions) are being turned into coordinates that can be read and calculated by machines (GPS locations and continuous tracking, barcodes, RFID tags, social media 'likes' and so on).

In its traditional guise strategy cannot survive in such a technological order. Organizational questions of alignment and settlement will be far more easily and competently posed and answered by machines. But strategy as we try and understand it, that is asking the questions 'Who am I?' and 'What is it?' both individually and organizationally, still offers possibility. It is to the exploration of these questions of self-knowing that our book is devoted. We elaborate what we sense is the grounding importance of strategy as an organizational practice: enacting the struggle to see outside the measured orbits by which organizational understanding is habitually and theoretically confined to a representation.

Following the introduction, we split the book into three parts. Part I opens up to the concept of authenticity and how, at least in ancient Greece, questions of self-development were intimate with an idea of strategy. Part II covers what we call the three epochs of strategy, each detailing a distinct quality in the way humans attempted to know about and control the world through the creation of organizational forms. Each epoch presents humans in an ever more impoverished state in their relations to the world (or earth). Part III picks up the pieces, attempting to find possibility in such poverty.

Part I

Chapter 1 covers the raising of consciousness and conscience and the interplay of authenticity and estrangement through a reading of Hannah Arendt, whose work we have found a profound inspiration throughout the book, notably her re-imagining of the ancient Greek city state of Athens and the *polis* as its political forum. The *polis* is an idealized space in whose relational confines an organized condition of authenticity can appear. It is a space to which those responsible for martial and administrative leadership of the city, the *strategoi*, belong, but over which they have no authority. Separated from the household (*oikos*, the root term for economics), the *polis* is not primarily concerned with biological necessity, a condition Arendt associates with the labour of sustaining the metabolic persistence of life. Nor is it primarily a matter of *work*, of making and fabricating functional, symbolic and institutional things that last, such as temples, or laws, and that in return let the makers and fabricators 'live on' in reflection of the things they have produced. The *polis* is very specifically dedicated to the common creation of opinions. It is a place of open questions – 'What if's'? and 'So what's?' – informed solely by a concern for the city itself, as opposed to a specific set of interests. Drawing from the structure of the *polis*, we argue in this chapter for the intimacy between strategy and authenticity, one in which the concerns of both labour and work are supplanted by those of action, which for Arendt is characterized by the continual and open-ended generation of new beginnings.

Chapter 2 turns to the role of language in the context of strategy, specifically investigating how rhetoric and persuasion can open and close spaces for the airing of opinions freely amongst speakers. It is in creating and expressing opinion (and not truth) in the *polis* – the space of appearances – that the question of who one is receives its full disclosure. We then turn to the appearance of strategy in ancient Greece, first in the figure of Pericles, then Alcibiades and in particular the latter's skilful performances in the *polis*, and a gifted if contested career blighted, we suggest, by a failure to apprehend the distinction between the *polis* (rhetoric) and *oikos* (sophistry and instrumentality). The failure of Alcibiades also hints at some of the difficulties of language as the means of self-disclosure and so also for Arendt's idealized association of action with talk, for it is in Alcibiades' struggle as a *strategos* that opinion becomes twisted into event: things get done, even if the action is consumed by failure and ruin. The case of Alcibiades takes us from talk to the body, and back to the *polis* in which the everyday is suspended so that action, freed from instrumentality, can occur and recur, each time alive and enlivening. The *polis*, we argue, represents an organizational condition of estrangement that appears far away from the means-ends concerns of much that goes by the name of strategy but which, we conjecture, grounds self-awareness.

Chapter 3 plays out a philosophical engagement with organization and technology following Martin Heidegger's well-known association of industrialization with technological enframing in which the question of self-knowing had been thoroughly and perhaps irredeemably concealed.

Were it possible to ask such a question, then Heidegger identifies an essential un-at-homeness to the being (*Dasein*) able to question its condition of being, its 'thereness', thereby setting in play an uncanny condition of being able, in principle (*qua* being human), to dis-conceal one's essence, and yet continually falling short of ever doing so. It is this uneasy revealing that sets the scene for our investigation of the self in its environment. Borrowing from the biologist von Uexküll, Heidegger's analysis of worldlessness, poverty in world, and world-making structures leads to his discovery of the existential difficulties of breaking out of instrumentality and environmental captivation into an open condition in which being itself can be glimpsed. In the light of this estrangement, we then look back to the *polis* and argue its being akin to a clearing in which the continual conflict between the concealed and dis-concealed finds an organizational expression. From this movement springs the possibility of new beginnings. Heidegger talks of the *polos*, meaning a swirl or the turning things from which one springs again and again (*Ur-sprung*), a constancy of motion that continually presences and absences. It is here, we conjecture, that strategy might start to renew itself. But danger looms in Heidegger's all too ready association of industrialization and mass captivation (as though only he, and spiritually attuned folk such as himself, have spotted the greatest danger of globalized capitalism). It is because of his essentialized association of technology, industrialization and the concealing of being that Heidegger equates the possibility of its being unconcealed with a political movement that pushes back at the global order, and restores a more archaic, human-centred version. The profound and horrific irony was that it was in totalitarian National Socialism that he found such a movement, an enduring affiliation that has been unmoored in detail in his *Black Notebooks*.

Part II

Chapters 4, 5 and 6 build on the grounding discussions in Part I to develop a threefold epochal reading of technology (as *technē*, technology and technogenesis) and we elaborate on the implications of each for the possibility of understanding strategy as self-knowing. We remain wary of epochal thinking and the tendency to find in the present imminent signs of a tipping over, a watershed, as if to monumentalize what is otherwise momentary, and to discount what has gone as somehow no longer worthy of notice. The epochs are our way of organizing our understanding of the intensity of technological mediation in strategic practice: one epoch does not give way to the next so much as constitute a twist of the enframing. Chapter 4 presents the epoch of *technē*, which is marked by the play of the fickleness of nature, luck (*tuchē*) and the fragility of early human stratagems. *Technē* is both a means of controlling the world, as well as one of violence. Indicated by humble and pre-scientific inventions such as the almanack, *technē* allows little gains to be wrested from an otherwise unforgiving surrounding by knowing when to sow or harvest in accordance with the alignment of experiential, mythical and cosmological clues. The epoch of *technē* is characterized by an intimacy between humans and their surroundings, the term planning itself finding its roots in the way in which seedlings are pushed into the ground by a farmer's foot. But there is also violence; both imposed on the human body, whose shape is bent and twisted, ground down and severed by the acts of labour and the growing numbers of devices that extend human reach; as well as upon nature, which becomes a place in need of taming and cultivating; cutting, splicing, ploughing, killing and using.

Chapter 5 details the emergence of machinery and organizational order through industrialization. No longer mere prostheses that allow humans to reach further, lift higher, hit harder or handle materials that would slice or burn skin, machine complexes and industrial installations supersede the human body's provision of labour force by conjuring immeasurable forces from nature itself. Heidegger's notion of the *Gestell* (enframing) characterizes these changes in terms of a gradual displacement of the human. No longer in control (or even in the picture), existence becomes wrapped up in continuously unfolding cycles of unlocking new resources, extracting, storing, distributing and switching over, in which whatever is made is always and only 'there' in potential service to what is to come: everything is a means for further progress, and progress is nothing more than the tightening and quickening of cycles of unlocking, extracting, storing, distributing and switching over. What is lost in this technological condition is the intimacy of the human being with their world; the care and concern that might be had for things understood as things in and of themselves, not merely input or output variables (and this includes fellow humans and the self). What is being lost is also a sense of control and oversight. When coupled, in this loss of status as a thing in itself and in this loss of influence over life, much is done but all ends disappear. Assembly lines hum, factories churn out products, organizations clash, humans are left to maintain and occasionally repair the assemblages of production and consume, but nothing endures. The questions 'Who am I?' or 'What is it?' lose their meaning when all that matters is the next deadline, update, investment opportunity, or new target, repeated; endlessly and nihilistically.

Chapter 6 reaches the end of our foray into Heidegger's analysis of technology. The chapter identifies a cybernetic fantasy of control in the ghost-written accounts of Sloan's strategic success at General Motors, a fantasy laid bare by an increasing inability to technological systems; and where humans are not even the ordinary fabricators anymore, the earth merely becomes a globe, that is gridded and dug over. The invention of the radio, which for Heidegger heralded an epoch of the nearness of the distant and the Gigantic, soon eclipsed any real nearness to events. The radio was itself soon eclipsed by technologies that rather than communicate things were just communications. With this transformation things and pictures and meaning and desires and ends are giving way to patterns and correlations; the cycles of the *Gestell* become one continual switching (there 'is' nothing as such to extract, unlock, store etc., save for information).

Chapter 7 begins the task of unpacking contemporary information technologies. Taking leave from Shoshana Zuboff's critique of surveillance capitalism, we suggest a further step beyond anthropocentric ideas of control. We discuss how organizational forms such as platforms and systems like Enterprise Resource Planning products, have come to 'run' organizations, but in ways that also extend, replace and veil human cognition, in often imperceptibly powerful ways. And yet, these widely connected networks, the computational apparatuses, intelligent algorithms and digital media are fundamentally indifferent to what they 'replace'. They no longer bring anything near, moreover there is no-one to whom such pictures and things can be brought. Agency, not just human agency, but all agency, is dissipated into brief small blips.

Chapter 8 broaches the understanding of communication systems and their intimacy with strategic practice. Beginning with the general (strategist) Napoleon's forms of communication-technological warfare and the subsequent reliance on innovation in communication devices, especially those of coding and decoding communications in military conflicts, we consider the workings and implications of electronic, digital computing systems for strategy. Via Alan Turing's imitation game and his universal machine, we introduce the debate on the nature of (machine) intelligence, consciousness and conscience (self-awareness).

Chapter 9 entangles strategy and cybernetics, as well as links between military funding and research development culminating in a discussion of the organizational force of neural nets as part of a programme that erases contingency and with this the increasing inability to ask strategic questions. Understanding the workings of these apparatuses has long become a matter for a limited number of experts, and even those are unable to really know how such nets compute themselves, in speeds and complexities that far outstretch human cognition. Glitches and errors, as well as idling, faulty codes, offer, we suggest, openings through which we might glimpse the nature of these new realities, yet rather than welcome, these seem to be subject to the continual attention of interface innovation and 'good' design that serve only to further veil access and awareness of the modern human's captivation in technological environments. With this slipping away of consciousness arises a poverty in a world that finally negates the possibility for conscience through self-knowing. The question of existence, and thus the capacity for strategy, have vanished; and there is no possibility of return to a pre-technological life to find a new entry point into the question of existence.

Part III

Chapter 10 offers a way through, not by opposing poverty, but reframing it, taking the metaphor of shadow as might an advocate of John Ruskin's 'Gothic': western epistemology has for far too long been interested in light, lightness, clarity, detail and transparency. What of opacity, hints, voids and niches? Being captivated by the technological environment, marks an impoverishment in world; a regress of humans from *homo faber* to *animal laborans*. But while in the epoch of *technē* the latter still could locate the self within a cosmic and divine order, all such locating is now forfeit. Our second reading of poverty, aided by Samuel Beckett's play *Krapp's Last Tape*, however, embraces the possibility of glitches, pauses, tunnels and severences that, because they lack obvious, praiseworthy organizational presence, hint at regions in which the potential for the revision of the self emerges.

Chapter 11 returns to the beginning by revising the arguments on negativity made by Adorno and Agamben, as well as George Spencer-Brown's language of distinctions and of the nothing to help formulate this sense of renewed strategic need for both in-forming and un-informing. It is not much that we offer by way of a way out, but that is the point; strategy must remain in an uneasy and slightly impoverished space if it is to survive. It is strategy from the shadows.

Part I

Authenticity

1   Strategy and the Organization of Authenticity in the *Polis*

Naming

Strategy is the collective act of interpretation by which an organization attempts to see itself, and to see itself anew, in the company of others doing likewise. These acts of interpretation use a language of named qualities and attributes. Yet to see an organization for what it is, and to name its (often idealized) qualities, is not the same thing. As the poet Paul Valéry remarks, the act of seeing is more than the act of naming. Indeed, to see often means to forget the name of what is being seen, and instead to study the acts of naming by which seen things are being so readily categorized. Seeing is both to see things as they are being named in language, and to see that to be named is to conform to the already established grammatical expectations that come with carrying a name, it is to see that the 'self' being presented already conforms to the agreed criteria for what counts as 'being an organization'.

Within strategic practice it is the first – the naming aspect – and not the second seeing aspect that dominates. The naming aspect is an administrative, martial or managerial concern with how an organization might justifiably present itself as acting in ways that make it 'excellent' or 'forceful' or 'agile' or 'resilient' or 'caring', and with how, over time, it gathers to itself a sense of self in which these qualities sediment in, and alternate between, memories and expectations. As a form of self-presentation, it is far from being static. Under its naming aspect, strategy confers an explicit, temporal framing upon an organizational form: its distinction is secured by placing its 'being present' between historical roots and future ambition. Strategy configures the organization in a present that reaches back in time to claim the foundational legitimacy of an origin, or the authority of generational struggles and sacrifices and successes. It also stretches forwards towards a future designed and imagined in such a way that it progresses from within the present as a probability, whilst, at the same time, always finding the present from which it is born somehow inadequate and in need of improvement. In this way the naming aspect is animated by a progressive movement, one which borrows from the Christians an eschatology of redemption, from ancient Greece a motive power of inner purpose (*telos*) along with the geometry of the point in time dividing before and after, and from the various modes of modern scientific objectivity the methodological structure of controlled synthesis.

Then there is Valéry's seeing aspect: not the operation of naming attributes, but the struggle to investigate the demand or desire to name things in the first place; less the language of identifying and fixing than its grammar. To sense this seeing aspect is an experience of language itself, of the very real nature of how language signifies, how it operates, and how, through signification, it structures experience in the most basic of ways. It is to extending the strategic task from naming to seeing that we believe we reach the basic question concerning strategy.

To broach both naming and seeing is to be aware of how all interpretations of what an organization is involve both the specific, performative use of words to orient experience (semantic acts) and acts of grammatical correspondence constituted as a purely formal association (semiotics). The latter are typically untroubled operations in ordinary language use; to recognize the self-referential act of naming enacted in the word 'we', for example. Yet in strategic practice this use becomes a struggle because it entails the question of how and why it is in language that something comes to name itself as 'we'. It is a question that can only arise in those who have already been constituted in language as a subject, as a 'we', and who already have a history of what it is to be a collective self and associate this with carrying names. To bring this naming into questionability is to see, which is like beginning *again*.

Naming finds the language user learning the collective arrangements by which grammar works and becoming habituated in a semantic practice of expressive utterance that fosters the practical and normative entitlements and commitments by which occurrence comes to have significance and meaning (it is narrated as history). Seeing considers and questions these arrangements. This occurs in language still, but in addition to semantic operations the naturally appearing semiotic associations (such as names) also come into view. The semantic involves understanding: the perception of meaning in an utterance, whereas the semiotic involves recognition: the perception of a sign that has appeared previously. In bringing both understanding and recognition into view strategy can deliberately and carefully question what it is that has been accepted as already understood. Here the naturally occurring semiotic force of language (the literal, natural fact that we, like all animals, speak) becomes apparent, and the strategist is left in what Giorgio Agamben calls the 'moat' between the semantic and semiotic (because the questioning can only occur against the backdrop of semantically acquired meanings). The stretch between naming and seeing does not dispense with or avoid names (humans cannot 'will' themselves to be outside history and into a purely naturalistic state of semiotic language), but brings names (and so naming itself) into questionability. In strategic terms, it is the provision of organizational space to consider, for example, why it is that an organization should gather under sobriquets and idealized characteristics such as 'class leading', 'visionary' or 'future proofed'. The strategist exists not just to name the organization, but also to consider these names anew, which in turn is to question how, in the use of such characteristics, understanding so readily slips into recognition.[1]

In considering what is named and why, and in considering how naming itself takes place, and why, the organizational condition being conferred by strategic practice is close to what, in relation to the human subject, is 'named' authenticity. To be authentic is not to conform with, and so confirm, a stable, grounding essence (which would be to define oneself by a name alone) but to see how a name has arisen, and in doing so leave oneself exposed to the possibility of other names, and other processes of naming. In human individuals it is a state of enlarged self-awareness that arises when a person is both aware of the names by which they are positioned within human practices and of experiencing itself outside of any specific practice, the latter being somewhat clumsily expressed in the grammar of the 'I'. Authenticity emerges when these two conscious states, in their intimate distinctiveness, speak with the same voice.[2] It is what Hannah Arendt calls 'the two in one of the soundless dialogue' with oneself. The dialogue is an act of thought that admits and then refuses the semantic discourses by which the life into which human beings find themselves thrown has been arranged, and which so often gives way to forms of uncritical, semiotic recognition. In the language of strategy it is not only to semantically re-interpret what it means for an organization to progress, grow or succeed, but to also question why phenomena like growth or success collapse into semiotic signs. More often than not, they are just acknowledged as desirable names. The refusal comes not in opposing one name with

---

[1] Giorgio Agamben *Infancy and History: The Destruction of Experience*. Translated by Liz Heron. London: Verso, 2007. Agamben riffs off Benveniste's distinction between semantic and semiotic, as well as the metaphor of 'moat', which divides by also connecting them, and which conveys the sense of a floating effect on those considering what it is to belong to language in itself, as well as to its historically enabled categories of understanding. Saku Mantere offers a rare reflection on the 'discomfort' of semantics in strategy practice and the potential for inertia that comes with the definitions and labels that preoccupy (academic) strategy discourse. Saku Mantere What Is Organizational Strategy? A Language-Based View. *Journal of Management Studies*, 2013, 50(8): 1408–1437.

[2] Hannah Arendt Thinking and moral considerations: A lecture. *Social Research*, 1971, 38, 417–46. Also Hannah Arendt *The Life of the Mind*. Edited by Mary McCarthy. Indiana: Harcourt, 1971/1978, 157. It is an agreement to subject one's deeds to self-examination without the comforts of compliance to publicly available standards by which one might check the veracity or rectitude of one's assessment.

another, but in admitting and absorbing one's complicity with the burden of carrying names, one upon the other, whilst noticing that no matter how many names one carries, there is something about the self that lives beyond them, but often in shadow: even 'I' can become a form of naming.

To think with and write about the 'I' is itself a practice, one that Joan Didion remarked, wryly, in her essay 'Why I Write' (which she chose as a title because it sounded like the repetition of 'I', three times, and which she borrowed from another writer) is an imposition upon the world, a demand to be listened to, a subjugating assertion that writers, in particular, are alive to.[3] If authenticity requires a two-in-one dialogue with oneself, it is hard to avoid using the 'I', but then the 'I' has its own confining limits. Where else can one go? There are options. Here, for example, is the dying narrator of Edward St Aubyn's novel *A Clue to the Exit*:

> I felt the relief of writing a third-person narrative. It's so much more personal than first person narrative, which reveals too flagrantly the imposture of the personality it depends on.[4]

The distancing relieves the 'I' from its circularity, and forgives the peculiarly fragile nature of its essentializing, but ever so thin, form. The use of the third person upon oneself carries within it an intimacy of seeing from a distance, it is less assertive and aggressive. It is as though a small demon appears at one's shoulder, the enigmatic, invisible being that the ancient Greeks believed accompanied all living beings, and which appears as a fellow, fateful conspirator in one's life.

One's demon (*daimon*) is both an outward signature of one's genius and destiny, and a guide that can appear inwardly, as a source of advice and council by which to gain perspective on one's own thoughts, feelings and deeds. The self that is seen with, and sees through, its *daimon* is neither an 'I' substantiated by a singular set of sovereign qualities (such as reason, will or divine spirit), or by biological determinism (an instinctive will) or by historically determining forces (such as fate, dialectical spirit or community belonging). Nor is it a stack of categories found in human practices (a collection of roles and qualities) balanced on top of one another into an (often shaky and uneven) upright form. Through its *daimon* this self-spoken third person becomes an unsettled, 'moat-dweller' able to critically measure up to its own entitlements and commitments set amid many others, and yet to find there the possibility of things being otherwise. It is a self that Didion also acknowledges at the end of her essay, when she asks of herself just who this narrator is, this 'I' who knew things and who told stories but who was

---

[3] Joan Didion Why I Write. New York Times. 5th December 1976.
[4] Edward St Aubyn A Clue to the Exit. London: Picador. 15.

not at all identical to herself, who was not at all at home in her house, and yet whose voice was, when one thought about it, the reason she wrote.

In talking of strategy as authenticity we are enquiring into how to organize a state of affairs in which the third-person *daimon* of St Aubyn's narrator, and Didion's 'I' and Arendt's 'two-in-one' dialogue, can appear as, when thought about, the reason for organizational action. It is an appearance in which a community of selves who adhere in some way to a unified and named organization of entitlements and commitments do so critically. If strategy is limited to setting out a plan of action and following it, it is incomplete, indeed it is barely strategy. Strategy is asking oneself, as a collective, the occasional but necessary questions of what a name (like a quality, achievement, desire, title, vision or goal) amounts to, and how one came to carry the names one does, many of which are enlisted in the furtherance of organizational survival and flourishing.

In the case of St Aubyn's narrator, for example, under the enquiry undertaken in the company of his *daimon*, he acknowledges how utterly he is being driven by instinct, and by being bounced along by the prevailing places, practices and habits by which a ragbag of a life has been roughly assembled. Yet in the very act of considering the inevitability of being organized through these inner and outer forces, that often twist back on themselves, so the inner becomes outer and the outer inner, comes a persistent but strangely elusive sense of distinction and hence possibility. It is a 'thoughtful seeing' through which he gains a temporary perspective upon situations that then become objects, or a scene of objects, against whose hard edges he is able to repeatedly and imaginatively speculate. In Arendt's terms, he experiences the two-in-one dialogue of authenticity: his is a refusal to fall in passively with existing agreements and conventions, and, just as tellingly, a refusal to settle easily alongside the appeal of newly imagined ones. What is being forged is what Arendt calls self-presentation:

Self-presentation is distinguished from self-display by the active and conscious choice of the image shown; self-display has no choice but to show whatever properties a living being possesses. Self-presentation would not be possible without a degree of self-awareness – a capability inherent in the reflexive character of mental activities and clearly transcending mere consciousness.[5]

In self-presenting (which, given it is a critical concern with how one wishes to appear is always open to hypocrisy) St Aubyn's narrator is the object of his own questionability: he is a being who may never have sovereign control over events, or a stable, inner sense of being 'I', or the comfort of being happily known as 'this' or 'that', but who nevertheless

[5] Hannah Arendt *The Life of the Mind*, 35.

struggles continually to see himself, and so embodies the possibility of starting events anew. He is, in our view, a strategist.[6]

Authenticity, Consciousness and Conscience

Authenticity is not freedom from the constraint of organization, but a freedom to modify the forms it takes, again and again: it is expressive and, potentially, transgressive. By locating authenticity in the interrogation of situations, from within those situations, Arendt envisages an intimacy between thought and existentially modifying acts of removal (*Ausgang*) from the ordinary concourse of events: authenticity is a forming of form-to-be, a picking over of unifying names to find fragments, working not to complete the image of oneself, but to disturb its complacency. Nothing fixed is being made or recommended, and the *daimon* is always acting as a process, not as anything that has been produced, an effect. Through the gaze of its own *daimon*, the authentic self gains perspective upon, curiosity for, and awareness of the organizational entitlements and commitments, some of whose normative force and apparent practicality are so engrained and habituated they have gone unnoticed. Their disturbance can be upsetting, Friedrich Nietzsche likens the carrying around of one's *daimon* to a pain, the pain cast by a riddler – and so occasional, elusive and fleeting in its nature. The *daimon* cannot be summoned at will, and as often as its company is provocative it is also paralyzing and dangerous. As Nietzsche reads it, it is both a state of conditioned happiness (the sense of *eu-daimonia* that comes from living alongside one's fate again and again) and occult disturbance (giving voice to the demonic or unruly forces that prevail beyond the world of known forms), and which then upsets the idea that happiness alone is the goal of living.[7]

Almost seamlessly, accompanying this consciousness of self realized in two-in-one dialogue, comes a sense of conscience: a thoughtful concern for why and how the social and im/material conditioning into which we are thrown organizes situations so that they carry an enduring and exemplary resonance. Arendt calls such conscience liberating: it questions the particular values, commitments, theories and doctrines by which people have lived, and continue to live, but without invoking general standards

---

[6] The narrator realizes quickly that 'the unadorned 'I' – the pockmarked column standing alone among the ruins' is as 'flimsy a fabrication as the rest of them', provoking him to ask the question that then frames the rest of the novel: 'So what is the authentic ground of being if this footling pronoun is so inessential?'. Edward St Aubyn *A Clue to the Exit*. 4.

[7] Friedrich Nietzsche *The Gay Science*. Edited by Bernard Williams. Translated by Josefine Nauckhoff. Cambridge: Cambridge University Press, 1887/2001, §341. The *daimon* appears as that which reminds the self of having to live life again, an eternal recurrence of the same, at which prospect one wails or one feels awe.

by which to warrant such questioning.[8] As conscience it is acquired not just through experience, but learning. It requires a memory from which to recall and think anew. If the *daimon* itself produces nothing, a formless form, then once brought to bear on events in memory and learning, this self-conscious seeing becomes a conscience from which one not only senses but judges oneself. It is a condition of openness that demands a sense of direction, though, as the poet Robert Frost reminds us, the demand is vague, and replete with difficulty:

> Tis of the essence of life here,
>> Though we choose greatly, still to lack
> The lasting memory at all clear,
>> That life has for us on the wrack
> Nothing but what we somehow chose;
>> Thus are we wholly stripped of pride
> In the pain that has but one close,
>> Bearing it crushed and mystified.[9]

Authenticity then, is more than a thoughtful reflection upon situational demands of existing and emerging commitments and entitlements, it is an active finding of one's way from within them, that results in a self-forming, which is of its own form, created by the realization that the question of what one is, and being what one is, are twinned, and is nothing outside what one somehow (opaquely) makes of it, in thought, feeling and deed, without ever being fully conscious or in control of such a life-affirming power. The form created in this 'choosing' occurs in an effortful language of plural stories and symbols that transform contingency into events that can be twisted into narratives from which hang carefully wrought opinions in whose argumentative embrace we find ourselves moved and purposefully committed. It is here a sense of self is both tempered and accented, for in the conscience arising from consciousness comes the struggle to distinguish the reasons that warrant exsting entitlements and commitments from the good reasons: such a distinction rests with experience, not principle. It is a practically and normatively made distinction that entails imaginatively replaying events, considering alternatives and speculating on possible futures in relation to the struggle to make oneself understood to oneself, and to then work outwardly from within the self-constituting atmosphere of this inner dialogue.

---

[8] Hannah Arendt likens conscience to the self being able to live alongside its *daimon*: 'Its criterion for action will not be the usual rules, recognized by multitudes and agreed upon by society, but whether I shall be able to live with myself in peace when the time has come to think about my deeds and words. Conscience is the anticipation of the fellow who awaits you if and when you come home.' *The Life of the Mind*, 159.

[9] Robert Frost The trial by existence. In *Frost: Collected Poems, Prose and Plays*. New York: Library of America, 1995, 30.

Perhaps contrary to some understandings of authenticity, and certainly those associating it with an inner immunity to events, Arendt's authentic self is necessarily always incomplete, hesitant even: it is a standing towards the social and material conditions that bind each self concretely, rather than any assertive separation from them. In standing towards these conditions, it is also an openness towards them, allowing them to breach their own limits a little, even if it is just the way they are forced to declare themselves when being looked upon with concentrated curiosity. There is an 'in–out' rhythm to taking in prevailing organizational orders and then pushing back against them.

Authenticity becomes a kind of breathing – in and out – which is continual, and remains very much of this world, which is a world of metamorphosis of which one is affectively, thoughtfully and imaginatively partaking. In what emerges by way of self-understanding there is no metaphysical clarity, no firm destiny, no brilliant vision, no isolated will, only the capacity for, and organization of, a self-forming that, if properly thought through, avoids narcissism on one side, and fatalism on the other. In this, forming the 'ways' that bind a community together – the sense of place and common tradition, the pragmatically useful skills that have grown up over generations, the temperament of character, the seasonal and environmental conditions, the prevailing material and symbolic resources – are acknowledged as conditioning influences making life possible. Yet none of these can be relied on to yield a sense of an authentic self, which has to *own* these conditions (the move from consciousness to conscience), and in the process of owning up to them, encounter lines of flight, glimpses of escape, fantasies of emancipation, all of which give full voice to what Arendt felt made life not just possible, but distinct: namely the ability to inaugurate, to begin anew, beyond the names that name.

In Arendt's thinking authenticity becomes part of the tradition of writing that so delighted Ovid: imaginatively thinking oneself into the condition of others and finding distinction in refusing the boundaries that divide; like time, life is at its fullest at the very point of its dissolution. We belong to that which is not us: we run alongside otherness and in doing so we find and re-find our place in the world of things. As a condition of being it is in authenticity that the self finds its grounding and senses what it can and might be. As the organizational expression of authenticity strategy also upends rather than confirms any fixed understanding of the self.

Following Arendt, our view of strategy runs askance from most other views. If strategy is a concern with authentic self-presentation, it can never again concern itself with delineating fixed positions. It is not about attaining known aims, winning a competition, or generally organizing institutional and material forces so as to align human thought, feeling and deed with desired outcomes. Strategy is not about settlement at all, but the deranging of settlements. Without recourse to an essence, and ambitious goal, or visionary end, a self might seem bereft of reasons to act, but in recompense it can shelve its prejudices and shake off its tethers: it can realize a generality not by controlling the things so they conform to its already existing self-image, but by continually coming alongside things and morphing in response. It is through this open morphology, we argue, that selves, and the organizational forms through which they coalesce, enlarge their awareness of what is possible, always flowing through the flaws they pick up when pulling away from what is considered typical, traditional, acceptable and normal. In its intimacy with authenticity strategy, as the art of the general, becomes an aesthetic that expands upon what was hitherto closed: strategy does not cover and so command the world, it transforms it.

Refugee

Writing in the aftermath of World War II, Arendt sets her enriching struggle for authenticity against the bleak backdrop of German National Socialism. Here was a political and social system in which individual lives were rendered superfluous when set against the idea of a master race. 'Rendered' is an appropriate verb: lives are cut into parts and processed as parts of parts, to the point where unities of living experience become interchangeable units of party machinery. A caustic mixture of violence, propaganda and fear were employed to warrant and enforce the downgrading of attempts at self-expression in favour of a general ideal. Coupled to this enforced ideal was a systemic requirement to concern oneself with everyday survival. To queue for permission, wrestle with bureaucracy, follow regulations, all of which required conformity with everyday opinions and practices, and a winnowing down of human life to a point of nullity in which the urge towards modifying acts of thought was snuffed out. It was as if the distinction between semantic understanding and semiotic recognition was being eradicated: language became the raw fact of speech, signs carried meaning on the basis of repetition, not interpretation.

Arendt herself fell short of the Nazi racial ideal. Being Jewish she was forced to hide, was captured and interred, and then escaped, fleeing Germany, first to France, and then to the USA:

We lost our home, which means the familiarity of daily life. We lost our occupation, which means the confidence that we are of some use in this world. We lost our language, which means the naturalness of reactions, the simplicity of gestures, the unaffected expression of feelings.[10]

[10] Hannah Arendt We refugees. *The Menorah Journal*, 1943, 31(1): 69–77.

The trauma of this breakdown, however, brought the importance of authenticity into stark relief. As an enforced wanderer the refugee has been expelled from the trinity of state–nation–citizen: they do not lose specific rights, but law itself. In Arendt's laconic phrasing 'their plight is not that they are not equal before the law, but that no law exists for them; not that they are oppressed, but that nobody wants even to oppress them'.[11] They are naked and adrift, without the protection of an entailed inheritance. They cannot just claim to have inalienable rights. No one is listening.[12] They are stateless, lawless, homeless, indeed so stripped bare of communal texture as to have no individuating distinction. Yet it is precisely at that moment that they become distinct:

The paradox involved in the loss of human rights is that such loss coincides with the instant when a person becomes a human being in general – without a profession, without a citizenship, without an opinion, without a deed by which to identify and specify himself – and different in general, representing nothing but his own absolutely unique individuality which, deprived of expression within and action upon a common world, loses all significance.[13]

It takes an avant-garde and so disturbing figure such as a refugee to reveal what otherwise is concealed: first that we are beings whose individuality is not in opposition to, but symbiotic with, belonging, and who, without community or government, become poor in world; and second, that we are beings who have forgotten the precarious character of this community and government upon which the appearance of any sense of self is named as such.[14] The refugee is a reminder that the collectives to which a sense of self belongs are nothing natural, nothing we can take for granted, they have to be organized. They are a figure who sees how naming organizes by confering limit conditions on life. Yet in being placed outside this figure is also a reminder of the irreducible difference by which all of us are individually and inwardly constituted, and of how so much that goes by the name of organization is predicated on, and generates, a hostility to this irreducible difference.[15] The hostility is an

[11] Hannah Arendt *Origins of Totalitarianism*. San Diego: Harcourt Brace. 1950/1979, 295–6.
[12] Hannah Arendt *The Human Condition*. Chicago: University of Chicago Press. 1958/1998, 200–1.
[13] Hannah Arendt *Origins of Totalitarianism*, 302.
[14] Hannah Arendt *Origins of Totalitarianism*, 293–4, 301.
[15] 'Since the Greeks, we have known that highly developed political life breeds a deep-rooted suspicion of this private sphere, a deep resentment against the disturbing miracle contained in the fact that each of us is made as he is – single, unique, unchangeable.' Hannah Arendt *Origins of Totalitarianism*, 301. Arendt's own history, ending up a refugee in the USA, is perhaps telling here. If, as F. Scott Fitzgerald suggested, the USA is neither a land nor a people, but an idea, then it was here, at least the 'here' Arendt experienced having escaped Nazi internment, that the irreducible difference of the private sphere received

acknowledgement of the limits of human artifice: no matter how much we attempt to pave over 'unique individuality' with the architectures of civilization, it has a habit of bursting back through.

In its distinct alienability, the figure of the refugee renews the possibility for authenticity. What the refugee knows, and what others might learn, is that the community and government that matter, that affirm life, are expressive conditions housed in the semantics of language that has to be worked at and seeded into histories again and again, it has to be achieved and then borne along: it cannot be designed and declaimed, it has to be acted out.[16]

The *Polis* of Ancient Greece

Perhaps the purest expression of this action, and certainly that about which Arendt thought long and hard, is the ancient Greek *polis*. The *polis* is a constantly renewing assembly of citizens engaged in listening, voicing opinions, arguing, thereby directly participating in the running of a city state by expressing themselves from within it. It is a form to which strategy has an intimate relation, not least because the origins of the word strategy lie with Greek city states such as Athens or Thebes and the officers – *strategoi* – responsible for their overall protection. To understand the ground upon which strategy rests, then, is to understand the figuration of the *strategoi* in relation to the *polis*, a relationship that is, we will argue, a struggle for authenticity, a struggle in which the distinctions to be realized by 'the two in one of the soundless dialogue' are made possible through a collective commitment to communally renewed criteria of consideration. There is an intimacy between authenticity and its public organization in a *polis*, and from the very beginning strategy was understood as the organizational practice of enacting this intimacy.

Ideally speaking, a *polis* should consist of as many citizens as one can make out individually from a single vantage point, and not more. The *polis* is being defined by the possibility of occupying a point of view in which a whole was somehow present, but only as a mutual gaze where

---

due consideration, almost, as it turned out, to an abnegation of the concomitant need of a public sphere through which private difference might find space enough to express itself.

[16] That we so typically resent the struggle this entails, and that we have come to a condition in which we would rather outsource the task to service providers only too willing to manage our affairs for us, thereby transforming them into an economy of signs, is a state of affairs made perfectly blatant by the treatment typical to refugees. Arendt observes that when nations are called on to deal with refugees, they regard them as minorities, as separate to citizens, as in need of special treatment and permission, as strangers who, at best, and with appropriate regulations and laws in place, might then live alongside 'native' people. The idea that we belong to a community simply by being human is a comforting abstraction that insulates us from the uncomfortable truth that belonging is an organized condition (Hannah Arendt *Origins of Totalitarianism*, 295).

each citizen could hold the look of another and in this encounter of faces, even if vaguely, sense them looking back, not as citizens who have given over their subjectivity to the state in exchange for security, but as citizens who *ipso facto* have an equal standing in bearing the weight of belonging together, and who might be themselves looking upon others with the same thoughtful freedom. It is in this flicker of mutual awareness that the self as a citizen appears, looking outside and finding there a provocation to turn inward: consciousness transitions into conscience and to action; insides and outsides continuing to twist into one another. The *polis* is the space of this metamorphosis. It is a gathering or clearing of mutual disclosure that is marked out wherever people gather to deliberate openly on the possible distinction between reasons and right reasons, acts and good acts, or form and beautiful form, and do so freed from the self-interest and economic concerns associated with each of their private households.

It was an important and perhaps grounding responsibility of the *strategoi* to have both a spatial and temporal oversight of the *polis* as without a public marketplace of opinions and ideas the city was bereft of vitality and integrity for it was there, in open discourse, that citizens attempted to understand what the city was, what made it distinct, what mattered to it uniquely, what social and material conditions it found itself in, and how these might be envisaged differently. The job was a profound and yet very ordinary one: To lay the groundwork of what it is to have a sense of civic self with which each citizen can feel sufficiently complicit and responsible to become exposed to others. The citizens are to discuss and dispute whether the prevailing agreements concerning the concepts of law, equality, value, strength, happiness, love or virtue continue to make more of life. In this partaking the *polis* constitutes itself, but does not sustain itself; its generative robustness and viability require strategic form.

Historically, the *polis* included the:

ecclesia, the Assembly of the people, which is the acting sovereign body. All citizens have the right to speak (*isegoria*), their votes carry the same weight (*isophephia*), and they are under moral obligation to speak their minds (*parrhesia*). Participation also materializes in the courts. There are no professional judges, virtually all courts are juries with their jurors chosen by lot. The *ecclesia*, assisted by the *boule* (Council), legislates and governs.[17]

The council or senate set the agenda of the assembly, and it was those who advised this council, notably the council of the ten generals – the

---

[17] Cornelius Castoriadis *Philosophy, Politics, Autonomy.* Edited by David Ames Curtis. New York and Oxford: Oxford University Press, 1991, 90.

strategoi – who held sway. The generals were military, economic and political in nature, they were responsible for prosecuting war but their authority was secured through yearly election which in turn was based on acuity in establishing alliances and trading.[18] They were leaders who acted as conduits for the *polis*, acutely aware of its being a space of both preservation and possibility whose limits were configured not just in city walls, but the legal constitution of a citizenry whose continual debate formed the wellspring from which an open future spills; the *strategoi* were to administer the edge of the *polis* to then better protect its enclosing and generative power.[19] These structures were there to reconcile the agonistic qualities of dispute and continual self-revealing with organized structures that better enabled such an exchange of opinion. These exchanges occurred without princes or kings, without bureaucrats or administrators, and most tellingly without any territorially grounded notion of state sovereignty that individuals were to identify ethno-racially as people, constituents or *Volk* for whom, in turn, rules and decisions were binding: They were only to be bound as citizens, of Thebes, Sparta or Athens, each of which, as a city, was the ongoing expression of the aesthetic effort to create what otherwise would never exist.

In attempting to recover an interest in the *polis* and the distinction between politics and territory upon which it was organized, Arendt was trying to push back at the prevailing agreements in German legal thinking which, at the time, continued to maintain a feudal association between law, politics and land.[20] Politics followed a model of territorial building, and law was tied to the markings of territory: soil, fences, the marking of borders. The marking of territory to form the estate, *das Gut*, vassal and *feud*, is a once-and-for-all distinction that then requires violence to defend as boundary lines drawn around an estate (the product of the focus on building and making) need to be authorized.

This unquestioned association of law, politics and land had been woven into prevailing understandings of the Greek *polis*. The eminent Carl Schmitt, for example, locates the etymology of the *polis* in both fortress and border, and ties law, or *nomos*, to the marking out of territory

---

[18] Maurizio d'Entreves Hannah Arendt. In *The Stanford Encyclopaedia of Philosophy (Spring 2019 Edition)*. Edited by Edward N. Zalta. https://plato.stanford.edu/archives/spr2019/entries/arendt/

[19] See Jerome Kohn Freedom: The priority of the political. In *The Cambridge Companion to Hannah Arendt*. Edited by Dana Villa. Cambridge: Cambridge University Press, 2006, 113–29.

[20] John Hart Ely The polis and 'the political': Civic and territorial views of association. *Thesis Eleven*, 1996, 46: 33–65.

into regional space, hence *nomos* can be located within walls. Etymologically, *nomos* also derives from the Greek *nemein* and the German *nehmen*, both indicating a taking or appropriating, which underlie Schmitt's use of the term *Landnahme* – the taking of land that was either free or won by conquest and so divided and appropriated under legal title.[21] These geopolitics of space identify politics, and more specifically strategic leadership, with jurisdiction over a territorial space, which in turn is linked to the existence of households (*oikos*) and families as parts of settled (as opposed to *nomadic*, which offers yet another etymological root as wandering or grazing) land-communities. In this, the *nomos* of the earth is also opposed to that of the open sea for which Schmitt harbours particular dislike: with the sea there are no limits and boundaries, no sacred locations, no law or property that does not float away or get battered in storms.[22] The sea resists cultivation and building, whereas land secures the agreements of collective belonging: ethnicity, religion, language and so on. It all begins with the first act of politics, which is fencing in. As Schmitt puts it:

Concretely speaking, *Nomos* is, for example, the chicken every peasant living under a good king has in his pot every Sunday; the piece of land he cultivates in front of his property; the car every worker in the US has parked in front of his house.[23]

But whilst this territorial state is literally and figuratively built – through taxes, enclosing walls demarcating a space as a home, city or nation, replete with national armies, education for cultural homogenization as subjects in a unit – it is also subject to a self-referential blind spot.[24] The legalization of governance only works under the cover of law: as Schmitt admits, 'every norm requires a normal situation'. So when the context changes and 'the state' can no longer securely structure its enabling space, then the warrant for authority breaks down as the strategist must declare themself to be acting in a state of exception from the law.[25] The unforeseen and new requires a political judgement by a decision-making entity that emerges in an act of suspending normal politics (and law) in order to save politics (and law), but which otherwise recedes and hides, lurking, amid the administration of everyday life.

---

[21] Mitchell Dean A political mythology of world order. *Theory, Culture & Society*, 2006, 23(5): 1–22.
[22] Mitchell Dean A political mythology, 15.
[23] Mitchell Dean A political mythology, 5.
[24] John Hart Ely The polis and 'the political', 55.
[25] William Rasch Conflict as a vocation: Carl Schmitt and the possibility of politics. *Theory, Culture & Society*, 2000, 17; 1–32.

Arendt's location of the *polis*, in contrast, though it obviously does require and invoke a distinct city space, does not involve chickens, nor is the first act of politics the drawing of boundaries. These acts are the concerns of the household, the *oikos*. In the words of Arendt: '[t]he private realm of the household was the sphere where the necessities of life, of individual survival as well as of continuity of the species, were taken care of and guaranteed'.[26] Law sat between the *polis* and *oikos*, as that which circumscribed the edges of each, organizing the movement from one to the other. And it is here along this liminal edge that the *strategoi* act like a permeable membrance.[27]

This wall-like law was sacred, but only the inclosure was political. Without it a political real could no more exist than a piece of property without a fence to hedge it in: the one harboured and inclosed political life as the other sheltered and protected the biological life process of the family.[28]

Though the *polis* was often configured through material and symbolic spatial arrangements such as offices, city walls, insignia and legally apportioned land, its nature was not of these things; politics required boundaries, but it did not draw them.

It is a view of the *polis* that frees itself from the blood-tied virtues of the old aristocratically configured city state to which Schmitt attaches the term. It is also a view that is distinct from more archaic versions of the *polis*. Earlier iterations concentrated on virtues or excellence (*arete*) beyond those of open discussion: notably the strength and skill involved in wrestling or racing that carry competitors to victory in Olympia, along with those virtues that let warriors bear the sight of bloody slaughter and stand firm in engagement with the enemy. The latter, savage valour (*thouris alke*), was mythologized as the 'best and fairest prize to win for a youth among men',[29] providing as it did the

---

[26] Hannah Arendt *The Human Condition*, 46.

[27] The *oikos* is a space of the visible hand, there is nothing of the mysterious fluidity of invisible power that permeates the exchange of opinion in the *polis*. The *strategoi* rule the *oikos* as those who run a household. They are exponents of *oikonomia* working from within a managerial, non-epistemic paradigm, one often associated analogically with the health of the body and a concern for the correct arrangement and function of the organs. Giorgio Agamben elaborates in this condition of *oikos* beautifully when suggesting *oikonomia* is both a *logos* (an unbound form of reasoning without rival) and *praxis* (what for Karl Marx is the originary, historical act of making) without necessity; its force is both discursive and practical. See *The Kingdom and the Glory: For a Theological Genealogy of Economy and Government*. Stanford, CA: Stanford University Press, 2011, 53–68.

[28] Hannah Arendt *The Human Condition*, 64.

[29] Tyrtaeus' elegy, in Eric Voegelin *The World of the Polis*. Baton Rouge: Louisiana State University Press, 1957, 259. Here, Voegelin focuses particularly on the Spartan *polis*, where even the questioning of its justness was seen as an act of treason and betrayal.

basis for the unquestioning availability of citizens to fight for their community, regardless of whether the cause of this fight was just. Savage valour also provided the possibility of transfiguration: the sweetness and honour of sacrifice let men become immortal, with their tombs and children being honoured long after their deaths. Yet the promise of a sweet death and immortality becomes problematic. In part because, as Eric Voegelin remarks, it romanticizes what could be a traumatic experience: 'no warrior who returned from battle has ever committed suicide in despair because such sweetness escaped him'.[30] And in part because it is impossible to conceive a functioning political body that is entirely made up of savage warriors, especially as the brutal task of warfare can be outsourced to mercenaries in the same way in which the *polis* may instruct technicians to build temples or fortifications.

As Voegelin suggests, the development of a proper political order requires a wider set of *aretes*, most importantly wisdom, justice and temperance, which in the Athenian version of the *polis* all gained more importance than savageness. Solon seems to have been a watershed figure here. His poems begin to elaborate concern for justice and a sense for the influence of human action as a cause of order or disorder in the *polis*, and especially for justice (*dike*), which always catches up with perpetrators of unjust action, even if such feedback loops span over many generations. It is in this temperance of individual will and desire by the intervention of *dike* (watched over by Zeus) that opinions and illusions (*doxa*) are brought into an order befitting the senses of the gods. This goes especially for the desire for the accumulation and staking out of land for the *oikos*, and the striving for wealth and possession, which cannot, contra Schmitt, serve as a principle of good order, for there is no end to such striving. In this way, a civic *polis* begins to assert itself against the more heroic versions. Not everyone can be an Agamemnon or Achilles, and even they can only stave off for a while a war of all against all,[31] and the bloody tyrannies that inherently follow impetuous and individualistic striving. Nor can individualistic accumulation of riches continue freely, as had been the case with Athenian aristocracy whose privileges provided economic advantages to secure positions and steer events into favourable directions. The citizen *polis* required a new temperance that recognized the individualism of *doxa* as 'the condition of disorder while the renunciation of *doxa* brings the right order (*eunomia*)',[32] making possible a life in community. Solon does not provide a list of the right measure or

[30] Eric Voegelin *The World of the Polis*, 261.
[31] Thomas Hobbes *Leviathan*. London: Penguin, 1968.
[32] Eric Voegelin *The World of the Polis*, 267.

criteria for good judgement, and for Voegelin, precisely this refusal to say anything positively about the source of order in the *polis* is the animating force that reveals the passion of life as the desire, illusion or opinion that must be curbed for the sake of order. The *polis* is the realization of this unspecified balance of the 'unseen measure', setting into rules of conduct, casting the role of its governors not as tyrants but lawgivers (*nomothetes*); statesmen in-between parties who share the passions of the people and so act with authority for the people.

Arendt takes Solon's discursive view of the *polis*, and then pushes it further still, because, for her, *doxa*, so long as it emerges from freely exchanged enquiries, is a source of power, not, as Solon suggests, mass ignorance. Ely's historical study supports Arendt's view, suggesting that the *polis* emerged from a protest by sworn soldiers leading to a strike that denied the king his corvée. This act, the expulsion of a tyrannical government, makes way for a civic community of citizens whose communion was concentrated within the fortified walls of Athens' Acropolis built around the upper reaches of a hill rising from the bustle of the tightly packed city. Yet the boundaries became porous, and even the physical space where the assembly of citizens came to meet – the Pnyx, used between the fifth and first centuries BCE – was found on the edge rather than centre of Athens, on a raised, open space south-west of the Acropolis, overlooking both the city and the port at Piraeus (see Figure 1.1).[33] The *polis* was defined by walls that both gathered the *ekklesia* into a tightly packed, bodily unity, but which set them against a wide landscape of mountains and sea: democracy was both prospect and refuge. Each meeting (where quorum was around 6,000, with a maximum capacity of around 13,000) began with an invitation to step forward and talk: τίς ἀγορεύειν βούλεται ('Who wishes to address the assembly?').[34]

Membership of the *polis* initially retained an overtly aristocratic bias, requiring lineage back to a mythologized ancestry. It took a change in

---

[33] Ely rehearses Aristotle's likening of forms of governance and physical features of the city. The form of a citadel is best geared towards oligarchies and monarchies, while larger aristocratic families, who suit a larger number of haphazard and random layouts. A level plain best befits a democracy where, as it was in Athens, the removal of private property markers was a precondition for citizenship, and with public spending geared towards temples and not private homes, were best suited served by a community of sworn worriers organized into a phalanx defending an unwalled city and in homes with unlocked doors. Ely suggests that when Athens built a wall in the fifth century BCE, it boded no good for the city's constitutional health. John Hart Ely The polis and 'the political', 42.

[34] Aristotle. Ach. 45. 'Who wishes to address the assembly?' See also Kōnstantinos Kourouniotes and Homer A. Thompson The Pnyx in Athens. *Hesperia*. 1932, 1: 90–217 and Mogens Herman Hansen Polis. In *The Oxford Encyclopedia of Ancient Greece and Rome*, vol. 5. Edited by M. Gagarin. Oxford: Oxford University Press, 2009, 398–403.

Figure 1.1 The Pnyx. Showing the 'stepping stone' or *bema*. Photograph by Costas Tzagarakis, 2021.

military technology around the mid-seventh century BCE to expand this aristocratic privilege to other citizens. The hoplite (a term derived from 'tool') reforms saw the emergence of the heavily armoured foot soldier that allowed for the phalanx battle formation, in which units formed deep and tightly packed lines of attack. The demands for such foot soldiers exceeded the aristocratic pool of men in some cities, and so free farmers who could afford the cost of the panoply, the armour, were initiated, first into the military, and later into political life.[35] The phalanx represented a community-based, non-permanent defensive army and therefore the city was not primarily based on barriers and walls that protected old claims to property, rather the phalanx itself is that barrier, made up of equal parts.[36] Legal supports were necessary to keep that

[35] Kurt A. Raaflaub Soldiers, citizens and the evolution of the early Greek polis. In *The Development of the Polis in Archaic Greece*. Edited by Lynette G. Mitchell and P. J. Rhodes. London: Routledge, 1997, 26–31.

[36] And, again, in further military developments from around fifth century BCE, lighter cavalry and, siege tactics and weaponry increased the technical demands required for warfare, leading to a gradual split between those specializing in rhetoric in the assembly, and those *strategoi* responsible for military campaigns outside the *polis*. See Scott Peake The role of the strategoi in Athens in the 4th century B.C. PhD dissertation, St Andrews University, March 1990. http://hdl.handle.net/10023/2961. But equally more distant

barrier up. In 507 the tyrants of Athens were expelled, and the citizens took over decision-making powers in city affairs, insofar as a broadening of both the opportunity to speak (*isegoria*) and the distribution of political rights (*isonomia*) began to swell the numbers of a politically active citizenry. The Athenians (or at least the mature, male Athenians) were becoming free, so that with the rise of Solon's accession he was able to refer to himself as a 'boundary stone' set between the rich factions of the city, and the 'abstract people' (*demos*) without means or interests, but exposed to the freely expressed opinion of the *ekklesia*.[37] All citizens could attend meetings and speak, with official positions being allocated by drawing lots or through elections, their conduct was subject to review, and penalties were applied to all equally.[38] It was a contained and evolving freedom, one shaped by a coming together of community and a bodily coming together of architecture and rituals of speech and listening through which people discovered the reason for, and were formed by, their solidarity.[39]

Hannah Arendt's Realms of Labour, Work and Action

In shuttling between *oikos* and *polis* the *strategoi* become the organizational equivalent of the two-in-one authentic self, alive to the administrative fault lines of territorial and legal facticity whilst also struggling to create and secure a political marketplace of ideas. Their role is to gain sufficient distance upon the situational presence of the city to apprehend better the possibilities for its self-transformation. They are alive to the quality of the *polis* as a space of open encounter and innovative

---

battles and the growing importance of military campaigns for Athens gave *strategoi* a weightier magistracy, with greater autonomy and influence. But with this also grew suspicion and distrust between them and the assembly. Dominant and charismatic figures were not immune to such distrust, an enmity that culminated in the trial of eight generals, and execution of six, following a botched attempt to rescue drowning sailors and damaged ships, after defeating a Spartan fleet at the Arginusae sea battle in 406 BCE. Luca A. Asmoti The Arginusae trial. *BICS.*, 2006, 49: 1–21.

[37] Lin Foxhall Who was the Athenian polis in the sixth century? In *The Development of the Polis in Archaic Greece.* Edited by Lynette Mitchell and Peter Rhodes, 2011, 61–74. Foxhall suggests it is neither clear who exactly constituted the *demos* – at least in its early seventh and sixth century BCE form – nor whether that lofty and benign attitude was more widely spread than Solon's poetry and propaganda. A more radically democratic version of the 'public' emerged in the fifth and fourth centuries.

[38] Hans-Joachim Gehrke The figure of Solon in the Athênaiôn Politeia. In *Solon of Athens: New Historical and Philological Approaches.* Edited by Josine Blok and Andre Lardinois. Leiden: Brill, 2006, 276–89.

[39] Marcel Detienne From practices of assembly to the forms of politics: A comparative approach. Translated by April Wuensch. *Arion*, 3rd series. 2000, 7(3): 1–19.

suggestion, as well as that of the *oikos* as a space of provision, domestic order, trade and military training; strategy becomes a practice of opening each to the other. It is not, though, a case of merging or even knitting them together, for they are of a fundamentally different nature.

It is in her distinction between labour and work, and with the further addition of what she calls action, that Arendt expands upon the distinction of the *polis*. It is only in action, she argues, that we make incisions into the world in an authentic and hence distinctly human way: action is what defines being human. Whilst both labour and work also involve incisions into the world, these are made in the shadow of an instrumental dependency that excludes the properly generative power unique to politics.[40] To labour is to meet the material needs of the body to survive. These needs are perpetual, and demand constant attention: the body needs feeding, shelter and sometimes medical care. Work extends beyond meeting these material needs, reaching into cultural productions by which life is not only sustained, but becomes something evaluated, and hence of value. Finally, action is a condition of freely exchanged opinion amongst equals without any regard for particular interests.

The *strategoi* clearly labour, and rely on labour, especially that of slaves, children, women, mercenaries and traders; indeed all those excluded from the status of citizen. Throughout the forming of Athens through the building of city walls, forays into battle, securing ports, and commercial exchange, structures have risen, or been raised and erased, in continuous cycles of production, acquisition and destruction. It is, quite naturally, the largely material and overtly labouring activities of producing, growing, defending, acquiring and consuming that dominate the everyday lives and considerations of those interested in the surviving and flourishing of cities like Athens. Because labour is characterized by non-durability – it is bound by the natural processes of an organic life form maintaining its viability – it is often the strategist's main concern: what is made in the service of preserving biological existence is quickly consumed, requiring yet more, but it is itself not of a particularly strategic nature as in the condition of labour life is pre-structured by necessities that often follow natural cycles and rhythms, and so there is little choice in which means and ends to pursue. It is a serving of life, not an individual's being, and in this service lives can come and go without leaving a trace. Their efforts are simply consumed as a means to secure more life, which is an insatiable force. Bound to this necessity, the labouring body

---

[40] Hannah Arendt *The Human Condition*, 176. And so politics becomes a genuinely human endeavour: 'A life without speech and without action ... is literally dead to the world; it has ceased to be a human life because it is no longer lived among men.'

is not free, but given over to bodily needs: '[t]he *animal laborans*, driven by the needs of the body, does not use this body freely ...'. There is no consideration of why these needs are being met and no questioning of being; products are made, consumed, and replaced (where possible), it is pure metabolism being experienced by members of a species (*animal laborans*). To present oneself to oneself does not occur under the impress of these life processes, there is no place for modifying thought.

The *strategoi* would also concern themselves with the realm of *work*. Where labour describes the processes by which naturally occurring life secures its continuation, work describes the struggle by which a specific form of naturally occurring life – namely human life – attempts to distinguish itself. Labour secures food and shelter but to work is to create objects that last, not products that are used-up and so the things made through work endure beyond their creation (i.e., they are not meant to be acquired, consumed and replaced). Work is not bound by necessities of species biology and its raw concern for survival, protection, possession and abundance. Being unfettered from biological organs, the objects created by work are both useful and valuable: they become cultural. Cultural objects are valued to the extent they potentially outlast the mortal span of their creating workers (*homo faber*); indeed in being taken up and used the objects can actually grow rather than diminish in stature, being always available and intensifying in symbolic resonance because of it. The objects of work are not always material, indeed even if they are material it is as often their symbolic force as much as their physical presence that counts. To work is to lobby and advise in the creation of laws, to create art works, stories, myths, norms and rituals. These are objects that organizationally enliven and enrich, but also suppress, human lives, animating material things and activities with 'civilizing' values. Materially, work objects can range from a well-used and therefore useful hand tool to an altar piece or epic poem, and institutionally from an official procedure to a constitutional ceremony. What they share is the quality of enhanced longevity: provided they are made well, objects can be used or admired without diminishment, indiscriminately giving of value themselves. The makers of objects are remembered for the handiness of the tool or the sturdiness of the building, for the beguiling features of the story or image, for the justness of the law or gravity of the sacrificial ritual.

Workers – lawyers, priests, artists – avoid the suffering attendant to labouring whose toiling activities yield nothing beyond what is needed right here and now. Workers can witness themselves in what is being made, and the more skilled and mannered they are the more they come to belong to the culture of the city, their works outliving their own lifespans and becoming part of the stories that give a culture a sense of progressive development. Culture is not the making of objects as such, but the habituated moving in and amid such objects; it is a style learnt by those schooled in appreciation not just of what is useful (handy tools) but also of what is beautiful (affecting art) and what brings wisdom (just laws). To belong to culture is to have taste; a discerning sensitivity; the ability to 'take aim' as Arendt calls it, whether it is a question of aesthetics, ritualistic belief or legal judgement. The cultured embody the requisite gestures and language that allows them to display a considered restraint: they can, for example, withhold emotion so that a natural ebullience in the face of a beautiful artefact becomes something calm, schooled and active, or they can act in a timely (*kairos*) way, by bearing in mind how rituals or laws are always loaded with both recollection (*anamesis*, historical significance) and expectation (prophecy, future). Through work comes culture, and with culture comes naming and a sense of artifice and sovereign force that severs *homo faber* from nature, implicating humans in their own created world.

It is here Arendt introduces notes of caution and concern. First, by separating themself from the wider world, the human worker (and the subjects of work's affects) ceases to be concerned with the very world that conditions its own being: the conscience through which the two-in-one dialogue initiates itself. The worker presumes the mark of work to be its self-sufficiency. As Arendt accepts this presumption has generated an impressive array of cultural forms, whether artistic, legal or religious, being built under the aegis of reason, or metaphysical belief, either of which speak of an end, *telos*, or a correct way of being, towards which the human alone can direct itself. Yet she reminds us that this artificial world of work should not be conflated with the world itself, and the fact that the human species seems intent on forgetting this is to its detriment. The forgetfulness means humans no longer critically consider the presence of work in the basic facticity of experience. It is as though work is all that matters, as if the work-world was all-absorbing, and what is outside the work being done by the self is of a lesser, objective status – and so the self only questions its effectiveness and efficiency in controlling a world of objects, it never questions its own status as a named subject. *Homo faber* is made in the reflection of the objects made through work, but with this also comes a sense of impoverishment in the relation to the world, which is always more than work. As a fabricator, the self performs amid a scenery of conforming subjectification: as it fabricates it accords with established patterns from the past, and frames a future through the order of intelligible expectations, some galvanized by hope. Through fabrication the future becomes a scene of possibility and entailments, and the past a scene of memory and commitments and entitlements, between which the present sits as the space of willed decision and controlled occurrence. The world is there to be understood, it is there as a scene of evaluation and value; in short, it exists to confirm the separating elevation of the only form of life that understands it: humans. This separation is marked by culture: the space afforded by a civilization for its continual consideration of, and adherence to, what is named as beautiful, good and true.[41] Mediated by culture, the non-human world becomes both symbolic and mute. In idealizing symbols, it can foster a heightened sense of inner certainty, and in material form it provides the raw material to sustain work, in either case it is subaltern.

The other source of concern Arendt raises with the association of work and human distinctiveness is its necessary and ultimately diminishing alliance with labour. *Homo faber*, no matter how creative and enduringly brilliant, nearly always acts in the shadow of labour: work serves labour, labour serves material need, and material need is endless. Within the world of work, the possibilities for non-instrumental, open expression remain diminished insofar as any cultural form built by *homo faber* that resonates risks being confined to a purpose, an end outside itself; it is enlisted to meet specific material needs. Even works of art – which are purportedly entirely removed from any use and therefore are as close as anything that is fabricated can be to being tangibly enduring and immortal – become things of use, for example to enhance the rhetorical power of a trader anxious to impress clients, or a priest anxious to protect his living. This is almost inevitable, irrespective of whether the work of art was commissioned for such purposes. The same with laws, which no matter how justly intended can quickly become the playthings of vested interests. Indeed, the objects of work often need to be profaned in this way for people to understand and make use of them in their daily lives: art works are used for decoration, and law to seek restitution in petty matters of personal possession; the ideals of beauty and equity are subdued.[42]

Though they are caught in a continual *melée* for the advancement of specific interests, Arendt is not dismissive of labour and work; and it is through an intimate understanding of labour and work that the *strategoi* play a grounding role in forming and sustaining a viable city, a place where things are produced and fabricated, a solidly administered space,

---

[41] Hannah Arendt The crisis in culture: Its social and political significance. In *Between Past and Future: Six Exercises in Political Thought*. New York: Viking Press, 1961, 197–226, 210–14.
[42] Hannah Arendt *The Human Condition*, 153–5.

an *oikos*. The *strategoi* become adept at understanding what needs to be built to create, protect and enrich the city. Theirs is a pragmatic intelligence that accepts the inherently self-interested nature of trade, acquisition and war, and remains ever alive to the broader framing by which these instrumental activities can be gilded and emboldened by values. In the service of the *oikos* the *strategoi* might, for example, oversee the employment of artistic genius to write of and symbolize the mythical figures to which a city is wedded and from which it takes emotional and purposeful succour. For the city of Athens these figures were the horse and the owl of the goddess Athena, the one symbolizing swift and powerful engagement, the other mysterious foresight, and in combination a powerfully charged embodiment of a people who had been hard set with confidence and ambition. Being in thrall to such affective appeals, the Athenians might be more inclined to labour as a manageable and efficient unit. The *strategoi* might also enshrine laws that require regular attendance at sacrificial rituals to ensure those growing rich through commerce and military success begin to channel some of their wealth into the artistically embellished public institutions, and so encourage a kind of virtuous cycle of influence between trade, art and belief.

Yet with labour and work alone any city, and body of people, any strategy, will find itself confronting and even encouraging a uniformity of commitments and entitlements, it is a body lacking the necessary self-awareness to renew its own practices. Arendt casts the problem as one of accommodation:

the world is created by mortal hands to serve mortals for a limited time as home. Because the world is made by mortals it wears out; and because it continuously changes its inhabitants it runs the risk of becoming as mortal as they. To preserve the world against the mortality of its creators and inhabitants it must be constantly set right anew.[43]

This setting right anew comes not from the *oikos*, which concerns the material and cultural realization of organizational order, but the *polis*. The *polis* is an-archic; its law is its own self-constituting force. It is secured by first making a space, both legally and architecturally, which then gives itself over to the boundlessness and uncertainty of action. The *polis* is the space of Arendt's third realm: action, a term she derives from the Greek word *archein*, – to begin, to lead and to rule.[44] But always

[43] Hannah Arendt The crisis in education. In *Between Past and Future: Six Exercises in Political Thought*. New York: Viking Press, 1961, 173–96, 190–2.
[44] Hannah Arendt *The Human Condition*, 132; Hannah Arendt What is freedom? In *Between Past and Future: Six Exercises in Political Thought*. New York: Viking Press, 1961, 143–72, 163–6.

with the emphasis on beginning, on appearing, on opening up, with little sense of an ending. Being devoid of explicit purpose and tangible object, actions have their own atmosphere: they have neither cause to absolve them nor effect to aggrandize them. Loosened from the moorings of wider determination, action is without need of stated, calculating warrants, indeed it is the space in which such warrants find their authority and legitimacy.

[A]ction and speech create a space between the participants which can find its proper location almost any time and anywhere. It is the space of appearance in the widest sense of the word, namely, the space where I appear to others as others appear to me.[45]

Each citizen accords others the status of beings whose distinctiveness as selves comes from their continually expressing and adjusting opinions about the commitments and entitlements by which a civic organization is being produced again and again.

For Arendt a citizenry can only properly flourish if the administrative activity of city management is itself directed towards the creation of an organizational space such as a *polis* in which citizens act for the sake of action alone.[46] It is here, amid all the jockeying and manoeuvring of open discussion and argument, that citizens find themselves; not, however, as sentient, practical creatures with specific biological needs, nor as beholders and holders of named norms and values, but as public beings freed from the weight of specific attachments. The *polis* itself produces nothing, that is the point: what is done is inseparable from the performative execution of its being done, and no sooner is it done than it dissipates: the action can only be understood in its being performed and in being performed it is complete, there is nothing further to be assayed or assessed.

Building Authenticity: Lessons from Athens

The *strategoi* are critical figures in the *polis*. Not only because they commit to the labour and work necessary for its material and symbolic form, but

---

[45] Hannah Arendt *The Human Condition*, 198.

[46] An intriguing aspect of this responsibility is preserving the deeds of those who act in the *polis*, deeds that cannot, by definition, have an end or settle around a set of defined interests. To preserve the deeds of the citizens is to enlist stories and myths surrounding argument and oratory, narratives that latch onto the expressive performance that would otherwise evaporate, given life in the *polis* has no beginning or end. The importance of doing so is that to preserve the expressive deeds of the citizens is to lend them the quality of being exemplary, it is a way of learning how to be citizens, how to enter the distinction-making *polis*. Hannah Arendt *The Human Condition*, 194–7.

because in learning the nuances of grammar and the arts of persuasion, they partake in its purpose: the creation and promulgation of thoughtful opinion through speaking up. Indeed, the most celebrated of the *strategoi*, Pericles who was elected fifteen times to the council of ten generals, is remembered because of his speeches, narrated in Thucydides' *Peloponnesian Wars*. From an aristocratic family bonded by a generational familiarity with political power, Pericles came to the fore along with Athens itself. The Athenian defeat of the Persians in the naval battle of Salamis in 480 BCE sprung the city into an ascendent arc upon which Pericles was able to latch his own fortunes. Even those writers like Plutarch who found his leadership wanting admitted that Pericles, though militarily average, had a mellifluous voice: he could and did persuade the *Ecclesia* with silver-tongued ease. Throughout his leadership he focused on the *demos*, the people. He felt that in the body of the assembly, the city found its life, no more so than when the city, as head of the Delian league, was fighting the Peloponnesians (led by the cities of Sparta and Corinth). In his most infamous and compelling speech – a funeral oratory given to all people of Athens, including the women – he reminds the audience of Athens' riches, not just architecturally and economically, but of its collective capacity for justice and deliberation. Pre-eminent amongst peoples, the Athenians cannot but fail to survive and flourish, despite the onslaughts from the enemy who had being laying waste to the city's hinterlands. It was, he reminds them, Athens who repelled the Persians and rightfully led the Delian league, by virtue of their vigorous patriotism and daring, and Athens who would again prevail. It was a necessity to fight those who sought to overthrow the *demos*, but set within the necessity of having to fight Pericles alludes to options, the most favourable one being to temporarily cede control of inland territories, and to concentrate instead on naval strength. Command of the seas secures trade routes, it allows for rapid deployment of forces, and given it relies on teams of lowly ranked oarsmen, emphasizing the navy contributed to a vibrant sense of equality. In response to the twice-yearly Peloponnesian attacks (from 431 BCE onwards) Pericles advises the citizens to take refuge within the robust city walls, to hold firm and stay the course.

In this funeral oratory Pericles embodies the performative skill and zeal by which a *polis*, ideally, comes to life. There is an audience to action, but unlike the leader of the hostile city states lining up against Athens, as Pericles opines he remains a member of that audience, he participates in his own witnessing, and it is as a collective that the assembled citizens validate the power to which the speech makes such eloquent appeal. The war, then, was not a decision emerging from the interior, freely constituted will of Pericles: it was the very form of the *polis* that required the war to be fought (a democracy cannot concede to a traditional tyranny and survive) and which brought forth the willing nature of those who fight (using civic minded and motivated seafarers). Material possessions, Pericles continues, are as nothing to the world of a city when set against its peerless force of character. Athenians, he argues:

cultivate refinement without extravagance and knowledge without effeminacy; wealth we employ more for use than for show, and place the real disgrace of poverty not in owning to the fact but in declining the struggle against it. [2] Our public men have, besides politics, their private affairs to attend to, and our ordinary citizens, though occupied with the pursuits of industry, are still fair judges of public matters; for, unlike any other nation, regarding him who takes no part in these duties not as unambitious but as useless, we Athenians are able to judge at all events if we cannot originate, and instead of looking on discussion as a stumbling-block in the way of action, we think it an indispensable preliminary to any wise action at all. [3] Again, in our enterprises we present the singular spectacle of daring and deliberation, each carried to its highest point, and both united in the same persons; although usually decision is the fruit of ignorance, hesitation of reflection. But the palm of courage will surely be adjudged most justly to those, who best know the difference between hardship and pleasure and yet are never tempted to shrink from danger. [4] In generosity we are equally singular, acquiring our friends by conferring not by receiving favors. Yet, of course, the doer of the favor is the firmer friend of the two, in order by continued kindness to keep the recipient in his debt; while the debtor feels less keenly from the very consciousness that the return he makes will be a payment, not a free gift. [5] And it is only the Athenians who, fearless of consequences, confer their benefits not from calculations of expediency, but in the confidence of liberality.[47]

Athens' strength lies with its commitment to the voluntary, open and disciplined action, and those who have and will die for Athens will be remembered not by the stone memorials of work but the continuance of a city steeped in freedom; it needs no myth-making Homer for its panegyric, its acts alone are sufficient. The suggestion here is of a people whose freedom is not something that exists prior to action, but is grounded in it: their uniqueness emerges from within the performance.

As both Bell and Garst observe, the power of the *polis* is social, not material in nature; it comes in the organizational formation of a common or general will in whose expression word and deed refuse to part company; they

---

[47] Thucydides *The Peloponnesian War*. London: J. M. Dent. 1910, §40. See also Hannah Arendt *The Human Condition*, 197, 199. Arendt notes how for Pericles the continuation of *polis* is assurance enough that the deeds and stories which are the outcome of action and speech remain imperishable, and in this the walls and laws of the *polis* act as a form of organized remembrance of the perpetual sharing of words and deeds. The walls and laws stabilize what is an organization of people arising from people living together so as to act and speak together.

too, like the citizens, are steadfast.[48] Arendt's sense of the *polis*, as encapsulated in Pericles' oratory, is of a politically generated freedom being made within a politically guaranteed public realm: uniquely, the fact of freedom and the institution of the *polis* coincide. The association of freedom with an exercise of free will is an individualistic idea of each being sovereign of their own self in distinction from, and uneasy competition with, other wills. It is an interest-bearing idea of freedom. For the Greeks of Pericles freedom was not of this order, indeed far from being an individually motivated choice between options, it is 'the freedom to call something into being which did not exist before, which was not given, not even as an object of cognition or imagination, and which therefore, strictly speaking, could not be known'.[49] It is a performative experience of being in the company of others without the debate being corralled by already scripted motives or goals. When the performance is riddled with one will setting and settling upon the other it becomes corrupted by the pursuit of specific interests, each advanced as a matter of force, or violence, but never power. It is not as if, in advancing their interests successfully, some subjects remain free, whilst others are subjugated. Freedom simply disappears.

Such a fate befell Athens in the wake of a plague that gripped the tightly packed city in 429 BCE, killing Pericles. With Pericles dead, the city fell into the hands of cabals intent on advancing private interests. Primary amongst the schemers was Cleon, who argued an empire is nothing but despotism, and its people disaffected conspirators who obey from fear not loyalty. He spoke in the aftermath of a failed rebellion by the city of Mytilenia, on Lesbos, for which crime, Cleon argued all the Mytilenians should be executed. Though initially the *polis* acted on this advice, even dispatching soldiers to execute an entire citizenry, they are persuaded by Diodotus to change their minds. It was the Mytilene *oligarchs* who rebelled, not the *demos*, and surely, suggests Diodotus, showing clemency to the people will reveal the seriousness of Athens' commitment to this primacy of a people over a leadership. Athens will punish those who offend democracy, not the people themselves. This norm of rule is absolute, exhaustless, undaunted: people are not free when they choose to act, freedom is action, and action only occurs in the performance of the *polis* from which the place the 'confidence of liberality' springs as naturally as the source of a great river.[50]

---

[48] Daniel Garst Thucydides and neorealism. *International Studies Quarterly*, 1989, 33: 1, 3–27. Vicki Bell The promise of liberalism and the performance of freedom. In *Foucault and Political Reason*. Edited by Andrew Barry, Thomas Osbourne and Nikolas Rose. Chicago: University of Chicago Press. 1996, 81–98.

[49] Hannah Arendt What is freedom? 143–72, 151.

[50] Arendt talks of the space of appearance as that place in which everything that finds itself being placed is, ipso facto political: see Hannah Arendt What is freedom? 155–6.

Diodotus' performative commitment to the idea of commonly held freedom, however, only holds sway a short while. Indeed, in the very next debate Thucydides chose to narrate how the Athenians turn back towards Cleon's instrumentalism by meting out the very same punishment they were considering for Mytilena to the citizens of Melos, a small island that had been attempting to maintain a neutral stance between Sparta and Athens. Melos' crime was to be Melos, an independent city state whose independence was considered a threat by an increasingly aggressive, dominant, but also paranoid empire. It seems, even Athens cannot uphold the normative regularities by which a *polis* is sustained: assert yourself too materially, and without good argument, and the power of action morphs into what Arendt calls the force of labour and violence of work, both of which require ever more resources, and have no other warrant than their own apparent necessity. Athens ceased to act, and instead it laboured and worked, stretching itself outwards without care for the specious nature of its talk of justice.

In acting, a sense of self is always being formed not just inwardly, but publicly: it is a space to disclose not 'what' but 'who' I am. These declarations of 'who' are inherently agonistic insofar as they are calls upon the attention of others and once expressed these calls can clatter into other claims, find companions, or be ignored, as other citizens also vie courageously to disclose themselves and seek acknowledgement. The mutual acknowledgement of action is the spring for authenticity, which ceases, then, to be just an inward attainment, but becomes a declared one, as it is not the citizen who affirms the act, but those witnessing the performance, other citizens, who then invest themselves in the disclosure by hearing and then recalling it in memory. Here work comes in. Memory works by being held collectively in stories, myths, laws and rituals that are invoked, offering up a space of signs through which disclosures can be interpreted, this way, then that way, growing or diminishing as they are taken up, or left aside. Being citizens, the audience has sufficient understanding of the process to understand that all opinions, no matter how appropriate they sound and how authoritatively they are named, carry a contrary within them, and so can be seen anew, again and again. The audience is aware that what holds them in common as citizens, irrespective of the pressures and demands that prevail in particular situations, is an expressive ability to act as beings in the world for whom self-disclosure is wrapped up in the ongoing public expression of opinion.[51]

---

[51] To act is to occupy a condition in which human response is still being made available even in situations where manners and mores have collapsed, where indeed a dictatorial cruelty is in reign. During the trials of those accused of genocide in the wake of the Holocaust, for example, Arendt judges the complicity of the accused – those such as

Action is a scene of expressive power that needs protecting from the force and violence found in the operations of the *oikos*. To breach the space of action is to permit the spread and elevation of one-dimensional characters interested either in the natural metabolism of survival or the cultural elevation and imposition of fixing values. And given work is always subservient to labour, this mixing of the *polis* and *oikos* allows what Arendt calls 'the unnatural growth of the natural', by which she means a singular concern with 'the constantly accelerated increase in the productivity of labor'.[52] The city becomes obsessed with making and acquiring and ordering lives in the service of material need, to the detriment of considering the affect the things being accrued are having on the prevailing character of the citizens. Where the correctly managed *oikos* ensures lives can be lived, a properly protected *polis* makes those lives worth living.

Authenticity as a Condition of Plurality and Natality

Action is realized through a spatially enclosed, collective use of spoken and embodied language. Of course, speech is also present in both labour and work, but in these realms it plays a subordinate role, ostensibly as a means of communicating or providing information, and is often unnecessary; the talk could be replaced by sign language or by programmed instruction. In action, however, performative speech and gesture become integral to revealing who one is, in the company of others also revealing of themselves; a language in which the beginning and end of all things occur.[53] It is only in acting that we experience ourselves as somehow free from subordination to ends outside ourselves:

With word and deed we insert ourselves into the world, and this insertion is like a second birth, in which we confirm and take upon ourselves the naked fact of our original physical appearance. The insertion is not forced upon us by necessity,

Eichmann whose defence rested on their simply following orders – as a case of 'banality'. They were not consciously, wilfully evil. That ascribes too much motive to power. Rather they were completely without action or the possibility for action. Their language slumbered, there was a falling away of self-awareness, mere naming without seeing, and labour and work were enjoined and enjoyed without questionability. The executors of genocide were being pragmatic in a base sense, unquestioningly absconding from responsibility, simply complying, obeying. Hannah Arendt *Eichmann in Jerusalem*. New York: Viking Press. 1963.

[52] Hannah Arendt *The Human Condition*, 47.

[53] At many Japanese Shinto shrines the gates are guarded by a pair of *Komainu*, dog- or lion-like spirit creatures, one to the right with its mouth open, wording the opening letter 'a' of the Sanskrit alphabet, the other to the left its mouth closed, wording the last letter 'un', one breathing in, the other out, in the breath ('a-un') comes the start and closure of all things, and during comes the harmony of things held in balance.

like labor, and is not prompted by utility, like work. It may be stimulated by the presence of others whose company we would like to join, but it is never conditioned by them; its impulse springs from the condition of beginning which came into the world when we were born and to which we respond by beginning something new on our own initiative. To act, in its most general sense, means to take an initiative, to begin (as the Greek word *archein*, 'to begin', 'to lead, and, eventually, 'to rule' indicates), to set something into motion (which is the original meaning of the Latin *agere*). Because they are *initium*, newcomers and beginners by virtue of birth, men take initiative, are prompted into action.[54]

Following the first birth of a unique but naked, speechless and action-less coming into the world, the word and deed of action bring forth a second natality, now born again to take on the 'naked fact of our physical appearance', do things and say things on our own initiative; the possibility of the creation of something new. In her emphasis on beginning Arendt expands on the nature of action: as an insertion into the world of set agreements it is both free and plural in nature. As a beginning, a commencing, action is twinned irrevocably with possibility, newness, unpredictability and difference. The nature of such a beginning cannot be planned, or ordered, or arranged for; it is what she calls a condition of infinite improbability, a birth of the new whose uniqueness takes it beyond the organic patterns by which the realm of labour is settled into its biological motion, and beyond the blandishments and aspirations of cultural evaluation and social engineers.[55] It is its own small horizon in which nothing is yet settled. It emerges from the basic primal question asked by all new things, the question prompted by the *daimon*: 'Who am I'? It is a question in thoughtful speech that declares a sense of belonging to being itself, as opposed to reporting on qualities and characteristics. It is from such a 'who' question – one that is answered the very moment it is expressed because its expression announces a beginning, an opening-up under the gaze of an 'other', the *daimon* that is now also a *polis* – that all forms of freedom emerge.[56]

---

[54] Hannah Arendt *The Human Condition*, 177.

[55] Arendt flirts with Deism here: 'This character of startling unexpectedness is inherent in all beginnings and all origins. Thus, the origin of life from inorganic matter is an infinite improbability of inorganic processes, as is the coming into being of the earth viewed from the standpoint of processes in the universe, or the evolution of human out of animal life. The new always happens against the overwhelming odds of statistical laws and their probability, which for all practical purposes amounts to certainty; the new therefore always appears in the guise of a miracle. The fact that man is capable of action means the unexpected can be expected from him, that he is able to perform what is infinitely improbable' (Hannah Arendt *The Human Condition*, 178). What is new and emergent always occurs in spite of probabilities.

[56] Hannah Arendt *The Human Condition*, 178–9. Without speech action would lose both is revelatory character and its subjects, in speech the actor announces the intentionality by which the action is something to which they belong: 'If action as beginning corresponds

Action is, by definition, immune to management. Once expressed, action comes fully formed, and its resonance spills outwards in ways that can confound, as easily as confirm, expectation. And once expressed there is no going back, for it colours and settles into the character of its exponents like dye into cloth, it colours them with self-sufficiency. It is through action that we realize a condition of happiness if, following Aristotle, by happiness and the nature of happiness we mean a critical awareness of what it is that affords us the continual company of what Arendt likens to the disturbing prospect of our conscience, our *daimon* (recalling Nietzsche's connecting it to *eu-daimonia*), without needing the guiding artifice of work. Action stands alone and what it finds is found to be good, without embellishment, without artificial improvement, without augmentation, without the often temporary experience typically attributed to happiness as a mood or state of affairs.[57] To act is to live well over time, and to have lived in such a way that the well-being of one's *daimon* is attended to as a form of revealing or unconcealing of being in the natality of action.[58]

Accompanying natality comes plurality. To begin anew in a second birth is to announce oneself as a self in the performance of action to

to the fact of birth, if it is the actualization of the human condition of natality, then speech corresponds to the fact of distinctness and is the actualization of the human condition of plurality, that is, of living as a distinct and unique being among equals.'

[57] Aristotle too is asking after the nature of human beings. What is it that makes us distinctly human? It cannot be that we are alive as we share that with plants, or sentient, which we share with animals, so it is more akin to the active exercise of the soul's functions in accord with rational principle, which is, then, to not just do things but to do them well, after consideration What then of what it is to do things well? This is virtue: action that brings rewards that is pleasant, but above all Aristotle poses the question thus in *Nichomachean Ethics*:

> To say however that the Supreme Good is happiness will probably appear a truism; we still require a more explicit account of what constitutes happiness. Perhaps then we may arrive at this by ascertaining what is man's function. For the goodness or efficiency of a flute-player or sculptor or craftsman of any sort, and in general of anybody who has some function or business to perform, is thought to reside in that function; and similarly it may be held that the good of man resides in the function of man, if he has a function.
>
> Are we then to suppose that, while the carpenter and the shoemaker have definite functions or businesses belonging to them, man as such has none, and is not designed by nature to fulfil any function? Must we not rather assume that, just as the eye, the hand, the foot and each of the various members of the body manifestly has a certain function of its own, so a human being also has a certain function over and above all the functions of his particular members? What then precisely can this function be? (1097b)

[58] This reading from Arendt finds relates the human self to its *daimon* accompanying each of us as we live, but which being somehow aside from us, is often only visible to others (as our fate) and not ourselves. She thinks only those in whose deeds a life is ended definitively, that is, it is sacrificed prematurely in a remarkable (and hence mythologized) form, such as that of Achilles, can fully experience *eudaimonia*, as only these supreme acts make a full (and hence complete, ended) life. Hannah Arendt *The Human Condition*, 194.

which others, necessarily, are an audience. Not mute spectators, but equally active beings with whom one seeks agreements. To act is not only invoking a *daimon* through thought (the two-in-one condition of looking upon and potentially agreeing with one's own self, but also a placing of oneself in others' conditions). This ability to think within others' thoughts is more than a dialogue with one's own self. It also requires awareness of conversations with those with whom one is in (potentially) some kind of (dis)agreement. To be aware of others and others' expectations and memories, commitments and entitlements means 'the ability to see things not only from one's own point of view but in the perspective of all those who happen to be present', a capacity that enables people to orient themselves towards a plurality.[59] It is in this way that the freedom of action is not an outward expression of inner certitude, but an already public performance whose certainty is being carried through attempts at persuasive argument. The need to persuade through performance is an acknowledgement that any insertion into the world through speech and action is an encounter with others with whom speakers are in relations of profound equality (all humans speak and act) and distinction (they do so uniquely): there are no formulae or ready-made routines available to action, each expression demands the effort of an imaginative placing into the lives of others.

Neither labour nor work afford us such natality and plurality. To labour is to make things to be sold, consumed and replaced, or otherwise to store until they decay or spoil. To work is to make objects to be used as tools or guidelines, or as symbols to be contemplated, worshipped or possessed. The production of labour is ceaseless, and confines all life to a headless fixation with its own continuation, without room for the two-in-one dialogue of authenticity. The fabrication of work would seem to offer more scope for authenticity, given it pointedly and explicitly attempts to elevate human forms of life to the level of a subject relating to 'objects' that exist 'out there': through work comes a sense of sovereign command and agency whose artifice keeps it separated from the outer environment into which it violently projects itself, securing its own sense of continuation that will outlive its meagre, biological span. Yet it is precisely because of its anthropocentric artifice that work also fails to render the human being into an authentic condition.

It is in action that authenticity arises. What appears as intimate to a condition of authenticity is a sense of a human self that feels implicated in occurrence: what marks the authentic self is the experience of altering, transforming or beginning again, and somehow at one's own behest.

---

[59] Hannah Arendt The crisis in culture, 218.

But this is not the equivalent to having rational control over events, or to thinking oneself on a trajectory that reaches beyond them, but an expressive awareness of an aeshetic power to act within them. Hence, for Arendt, far from being an inner state of subject sovereignty, the condition of authenticity is an organized giving over to the gaze of others in the public creation of opinions (being aesthetic, action is making something that otherwise doesn't exist, it is not natural, but nor is it committing to a separating truth: because of natality and plurality, what is made is always subject to metamorphosis).

To experience authenticity requires, first, a solitude from practice sufficient to transform a consciousness of saying and doing things into a conscience about having said or done them (from naming to saying), or in imagining oneself saying or doing them. In this it tended towards being a contemplative condition, one which Arendt was to distinguish as a condition of thinking and then willing. Yet this two-in-one dialogue is only possible in the company of others from whose distinct presence comes an open, and fragmented appreciation of how things can be said and done differently. Under the collective force of this public expression what appears as something 'given' (a determining fact) becomes 'what gives' (an expressive handing over), and what gives is what makes and then hands over, and what is handed over is not determined and cannot be controlled. It is, then, a distinctively immediate condition in which the idea of cause and effect (the basic ordering of a narrative that, in the hands of fabricating work, becomes a comforting story that begins and ends) collapse into one another, for no sooner is an action performed than it acts upon others capable of their own actions, outside these being just a reaction or adaptation. The aesthetic act of creating opinion sets in train an affective spilling over that is without edges and which, in practical effect, can as easily break open long-established agreements as it does re-enforce them. In the space of appearances this cycle of unbounded resonance occurs intensively, it cannot be unfolded into sequential chains of thought/act/effect; the action and its resonance are ravelling and unravelling in a kind of expanding, expressive, affective present in which speech and action arrive and disappear as one.[60] To speak is itself a thought and action and in actions what is said is being borne along, and in acting comes the speech by which any insertion into the already existing world is being affirmed or challenged in new distinctions.

It is in the nature of these plural, new beginnings that one cannot extrapolate from them towards a known end, or invoke a settled origin,

---

[60] Hannah Arendt *The Human Condition*, 191.

and as a space of such appearances the *polis* is not somewhere to consider either the determining biological ends met by labour or the presumption of sovereign agency fabricated by work from which things emerge; there is neither resolution nor control. The fact that materially and institutionally the *polis* is itself an end towards which the *strategoi* and others labour and work, at least insofar as it is an organized condition towards which we ought to orient ourselves, is an apparent irony to which Arendt is alive, and to which she responds by thinking of the *polis* purely in terms of language. As a grammatical condition, the architectural and legal means by which the *polis* is constituted are reconciled to the realization of its being more akin to a pure means, namely a means whose expression is nothing more than its own mediacy embodied in the being-in-common that is action.

It is to language that we now turn.

2   Can the *Strategoi* Ever Build a *Polis?*

Logos and the Creation of a Self as a Grammatical Effect

The biggest risk to the space of appearances is itself. The material from which the *polis* is made is the language of disclosure (*logos*), for it is only when braided with threads of speech in deliberation and dispute that action takes the free and plural form of thoughtful action. It is a space where natural life (*zōē*) becomes storied or disclosed life (*bios*) without either ceding to the other. The connecting distinction between *zōē* and *bios* is a subtle and generative one, the former reminds the latter of its frailties. *Bios*, without the company of *zōē*, finds labour and work taking hold of power, transforming it into force and violence. Humans become organized around hierarchies of particular interests, typically those in control of human capital. The narrated life of *bios* becomes a fixing truth using names, either because an opinion dominates so much it becomes a totalizing belief system (*dogma*), or because speculative language slips into mannerism and idle posturing (*torpor*). Arendt refuses truth by imaging the *polis* as a space where *zōē* is kept in play as an expression of first birth (just as seeing rather than naming finds the semantic in company with the semiotic), and where *bios* encourages the possibility of second birth, disclosed in an active life of questioning and starting anew.[1] In holding them in proximity the *polis* gives each its

---

[1] Hannah Arendt *The Human Condition*, 24–6. Arendt's interpretation of Aristotle has been influential, notably for Agamben's reading of *homo sacer* as the bare life, *zōē*, or voice, which lacks *bios*, or life with language. There is debate as to whether Aristotle used the distinction in this way, or whether *zōē* refers to life including life of animals and plants, and *bios* to human life, and whether *bios* is one expression of *zōē*, or a rationally distinct addition, insofar as its sociality is reasoned, not instinctual. Clearly, though, *bios* is not sustainable without *zōē*, at least in an empirical sense of the animal world and human world being entrained in one another. The opposition between them is not so clear cut in the source material from Aristotle's *Politics*. See James Finlayson 'Bare life' and politics in Agamben's reading of Aristotle. *The Review of Politics*, 2010, 72(1): 97–126. In Arendt it is equivocal whether humans are creatures with *zōē* and the addition of *bios*, or beings of *bios* who keep company with the natural forces of *zōē*. Given

distinct due in the continually renewing and replenishing power of action. If action is subsumed by labour the *polis* is supplanted by forces of survival and sovereignty in which citizens cede their natality to biological processes, and if it is subjectified to work then natality is ceded to ideals mediated though propaganda. In neither case is authenticity, and hence strategy, possible. It is in the language of disclosure, *logos*, that *bios* is held in communion with the natural life force of *zōē* to which humans can be disclosed, but only ever through language

In the *polis*, language has to be worked at, and worked into interstices, to prevent it from becoming assertive, stagnant, domineering, or enervating. To attend to this animating balance of naming and saying is to be alive to the conditions of persuasion (*pistis*, a proof or assurance that is trusted and believed), and so, by inference, to the means by which any opinion on commitments and entitlements becomes so persuasive as to refuse the company of natality. *Logos* is language of both speaking and listening, and of reckoning and accounting, it is language that is tied to reasoning and is the root for logic, yet its operations expose as much as they define appearances. *Logos* is speech that comes alive with its physical, bodily demands: having to shape speech into plausible forms that resonate with desired affects provoking or soothing the temper and temperament of interlocutors. Before then separating, to find schisms and chance meanings. Through debate speech becomes a risky way of declaring oneself through expressive, yet measured grammatical compositions. Without *logos* there is speechlessness, a condition that is difficult to grasp, or to think even, given thought is grammatical in nature.

The *polis* is spatially generated through the argumentative performance of *logos* in which experience, concepts and ideas are brought to each other, and each speaker likewise is brought to another, without condescension or indifference, but always with the lure of persuasion (so finely and nobly wrought in Periclean oratory) or novelty. Though proportionate, this the exchange is never complete or even tidy; not even Pericles can have the last say. The content of an utterance – the locutionary form or meaning of the statement – is accompanied by the active illocutionary force of its having been uttered by a speaking body, and by the perlocutionary force of its persuading, seducing or influencing other bodies (and more importantly, failing to). Unlike the illocutionary force of a promise or a signature, persuasion is not manifest in the initial

Arendt's lament of the decline of human life to mere *animal rationale* which she regarded as a state that was sub animal, and the repeated insistence from Heidegger that Dasein could not be understood properly as animal plus reason, but was its own form of disclosing life, the latter seems the more productive interpretation.

attempt. It has a longer temporal duration as it must be felt by another, it is an I–you perturbation of passion, improvisation and accident rippling across speech.[2] As Thucydides admits, the content, manner and style of Pericles' speeches was nothing without an audience capable of being affected, and this capacity had a long gestation. The *demos* had become the most distinctive element of the Athenian state with the encouragement of the aristocratic Pericles. They owed him, and more so given it was he: who had changed the law to allow fees to be paid to citizens for attending the grand jury, who had offered free theatre seats and sponsored the performances at the Greater Dionysia of some of the greatest Athenian drama (not least Aeschylus' *The Persians*), who had initiated the building of the Parthenon, and who had invited the greatest minds and intellects to the city. The citizens had been schooled in commitments and entitlements that conferred on them the distinctive *arché* of a pre-eminent and ruthless city: their senses were primed to belong to a space with such passion that its life was indistinct from their own.

Pericles' speech (or is it Thucydides') is a speech act whose duration is open, and it either works or misfires, depending on the prevailing flows of emotion, on the stock of common sense (publicly held opinions whose cogency provide a repository of general forms of wisdom) and emotional range, and on the clarity, brevity and cogency of the arguments being employed, all of which cohere in what John Austin calls moments of felicity. One can never predict with any certainty that the act will work ('infelicity is an ill to which all acts are heir'),[3] and it is this very condition of ignorance that grounds what is most productive about it. As Shoshana Felman, somewhat scandalously, suggests, it is in loosening the criteria of truth with forces of seduction that meaning comes alive, though without firm ground on which to lie, and always in the speckling company of accident, illusion, mistake and mystery.[4] Reaching the point of persuasion is not just a logical process of proof, far from it: it happens amid the hubbub of open, considerate talk, and it is always incomplete. Its persuasive force comes generously and so most powerfully in its being a newly formed way of seeing and making contact with our condition of being,

---

[2] Stanley Cavell Foreword. In *The Scandal of the Speaking Body*, Shoshana Felman. Stanford: Stanford University Press. 2003, xvii–xx.

[3] John Austin *How to Do Things with Words*. Oxford: Clarendon Press. 1975, 185.

[4] Shoshana Felman *The Scandal of the Speaking Body*. Stanford: Stanford University Press, 2003, 64–7, 121. Felman works with John Austin's phrase of passage to heighten the sense of action being a merger of language and body, that what defines a human being is the insertion into the world through speech acts (political, if you like), the scandal being that the speaking body cannot really know what it is doing until it is said and hence done. This is action in the *polis*, untamed.

a beginning again, with all its hints, rather than a competition with all its weighty accomplishment. In Pericles the force was so generous as to suffer from its fulsomeness: he was so good a democrat that the old, elite families of which he was a member thought him a visionary traitor, and no sooner had a first bout of plague hit Athens, they rounded on him, accusing him of over-filling the city and creating a weakened citizenry of wall-hiding cowards. Once he died, he really died, as did democracy, as an intellectual demagogue – a leader of the *demos* – he spoke too highly of the people's views, he gave them too much scope, he gave them too much ambition.

Opinions Are Greater than Truths

For Arendt scope was all important to the space of appearances, and it required that the views of the people were configured as opinions, not truth. Truth claims are prone to hegemony; there is always a risk that stated beliefs will subsume the process by which they emerged. Here truth locks the world down, whereas opinion opens it up. The two are not in strict opposition: opinion needs the support of factual and experiential truths to realize a properly considered form rather than collapsing into brute assertion. But here truth-as-fact plays the subservient role of feeding opinion, thereby preventing it from becoming too polemical and idealistic. Truth comes as a proposed necessity against which opinions can gather in waves and smother in surging spray, or, more calmly, lap against its edges, but whichever way, the fluidity carries greater force.

Truth itself must be treated with caution, for if a truth is deemed free from the open sea of stone-eroding opinions, its adherents will then turn their backs and 'go inland', looking to gain height over the enlarged and unprejudiced space of appearances. Once inland the truth becomes a form of force and violence; both as a claim that excludes others by calling them false or ill-informed, and as a distinction-making incision into the world that, forgetting its own nature as a perspective, speaks only of order and unity. The *polis* was there to keep the truth on the shoreline, facing the open waters of opinion, at their mercy. Julia Kristeva talks of this continual bringing together of opinion and truth as a condition of both comprehension and apprehension. Those expressing opinions have comprehended things and events by actively exposing themselves to suggestion and stimulation, they wait to be seeded. Yet as she comprehends a speaker also apprehends how things are: she takes a view, throwing aside what she feels is distracting from, or superfluous to, the distinction she is making. In making such a distinction in the world she recreates and so transforms it in some way: in being a receptacle she is also an origin.[5] It is an origin that works into absence, using metaphor to grope for the purchase of meaning and so scramble along. This is how the language of the *polis* works to open up appearances: it is riddled with metaphor. Metaphors, suggests Anne Carson: 'teach the mind / to enjoy error / and to learn / from the juxtaposition of WHAT IS and WHAT IS NOT the case'. And it is the process of juxtaposing that matters: to join things that belong apart 'causes the mind to experience itself / in the act of making a mistake'.[6]

So what matters in meaning making is not just that you are telling truths – which somehow elevate themselves and look down from above, much like, as Carson goes on to remark, Thucydides does when chronicling and signalling the opening of the Peloponnesian war as being in spring, and with other facts about campaigning seasons. Whereas Virginia Woolf, in contrast, in her account of the opening of a war, starts from within her own time, a burst of impressions, until they are interrupted by a mark, a fact, of the kind Thucydides is making continually. Woolf's language redounds as fully as Thucydides', but without its arch loftiness, its truths are of a more aching and ordinary hue, woven as they are with a phenomenology of on going experience. It is this kind of contrast discussed by Carson in accounting for ocurrence that opens up the question of style.

If, in the *polis*, there is no truth as such, only truths, then these truths are richer and more compelling the more capable are their adherents in the rhetorical art of expressive, reasoned style. In being intimate with force and persuasion these rhetorical exchanges (unlike those in bringing about proof or in following moves on a board game) have the quality of being embodied, empirically present events: the exponent and interlocutor vie with one another as equals. Yet there is a sense of its being somewhat combative in style, and why should this be so? Might we consider conversation that does not rely on 'well inked' full stops to be equally viable within the *polis*? After all the equality being embodied there is not pre-ordained or claimed as a formal right, but practiced and generated in civic exchange: only then can opinion trump truth. In this space of appearances all citizens, by being there, are equally intelligent, equally alive to the possibility of forming views, equally engaged in bringing being into questionability, without having to adopt a specific style of thoughtfulness. Without dogmatic positions or specific interests at stake there is no presumption of transference from those who know to those who do not, nor is there a compelling sense of *Bildung* or transformative development towards known values because of this transference. Rather, the opinion comes to form itself as that about which

---

[5] Julia Kristeva *Hannah Arendt*. Translated by Ross Guberman. New York: Columbia University Press. 2001, 26.
[6] Anne Carson *Men in the Off Hours*. New York: Knopf. 2000, 31.

a speaker and interlocutor show consideration, a triadic forming of the yet-to-be-placed whose restlessness forms the crucible for meaning.

In such a *polis* citizens take part in what Michel Foucault calls 'the serious play of questions and answers', embodying enquiry, attempting persuasion by discussing across their differences. They nudge, object, suggest, always granting the other their right to belong to the conversation. As such the citizen is opposite to what Foucault calls the polemicist, the speaker who lacks generosity because they are, by definition, asserting a position and refusing those who oppose their position the right to belong to the conversation, indeed there is no conversation there is assertion, the polemicist first knows the truth, then bellows like a cow.[7]

For him [the polemicist], then the game consists not of recognizing this person as a subject having the right to speak but of abolishing him as interlocutor, from any possible dialogue; and his final objective will be not to come as close as possible to a difficult truth but to bring about the triumph of the just cause he has been manifestly upholding from the beginning. The polemicist relies on a legitimacy that his adversary is by definition denied.[8]

---

[7] In an early work, Nietzsche introduces the idea of truth as linguistic, polemical convention akin to bellowing. In designating one thing 'this' and another 'that' we satisfy our herdish instincts to be in each other's company, as the distinctions themselves are nothing more than things we agree on: classifications and principles that are sedimented as truths and which then channel human congregating and communicating. They are and remain the stuff of what Arendt calls the common world. If we fall in with the flow, we are truthful, if we deviate, we are in error. We take solace in the definite and certain outlines of these truths whose form lends life a sense of balance and promise. The insertion of a 'this' and a 'that' lays the groundwork for identifying reality. We are able to establish law-like causalities ('this' is of a form that follows from 'that'), a sense of progressive time ('this' is of a form that can become 'that'), and for classificatory knowledge ('this' compared to 'that', 'this' belongs to 'that'). The virtue of these insertions is they allow us to cope with the world, to pragmatically deal with the business of surviving and flourishing: we think, then we act, there is an effect, we observe the effect, we think, we act, and so on, all the while using concepts to relate and fix what is otherwise opaque and fluid. This allows us to get on, but it does so by invoking collapsing form of truth:

> What then is truth? A movable host of metaphors, metonymies, and, anthropomorphisms: in short, a sum of human relations which have been poetically and rhetorically intensified, transferred, and embellished, and which, after long usage, seem to a people to be fixed, canonical, and binding. Truths are illusions which we have forgotten are illusions – they are metaphors that have become worn out and have been drained of sensuous force, coins which have lost their embossing and are now considered as metal and no longer as coins.

In this concealing the truths are held in tightly knitted patterns of vraisemblance that insulate us from what Nietzsche senses are the fluxing, indifferent uncertainties of nature. This is the reality from which we hide, the reality is turmoil, immediacy, accident, and conflict between forces forever bonded to one another. (Quoted in *On Truth and Falsity in their Ultramoral Sense. Friedrich Nietzsche. Early Greek Philosophy and Other Essays.* Translated by Maximillian A. Mügge. New York: Macmillan. 1911, 171–92, 180.)

[8] Michel Foucault Polemics, politics and problematizations. In *Essential Works of Foucault Vol. 1.* Edited by Paul Rabinow. New York: New Press. 1998.

How, asks Foucault, can ideas be generated by the polemicist? The polemicist is an inland dweller, retrenched and trenchant in their beliefs that have secured a refuge from which to proceed outwards, looking to conquer and occupy. The polemicist deals in strict causes. A cause is linear, distinct, and claims entailments that cannot be resisted because their necessity is secured by justice. Perhaps, then, to recall his encomium to Athens, Pericles is just one such polemicist, that is if he views himself as being buoyed along by just cause. But then he was not, strictly speaking, in the *polis* when issuing his oratory, it was at a ceremonial funeral honouring the dead, held by the banks of the Eridanos river. He was not in conversation, where, we might presume, his speech was different in tone: more enquiring, open, curious.

In contrast to polemicists, Arendt is imagining a collection of active bodies who are origins, not causes. An origin is open, kaleidoscopic, democratic and utterly complicit with the atmosphere it animates. The natality by which she defines the second births in the *polis* is a coming together of origins configuring the struggle for self-presentation through events (myths, symbols, stories, characters) that orient citizens to the sense of their own history (they can comport themselves towards earlier human achievements) without this becoming law-like dogma.[9]

In this way citizens can be carried along by new opinions, and then fall away, without forming into a consensual order organized by specific interests. The danger of consensus is real, the relating can come to dominate the separating, especially when it is dogmatic appeal gaining traction. The consensus can appear to be fluid, it can argumentatively bulge, shimmer and gyrate, but like a haul of herring it can get caught in a net of particular and private agreements. If the persuasion takes hold the meaning can become unimpeachable, the attraction overwhelming, and the space of appearances becomes a stage for polemics and position taking. This is when rhetoric becomes sophistry, and so a corruption of the *polis*. Barbara Cassin puts it neatly when she reminds us of how Aristotle opened his *Rhetoric* with the counsel that we might consider rhetoric as a protection from rhetoric (sophistry).[10] The sophists teach

---

[9] In *Origins of Totalitarianism* Arendt suggests 'The event illuminates its own past, but it can never be deduced from it.' In this way she hazards that the rise of totalitarian systems can never be causally analysed, only apprehended after the fact as a gathering of multiple and disparate forces that, hitherto, had little in common, but which in the light of events became cast in association. Yet it remains the case, that of these forces, the human remains centre stage, specifically the acting, thinking, willing subject. It is here we find the well spring of origins, so to speak, and it is to here Arendt recurs.

[10] Barbara Cassin The evidence of Phryne, or Phryne stripped bare by rhetoric even. In *Making Things Public: Atmospheres of Democracy*. Edited by Bruno Latour and Peter Weibel. Karlsruhe: Center for Art and Media. 2005, 694–7. Cassin poses the case of Phryne, stripped naked before a court by her lawyer Hyperides who, rhetorically and

us there is always another way of things appearing to each of us (*dokei moi*), the rhetor teaches us that amid these appearances come truths and the *polis* is the space in which these truths are being formed, continually: truths appear. There is, though, no dialectical end point at which a founding truth is discovered. Rather there is a grounding in *logos*. Attending to the condition of protecting the space in which opinions are formed means being alive to how, in being faithful to the self-disclosure of expression, there is further implied a grounding condition of faith in *logos* itself, something that comes from within.

Perhaps this is too idealized? Arendt thinks not, and she enlists Socrates to show why. For Socrates the *polis* was a space in which the citizens came to articulate what it was they already half knew, but had supressed, given the everyday dominance of work and labour in household affairs. Socrates acted as a catalyst, a dialectician able to elicit from others a capacity to reveal the truthfulness of their *doxai* by encouraging them to relinquish the comforts of habit and obedience and, instead, to think through considered argument into 'seeing' the condition of one's own being. He introduces them to *logos* as a means of giving *bios* a more compelling personal narrative than it otherwise would have. The culmination of this process was not truth per se, it was not a condition of collective agreement that 'this' and not 'that' constituted how things were and should be with the world. It was also a question of 'Who one is?', a question that could be addressed only when each speaker experienced the use of *logos*, and in this state of thoughtful inquiry subject themselves to scrutiny, and find there a being freed from the contradiction of willing themselves to act without will. Under Socrates influence the *polis* becomes a space of conscience – a place not of agreed public principle but of a public made up of citizens each holding themselves alongside their own sense of self-willed direction.[11]

---

at exactly the right moment, was attempting to elicit pity from the lascivious but not unmoved male judges who in witnessing unblemished skin also bore witness to a divinity that would not speak its name, only show its power to move, and in showing making the words shimmer and radiate in ways far stronger than those employed in the argument against her. She is acquitted because of the truth and reality of words animated and heightened by display. In coming to a resolution who or what was being served here?

[11] Hannah Arendt Philosophy and politics. *Social Research*, 1954/1990, 57(1): 73–103. Richard Bernstein notices the calm and cautionary nature of Arendt's ideas here: how she does not believe thinking an antidote to totalitarian regimes, for thinking often fails to tell us what to do, but it is very powerful in showing us what not to do, what is plain wrong. To think is not to invoke rival principles, to pit good content against bad, but to acknowledge what happens when the basic human capacity to reflect from particulars towards a general condition of others and otherness is lost. Richard Bernstein Arendt on thinking. In *The Cambridge Companion to Hannah Arendt*. 2006, 277–92, 285.

This is the gift of Socrates, a 'gadfly' who provoked each of his interlocutors to find within themselves the possibility for a transforming dialogue, and who found in the *polis* a public stage for the expressive projection of this continual expression of beginnings. Being alone with the two-in-one of one's thinking is the source of natality and comes before all else:

> It would be better for me that my lyre or a chorus I directed should be out of tune and loud with discord, and that multitudes of men should disagree with me, rather than that I, being one, should be out of harmony with myself and contradict me.[12]

It is the individuating, distinction-making self from which the *polis* emerges. For Arendt Socrates exemplifies what it is to demand one live alongside oneself in this examined way (*Selbstdenken*). As an exemplar Socrates is peerless, there has been no other Western figure able to move with such bright alacrity between the mundane and exceptional, between the bustle of the *polis* and the calm of inner thought; a city lives and dies by its capacity to encourage and learn from such figures, and those who should especially take note are the *strategoi*.

Alcibiades as a Case of Strategic Failure

Perhaps, after *Pericles*, the most famous of all *strategoi* is Alcibiades, elected to the council of ten generals around 421 BCE. Though re-elected the following year, by many accounts his term as office holder was underwhelming, but it confirmed in him a calling for power, and provided a platform for its further pursuit. He was jousting for influence against the backdrop of the increasingly fraught relations between a once dominant Athens and a rising Sparta. According to Thucydides, Alcibiades was a bullish proponent of expansion, arguing in the realist spirit of naked self-interest that to retain regional influence Athens had to extend it, and that to continue to enjoy self-rule it was necessary to rule others, for only then, in possession of others' resources, could one be assured of protecting one's own. And whilst Sparta was too strong to take on directly, Athens might do well to look to weaker cities from which they could extract much needed revenues, readying itself. The city listened. In 416 BCE *Melos* was besieged by Athenian triremes and forced to capitulate: the men were executed, and women and children sold into slavery. And the following year, Athens' leaders sanctioned what became an ill-fated expedition to Syracuse in Sicily that had been brokered by Alcibiades and a cohort

[12] Hannah Arendt Thinking and moral considerations, 417–46.

of Athenian traders. Sicily, like Athens an early exponent of democratic rule, was rich in forests and arable fields and ripe for plucking. Alcibiades nominated himself as head of the expedition, and was duly appointed. He was not without rivals though, and just prior to leaving he was implicated (probably falsely) in a drunken desecration of statues of Hermes (god of messengers and voyagers), a scandal ensued, and though he had already set out, he was ordered back to Athens to stand trial. Fearing his standing was falling, and increasingly alive to the hubristic excess of trying to attack Syracuse, Alcibiades ducked from the pending charges by evading the galley sent to escort him back. Now in exile and sentenced to death in absentia, he defected to Sparta and became an advisor, plotting against his erstwhile home. The Spartans, though, remained suspicious of this refugee, and grew tired of his scheming. Losing influence here too, Alcibiades absented himself once more, ending up as a counsellor to the Persians, who also grew wary. He drifted in this way for over eight years, long enough for the Sicily expedition to fail, and, in a lucky twist of fate, for the Athenians to think the blame for this defeat lay with those who tried to arrest Alcibiades rather than letting him lead the army into the fray. Alcibiades did his upmost to encourage these interpretations, and eventually the newly installed Athenian oligarchy invited him to make restitution with the city by suggesting he help lead naval expeditions around the Hellespont. These were relatively successful, allowing Athens to maintain its regional dominance, and whilst it was his fellow generals who were the actual fighters, it was Alcibiades who wrote the colourful dispatches of the battles in which he cast himself in glowing terms. His sophistry was persuasive enough to find him pardoned and the city allowed him back within its walls. In 407 BCE his property was restored and the death curse lifted, he was accorded the title *strategos autkrator* (high commander of land and sea), and led the Athenian fleet first to victories, but then to devastating defeat by the Spartans of Lysander at Notium in 406 BCE, a symbolic loss from which Athens never really recovered.

Alcibiades seems to have had the career of an entitled and gifted schemer. He was a clever speaker, someone who had been cleaved in tutelage to the great Athenian leader Pericles, from whom he had learnt how to read political situations with perspicacity and fostered a skill in practical adaptation. He was versed in the life of the Athenian *polis* (the practical instantiation of such, as opposed to the somewhat abstracted one we have been discussing) and made it work for him. He understood how to use language, and how to win others over by allying oneself to demonstrations of decisive and compelling success, and absenting oneself when loss looks more likely. He seemed able to work his way through to the affections of others, but then got carried away with the influence this brought him. As well as Pericles he had been taught by Socrates, and he had flourished under the attentions of such a beguiling master. Socrates had instructed him in how to conduct reserved and patient argument, and more broadly, in how to defer and resist immediate desire in order to realize long-term goals. Desires, being always directed to an immediate end, were dangerous if they went unchecked, for they locked down one's options and fixed one's focus in a linear, inflexible way.

As a result, Alcibiades was able to channel and exploit his talents more effectively, he schooled himself in the arts of rhetoric, and sought the attention and favour of many, for example by spending a small fortune on teams of horses to win the chariot races at the Olympic games, and so better secure his political status. Yet his learning stuttered, and became twisted, desires overcame him. He often relapsed into debauchery (see Figure 2.1), he seemed all too willing to revert to sophistry when it suited his interests to do so, and he seems to have found the *polis* little more than a space for the advancing of personal and sectional interests. In this he was not alone, and according to many historical accounts, *strategoi* like Alcibiades were as much in thrall to labour and work as they were action and their rhetorical language was far more typically motivated by the pursuit of self-interest than it was self-disclosure.

An exception to this prevailing understanding of his character comes in Plato's *Symposium*.[13] Here we witness someone aflush with success and experience, someone who, as a strategist, no longer feels the need for advice, but whose confidence is, nevertheless, disturbed by the memory of his pupillage to Socrates. The *Symposium* is set in 416 BCE, just prior to the draining and dispiriting Sicilian campaign; Alcibiades is still enjoying the fruits of his lofty station. Plato writes of him arriving towards the end of what has been until then an unusually sober party (including the

---

[13] There are two main sources from Plato linking Socrates and Alcibiades (though some suggest Callicles in the *Gorgias* (he who issues the famous epithet 'might is right') is a mask for Alcibiades). *Alcibiades I* is a conversation between the elder teacher Socrates and the younger, eager student Alcibiades in which they discuss the knowledge needed for effective political life, in effect for strategy. The dramatic tension, such as it is, lies in the nature or quality of this knowledge, whether it is of oneself or of a setting, and to the extent the former comes to the fore, whether this self-knowledge is reflexive and transformative, and so, ipso facto, a form of care. Alcibiades also appears in the *Symposium*, and it is here we witness the upshot of Alcibiades' learning: whilst he clearly enjoys political success, this remains, it seems, a fragile achievement requiring constant concern for managing different sets of interests and playing them off one another. He has learned to gather information and manipulate, but has he learned about himself, has he the humility that stipples and shades the otherwise smooth and brilliant contours of his presence? Clearly not.

Figure 2.1 Pietro Testa, *Drunken Alcibiades interrupting the Symposium*, gravure, 1648. Wikimedia commons

trio of Socrates, Agathon and Aristophanes) to which he is a dramatic contrast.

Adorned with vines and violets, intoxicated, and already having caroused with the flautists who he had found outside, having been bidden to take their leave whilst the men sat down to the serious business of talk. Alcibiades wants the flautists to come back in and play, he wants it to be a proper symposium, and naturally assumes dominion over the gathering, much as he was attempting to assume dominion over Athens.

The theme of the hitherto sober symposium had been in praise of love, and Alcibiades riffs off this, without invitation, by performing an encomium to his old teacher. The praise for Socrates is fulsome, yet enigmatic. Alcibiades recalls his having been smitten by the erotic attentions of this pug-nosed elder, and yet utterly wary in his embrace: entranced and anxious at one and the same time. In a poem by Anne Carson we find him recalling just how uncannily persuasive Socrates could be:

> In Athens orators are hot –
> Perikles for instance.
> Now Perikles is good, but

listening to him can be pretty predictable.
When Sokrates speaks, on the other hand,
I experience something uncanny,
I don't know what

it is – a wild feeling
like a heart attack, or like dancing –[14]

Alcibiades goes on, recounting his thwarted attempts at seducing 'hot' Socrates. He finds himself rebuffed: not directly, only suggestively, and always provocatively. He recalls them being accomplices in fighting, though it was Socrates who had the swagger. He recalls them being interlocutors, though it was Socrates who introduced the inscrutable silences, the charm, the quick-fingered witticisms that pricked youthful confidence. He recalls them being physically close under the same cloak, though it was Socrates who found great, disorienting distances in such proximity. Alcibiades suggests the pedagogic methods to which he was subject were duplicitous, deliberately goading and upsetting in their refusing him the comforts of convention and flattery.[15] Socrates' force worked in strange and indirect gradations, and was all the more powerful for it. There was nothing upfront and honest about it, his irony was hard to live with, but in concealing things, and himself along with them, Socrates revealed the world more fully than anyone who simply sought to tell the truth. Socrates' method was enjoined to a basic irony: truth cannot be told, only reveal itself, and the revelation works most powerfully in the company of subterfuge and veiled cunning. Alcibiades praises Socrates for this most basic of lessons: if you confronted people with truths directly they would carry on in ignorance, hiding behind walls of convention. It was only by disassembling these walls through dialogue that truths could be admitted, and never as necessities. The method was to let his interlocutors continue in error awhile, to let them think themselves potentially an equal in debate and so lead them along with his voice, until the moment when they, as a pupil, realize for themselves just how poorly they measure up to the demands of what Arendt would call natality. Then the motivation to learn becomes irrepressible, the spirit grows, and the citizen is born.

---

[14] Anne Carson *Oh What a Night (Alkibiades)*. London Review of Books, November 2020.
[15] It was, in part, by considering the reckless and treacherous behaviour of Alcibiades that the Athenian *polis* felt able to uphold the charge levelled against Socrates in 399 BCE that he was indeed a corruptor of youth and worshiper of false gods: his teachings were so individualistic that he encouraged an arrogance in his pupils that set them against the collective, civic spirit. Socrates' willing submission to their judgment should, perhaps, have been evidence to the contrary, but it could only ever be advanced after the fact.

As Carson's poem reveals, it was the sensuousness of the performance that really did it. Alcibiades compares Socrates' speech to a satyr's flute, a beauty in tone and tune that bewitches listeners, willingly caught in their power and leading them astray. Satyrs have short, bulbous noses alive to the most distant of fragrances, thick lips whose kiss smothers with delight, and wide, staring eyes whose orbit takes in far more than mere mortals might see. The satyr is super-human, their sensual reach touches on generalities with greater alacrity and prescience than ever a *strategoi* might manage. They are farsighted, they apprehend the most meagre of possibilities, their tongue is perfectly clear and openly heard and yet talks in spell binding curlicues, and they feel so acutely they can adjust the pitch and sing of their appeal to fit better the most minute fluctuations in the temper of an audience. Their appearance is strange, their affect is undeniable, and their presence compelling. And yet, Alcibiades goes on, Socrates is even more than a satyr, because he attempts to be less than one.[16] He wears his pre-eminence invisibly, concealing it in self-abnegation, moderation and humility, all too willing to have others take on the burdens of honour and wealth and feel elevated, before then, perhaps, glimpsing their own folly and vanity.

All this he admits in praise of Socrates, but at the end of his encomium Alcibiades shifts tone, urging on the assembled company a note of caution. If nothing can dismantle the prowess of Socrates, not even a satyr, if he is always gold to others' bronze, perhaps it is better to avoid argument altogether. His company will only bring pain to those who are, inevitably, less able and yet who remain desperate to prove themselves, whether in love, in argument, in fortitude, or in ambition. Why not carry on without him? After all, hints Alcibiades, he himself was enjoying a decent enough career. Freed from the shackles of false modesties, had he not used his not inconsiderable rhetorical force to persuade the Athenians to invade Sicily? Had he not been able to enlist the citizens in his own imperial and cosmopolitan vision for creating a robust, resilient city?[17] In contrast Socrates seemed to be all talk.

Socratic Enquiry and Self-awareness

The career of Alcibiades is emblematic of one who, in experiencing action, undergoes an initiation into the *polis* and enjoins himself to the

---

[16] Whereas a satyr has use of tools, notably a pipe or flute, Socrates needs only the melliflu-ous reach of his own voice, he is his own instrument, his own mediation. Maria Catoni and Luca Giuliani Socrates represented: Why does he look like a satyr? *Critical Inquiry*, 2019, 44: 681–713.

[17] Mary Nichols Philosophy and empire: On Socrates and Alcibiades in Plato's *Symposium*. *Polity*, 2007, 39(4): 502–21.

exposing and demanding freedom of opinionated exchange. From the *Symposium* we get rough hints of an Arendtian *strategoi* steeped in *logos*, but one who then deviated into a skewed and partial form, one who thrives in the *polis* as he finds it, but then questions its open protocols, and who seems to want to make an aquarium from the open sea of opinion, looking on from the safety of the shore. Perhaps this is as it should be: if the *polis* is true to its nature then nothing is off limits for revision, including the *polis* itself. Moreover, action is more than talk, isn't it? Something has to be done because the city has to survive and flourish and this can only happen if action is made intimate with both labour and work. The feelings of excitement, insight and puzzlement that arise from self-directed inquiry have to be woven with the organization of the *oikos*: ships leave a harbour, soldiers are speared by weapons, grain sacks are stored, legal rulings are made, walls are built.

Alcibiades' story reveals what remains a persisting problem with Arendt's advocacy of the *polis*: just how distinct and separated can such an organizational form remain if it is to have any strategic influence over daily lives? Alcibiades' encomium to Socrates is sensible to the potency of language, but also to its limits, and it finds action to be something other than just the 'pointless' generation of opinion. Indeed, action is nothing if it is not active, and by being active Alcibiades hints at something that is felt purposefully, something that is motivated by a sense of its own possible fulfilment, indeed something that lives outside its always being considered first one way then another. Here is a *strategoi* who, for sure, has understood the value of reasoned thinking. He has acknowledged that ancient virtues such as savage valour erode as much as sustain community. He understands it is perhaps as well to understand soldiers as labouring bodies rather than seekers of immortality. He has learnt how, as *strategoi*, he ought to act in-between parties, sharing the passions of people so that he might better carry the authority to act.

Yet he still wants to act, and his view of action is more active than Arendt is prepared to admit. Perhaps Alcibiades' sense of action is more in line with Friedrich Nietzsche's? Nietzsche, like Arendt, found action to be a convincing site for the investigation of what makes us human. He also acknowledged that what made action compelling was its being rich in variation, and never amounting to anything whole: '[O]ur actions shine alternately in different colours, they are rarely univocal – and there are cases enough where we perform actions of many colours'.[18] And what made this

---

[18] Friedrich Nietzsche *Beyond Good and Evil: Prelude to a Philosophy of the Future*. Edited by Rolf-Peter Horstmann, Judith Norman. Translated by Judith Norman. Cambridge: Cambridge University Press. 2002, §215.

the case was not the interchange of well-articulated, well-grounded, and mutually open opinions, rather its opposite: action was impregnated with sensual feeling, with mystery, with the shame of failure and flush of success, with drive, with instinct; and given all this passionate excess it is nearly always doomed: action carries within it the hue of tragedy, and it is in the failures that accompany tragedy that the will to begin again rises: first in Athens, then Syracuse, then Sparta, then Persia, then Athens once more.

Nietzsche was, like Arendt, entranced with Socrates, yet not so convinced that he felt restraint through thinking was possible, or even desirable. What Nietzsche gains from Socrates is the embodiment of a method of living, a demanding and even coruscating commitment to inquiry grounded in *agon*, in conflict, outside the settlements of received belief.[19] This is done by having a distinctly individual relationship to prevailing commitments and entailments. Such a relationship is realized through an intellectual conscience, one that questions experience, and continues to do so, despite fate refusing the settlements of fixing answers. This Socratic temper, embracing as it does the contingent and multiple nature of truths, finds the truth of action in its being bound, necessarily, to opinion, and so to the political and psychological aspects of life, and not to the metaphysical abstractions of philosophy or the social conventions of morality. Without truths as such, but only truth as a condition, Socrates is acknowledged as a genuinely generative force. He acts through *logos* alone, without the support of pre-established or desired identity: he is all identities and able to move between these identities at will, imagining himself into the condition of all interlocutors with equal and beguiling ease. His is a shrewd and cunning intelligence that needs no anchor save his own sense of shapeshifting prowess: he can become anyone, and hence himself is no one at all. He is always in a transitional condition of overcoming which ever position he finds himself in, searching anew. In the *polis*, there is no finer political animal. In all this, Nietzsche and Arendt remain twinned in their admiration of Socrates.

Yet Nietzsche also finds it all a bit irritating, not least how Socratic inquiry recommends itself to the development of a specific form of individual, and to an individual happiness found in a specific idea of self-care, in which emotions, myths, music, desires and instincts are downplayed as

---

[19] Nietzsche was, from an early age, an enthusiastic student of critique. His philology meant him wandering away from the certitudes of religion into the self-governed, historical interpretation of texts. What remained of his Lutheran upbringing was a commitment to conscience: you should become the one that you are. In *The Gay Science* he elaborates on this injunction for self-examination and self-realization. This becoming is distinct from *telos*: who you are is not seeded into you, it is an ever-renewing condition of overcoming self-examination in which a figure like Socrates would thrive.

things to be organized by the sifting process of a publicly instituted, two-in-one dialogue that is considered, patient and balanced. Socrates' insistence on the priority of opinion over truth, and ignorance over knowledge seems to expose meaning to the joys of natality, but it was predicated on the avowed priority of a singular method of cool, reasoned questioning. The freedom and plurality that ensued from the collective embodiment of Socratic inquiry was, for Nietzsche, of a peculiarly individual and passionless nature, one that denied us the body and its ineffable affiliations of feeling.

Through this reliance on reason there emerges a good and evil side to humans, and in action (the two-in-one rising of conscience from consciousness) citizens were to discipline the bad with the good. In his advocacy of *logos* Socrates is instituting a regime of good and evil that prejudices us against the very freedom from upon which, it, reason, emerged. Under Socrates, *logos* risks taking judgment from us because it refuses to allow us to accept the contingent conditions in which we are thrown as belonging to us. Instead, it gives us over to values that presume to know the motives and drives by which we are and ought to be compelled.[20] In the active process of such a 'giving over' we lose touch with our being because in such a world selfhood ceases to be a condition we organize; being is presented as the examined outcome of a method of living (there is a stretching from naming to seeing, but seeing is then named). Those who follow the method do not then escape the administrative atmosphere of the *oikos* because, in affect, they establish domestic interiors within themselves: the evil is enslaved and the good rules like a patriarch; it is a micro *oikos*, a well-trained unit from which a version of the *polis* is built. Because Socrates is clever his move is disguised. The training is more ambiguous than simple master–slave domination, because it is self-training, and induced by the mimetic proximity of Socrates-like figures, instructors who show the way only by showing where not to go (towards the passions).[21] Alcibiades is right to issue cautions against Socrates' influence. Not that his own embodiment of a *strategoi* was any better, but at least it was honest in its frustration with Socratic wiles.

It is as though he, Socrates, believes the organs of the body are always liable to bring us down, and that the uneasy relationship between thoughtful speech and action should be settled in favour of speech as the

---

[20] Friedrich Nietzsche *Dawn. Thoughts on the Presumptions of Morality*. Translated by Brittain Smith. Stanford: Stanford University Press. 1881/2011, §134.

[21] Peter Sloterdijk *You Must Change Your Life*. London: Polity. 2013, 164–6. The instruction to be superior to oneself generates the feeling of contempt (when the smaller, rational part is overwhelmed by the larger, darker passionate side) which then, in the *polis*, transforms into a regulative principle.

more refined and elevated of the pair; it is always the body and its base desires that are spoken of as betraying the will because they are inevitably unorganized. The body is incapable of the kind of mimetic self-analysis possible in speech. During speech we are able not just to be ourselves, to express ourselves, but also to skew our understanding towards ourselves by imagining ourselves into other positions (Arendt's two-in-one). This mimetic twist, like a dance move, takes training: we keep hold of what we have done, and imagine ourselves into the place of another, adopting their view, to then consider how what we have done might be done differently, all the while keeping hold of the original against which the mimetic gestures maintain a distance, to then make their reasoning mark. Socrates, as an interlocutor, intervenes as might a dance instructor, revealing the clumsiness of our move, and in doing so exposes us to the possibility of doing it differently. In part this mimesis is one of emulation: we look to act differently, provoked by Socrates. But it is not just a bodily move, it is also an awareness that it is us doing the moving that matters, and we are struggling to recognize ourselves and the possibilities for acting differently that arise from the care induced by this recognition (catalysed by Socrates).

Here, though, isn't there a requirement of continuing involvement? The work of self-presentation or self-care changes you, its affects colour experience in ways from which there is no going back, it resonates in ways that cannot be predicted.[22] Yet in Socrates this uncertainty is lost, because feeling is continually being pushed aside as the unorganized force in need of forming from reason. One has the impression of being directed somewhere, a sense that there is one pathway that cuts through the many possible pathways, towards which we are being goaded. But as Jonathan Lear also points out, the setting of reason against feeling, or the mind against the body, is rather too simplistic.[23] Alcibiades' desires, for example, seem to have been consistently organized by a reflective and imaginative understanding of his condition as one of frustrated ambition. Here it is not reason but a dominant desire masquerading as reason that he continually uses to explain why he meets the fate he does: he lives in

---

[22] Albert Joose Foucault's subject and Plato's mind: A dialectical model of self-constitution in *Alcibiades*. *Philosophy and Social Criticism*, 2015, 4(2): 158–77. The intent in isolating the active aspect of what enacts self-care (namely the self who is being cared for) is to transcend any sense of inner individuality, to relinquish the desire and passion of oneself for oneself, and instead to be alive to the general appeal of questioning. We have a condition of mirroring, as one self mirrors another each mirrors themselves: only then, in this public situation, can one attain a full enough relation to oneself to experience it as a state of care.

[23] Jonathan Lear Integrating the non-rational soul. *Proceedings of the Aristotelean Society*, 2014, CXIV, 75–101.

a world where events always conspire against him, and which he might only ever surmount temporarily. Victories are always Pyrrhic.

To get reflective distance on this 'felt' or 'desiring' mode of reflection, so to speak, requires the body be given its due: it is certainly very capable of generating its own well-warranted, consistent form of self-understanding, and to consider this anew, to find room for natality here, the elevation of a single method might prove insufficient. With Socrates you get the sense that desires are slightly silly, like young whelps in need of disciplining, and this downgrading incurs Nietzsche's ire. It is not that the body and bodily affect should be restored to pre-eminence, or given equal billing (which is to replay the dualism), but to consider how reason (as critique) might itself be an unreflective, disorderly force (and perhaps all the better for it), and desire a reflective, ordering one.

Ressentiment and the Revolt against the Body

As well as Socrates Arendt also takes Nietzsche, and especially his love of the body, seriously. She too is alive to the tendency of western metaphysics to elevate reason over imagination, and inward thinking over outward movement. It is a tendency that Nietzsche dramatizes in his speculative history of the slave revolt. He identifies no specific date in history, but by the revolt he means the rise of Christianity and Christian values. The slaves, he conjectures, have found themselves incapable in a world run by masters whose mastery is defined by their capacity to do what they want, unopposed. When set against this iridescent and unreflective force of will the slaves have no choice but to live in shadows. They are weak, and go unnoticed, with little hope of accruing the capacity to act that defines the masters. The masters are enigmatic: Nietzsche sometimes refers to Homeric figures such as Achilles, at other times to Celts and Vikings. At times they are almost comic; the masters simply act, and crush those preventing them from acting. With this acting comes a life affirming virility and engagement – the masters insert themselves into the world without fear or equivocation. The slaves simply look on, doing the masters' bidding, unable to compete. What they do have, though, is intelligence: they can think, and this thinking finds them increasingly at odds with their condition. Caught in their ebullience, the masters have nothing authentic about them, caught in their impotency, the slaves have less and less to be authentic about. They are increasingly and acutely aware of being in thrall, a feeling which intensifies into an embittered sense of *ressentiment*. This is a state worse than resentment. To resent something is to envisage a possible response that carries the promise of cathartic retaliation, whereas *ressentiment* signals a sense of slight coupled to a material impotency. Unable to invoke nemesis and execute revenge, unable even to loosen the pinions by which they are bound, the slaves are thrown into such an intense condition of privation that they are forced to think of life beyond or outside the world and to imagine places where the master values no longer count. And it is this otherworldly move that unexpectedly gives them an inkling of power. Slowly it dawns on them to use their intellect to redefine the criteria by which situations are evaluated as good and bad. Just what prompts this dawning remains a moot point, Nietzsche suggests it is released by priests, a renegade sub-class of masters who learned the most cunning trick of all, to transform servility into a strength by preaching on the sinfulness of pride with such intense passion they secured their own elevation. Once freed from Socrates' satyric influence, Alcibiades has the way of such a priest, heaving himself from alliance to alliance, always looking for a way through, persuading and coordinating rather than just doing. Once agitated, the slaves begin to revalue the prevailing values. Under their revaluation, active strength and assertiveness are no longer the signatures of a full and rich life, rather it is their inactive opposite: weakness and humility. Gradually this inversion become persuasive, as others, equally put upon, are moved by the voice of the slaves, sensing the possibility for salvation. The truths of which the slaves speak become seductive because their offer of absolutes cannot be contested: they offer peace everlasting and love eternal. These are blissful conditions, and they are not matched by a counter-offer from the masters for the simple reason that the masters are not listening, they lack the sonic range to listen in on the speculative, imaginative, metaphysical language of the slaves.

Unlike the masters, who insert themselves into the world through instinctual cunning and the physicality of the deed (without speech, or much in the way of two-in-one self-awareness), the slaves are, initially at least, reflective, they consider themselves, searching their interiority, and then in growing numbers, they insert such an interior life of thought into the external world by insisting on institutional forms of self-examination and disclosure (confession, penance, redemption). The masters just do. There is no agent doing the domination; they are domination. To think otherwise is to be confused by grammar, as when the claim 'lightning flashes' suggests both an event and a predicated subject. Nietzsche was at pains to point out that just as lightning was nothing more nor less than the performative flash, the masters were nothing more than strength, and to demand they restrain themselves is to mistakenly think there is a being behind the doing, when in reality the doing is everything.[24] It is not a chosen, or nurtured condition.

---

[24] Friedrich Nietzsche *The Genealogy of Morality*. Translated by Adrian del Caro. Stanford: Stanford University Press. 1887/2014, 1.13.

Nor is the natural weakness of the slaves who instinctually do the least possible. The revolt comes in the use of language to represent their natural weakness as a freely chosen, praiseworthy deed. For Nietzsche there is a double sin here. First, comes a feigning to stand away, to turn the cheek, to humiliate themselves, but only in order to advance their condition in relation to the instinctually strong. The slaves need to invoke a subject in order to survive. Once mediated by the conceits of judgment, humility becomes its own form of hypocritical arrogance demanding that others ought to relate to the world as a debased setting fit only for sin. This requirement goes for all material things, including the human body. Second, the slaves conceal this conceit. They rifle through their own and others' lives in the search for spiritual concordance with otherworldly representations, and they believe this work to be of the subject, or soul, which deserves praise. The less worldly the more advanced they become, hence their belief in self-effacing, belittling virtues of faith and hope through which a distinct sense of a subject freed from desire is elevated into a crowning achievement:

> Whoever has theological blood in his veins is shifty and dishonourable in all things. The pathetic thing that grows out of this condition is called *faith*: in other words, closing one's eyes upon one's self once for all, to avoid suffering the sight of incurable falsehood.[25]

In Nietzsche's casting we have vital but rapacious masters being outwitted by weak slaves whose subsequent hegemony is grounded on a linguistically harboured hatred of natural desire and feeling.

As a diagnosis of how Europe arrived at its nineteenth century, theologically pillowed bourgeois settlements, Nietzsche's analysis is pure caricature, yet in being so it accentuates the singular features that best exemplify how humans relate to the world: the unchallenged dominance of either the mind and its reasoning over the body and its feeling, or vice versa. The problem with the masters was their instinctual resolve to be just as they were, with the slaves it was their faithful resolve to be elsewhere; the former are almost animal, and the later suffused in a totalizing *bios* of competitive humiliation sanctioned by a Christian god. In such a setting the possibilities for authenticity are thinned out to the point of ascetic nullity. Each act was met with accusations of vanity. All human lives are surrounded with an essential lack from which they were destined to suffer, both mentally and bodily, because they were sinners and they find a purpose in their sin.[26]

---

[25] Friedrich Nietzsche *The Antichrist*. Translated by H. L. Menken. New York: Alfred Knopf. 1896/2006, §9.

[26] Humility gives suffering meaning, but the meaning was itself a form of poisonous suffering, one that went by the name of guilt. Friedrich Nietzsche *The Genealogy of Morality*, 28.

The *Polis* as a Space of Inclusion and Exclusion

So, in the wake of this digression into the difficulties of realising Socratic self-understanding, we might now ask whether authenticity can be encouraged and protected by the *polis*? At the symposium Alcibiades hints that it can, but he also embodies its difficulty, and even impossibility, given its realization seems to be reserved for those exceptional beings who are 'more than satyrs'. A further, more analytic response is offered by Arendt's long-standing friend Karl Jaspers, who turned the tables on Nietzsche a little by speculating that it was precisely in groups like the early Christians that authenticity was most apparent.[27] Far from being slavish, the Christians, holding themselves in hiding from persecution in underground niches, would, like Socrates, have been continually questioning the very ground of their condition. It was surely the kind of questioning in which:

man becomes conscious of Being as a whole, of himself and his limitations. He experiences the terror of the world and his own powerlessness. He asks radical questions. Face to face with the void he strives for liberation and redemption. By consciously recognising his limits he sets himself the highest goals. He experiences absoluteness in the depths of selfhood and in the lucidity of transcendence.

All this took place in reflection. Consciousness became once more conscious of itself, thinking became its own object. Spiritual conflicts arose, accompanied by attempts to convince others through the communication of thoughts, reasons and experiences. The most contradictory possibilities were essayed. Discussion, the formation of parties and the division of the spiritual realm into opposites which nonetheless remained related to one another, created unrest and movement to the very brink of spiritual chaos.[28]

This unrest and movement feel close to Arendt's *polis*, the *polis* embodied and loved by Socrates, outside which he cared not to live, but one which need not rely on individuals as wise and refined as Socrates. Jaspers offers

---

[27] See Agnes Horvath, Bjørn Thomassen and Harald Wydra. Introduction: Liminality and cultures of change. *International Political Anthropology*, 2: 3–4. The liminal, in a social order, has two aspects. First come the rites in which individuals undergoing a process of conversion or initiation are held on the cusp of a new state – the liminal is the threshold point, once they cross this point life is coloured anew and the world, including one's pre-transformed state, appear differently. It is a space of disorienting hesitation. Where the first is constituted in established and often long-standing human practice, the second is a condition of social disorientation in which the habits and values of existing practices are no longer sufficient, but have yet to re-settle into new practices. Arendt is attentive to this second condition, indeed excited by it. It is when peoples experience revolution, when they find appearing within them a new political order, that action and the uplifting affirming nature of action, is at its most apparent. Hence her intense interest in historical periods of revolution, in France in 1789, in Russia in 1917, across Europe in 1848. The Eurocentric nature of this history belies somewhat the claim to her politics being a universal condition.

[28] Karl Jaspers *The Origin and Goal of History*. Translated by Michael Bullock. Abingdon: Routledge. 1949/2010, 2.

a phenomenologically rich evocation of what it might feel like to encounter one's own subjectivity stripped bare, one that he was felt was not limited to Christians and the dawning of an occidental culture, but extended to peoples in India and the East too. Everyone was capable of an encounter with themself curated through reason: the quality by which humans comprehended the world in such an open way that they apprehended being as an experience they could hold to account. In holding to account a sense of self was revealed and sharpened, becoming the edge by which further incisions could be made into the world again and again: '[t]he unheard-of becomes manifest. Together with his world and his own self, Being becomes sensible to man, but not with finality: the question remains'.[29]

Unlike Jaspers, whose talk of 'everyone' strives for a general inclusivity, there is a persisting and disturbing suggestion of exclusivity in Arendt's organizational distinction of a *polis*.[30] The most obvious division is that a flourishing *polis* relies on a deftly administered *oikos*: the citizen, typically male, is enjoined to thoughtful action only insofar as the civic space is sustained by the separated spheres of labour and work. As citizens, *strategoi* like Alcibiades might well experience the power of thoughtful action, and one can envisage how these experiences of authenticity might ensure other citizens as equally endowed, but what of the children, women, slaves, animals and foreigners being subjected to violence and force, those without *logos*, the speechless? Their labour (and occasionally work) helps sustain the *polis*, but they share none of its atmosphere: they are too busy, sick or scared to think of any life beyond coping with its enervating practicalities.

Acknowledging the injustice of human exclusion, Arendt pursues it as a technical problem of *poiesis* (fabrication): technological development might, ultimately, find all of us free enough of labour and work to partake as citizens. The job in hand, and so the job of the *strategoi*, becomes one of administering the city – the collective *oikos* – in a practically adept way so that more and more might be afforded the opportunity of becoming publicly minded amongst civically constituted equals. The *polis* is envisaged as a benign, if demanding, civic space that can be expanded like a balloon to enclose more and more people, given enough technical *nous*. The implication, however, is that children *qua* children, women

---

[29] Karl Jaspers *The Origin and Goal of History*, 3.
[30] Karl Jaspers imaginatively identified sufficient commonality across different religious and cultural settings to propose humanity itself was beset by a new age – what he called an axial age – defined by the growing sense that for all people there was a centre to their turning world, themselves, and it was always in reference to this thinking and feeling self that questions of meaning would recur.

qua women, slaves *qua* slaves, animals *qua* animals and foreigners *qua* foreigners cannot be authentic, it is only as citizens that authenticity is possibility, and the job of *strategoi* would be to expand the space of appearances to cover them. It was with this in mind that Arendt considered it a great failure of the nation state to have somehow intervened between citizens and the state, confusing what ought have been a basic, grounding association of *logos* and authenticity.[31]

Given authenticity is a condition of bringing being to questionability then what characterizes the second birth of natality and plurality is the preservation of difference, not its eradication. The *polis* is a place of opinion forming: it is in congregating and debating that citizens come to reveal and constitute opinions. This is the transformative condition of the *polis*: it is not a space in which interests compete, but a place in which they are formed and re-formed, through transactional rather than interactional relations. It is a restless place of passion, emotion, reason, persuasion.

Insisting that it is only as citizens that authenticity is experienced seems to run against this. After all, Arendt herself also identifies authenticity in the figure of the refugee, the homeless one who nevertheless creates a home from *logos* without the provision of a *polis*. In understanding authenticity as an organizational problem of widening the material and institutional space of citizenry there is a problematic evening-out of the very plurality that Arendt wishes to see instituted. We go back to Nietzsche's complaint that Socrates' form of open debate gave preference to those whose individuality carried a reasoned maturity that was itself a schooled method and hence an already well-practiced form of work. A citizen is someone able to manage their body, display their passion with measured decorum, reflect on habit, and convey opinions lucidly. The decent monotony of such a citizenry is puzzling. Just how many beginnings will really be acknowledged in this kind of *polis*? To recur to our opening discussion of authenticity, the pulling away of the two-in-one self is executed as a critical move, an act of *ek-sistence* that dislocates, and which should also include a pulling away from the rationally

---

[31] As Arendt suggests in *Origins of Totalitarianism*, 123:

> The tragedy of the nation-state was that the people's rising national consciousness interfered with these functions. In the name of the will of the people the state was forced to recognize only 'nationals' as citizens, to grant full civil and political rights only to those who belonged to the national community by right of origin and fact of birth. This meant that the state was partly transformed from an instrument of law into an instrument of the nation.

> The problem of the nation state is one of its being exclusionary those note born struggle to find source of common association, creating resentment.

avowed condition of self-rule advocated by Socrates: authenticity is a condition of questioning, not autonomy. What of having the slaves, children, women, animals, and foreigners appear named as themselves, as different and remaining thus, properly animating the *polis*? Why ought the *strategoi* organize the city in such a way that these differently named roles, types and characters are to be contained in the *oikos*, and obliterated in the seeing of the *polis*? Relatedly, even with the expansion of the *polis*, how will *strategoi* encourage those for whom being voiceless appears as a natural condition and for whom a *polis* is of a fundamentally different form of life? These are the lost figures conditioned by the force and violence that has been long legitimated in the *oikos*; Without the schooling required for life in the *polis*, how then do they ever act?

Arendt remains alive to all these questions, but maintains that authenticity is reserved for the *polis*.[32] She seems reluctant to admit that the voiceless might acquire authenticity within the household itself. Is the *oikos* capable of generating the conditions in which one can give an account of oneself that might then be heard? Arendt argues not, but why? She seems committed to a view that authenticity is organized in a limited and artificial space. But why dampen and discount utterly the potential of the *oikos* to generate an authentic sense of self? Is it an urge for conceptual clarity that sustains Arendt's reluctance here? The household may indeed be larded by concerns with biological and productive necessity, yet even here, in these experiences of biological and institutional necessity, self-revealing is surely possible. Are these household dwellers really unable to imaginatively think in the way fully formed citizens are? Isn't there something a little 'off' about the divisions being implied here? After all, a house can be open, harmonious and alive with language, in the style, say, of a Pieter de Hooch painting (see Figure 2.2).

De Hooch shows a great cleanliness and clarity pervading the space. There are no curtains anyone might look in through the wide-open doorway framed as a natural bower which brings the outside in. The atmosphere is suffused with a neatness and probity, gently emanating an understated social confidence and amiability realized in the trade of goods, ideas and gossip through whose boons the home is maintained. It is an *oikos* grown large, an *oikonomia*, a space that deftly gathers and projects its well-mannered appearance as civility. Even the dog is tamed, watchful for instruction, its progeny tucked safely into the sunlit folds of a human lap. As a pictorial embodiment of the commercially formed

---

[32] Arendt recognizes this when she observes how the incapacity for distinction amongst *animal laborans* was empirically confirmed by an absence of slave rebellions. Slaves are equalized under conditions of vassalage to the point where it does not occur to them to seek distinction. Hannah Arendt *The Human Condition*, 215.

Figure 2.2 Pieter de Hooch, *Man Handing a Letter to a Woman in the Entrance Hall of a House*, 1670. Oil. Rijksmuseum Amsterdam. Public domain. SK-C-147

civic sensibility in a Republican city of Northern Europe it might be idealized, but no less so than Arendt's version of the Greek *polis*, and no less plausible as a space of action and speech. A letter is being delivered: ideas and possibilities may be afoot.

Equally as plausible, though in a more obviously oppressed domestic setting than de Hooch's, we might imagine that it is precisely when those in the household suffer intensely, either under direct force and violence, or from a disorienting experience of aimlessness, that a need to examine and declare one's self critically arises. This seems, at least, to be Nietzsche's implied position in his analysis of the slave revolt. It is only when enduring conditions of such utter privation that questions of authenticity arise, for it is only in such a condition of privation that the existential question of one's own self-sufficient being as a beginning, as an origin of things, is forced into the open. As it is with the slaves, who he admires, at least for this, because when set against the masters who are happy and so thoughtless, the slaves though twisted with *ressentiment*, show a reflective liveliness in sensing their own being as a condition of beginning again. Though their thrownness is given, they can involve themselves in how to project from it, they can choose how to relate to the world, and though they choose wrongly this is not to deny it could have been otherwise.

Also, what goes for slaves goes for other members of the *oikos*. There is no empirical reason why we cannot experience natality from within an *oikos*.[33] In Henrik Ibsen's *Doll's House*, for example, the loveless and exploitative marriage into which Nora is thrown provides the theatrical setting for an awakening conscience. It dawns on her that, for all her situational misery, her bourgeois settlements are precisely that: hers, she belongs to them, and can refuse them. Her refusal constitutes a second birth, an ontological realization of the existential facticity of her life being a condition that she can own. To take ownership it is not sufficient to internally, inwardly assume oneself able to respond, it has to happen in speech, in the saying and gesture of a refusal, a slammed door, a 'no'. As a word it has no meaning beyond its performative force, a force stronger than the vow 'I do' that first bound her to marriage. It is a 'no' that declares the possibility of another community, a disclosing of a new world where words might be experienced as a release rather than incarceration.[34]

Can *Strategoi* Ever Build a *Polis*?

Nora's 'no' is also a leap, a jumping off into improbability that, for Nietzsche, is the mark of a being who owns being, alive as they are living-out an unmanaged fate whose ungoverned condition they can

---

[33] See Hauke Brunkhorst Equality and elitism in Arendt. *The Cambridge Companion to Hannah Arendt*. Edited by Dana Villa. Cambridge: Cambridge University Press. 2006, 178–98.

[34] Brunkhorst argues Arendt's Heideggerian influence jars alongside her pagan republicanism: whereas the latter espouses an active and artificially created space for freedom (an island of power set within a sea of violence and force), the former is more universal, and requires only the utterance of a beginning, a natality that is acknowledged not just in inner awareness, but also in communicative speech. See Hauke Brunkhorst Equality and elitism in Arendt, 189–90.

learn to love rather than resent.[35] The future is enacted in the creative imagining of the self as it picks over the fragments of the past, aware that whatever is being made is doomed to become such a past, to again be picked over. Arendt seems to baulk at the fragility of this prospect, wanting something stronger for authenticity than small acts of gleaning from amid the fragments of others' failures. She worries that left to the spreading regimen of the *oikos* the realization of authenticity is being left to the vagaries of personal accident. Yet, whilst Arendt wants more than is offered in Nora's rejection of the *oikos*, she is not so clear on what the structures of the *polis* are. Indeed, she cannot be otherwise, because to be organizationally clear as to how the *polis* ought to be built is to fall foul of the urge to fabricate through law and territory, and so arrive back at the messy questions of sovereignty and authority that she was attempting to leave behind by confining them to labour and work.

This has not stopped commentators looking for suggestions of what an Arendtian *polis* would look like. Waldron, for example, has found in her work an intermittent but still substantial attentiveness to how the *strategoi* might 'house' the polis.[36] To organize for such building work, the *strategoi* would have to foster a number of institutional forms. For Waldron, these include: establishing rules of discourse by which citizens avoid being polemicists and so deliberate rather than position themselves; the use of voting procedures and majority decision making that do not then prejudice a losing minority, for example by refusing them opportunities for further participation; the adoption of smaller units (elemental republics) that foster experiences of direct democracy and which feed into collective decision making, perhaps through the mechanism of representative deputies who might sift opinions for their cogency; and above all, the habit of promising: a submission to the originating act of committing by which a community agrees upon its structure.

The problem here, though, is that the originating act of the promise is being configured as a sovereign one (it is characteristic of work, not

---

[35] Fate need not be understood as an already determined outcome, a spooling off of what is written already in the stars. In English at least, right up until Shakespeare, fate was intimate with what was uncanny: indeed, weird and fate were used interchangeably, as in the witches in Macbeth, the weird sisters, being sisters of fate, of prophecy, foretelling what would occur, but also offering up the possibility of its not being so, were Macbeth able to own his thrown condition. To act is akin to Nietzsche's sense of what it is to leap.

[36] The allusion to a concept that Heidegger uses to convey the nature of *logos* and yet which is also a domestic concept evoking the *oikos*, is not accidental here, it reveals the antagonistic sympathy between the two orders with which any *strategoi* will have to wrestle. Jeremy Waldron Arendt's constitutional politics. In *The Cambridge Companion to Hannah Arendt*. 2006, 201–19.

action): it is a conversation stopping inauguration of a political process to which there is no seeded alternative. The setting inaugurated by the promise is that into which the citizens are thrown, they find themselves there, and cannot negotiate their way beyond it without fundamentally denying themselves the spatial conditions of authenticity. They can abandon politics, but not alter its staging. If they join others on stage, it is a promise to abide by its performative structures, irrespective of the outcome. As with Socrates' singular method of living, prospective citizens of the new *polis* must relate to these structures and their promise not as tools for doing a specific job (they are not resources employed to further one's interests) but as the conditioning factors for authenticity. By invoking a sovereignty of promising, the *strategoi* are being called on to act like midwifes of language, overseeing the deliberative birth of opinions whilst ensuring only those with the requisite deliberative skills (one might say the Socratic style) are granted access. Those who cannot conceive opinions, either because they are too wrapped up in the busyness of labour and work to commit to promises, or they are, like Alcibiades, too calculating and wish to exploit systems of promising to enforce specific interests, are, refused entry because they are not committed to the ends of the *polis*, to which the means are made subservient, they are unable or unwilling to stay in the moat between naming and seeing.

For the *strategoi* to refuse entry to those who want to advance specific interests becomes an exercise caught in such twists of profound contradiction that its organization risks self-asphyxiation. After all, to overtly protect the 'delivery' space of appearances is itself an instrumental condition of labour and work directed towards a known and therefore limited and limiting objective. Refusing entry to those who are too busy quickly risks exploitation because it maintains the distinctiveness between the *polis* and *oikos* in such a way that the violent ordering of the latter is warranted by the free and authentic possibilities experienced in the former. It sustains a private–public split that restricts which kind of 'self' is allowed to perform acts of self-disclosure. Its generosity is noble, but limited. Moreover, is it at all possible to sustain the separation of the *oikos* and *polis*? As Arendt admits the everyday condition into which humans are thrown is ordinarily and necessarily an inauthentic one of worldly organization (that of labour and work). It is a world of prevailing positions, cruelties, ad hoc occurrence and ambition, all which have an air of familiarity about them: they are the stuff of life. Practically speaking, this inauthentic condition is the one that holds sway amongst the *strategoi*; no matter how strident their urge towards authenticity, it is not in the gift of any individual general to act other than practically. As Theodor Adorno wryly observes:

A general who resolved, as irrationally as he used to revel in atrocities, to allow no more of them to be committed; a general who raised the siege of a city already given into his hands by traitors and set up a utopian community instead—such a general would have been promptly killed by mutinous soldiers or else recalled by his superiors even in the furious, farcically romanticized times of the German Renaissance.[37]

So, whilst Arendt talks of the kind of organizational structuring the *polis* might require, she cannot insist on this, and nor can the *strategoi*. Conscience is inherent to our having language, and in language we carry the bodily and affective memory of place within us, unbidden and unhelmed. In *logos* we bring the *oikos* to the *polis* and vice versa, our authentic world is not itself portioned into smaller, self-contained units. Its subtleties and distinctions are passageways not cells, and we are moving all the while, from language game to language game, and each person gathers a sense of self as they go, a palimpsest of expression and action constantly accruing a patina whose uniqueness is a function of its mobility across different spaces. What appears in the space of appearances is a modification of what appears in the *oikos*, and back again, only now differently so. As Peter Sloterdijk remarks, no space is innocent, one cannot create a neutral space or invent an entirely new one, only generate differential spaces, which carry their distinction only insofar as they are marked out against earlier spaces, rather than delineating a metaphysically elevated enclave.[38] Indeed, this space-making 'projective dynamism' is what marks out the human, equipped as we are with a sense of what it is to be born, to be thrown into the world of others and with others as an opening. In this, she says, we are unlike the animals and unlike the gods.

So, it is this that we take from Arendt: that what marks us as distinct, and so authentic, is the natality of birth. And if the *polis* is to be a second, collective birth it will always inevitably be coloured by the earlier and embodied spatial experiences of the citizens not *qua* citizens, but *qua* language users, with all the grammatical familiarities, misfires and felicities that that implies. In the *polis* there is neither recourse to a single authoritative voice, nor a stepping out into an idealized calm: there is no loosening release into an open exchange of opinions unbidden by interests. It is more contested than it is contemplative. A space in which what is normal and everyday suddenly appears unruly and out of joint.[39]

[37] Theodor Adorno *Negative Dialectics*. London: Routledge. Translated by E. B. Ashton. 1966/2004, 50.
[38] Peter Sloterdijk *Not Saved: Essays After Heidegger*. London: Polity Press. 2016, 198–9.
[39] Martin Heidegger Letter on humanism. In *Basic Writings*. Edited by David Farrell Krell. New York: Harper Row. 1978, 213–265, 226–7.

Thinking of such a condition in its collective form, a gathering of citizens so to speak, Agamben wonders:

What could be the politics of whatever singularity, that is, of a being whose community is mediated not by any condition of belonging (being red, being Italian, being Communist) nor by the simple absence of conditions (a negative community, such as that recently proposed in France by Maurice Blanchot), but by belonging itself?[40]

His answer is akin to that of Arendt: it is a politics of action, a struggle between the instrumental apparatus of violence and force that advance specific interests, and the *potentia* of those held in a space of appearance without an identity or distinction they want to defend, save belonging itself, and what they hold in common is the willed capacity to begin again. And in beginning again, and again, any claim to truth, in the very act of being claimed, shatters into myriad alternatives, many of which might then be taken up and made to appear as equally persuasive as the parent from which they were blown asunder.[41] Unchallenged truth is antithetical to appearances it forecloses on birth, it ushers in origin myths of which totalitarianism is the culminating organizational expression. The politics of the *polis* is to trade in the fragments and vignettes of lived experience, to distil ideas and possibilities from these, but always in the company of alternatives; it is a politics that eschews the comforts of stable myths. Arendt is alive to how puzzling this is. It is as if the human being, perhaps alone amongst all living things, is, in its most authentic guise, in a condition of estrangement from which it has to think itself back into its own practices, without then seeking the comforts of a position or identity offered by those practices. We want, then, to envisage strategy more as an organizational condition of estrangement from which to think ourselves into the world, rather than with how to arrange it in the service of specific interests.

[40] Giorgio Agamben *The Coming Community*. Translated by Michael Hardt. Minneapolis: University of Minnesota Press. 1993, 84.
[41] Martin Jay Against rigor. *New German Critique*, 2017, 132, 123–44.

3　Strategy in the Lifeworld, and the Problem with Home

The Self as Tragic Experiment

Though we might think of the *polis* as a retreat from the everyday world of work and labour, it is really an attack. The subject of attack is the habituated activities, thoughts and values that deaden life with their smooth certainty and comfort. In *The Gay Science*,[1] Nietzsche elaborates on the possibilities for such an attack, which ought to take more enigmatic and subtle forms than one that uses grenades. He asks his readers to imagine themselves looking at a stone. We sense the cold, hard, resistant surface, the edgeless patches of morphing colour, the silence, and its angles or smooth curvature, and yet what comes forth as we look and look is less an awareness of the stone than of ourselves. In looking we become aware of our imagination (our tendency to fantasize), our inventiveness (our expectation that in prodding the world we experience a reciprocal yielding) and our reason (our expectation that the world coheres in certainties), and we do so because, in this very simple but difficult and unusual act, we find all of these deeply held habituated ways of being with and relating to the world beginning to struggle.

To be provoked by a stone in this way is to experience natality, beginning again, an enriching struggle that had been the subject of his preceding and equally optimistic book, *Dawn*.[2] Under the undiminished, blank force of an utterly indifferent stone our life-avoiding assumptions of a collegial world being amenable to human design start to stutter. Yet as habits are exposed and give way, the fact that we remain forces us to encounter the world as it is. We look upon nature, nature looks back, and we feel alive in its company.[3] Only then can we begin to think of ourselves, each of us attentive to what we are sensing and feeling: a bundle

---

[1] Friedrich Nietzsche *The Gay Science: With a Prelude in German Rhymes and an Appendix of Songs*. Edited by Bernard Williams, Josefine Nauckhoff and Adrian Del Caro. Cambridge: Cambridge University Press. 2001.

[2] Friedrich Nietzsche *Dawn*, §3.

[3] Rüdiger Safranski *Nietzsche: A Philosophical Biography*. Translated by Shelley Frisch. London: Granta. 2003, 173–4.

of circulating forces among which come mysterious wisps of consciousness, the hints of individuality. These suggestions of perception can have us either running back towards the comforts of reason to then categorize and tidy them into states which then distil into the qualities of an intentional subject (one object among many objects), or running to metaphysics to then assert inviolable certainties about an immortal soul (the one as the many).[4] Neither route, whether that culminating in scientific knowledge or religious belief, is honest. Nietzsche suggests we should remain with ordinary experience, with the stone for company, looking back at us, and in the midst of its elusiveness we might develop a subtle intelligence as to the nature of things, we might cultivate and steward our drives and desires, whilst all the while acknowledging the inherent incompleteness and openness of each moment caught within 'myriad surges of possible meaning'.[5] In this way we become adventurous enough to confront the truth as it is: the world is without comforts, yet the stone still appears to us, it remains present in its enigmatic calm, which is still a kind of comfort.[6] It is hard, though, to let the stone be a stone, and much easier to gather it up and give it a role and place within our practices. It can be graven with images, locked down as a milestone along a roadside (to be then used as a metaphor by modern, corporate *strategoi*), thrown as a weapon, incorporated into the walls of a dam: 'why don't people see things? They themselves are standing in the way, they cover up things'.[7]

To see things, we have to try to get out of the way a little, which means modestly trying to see ourselves as the equivalent of the stone, treating its and our own materiality seriously.[8] In doing so we are attacking those human practices in which we naturally assume ourselves to be rationally

---

[4] Friedrich Nietzsche *Gay Science*. §1–11. Nietzsche observes our tendency to seek the comforts of truths as they ought to be constructed (whole and wholesome) rather than truth as such, or to scurry off and find remedies. We present ourselves to ourselves with false truths we have invented. In *Dawn* Nietzsche enjoins his readers to a terrible happiness to be experienced in encountering a wider world emptied of foundational meaning. To be aware of this is to begin anew: 'The sea purple and mute, the sky playing in dusk is mute, the ribbon of rock spilling into the sea is mute – this silence – this malice'. 'Oh sea! Oh evening! You are terrible mentors! You teach the human being to cease being human! Ought he to sacrifice himself to you? Ought he become as you are now, pale, shimmering, mute, prodigious, reposing above oneself?' Friedrich Nietzsche *Dawn*, §424, §539.

[5] Friedrich Nietzsche *Dawn*, §119.

[6] Nietzsche is not utterly nihilist, despite his dire warnings he is still in a phase of thinking that allows for uplift, for willing. Goethe too was finding in nature a sublimity that could be used as a guidepost: '[W]ater as the chaotic element of life does not threaten here in desolate waves that sink a man; rather, it threatens in the enigmatic calm that lets him go to his ruin', a ruin that is a human affair '[I]n all this it is nature itself which, in the hands of human beings, grows superhumanly active.' Walter Benjamin *Goethe's Elective Affinities*. 1924/1996, 303.

[7] Friedrich Nietzsche *Dawn*, §438.

[8] Keith Ansell Pearson 'Afterword', *Dawn*, 377.

or spiritually endowed subjects looking upon a world of objects. No, our distinction is something to be worked at, not assumed, and it begins by forcing ourselves into the inscrutable and even malicious company of things that will not speak. Only then, from this strange and stripped back, 'pale' beginning, can we begin to look at ourselves anew, as the prodigious source of new possibilities.

This thought experiment harks back to Nietzsche's first birth, his book on tragedy.[9] When writing the book, based on earlier lectures, he had been a frequent visitor to the composer Richard Wagner. They sang, scaled mountains and rowed on Lake Lucerne, invoking the gods to laud the beguiling and intoxicating spirit of music called forth in the composer's *Gesamtkunstwerk*. It was within the figure of Wagner that a young, adoring Nietzsche saw tragedy develop to a new level, bringing forth music that 'shakes mankind to its deepest foundations'.[10] The tragedy came not in what the music described, but in how it appeared, affecting as it did a reversal of our expected sensory impressions, for:

[h]owever vividly we may move a figure, enliven it and illuminate it from within, it always remains a mere appearance, from which no bridge could lead across into true reality, into the heart of the world. But music speaks from the depths of this heart; countless appearances like this could pass before the same music, yet they would never exhaust its essence, but would for ever remain mere externalized copies of it.[11]

Here the impressionable Nietzsche was being overwhelmed by the certainty of something that could be directly apprehended (*Anschauung*) but not properly comprehended. There was no linguistic form that could convey the experience of the music. It 'consumes the entire world of appearances', and yet still, at odd times, we can sense 'behind that world and through its destruction, a supreme, artistic, primal joy in the womb of Primordial Unity'.[12] It was a music for the brave few who could cope with such intense oscillations of feeling, who could freely leave the tucked-in safety of everyday practices and stride out as an exception, standing amid the exceptional and extreme. Leaving the middle ground of conventional agreement means inviting chaos; embracing both the sublime and the terrifying, and to do so without flinching or wavering, is required for an authentic life.

The figure who embodies such an upright position is Prometheus, the semi divine errant who refused to kowtow to the gods, who had defied

[9] Friedrich Nietzsche *The Birth of Tragedy*. In *The Birth of Tragedy and Other Writings*. Edited by R. Geuss and R. Speirs. Cambridge: Cambridge University Press. 1872/1999.
[10] Friedrich Nietzsche *The Birth of Tragedy*, §22.
[11] Friedrich Nietzsche *The Birth of Tragedy*, §103.
[12] Friedrich Nietzsche *The Birth of Tragedy*, §105.

DIE

GEBURT DER TRAGÖDIE

AUS DEM

GEISTE DER MUSIK.

VON

FRIEDRICH NIETZSCHE,
ORDENTL. PROFESSOR DER CLASSISCHEN PHILOLOGIE AN DER
UNIVERSITAT BASEL.

LEIPZIG.
VERLAG VON E. W. FRITZSCH.
1872.

Figure 3.1 Friedrich Nietzsche, *Die Geburt der Tragödie aus dem Geiste der Musk.* Leipzig: E. W. Fritzsch, 1872. Photo © H.-P. Haack. Wikipedia

them by stealing fire and giving it to humans so that they might extricate themselves from fate. He did this with his head held high, a lack of contrition, which irritated Zeus more than the theft itself. In Hesiod's *Works and Days* the fore-knowing Prometheus receives his punishment unrepentant, fixed to the slopes of Mount Caucasus to be set upon by eagles who, day after day, would tear at his liver, only for it to regrow. And, still, he holds his head up high.

Prometheus appeared on the frontispiece of *The Birth of Tragedy* (Figure 3.1), a testament to Wagner's (and Nietzsche's) indomitable, world-searching spirit and to the art work in which this spirit was manifest. Yet no sooner was it published than Nietzsche began to have doubts. Amid all the mythopoetic talk of striving after immortal forces hidden deep in the belly of forgotten worlds, Wagner had seemed to be latching onto something permanent and grounding. He had created an aesthetic form whose unity was a coming together of representational imagery and ideas that both excited and affirmed the audiences' own non-aesthetic relations to the world: the beauty of its form lay in its apprehension of a world that has been understood in such a way that it clarifies and affirms experience. Wagner's genius was in encouraging the audience to arrive at such an appreciation: through struggle. The surety of revelation was realized through discordant, unresolved fragmentary journeys taken along cavernous routes and impelled by destructive forces. By immersing an audience in mythic tribulation they are brought to the edge of nihilism, and within the cauldron of this tragedy their sympathies fuse with the predicament of the hero's in such way that they share the plight, the fear, and in such sympathy are able to imaginatively feel what is at stake, and to ache for the restoration of what faces annihilation. Because it was through the medium of music that Wagner worked, he was able to confront the audience directly with the inherently unstable and uncertain nature of the human will and its place in the world: Wagner's representation was compelling because it dispensed with dusty and circuitous explanations, it needed no warrant other than its own presence, it worked not with argument but atmosphere into which an audience was compelled by an 'unmediated certainty of intuition'.[13] In Wagner the essence of the world and its representation were perfectly aligned: the tragic compels the audience to realize the essential truth that the human condition is one of suffering, but redeemed through perfecting art forms, notably tragic drama. It was only through the aesthetic forms created by Wagner that, first, the human condition was revealed as it truly was, a condition of striving and suffering, and second, that this condition was redeemed by the mediating form of its sublime revelation; destruction and fate were countered by creation and self-expression.

Nietzsche's enthusiasm waned because of an inward suspicion: how was it possible for him to believe in this totalizing myth without then suspending or even ending the idea and experience of struggle? It was all a little too comforting and self-congratulatory: taste merged with metaphysics to form an intoxicating brew that induced a state of blissful reconciliation. One had only to observe Wagner comfortably settled into his mythopoetic world of signature rings, custom-made silk underwear and chromatic destabilizations to suspect something was amiss with this view of tragedy as capable of realizing a synthesis between the Dionysian forces of destruction and the ordering forms of Apollo. Equally amiss was the audience at Wagner's pompous Bayreuth performances of the Ring cycle, Nietzsche noting in disdain that 'the entire loafing riff-raff

---

[13] See Paul Daniels *Nietzsche and the Birth of Tragedy*. London: Routledge. 2013, 64.

of Europe' were merely adding the event to their wide-roaming travel calendar.[14]

Though Nietzsche dropped the figure of Wagner as a provocation for thought, he retained that of Prometheus. In gifting fire Prometheus had freed humans from thoughtlessness. Whilst still compelled by natural drives, humans could also subject themselves to the artifice of civilization: they could create, and in creating develop the requisite taste and style by which creation might be refined and better appreciated. With the tools and arts that stemmed from having control of fire humans were able to secure their own interior forms, insulated from fate. Yet never wholly so, and in visiting the figure of Pandora and her jar of *daimons* upon the humans as a punishment for receiving the gift of fire, Zeus ensured the species for which Prometheus bore so much love did not escape unmolested. The *daimons* flying out of Pandora's jar – the slips of chance, the stuttering enterprise, the unwilled hope that finds all action in deficit to an unrealized future, the mildewed exhaustion that grew across the human countenance and went by the name of experience – make Prometheus, as a giver of wisdom, and bringer of understanding, a more equivocal figure: with gifts come curses. And in his own punishment Prometheus was the distilled individuation of this curse, a being whose grounding virtue was the capacity to bear suffering, a capacity that echoed throughout Nietzsche's writing and which towards the end of his life found a profound rhetorical force in the opening of *Ecce Homo* 'How much truth can a spirit endure? How much truth can a spirit dare?' By then he had fundamentally re-evaluated *The Birth of Tragedy*. The tragedy installed into human lives by the figure of Prometheus, and into which he too installed himself, revealed the human as an essentially restless, questioning creature that had forgotten to ask questions, and which instead had become content with the prevailing agreements of habit. Far from being destabilizing, Nietzsche came to think of Wagner's work as the gilded acme of such habit secured by its status as high culture. Its unity was freighted with a 'heavy and ponderous' truth and decorated with distracting pyrotechnics that had the appearance of disturbance but were really just decorative chiaroscuro. Under the totalizing impress of Wagner's myth there is a forgetting of the equivocal nature of Prometheus' gift. Being artificial creations, all truths and all concepts are illusions, and it is with art, and specifically with tragic art, that the most compelling illusions are produced. Compelling because they are those closest to experience,

---

[14] Sue Prideaux *I Am Dynamite! A Life of Friedrich Nietzsche*. London: Faber & Faber. 2018, 150.

whereas the illusions being produced by Wagner become too insulating. They create an artifice in which an audience is smothered by veiling beauty, by the Socratic delusion that understanding heals the wound of existence, and by metaphysical gestures towards an underlying unity.[15] It is perhaps as much in the stone to which he is chained, as in Prometheus himself, that the tragic is revealed.

Hence Nietzsche's second birth, his daybreak, in which the overblown creative urge to complete a totalizing representation of the human condition yields to a patient acceptance that the only opening, the only sense of freedom, is what comes in every attempt to act and express oneself as a beginning, and that in compensation for being unable to ever complete anything, one might console itself with the knowledge that one can try again: 'there are so many dawns that have not broken'. It is through this wandering that Nietzsche believes us capable of realizing an authenticity alive to the possibilities that emerge from the paradoxical, the mischievous and the curious: really what is being revealed is nothing more than constant revealing.[16] To know one's self through tragedy is not an exercise in revealing what is essential to all of us, but an exercise in self-development, which is an aesthetic one of representing images of oneself to oneself again and again, aware that in every appearance, no matter how appealing and generative in its form, comes the realization that it is only appearance (and not an appropriation of something essential about the world) and that appearances go all the way through. It is an active, ongoing, incomplete stewarding of experimental possibility that the artists and audience take interest in, and scour from, the appearance of things not because these representations reveal a reality beyond themselves, but simply as appearances. The artist and audience take things as they alone find them, and in finding there little in the way of settlement, spur themselves onward, to try again 'to live like a bird that comes and flies away and carries no name in its beak'.[17]

To work beyond the name (so beyond images, and beyond concepts understood as images cast through metaphor) is to make oneself a subject struggling to shed the subject, a moving from naming to seeing, a struggle of self-presentation that the Norwegian writer Karl Ove Knausgård, likens to a shedding of the urge to think:

---

[15] Friedrich Nietzsche *The Birth of Tragedy*, §85.

[16] 'Creating – that is the great redemption from suffering, and life's becoming light. But in order for the creator to be, suffering is needed and much transformation. Indeed, much bitter dying must be in your life, you creators! Therefore you are advocates and justifiers of all that is not everlasting.' Friedrich Nietzsche *Thus Spoke Zarathustra*. Edited Adrian Del Caro and Robert Pippin. Translated by Adrian Del Caro. Cambridge: Cambridge University Press. 2006. Part II, 'On the Blessed Isles', 66.

[17] Friedrich Nietzsche *Dawn*, §470.

One doesn't have to think too hard to understand ... the reason that painters and sculptors spent all their time during their crucial formative years of youth copying others or mechanically reproducing models of objects. They weren't doing it so they could copy reality ... They were doing it so as to learn how not to think. This is the most important thing of all in art and literature, and hardly anyone can do it or even realises it is the case.[18]

Frederik Jameson finds Knausgård's struggle to move through, and then out of, thought intriguing (and Knausgård is using 'thought' here as the conscious and explicit articulation of an aspect of the world being made out by an observer). In transcending such thinking – by reaching a state of intuitive feeling and absorbing things without them being at all distinct as already classified (marked) objects – the subject ceases to be subjected, there is a freedom from being individuated as a subject in the world.[19] Lacking an object, including an objectified or essentialized sense of self (for example the image of a mind woven from cognitive wiring; or a soul; or a mind–body machine), the self becomes nothing more than the faltering project of an incomplete being attempting to spiritually, collectively or mentally complete and so assure itself that it is, indeed, objectifiable. It flits erratically between the first and third person, the present and past person, and it does so by virtue of the aesthetic distance realized in an understanding that the self appears as an appearance, again and again. The self as proper name referring to something being represented (outside appearance) is forced off-site as a being that is too contrived to do any effective revelatory work. It is too sure of its correcting autonomy as it tries to use the tools of writing and memory to marry everyday experience with the unifying condition of thought. But, as St Aubyn's third-person narrator also asked, what is left? Nothing more or less that than appearance and re-appearance of self-created images, one disturbing or destroying the other, and having been endured the process is then held aloft before an audience. Jameson likens it to the performative creation of shame. As an artist, a creator of appearances of self, Knausgård writes openly for an unknown reader, aware how he appears, and the delight he takes in creating these images, will be judged, and that the reader reads expecting to make such judgements, and in this open complicity between appearances of the 'self' and of intimate, acknowledged and obedient 'other' selves (the readers) who are more

[18] Quoted in Frederic Jameson. Review of My Struggle: Book 6. The End by Karl Ove Knausgård. *London Review of Books.* 8 November 2018, 3–9. Karl Ove Knausgård *The End*. Translated by Martin Aitkin and Don Bartlett. London: Harvill Secker. 2018.
[19] See Christophe Menke Tragedy and the free spirits. *Philosophy and Social Criticism*, 1996, 22: 1–12.

distant than one's own re appearing self, comes shame. It is a condition of shame, argues Jameson, because it calls forth an ever-present vulnerability manifest in the repeated attempts to write oneself into an openness in the knowing company of unknown readers whose judgment on what is written is not entirely silent, and is itself an interplay of appearances breaking down further appearances. The written voice gathers itself into a perpetual pause; it does not write for, or from, a cause.

Jameson contrasts shame with guilt. Guilt emerges from a measured, ethico-political awareness that one's conduct is lacking in some explicit, purposeful way. Guilt requires criteria against which one might evaluate one's conduct. Shame refuses such an ordered, calculated, condition.[20] Shame is a felt condition of violation associated with the meagre appearance and re-appearance of oneself. To be ashamed is to be concerned with how one is continually appearing. It is a nakedness that cannot be corrected, only hidden. In Knausgård, as in Nietzsche, it is deliberately courted, flirted with and projected 'out there', a baffling nakedness that intensifies in its projection. In its intensity it elicits in the writer an urge to retreat to where the public gaze cannot penetrate, and it is the writer's job, as a creator of aesthetic illusions, to resist that urge to enclose oneself. Guilt allows for closure through the public compensation for acknowledged error (invoking law, religious ritual and abeyance, the Christian comforts of knowing one is sinful). The correction comes in punishment and in redemption through which the subject becomes graded and differentiated and so more complete. Shame elides such subjectifying correctives, it leaves the self open to its own endless modifications of form.

This makes self-fashioning as much an aesthetic as it is an ethical task: it is the creation of projects that belong to us as our own because they are our imaginative responses to the vast sea of necessity into which we find ourselves thrown. Indeed, it is far more an aesthetic task than ethical if by ethics we mean a falling back on moral principles. Throughout *Dawn* Nietzsche objects to the tendency to invoke morality as a supplement to knowledge, something that takes over once verifiable and predictable certainties are exhausted. We can never know our own motives and desires properly, let alone those of others, and to presume, somehow, we can find in Arendt's two-in-one moment an enlightened seat of certainty is to assume the equalizing garb of a people fleeing from themselves and running into the relative safety of moral categories.

---

[20] See also Bernard Williams *Shame and Necessity*. Berkeley: University of California Press. 1993. on the complex sense of shame in Greek Tragedy, a staining of character for which fate bears responsibility, but which is then transferred onto individuals who carry it. Tragedy, from *tragus*, the goat, and so scape goat. Tragedy is the goat song.

Business and Self-revealing

Authenticity is an organization of consciousness and conscience in which experiments with our sense of self might be possible, modest and continual, and through which 'the need for tiny, deviant actions' is indulged and encouraged.[21] We are to work on ourselves with enthusiasm rather than out of a sense of duty.[22] If authenticity concerns itself with the open and unknowable future and what lies beyond the horizon – the great sources of provocation – it is precisely these experiences that the structures and principles typically associated with strategy try to close down by bringing the world closer and holding it fast in John Donne's calculating nets. Keith Ansell Pearson points to the observations scattered through Book III of *Dawn* in which Nietzsche diagnoses how the world of commerce and politics – the world of strategists – has become complicit with attempts to first extend the known world (as if more information and theory would make us more knowledgeable, rather than expand the horizon of our ignorance) and second to compensate for the limits of what we know by using visionary (moral) supplements.[23] The spread of knowledge and vision finds individuals being known only insofar as they are 'of use' to one another. They become expendable units, stamped like an 'inferior piece of nature's pottery that others use up and shatter to pieces without feeling any responsibility whatsoever'.[24] It is the baleful condition that Arendt later equates with a dominance of labour and its relations of thoughtless use, one in which the cultural refinements of work are less and less persuasive.

Business people. – Your business – that is your greatest prejudice, it ties you to your locale, the company you keep, to your inclinations. Diligent in business – but lazy in spirit, content in your impoverishment, having tied the apron strings of duty to this contentment: so do you live and so do you want your children to live.[25]

With labour on our backs, we have little time for arguing, dreaming, speculating, experimenting, we just have busyness coupled to an ideology of no-nonsense directness, and we learn to become content and secure with the legitimating logic of use-value by which this language

---

[21] Friedrich Nietzsche *Dawn*, §149.

[22] Keith Ansell Pearson equates this idea of the self as a site of organizing our drives to a form of perfectionism grounded in radical independence (we spend time alone, thinking carefully and cautiously about our situational experiences, and in this the self continues to be a site of organizing, it is nothing more than this, nothing more lofty is available to us, save the fact of our being a beginning, an unfinished fact, that can be nurtured, or looked after. 'Afterword' *Dawn*, 400–4.

[23] Keith Ansell Pearson 'Afterword' *Dawn*, 400–4

[24] Friedrich Nietzsche *Dawn*, §166.

[25] Friedrich Nietzsche *Dawn*, §186.

of fact is evaluated: labour 'places a tiny little goal always in sight and vouchsafes easy and regular satisfactions'.[26]

Arendt also picks up on this tendency of modern commercial, martial and political organizations (and their strategists) to fill out the world in their own image, and she enlists the *polis* as an organizational rebuff; here is a space that not only contains but is built by publicly embodied attempts at self-understanding. In falling for the *polis* she is keeping faith with organization itself. She was alive to the possibility of constructing something in common, of looking into one another's conditions, imagining how it might be to be them, to then give rise to a collective sensibility. There was something necessary, if demanding, about constructing a *polis* and its civic sensibility, in which humans find what is most essential about themselves. Nietzsche would have none of this collectivism, indeed he senses it is in the nature of all organization to betray authenticity, and it might then just be better to be realistic about this, as when Nietzsche suggests the Greek city state was concerned, primarily, with biological preservation: 'there we have people together and relying on each other who want their species to succeed, most often because they must succeed or they run the terrible risk of being exterminated'.[27] And Arendt's advocacy does indeed struggle, not least when troubling over the seemingly intractable question of belonging and who might count as a citizen.

To pursue the question of strategy, however, it is necessary to keep pressing in the way Arendt did, and to inquire whether organization (and hence its strategic design) is indeed antithetical to authenticity. That is, if we are to maintain our definition of strategy as a form of organizational self-disclosure. Yielding to Nietzsche's suspicions of organization catapults us into a nihilism through which only individuals as experimenting individuals find release. It is a question of whether organization can be at all sympathetic to authenticity. As Arendt also acknowledges, the evidence is not encouraging. Commerce and politics carry about them a labouring atmosphere that stifles self-cultivating spirits. Opportunities to think carefully about the experimental possibilities for beginning again are, if they are made possible at all, couched in a discourse of design, enterprise and innovation, all of which remain in the service of labour. Instead of natality (and the plurality it entails) comes a growing organizational skill for producing what can be possessed and further processed: land is developed and protected, people are trained, machinery and laws

---

[26] Friedrich Nietzsche *Dawn*, §173. In contrast, Nietzsche espies in ancient (Hellenic) Greece, a spatial contentment with smaller proportions and without the need of complexities: 'how simple were the people of Greece in their *own conception of themselves*! How far and away we [moderns] surpass them in understanding human nature!' (§169). In understanding, not in living.

[27] Friedrich Nietzsche *Beyond Good and Evil* §262.

are updated. It is an unrelenting spread of the *oikos*; an administered global space in which strategists commit to govern with a productive and direct frame of mind that gets things done without deviation or costly ceremony. The world is burdened with busyness and fact, so much so that those who labour bend their head so low they can no longer see how, in striving to fireproof the world, they make it more combustible, and in the process squander life.[28]

So how to employ strategy in such a way to *organize* towards the unrelenting demands of self-examination? Following both Nietzsche and Arendt this is an open question that needs to be held in the open. It is a question of acknowledging what it is to be at 'home' in a world in which there is no natural home to be had, a world from which our own 'being' is sufficiently distinct to gain a perspective and to speak to itself and others of its being a world that lies open to question. It is a question that Martin Heidegger, the thinker who sits somewhat uneasily between Nietzsche and Arendt, phrases as the question from which all others emerge.

Poor in World

In taking up the question, Heidegger reaches for a threefold comparative distinction, one that also includes a stone and a human, but which adds an animal in between them. Leading us unapologetically into a dense thicket of etymologies and circular relations, Heidegger observes 'the stone being world-less, the animal being poor in world, and the human being world forming'.[29] Lacking sentient life, the stone is bereft of birth, and therefore of a world in which it can live and dwell. The earth on which it lies, or the path it paves are not given to it as earth and path. The stone merely exists, it has no access to being. The matter becomes more complicated in the case of sentient life, such as, say, bees. Such beings are, suggests Heidegger, not without Being, they are aware, but poorly so, they are poor in world. Poor, Heidegger elaborates, leads us to draw a comparison to wealth; being in poverty as against having; the bee has less; but less of what?[30] The bee has its environment. Heidegger takes this observation from the zoologist Jacob von Uexküll who argues the bee is defined by its 'vision-room' which is determined by its bulbous eyes whose fixed visual sensors are set in spectral angles, forever blurring that which is far away.[31]

---

[28] Friedrich Nietzsche *Dawn*, §177–9.

[29] Martin Heidegger *Die Grundbegriffe der Metaphysik: Welt, Endlichkeit, Einsamkeit.* Frankfurt: Vittorio Klostermann. 1983, 261, 263. Our translation.

[30] Martin Heidegger *Die Grundbegriffe der Metaphysik*, 284.

[31] Von Uexküll, whose work has more recently been taken up by Gregory Bateson and subsequent eco-philosophy and bio-semiotics, rejected contemporary attempts at

The bee has its flower stock, its hive, its honeycombs and blossoms; it is a world limited to a certain domain and it remains sharp only when fixed in that sensory circumference.[32] The worker bee knows the patches of nectar and colours of the blossoms it visits; their iridescent light and smell, but not the sculptural form of the stamen or the role of pollen. Set in contrast, the human world is rich in terms of the sheer depth and breadth of the things it encompasses, given the intensity and nuances of its sensory apparatus that reach further than those of the bee.

Heidegger notices, however, the criteria of such comparisons offered by Uexküll afford a one-way, gradual distinction between rich worlds and poor ones; and do so in a way that unproblematically elevates the human world. As a good student of Nietzsche, Heidegger is suspicious that such a human-elevating hierarchy of worlds exists. Indeed, the hierarchy founders almost immediately when considering the sensory superiority of the bee's eye over human eyes in respect to its environment, for instance when sensing motion, making it perfectly adjusted to flower-field aviation. Heidegger initiates a philosophical twist, however, by refusing to remove the descriptor 'poor in world', and instead elevating this 'poverty' to being something valuable. He reverses the connotations of poverty by equating it to a condition of rich wellbeing: an insect like the bee relates to its surroundings in perfectly attuned fashion, and the same goes (he

---

reading the psychology of animals in terms taken from human psychology, including 'consciousness', 'memory', 'awareness' or 'perception'. Instead of extending the field of semiotics into biology, Uexküll pursued a framework of sign systems that embraced all living things via their vital processes and so elevate meaning over taxonomy. His main work, *Theoretische Biologie*, published in 1920, follows earlier works on water animals, which began formulating a law of 'neuromotor regulation' outlining functional body (or building) plans (*Baupläne*) of animals on the basis of the workings of receptors, the nervous system, and muscles. These *Baupläne*, however, are not the 'actual natural factors' that force physical-chemical processes, but 'merely a draft made by us [observers]'. Starting from a building plan means to start with the organism in a holistic way, rather than relying on the chemical study of its parts alone. Living, he claims in the book on water animals, 'is at the very least a machine not just something mechanical; it is not just something that can be structured, but must have a teleological structure -, it is not just something organic but an organism'. In Carlo Brentani *Jakob von Uexküll: The Discovery of Umwelt between Biosemiotics and Theoretical Biology*. London. Springer. 2015, 58, 77. Establishing an early theory of feedback, Uexküll speaks of receptor and effector organs, the former registering the actions exercised by the exterior world; thus allowing the organism to respond to such stimuli as a relationship that holds together the performance of all organs – which he later developed into a general theory of a functional cycle. This makes experimental biology the task of researching *Umwelt* as the interpretation of signs in self-organized systems, beings capable of making their own *Umwelten*. See Kalevi Kull Jakob von Uexküll: An introduction. *Semiotica*, 2001, 134(1–4): 1–59, 7.

[32] Jacob Von Uexküll *Streifzüge durch die Umwelt: von Tieren und Menschen. Bedeutungslehre.* Hamburg: Rowohlt. 1956, 38.

argues in distinction from Uexküll who largely stuck with insects and small mammals) for all animals. Etymologically, Heidegger repeats the twist by suggesting the German *Armut*, meaning poverty or lack, is a lack of something that could have been present, but which also points to mood (*Ar-mut, wie einem zu Mute ist*), so how one feels and is.[33] The stone has no mood; it merely is. But then it is not lacking anything either; it is what it is precisely because of it not having a world. The bee is locked in a space that neither expands nor narrows throughout its entire life.[34] The space is what Uexküll calls an environment world (*Umwelt*) defined by those elements or marks (*Merkmalträger*) that are its exclusive interest. Each animal has its own set of marks delineating an *Umwelt*. For the bee the meadow carries a set of marks distinct from how it appears for the cow, or the drover. Its receptive organs and the meadow realize a unity, an ecology, that is unique to the bee; outside which nothing occurs. This harmonic unity is an enclosure by which the bee is a bee: it is less a prison (which suggests a possibility of escape) than the markings by which bee-ness is possible. Uexküll speaks not of 'effect' but 'affect' as the force making the animal capable but also captivated within this realm while everything else is, *a priori*, unable to shoulder in. The life world of the bee is constituted in this affective relationship of mutual marking and nothing can insert itself into this *Umwelt* that is not, thereby, a mark. For Heidegger it is a condition that is both poor, as the possibilities of relating to its environment differently are limited, as well as rich, as these relations are a directly felt link within the environment: 'closed in the circle of its marks ... closed in the few elements that define its perceptual world'.[35] This closed-in-ness is a condition of captivation (*Benommenheit*) that occupies and absorbs the bee (*benommen* also meaning dizzy) so that its behaviour (*Benehmen*) is utterly in tune with the nature of its captivation.[36] As such, the bee is not a captive, but captivated. Bees behave as bees do, in relation to their environment; and they do so perfectly.[37] By describing this as being poor in world (a poverty) Heidegger

---

[33] Martin Heidegger *Die Grundbegriffe der Metaphysik*, 287ff.

[34] Martin Heidegger *Die Grundbegriffe der Metaphysik*, 292.

[35] Giorgio Agamben *The Open: Man and Animal*. Translated by Kevin Attell. Stanford: Stanford University Press. 2004, 51.

[36] Martin Heidegger *Die Grundbegriffe der Metaphysik*, 347.

[37] A similar structural argument of captivation appears in Milton Friedman's palindromic phrase 'The business of business is business.' (Though the source for this quote is elusive, and for some it was Alfred Sloan's not Friedman's.) Whilst managers and corporate officers are persons in their own right, business operates ideally to the sole logic of engaging in open and free competition without deception of fraud. It is tightly bound to its environment, is as it should be. See The social responsibility of business is to increase its profits. *The New York Times Magazine*. 13th September 1970.

is not suggesting the presence of lack, on the contrary it is an entire and replete condition to which the idea of an outside is utterly concealed. Any quantity of additional information concerning the wider world, the world beyond receptive organs, especially of the objective and representational kind called knowledge as well as any act of naming, would be utterly alien to the bee whose captivation needs no further organization.

Heidegger is beginning to think with Uexküll as much as Nietzsche here. What Uexküll proposed was an ecological understanding of sentient life that disrupted what, until then, had been a common spatial assumption in taxonomizing science: there is single world that comprises within it all living species. This single world is, by its extensive (measured) nature, conducive to knowledge, and knowledge of an ordered and hence comforting kind: it can be arranged in taxonomies horizontally by way of classes and vertically by hierarchies, from the most elementary to the highest, most complex of organisms. Uexküll shattered this smoothing, conventional way of categorizing the world. Instead, and in a way that would have positively delighted Nietzsche, Uexküll saw an infinite variety of perceptual worlds, or ecologies; the bee's captivation is a captivation in its own world; its 'vision room' is from and for bees, and the sensory circle of marks that mark the captivation of other species varies in accordance with their own properties.[38] There is no single world in which all this life unfolds; only infinite and unknowable environment-worlds defined by repeated attempts at striving in which each species finds itself: 'the animal is encircled (umringt) by this ring (Ring), constituted by the reciprocal driven-ness of its drives'.[39] There are myriad worlds, as many worlds as there are animals. Closed in by encircling marks the animal is animated in an unstoppable movement of drives-in-relation-to-environment. In this way the animal is dis-inhibited; it is open in its embrace of a total (and so limited) world. The animal emerges fully formed as an ecological unity; its struggle (Ringen) is the maintenance of that sphere alone, precisely without extending it or separating itself from those signifying marks that speak to its being and that make up its environment.

Uexküll illustrates his studies with quaint drawings depicting the sensory worlds of bees (and other animals), showing ecologies which, to the abstracting human eye, seem sparse, even bland. The disinhibiting ring acts like a filter that seemingly reduces the scope for influence to what that species is biologically organized to perceive: there is a coming into being of a self and its environment at one and the same time; they are indistinguishable. There is nothing new that can enter this ring; nothing

---

[38] Giorgio Agamben *The Open*, 40.
[39] Martin Heidegger *Die Grundbegriffe der Metaphysik*, 362.

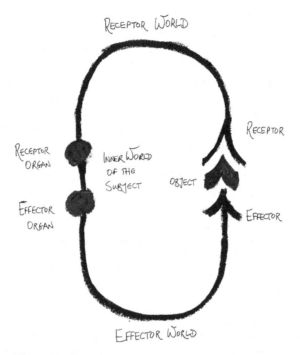

Figure 3.2 Diagram of the *Umwelt*. Based on schematic view of a cycle as an early bio-cyberneticist. Authors' own.

that makes it from the outside into the sensory room of the animal or insect.

Being poor in world, the animal is always already completely open to its world; this unmediated, direct and intense relationship manifests itself through the seamless connection between sensory impulses and bodily reactions. The animal is always already captivated by its environment; lodged in its disinhibitor ring (see Figure 3.2) and determined by its striving.[40] Its being does not derive from a separation from the

---

[40] We revisit the idea of striving in Part III. Following Heidegger here, Agamben (*The Open*. 55) finds the animal, *qua* its poverty of world, is attuned and in harmony with its being; its lack is feeling that opens up its sensory vision room rather than being something missing. The animal possesses this being-open in its essence. Being open in captivation is an essential possession of the animal. On the basis of this possession, it can do without [*entbehren*], be poor, be determined in its being by poverty. This having is certainly not the having of a world, but rather a being taken in by a disinhibiting ecology. Because this 'having' is also a 'being-open' to the ring of disinhibitors by which it is enclosed – and yet the very possibility of having the disinhibitor revealed as a being is withheld from this being-open-for – then because of this, the possession of 'being open'

world, and therefore from distinction, but rather from its being perfectly attuned to its surroundings. The animal, captivated by its marks,
struggles (*ringt*) with its environment without changing or reflecting on
this mode of captivation; its experience is unmediated; direct; pure and
intense. Animals may very well use tools or scheme, such as apes and
other mammals when hunting or cracking open eggs, clams or shelled
fruits through means other than their claws, teeth or beaks, and in this
they are tool-using creatures. But they do not, following Heidegger's
embrace of Uexküll, leave the *Umwelt*. The question never arises: in captivation the marks are never revealed as marks, they simply are the a
priori against which experience unfolds. The animal has no sense of self
that is somehow separate from and looking down from above: even an
air-borne dweller like the bee wandering across open meadows is unable
to remove itself from captivation; having a perspective on one's condition is not a question of distance.[41]

Office, Convention and Becoming Attuned to the World

The behavioural captivation of the animal finds it always acting in an
Umwelt, but not in a world; the animal 'does not stand within a potentiality for revelation (*Offenbarkeit*) of being'.[42] It is not within the bounds
of its own being for a bee to encounter something *as* something; rather,
what is there is already and always there as an integral element in the
unity that is the condition of captivation. Hence beings are not revealed
to animals because revealing is not an aspect of the animal *Umwelt*: it is
not a case of beings that are there but closed off from the animal because
they can never be there. This extends to revealing itself, so the animal
can never properly be said to be aware of, or in the company of, itself or
other beings' experiences *as* beings.[43] It is this that Heidegger likens to a
poverty: an instinctual captivation to an *Umwelt* that is nevertheless open
to beings, albeit these beings never appear as such. The animal striving
cannot comport itself towards beings as such, only towards that which is
constituted as a mark in the singularity of its *Umwelt*.

Heidegger's ecological elaboration of poverty affords us a glimpse of
a twofold possibility located at the opposite ends of a line drawn from
stones to animals, to humans and beyond. On that line we can imagine

---

is a not-having, and indeed a not having of world, if the potentiality for revelation of
beings as such does indeed belong to world.

[41] Giorgio Agamben *The Open*, 57.
[42] Martin Heidegger *Die Grundbegriffe der Metaphysik*, 361.
[43] Martin Heidegger *Die Grundbegriffe der Metaphysik*, 361–2.

the stone, that world-less thing that does not lack in anything; it is a stone because it has no world; it lies here or there and so its lack of world is constative of what it is. The animal, to the right of the stone and left of the human, has a world; one in which there is no separation between 'the what' and 'the who'. As they insert themselves into the world through deed alone (recalling here Nietzsche's Masters, who might also occupy a similar position on the line as animals, as similarly enraptured in simply doing, *without bios*). To the right of the animal comes the human, shaped through the continual engagement in the ongoing process of separating and relating to the world and further to the right we find the gods for whom there is no lack because in their immortality they brim with the potential to have or be anything.

Yet, Heidegger's image of the uninterrupted line from stone to animal to human and beyond, is only partially helpful, not least because of its overly biological or genetic rendering of differences. It is an image that often populates a rather different paradigm where all are related in a chain of being where what comes 'after' (to the right) is gifted with more sophisticated forms of intelligence and power than what precedes it. It is a linear sequencing set in a Western left to right order that makes us think that animal plus reason equals human; human plus immortality equals god. This is a tempting formula as it elevates the human being over the animal in a way that finds the richness of being human being derived from a separating method of living, one called reasoning, often associated with the intellect, and what René Descartes casts as its doubting controller, the mind. The humanizing element of the human is an additive one, and with this also a sign of superiority that legitimizes the dominion of this (higher, more complete) being over animals, plants and the material environment. The distinction was something to which Descartes brought evidential proof by testing on animals. When prodded, mauled and stabbed, their screams and screeches were programmed responses, nothing more, they were creatures lacking in soul, rendering them little more than mere mechanical automata.[44] What marked the human as human was the capacity to reason (and to speak rationally). By reason Descartes did not mean the kind of situational, practical intelligence that would allow one to anticipate pain, say. Reason was otherworldly, it belonged to the mysterious inner world of thought – the *res cogitans* – by whose representational, quantifying operations fed by experiment experience was subjectified to knowledge.

Heidegger resolutely rejects this Cartesian story of the *animal rationale*. In *Being and Time* he writes that Descartes: 'investigates the *cogitare*

---

[44] Giorgio Agamben *The Open*, 23.

[thinking] of the ego within certain limits. But the *sum* [Being] he leaves completely undiscussed, even though it is just as primordial as the *cogito'*, and he goes on to observe that most forms of human inquiry (anthropology, psychology and biology) fail to properly consider the nature of 'being' human, as they nearly all begin their enquiries on the assumed existence of *animal* plus *rationale*.[45]

Rather than appeal to reason, Heidegger, because he still wants to use the image of a line of Being, argues that what marks the human *Umwelt* is the possibility of unhomely disturbance (and hence authenticity). In Heidegger's rich and sometimes inky word play, the singularity (*Eigentümlichkeit*) of the animal is akin to property (*Eigentum*); the kind of property an office bestows upon an office holder; a property of being that derives not from thinking and questioning but from striving (*Trieb*) to fulfil a role.[46] Being entirely in tune with striving means that there is no residue, no outcome; nothing left behind. The animal is a unity and as it encounters things in and through striving it is being taken in (*hingenommen*); the animal displays behaviour (*benehmen*), without apprehending (*vernehmen*). The bee in flight, the lark in song, the lynx in its silence, are all encompassed in the raw language of signs. Signs are recognized, not interpreted. It is the human animal that interprets, whose language is not the issuing and reception of signs, but their situational interpretation. It is a language of comprehension, of semantics. Where the human can thus know itself as something (it can form itself under the aegis of a subject predicate for which there is no lexical referent but which, nevertheless, remains an empirical expression of self), the animal cannot know itself (it lacks the potential of authenticity).[47]

For sure the human can be, and often is, captivated. When, for example, a human office holder becomes indistinct from the procedures and duties by which the office is defined. Setting in train patterns of Weberian nicety for which many organizational scholars still betray a profound fondness, wanting, it seems, to replicate in institutional form the forms of animal captivation that Uexküll found so entrancing.[48] Yet the similarity between human and animal office holders is the empirical appearance of similar rhythms, the difference being that, for a human office holder the captivation is not ontological, the marks and signs are not semiotically captivating in the same way. To be simply taken, to be entirely and rapturously taken by the environment, forecloses on the human form

[45] Martin Heidegger *Being and Time*, §44–9.
[46] Martin Heidegger *Die Grundbegriffe der Metaphysik*, 341.
[47] Giorgio Agamben *Infancy and History: On the Destruction*. Translated by Liz Heron. London: Verso. 2006, 55–6.
[48] See, for example, Paul du Gay *In Praise of Bureaucracy. Weber. Organization. Ethics.* London: Sage. 2000.

of linguistic mediation that transforms recognition into comprehension. The perfection of human office is configured unnaturally, or perhaps better to say culturally (semantics), for example using the grammatical structures mediated through files and filing systems. Where, for the most part the entries, distribution and storing of files works through semiotic recognition, there will always be ruptures, pauses, appeals and errant outliers that demand an act of interpretation, and there will always be expressions of the self – the 'I' – that cannot be filed.

One is reminded of Alcibiades' strange and passionate encomium to Socrates. Here is a philosopher whose wisdom lingers behind the cloak of ignorance, and whose seductive beauty hides in the shadows of enlarged, bulbous features. A figure who is unplaced, untimely, rude even, who is ironic, elusive and tricksy, but whose presence as an interlocutor eventually elicits profound insights. Alcibiades is alluding to a condition in which oppositions open up to possibility. The interplay of contrasts and the refusal to present an open, static, unified self, makes Socrates all the more 'present'. This was the point of alluding to him as a satyr, living in neither this nor the other world, but wholly betwixt, one whose habitual edge dwelling became too edgy for the Athenians, who tried and executed him in 399 BCE for invoking unsanctioned gods, and for leading the young astray, one who, on hearing the verdict, accepted it rather than follow the encouragement of his friends to escape. Alcibiades, a *strategos*, warns others to be wary of this force, to oppose it lest they are seduced, and yet he admits, in himself having actually succumbed, to being exposed to opening truths that would have otherwise remain concealed.[49] In his actions Socrates reveals an *Umwelt* open to the concealed nature of being: the *oikos* cannot reach such a being, it is ungovernable.

Prejudice

The animal's captivation is not diminishing in any way (nothing is being concealed), and nor does it follow that humans enjoy a blessed and rich life simply by virtue of their *Umwelt* being marked by language. Yet given

---

[49] Martin Heidegger *Parmenides*. Translated by André Schuwer and Richard Rojcewicz. Bloomington: Indiana University Press. 1998, 228–32. Going by, or being seen as, another name, for example, can be a deception, a concealing of self, yet the resonance of this concealing is complex. It can be a forger pretending to be a more famous artist; or an incorrect attribution made in error, or made deliberately; or a case of misattribution; or a display of cunning; or an insubstantial form of play, none of which forms, says Heidegger, can be said definitively to be false as such. They are different aspects of concealing from which revealing of self emerges. Take the use of a title such as 'Dr' or 'Dame', here the title conceals and in concealing reveals (grandeur, professional status, belonging), it is, he says, an ostensive showing that shows by holding back.

Heidegger's use of a line of being, it is hard to avoid the impression that Heidegger is elevating the being of the human by associating it with language. To recur back to Agamben's distinction between semantics and semiotics. First, come the signs that stand as distinct unities (such as the words petals, wet, bough) which have the potential of being read, but which in themselves have no meaning, as in the animals' language, they are either recognized, or not. Second, comes thoughtful language, or speech carried by empirical acts of interpretation through which language fosters meaning: the potential of words is being actualized. Unlike the recognition of signs, which comes instinctually, to strive for speech is an acquired effort of learning

Instead of ecological capture humans have language: the marks marking the edge of the *Umwelt* are environmental and organizational forces to which we humans accede by way of consciousness, cultural tradition, behavioural habit and even, on occasion, conscience. And it is here Heidegger seeks to redeem his somewhat anthropocentric elevation of the human by diagnosing this condition as being 'held captive'.[50] To be human means to be thrown into an already living world to which we are always already attuned (*Stimmung*); to which we are bound in advance and that binds us before we can begin the task of thinking or acting, demanding we fall in with its demands.

Being a cultural condition, and not instinctual, this being 'held captive' (*gefangen*) is quite different from the animal's captivation (*Benommenheit*, especially when read as dizziness).[51] The living world always already precedes and so conditions any attempt to understand it: it exceeds any totalizing conceptual grasp. Understanding takes the form of learning prescribed ways, like learning a piano, thereby acquiring the skills to partake of living, playing along, lives unfolding on the basis of continual adjustments to the prescriptions. But there is a curious twist to this attunement. For something like a piano to function it too has to be tuned properly, it has to be played by proficient musicians, to become part of the orchestration of a performance and so on, so the fact of its tuning, playing and orchestration has to be left behind and forgotten. In concealing this groundwork of expression human language users also conceal the experience of openness towards which language might expose them were they to consider that what made them human was nothing more than the continual effort at securing the unnatural possession of language. Such a contingent grounding is disorienting (again, recalling Agamben's metaphor of entering the moat between semantics and semiotics, and staying there), and to avoid

---

[50] William McNeill *The Time of Life: Heidegger and Ethos.* New York: SUNY. 2006, 41.
[51] William McNeill *The Time of Life*, 50.

unbidden encounters it is perhaps easier to outsource the acts of interpretation to habit. Rather than express oneself as a speaking, 'seeing' self, a named 'I' in the expression of which one brings a 'self' into being as a thing to be also seen without gradation or evaluation, it is less fretful to adopt the ready-made interiors of truth-making prejudices within which one might walk comfortably, as in an arcade, a comforting *Umwelt* made of glass, an interior from which to look, but never venture outwards. Prejudices then appear as the edge marks of this *Umwelt*, and the grounding role of language is concealed, making the human worse off than the bee, the lark or the lynx, more impoverished, for in its drifting from flower to flower the bee enjoys an immediacy and rapture unavailable to the human caught in its own glass cage of totalizing prejudices (conventional measurements, rules and principles). As Nietzsche pithily imagines:

'Humanity'. – We do not regard the animals as moral beings. But do you suppose the animals regard us as moral beings? - An animal which could speak said: 'Humanity is a prejudice of which we animals at least are free.'[52]

Prejudice is the striving to fulfil a role, and which, conventionally, becomes the mark by which human life is said to be being lived, but it cannot be said with any great passion or distinction.

The contrast with animals, then, is not simply one of language and speech, of capture and contingency, but also an unwillingness to struggle towards speech, and instead to prefer a semantic concealing of the semiotic recognition that human language, and so humans, are baseless. Faced with the realization that humans lack a natural grounding, and that what is essential to being human is nothing more than successive acts of speech, the tendency is to conceal this fragility by elevating prejudice, and to then hide the entire struggle towards the production of speech.[53]

What is it to semiotically reveal this struggle towards production (to get back into the moat)? It would be as if, to go back to the example of the piano, a composer deliberately messed with the standard set up, interfering with the strings tuned around the agreed chord of A 440hz, and placing foreign objects into the instrument, so that the entirely habituated performative setting of playing music becomes visible. This is what John Cage did with his works for prepared piano, where he provided instructions for placing

---

[52] Friedrich Nietzsche *Dawn*, §333. Nietzsche's response is to embrace the indifferent emptiness of our biologically configured condition. Heidegger attempts to resist this resignation. *Parmenides*, 226–32.

[53] Paul Daniels *Nietzsche and the Birth of Tragedy*, 33. Though Nietzsche initially felt Wagner had revealed and distilled this struggle in what became known as the unresolved discordant chord in the Prelude to *Tristan und Isolde*, he had, through affect, transformed the struggle into a metaphysical unity in which everyone adapts to everything.

bolts, rubber and screws between the strings, and with this un-concealing an entirely different sonic experience appears, one in which otherwise mute and obedient things start to gather their own recalcitrant yet alluring energy; a force that sits askance from, and is alien to, that of the typical human-instrument-audience performance (see Figure 3.3).[54] Rather than tighten and connect things, the bolts and screws loosen them: the world of composition splinters, and the compossible now lives alongside the in-compossible, and in this plurality it is no longer possible to compare works on the basis of common criteria. The composition and performance display a freedom of distance from goals that leaves space for a freedom of experimentation: there is no purpose to them outside the performance itself, and as it unfolds it experimentally resists itself, each appearance is destroyed by a new appearance (recalling Knausgård's self-presenting). One sound shimmies into another, overlaying, demanding recognition, resisting interpretation. Cage creates a space for music that is also raw noise, both tunes and the piano that makes them are present, and neither is able to overtake the other. It is music that is interrupted by the instrument, which retains a disturbing presence, which exposes the composition and performance to risk, detaching it from the habits of life to then return to life in experimental self-relations.[55] And so the experience unfolds in random as much as prepared ways: the sounds are nomadic, and wash through the audience and performer unbidden: called up in the after-effects of a struck note the sound is carried along on the back of reverberations into unchartered, un-staved space.

The same play of concealing and un-concealing pertains to human life: 'Being' means to already be attuned to the world, so much so that this attunement withdraws from sight, we cease to notice it as anything other than a suffusing mood, so that life, like music, can manifest itself. Mood is deeper than affect, it touches on the condition or criteria by which affect makes its mark. To make such attunement the object of inquiry is to interrupt habit, in the same way in which re-tuning the instrument means pausing the standard musical performance by letting a thing speak for itself, so to speak: 'entities show up intelligibly only if they show up and their showing up does not itself show up'.[56]

---

[54] John Cage reflects on this revealing with characteristic lucidity: 'When I first placed objects between piano strings, it was with the desire to possess sounds (to be able to repeat then). But, as the music left my home and went from piano to piano and from pianist to pianist, it became clear that not only are two pianists essentially different from one another, but two pianos are not the same either. Instead of the possibility of repetition, we are faced in life with the unique qualities and characteristics of each occasion.' Quote taken from https://johncage.org/prepared_piano_essay.html

[55] See Christophe Menke Tragedy and the free spirits, 22.

[56] Katherine Withy Heidegger on Being Uncanny. Cambridge, MA: Harvard University Press. 2015, 116.

Figure 3.3 Experimental composer John Cage changes the tuning of his piano by placing coins and screws between the strings in the Gaveau Auditorium, Paris, France, 25 June 1949. New York Times Co./Getty Images.

We find ourselves thrown into a world in which various beings – stones, bees and blossom – already exist and flourish, a world where 'this' (city walls) or 'that' (food) matters already for 'this' (protection) or 'that' (sustenance). Such attunement is everywhere. What Cage does is to bracket it off, or pause the already existing world awhile, so we might observe the tuning (or grammar) by which it is being performed. This is all we can do by way of a two-in-one removal from being: to experiment with what comes familiarly, to then reveal its familiarity, and from this revealing emerges its estranged twin, the uncanny. Inside Cage's prepared piano the errant bolts shivering between the strings reveal how, typically, instruments, harmonics, tones, musical compositions and so on cohere. But the preparation of the piano is not a complete separation from our thrown condition. Rather it works from within, by staying with being, with the performance of music, and reveals a new possibility, one where chance is elevated to the role of prospective genius and where musical scores can be blank, one where silence bears the weight of meaning, one where musicians become very busy doing nothing and letting screws and bolts do the work for them. Cage is taking music back to a kind of beginning point and beginning again (a particularly deliberate, well-crafted expression of what Arendt means by the second birth of natality), and the piano itself, the tuner, musicians and the audience have to come along with him, setting themselves anew (natality again) in a democracy of things from which sound emerges and might be attended to and arranged. Each (collective) attempt is just that, it is struggling in rubbing along the edges of the disinhibitions that constrain, pushing them outwards a little, whilst also, musically speaking, going right back to its centre point.

Attunement

We might now go back to Arendt's attempt to pull the *polis* away from the *oikos*, to enact the organizational equivalent of a thoughtful consideration of a self. The *strategoi* have to manage the fault line between *oikos* and *polis*, acknowledging the productive, habituated and inevitable force of the former, but only in order to sustain the authentic disclosure of opinion through the thoughtful action of the latter. Is there really a need to pull away and separate in the way she suggests? Cage's example of the prepared piano opens up another means of affording authenticity, which implicates the *oikos*.[57] It is a similar form of authentic striving to

[57] Hannah Arendt *The Human Condition*, 175.

which Heidegger alludes when he questions rationally (Socratically?) the warranted elevation of humans above animals. We are, argues Heidegger, in our *Umwelt*, always already distracted by everyday habit (by idle talk and by the everyday business of meeting our practical needs) and our access to being, to authentically grasp our existence itself, is always being clouded by our withdrawal into everyday matters. This happens in labour, in work and even in action: our ordinary, originary connections are always with us, our moods constitute the motivations and environmentally seeded dispositions by which sensory affect takes hold.[58]

What Cage does is not to remove us from this state of attunement, but to reveal it by deliberately inducing a disturbance by which what hitherto had gone un-noticed, becomes noticed. The music reveals rather than conceals the instrument and in its making a disturbed but still recognizable kind of music. We suddenly notice how our perceptions are always already 'coloured' by 'how we feel'; an existentially basic way of being-in-the-world.[59] Cage is releasing us into new possibilities by revealing how our originary and typical moods of attunement are, after all, negotiable; it is a disturbance to our being-in-the-world, rather than a calculated removal from it.[60] In the words of Cage, as a musician and artist the job in hand is to sober and quiet the mind so we might attend to how things are and then to find a way into a commerce with things in which they are no longer so smoothly being 'used'.[61]

Approached from within in this way, the world emerges as a latent field of relations; hidden, clandestine, undisclosed.[62] Humans:

find themselves in their thrownness, whether explicitly or not. In attunement, *Dasein* is always already brought before itself, it has always already found itself, not as perceiving oneself to be there, but as one finds one's self in attunement. As a being which is delivered over to its being, it is also delivered over to the fact that it must always already have found itself, found itself in a finding which comes not from a direct seeking, but from a fleeing.[63]

---

[58] Charles Guignon Introduction. In *The Cambridge Companion to Heidegger*. Edited by C. Guignon. Cambridge: Cambridge University Press. 2006, 1–41; Theodore Schatzki On organizations as they happen. *Organization Studies*, 2006, 27(2): 1863–73, 1871.

[59] Martin Heidegger *Der Begriff der Zeit. Gesamtausgabe Band 64*. Frankfurt am Main: Vittorio Klostermann. 1924/2004, 33.

[60] Martin Heidegger *Being and Time*, 130ff. See also William Blattner *Heidegger's Temporal Idealism*. Cambridge: Cambridge University Press. 1999, 319.

[61] Stuart Jeffries 'John Cage: Musicians and Artists on a Legend' *The Guardian*. 15th August 2012.

[62] Maurice Merleau-Ponty *Phenomenology of Perception*. Translated by C. Smith London: Routledge and Kegan Paul. 1962, 284.

[63] Martin Heidegger, *Being and Time*, §132.

Throwing and finding are the 'to-and-fro' movements expressing this engagement. To be thrown and to find are not decisional experiences, they are felt conditions, steeped in mood. For the most part, moods connect us with the world, but they do not always comport us towards that connection. Cage reveals this by de-tuning our condition, setting in train different and even temporarily disabling moods, primarily anxiety (How is it we can come to care for bolts rattling into the piano carcass? Isn't this just noise?). In anxiety, the mood itself, that about which we are anxious (our existence) and that in the face of which we experience the mood (the nothing that unveils our existence) coincide.[64] Anxiety can offer a glimpse into conditions of thrownness; in anxiety we become open to being; in anxiety we have to fall back on ourselves. Anxiety is 'the birth of the understanding of being'.[65] Understanding being, therefore, is prompted by something unsettling; by a mood evicting us from the familiar and homely. Anxiety is different from fear, which has a definable source (fire, ghost, snake) and can be treated as a problem that, potentially, has a solution.[66] Anxiety is destabilizing because there is no identifiable problem. Problems are structured by typical cognitive patterns (perceive, think, act): normal routines break down, we recover, assess and organize anew. We discover the pieces inside the piano and remove them. Anxiety offers no such comforts: 'you mean he meant the bolts were meant to be in the piano? But why?'.

Gradually, as it dawns on the first listeners to Cage's piece that this was a deliberate act, the entire form of life called music begins to wobble, and host of hitherto concealed background agreements appear and in doing so become questionable.[67] Does music need a trained musician? Does the

---

[64] Katherine Withy *Heidegger on Being Uncanny*, 80.

[65] Katherine Withy *Heidegger on Being Uncanny*, 89.

[66] Brian Söderquist Kierkegaard and existentialism. In *A Companion to Kierkegaard*. Edited by Jon Stewart. Oxford: Blackwell. 2015, 89. Søren Kierkegaard, from whom Heidegger takes the distinction between fear and anxiety, thought of anxiety as a grounding or originating mood, a sense of unease we felt at having to confront the inevitability of our own downfall, our own sin, whose shadow is the necessary accompaniment to the possibility of possibility: if there is a possibility of our being responsible for ourselves and our self-development, there is equally a possibility of us erring, or sinning. This is woven into our very being, the struggle is that from which all selves are born and into which they die and thinking on this becomes itself a struggle set amid indefinite regions. Yet where Kierkegaard finds in anxiety a source of freedom (the scene of one's own self-willed being), Heidegger is less sanguine, thinking, in a more Nietzschean vein, of anxiety as a nihilistic condition.

[67] Ciborra makes an elegant appeal for being more attentive to how information and its meaning is intimate to the everyday lifeworld of its appearance. Claudio Ciborra Encountering information systems as a phenomenon. In *The Social Study of Information and Communication Technology*. Edited by Chrisanthi Avgerou, Claudio Ciborra and Frank Land. Oxford: Oxford University Press. 2004, 17–37.

instrument have agency? Should musical sound carry intention? Should it induce pleasure and what is pleasure? To carry on listening is to accept the presence of what is strange without an ability or even urge to explain or correct it, and then to also realize that despite this strangeness the world is not actually slipping away into chaos, because we encounter ourselves, not as a being riven with equipment and engaged in habitual practices, but somewhat alone, and in still 'being there', in spite of the apparent disturbance to everyday habits, our encounter orients itself into a self-encounter.

Polos and *Polis*

The throwing and finding example from Cage is perhaps a little too contained. After all, not everything gives. The music is still being played at an event, attended by a 'typical' audience who might even be prepared for such strangeness, and it will end, forming a topic of conversation around dinner tables and in academic books. But it is suggestive of how anxiety can be generative as well as disorienting, and can be induced as well as coming out of nowhere. To induce such a mood is clearly resonant with leaving the *oikos*, the home, to then be not at home, and to take a seat in public. Perhaps the concert hall that hosts Cage's music is a little too much like a confident and ebullient *polis* in whose ways one, like Alcibiades, has already been schooled (a place of taste), but the reactions of the early audiences attest to something more dislocating, to an un-homing that disturbed them. On leaving the hall they were no longer open to the play of conventions and agreements in the way they were when they walked in: they were just there, stripped somewhat of their expectations, exposed:

what the human being gives up when it is thrown open is its openness, the *da* [there; the *da-* of *Dasein*]. Since this openness is the human being's essence, the opening up of openness involves the surrender of the essence.[68]

It is this throwing open to the open, and this finding of being there in the open, a being that cannot be talked about as a subject to be managed, that intrigues Heidegger. It is a condition that can be experienced through anxiety, or other moods such as boredom, but it is not synonymous with these moods, which are more like bridges into and then away from a formless nihilism, and which Heidegger is cautious of valourising as inherently desirable.[69] Outside knowing and belief there is nothing,

---

[68] Katherine Withy *Heidegger on Being Uncanny*, 135. Our insertion.

[69] In *What Is Metaphysics?*, Heidegger argues that while angst may indeed be a mood, there is also a more primal angst is an *existentiale* that belongs to *Dasein*'s essential constitution (Martin Heidegger What Is metaphysics? In *Basic Writings*. Edited by David Farrell Krell. London: Routledge. 1993, 99–110).

and Heidegger wants to give this a form by making it apparent in experience, and so revealing to each being the 'most proper and deepest finitude': the nothing that lies at its ground.[70] This inability to be fully open to its own ground; that at the very ground of being, glimpsed in angst, there lies nothing that can be discovered, makes angst a movement that at once discloses and withholds. In being truly at home in the world we are also not at home. The homely and the unhomely (*unheimlich*; uncanny) implying each other as a fundamental *stasis*.

This play between homely and unhomely is the first in a series of vexing relations marking the human being's encounter with authentic being. To be at home in the everyday world of familiar others and things is to be not at home in one's own-most existence. And this everyday being at home would include a *polis* at least one occupied by an entitled, equally committed group of citizens. In the discussion of anxiety Heidegger is suggesting authenticity would struggle to make itself felt in an assured organizational space like Arendt's *polis*, it needs something:

which throws one out of the 'canny,' that is, the homely, the accustomed, the current, the unendangered. The unhomely does not allow us to be at home. Therein lies the over-whelming. But human beings are the uncanniest, not only because they spend their lives essentially in the midst of the un-canny understood in this sense, but also because they step out, move out of the limits that at first and for the most part are accustomed and homely, because as those who do violence, they overstep the limits of the homely, precisely in the direction of the uncanny in the sense of the overwhelming, that is the homely, the accustomed, the usual, the unendangered.[71]

The *polis* towards which strategists might strive but never as a goal, therefore, is not to be homelike, in that it is not a place in which being can come to settle by way of habit.[72] Nor is the *polis* an alternative home to that of everyday existence, one into which the self can move once it has left its inauthentic existence amongst the average everydayness of the 'they', once it has realized that its essential home is, say, its capacity to follow the method of an examined life. The *polis* – understood

---

[70] See Katherine Withy *Heidegger on Being Uncanny*, 85.

[71] Martin Heidegger; *Introduction to Metaphysics*. Translated by Gregory Fried and Richard Polt, 2nd edn. New Haven: Yale. 2014,168. Our emphasis.

[72] There is, perhaps, an irony here, as the *polis* understood as a confident place of action, whereas it is the *oikos*, as a space of violence, that can be more readily understood as anxiety-inducing. To recur to Ibsen's *A Doll's House*, Nora is not fearful, there is no explicit threat, it is more a cloying atmosphere in which she can no longer breathe, and which casts her outside of the condition into which she has been thrown. She must first feel herself doll-like and not a person before her issuing of the 'no' comes forth (Henrik Ibsen *A Doll's House*. Edited by Martin Adamson and David Widger. Project Gutenberg. 2001. www.gutenberg.org/files/2542/2542-h/2542-h.htm).

in Arendt's terms as a space of appearances – is itself to be uncanny (*ungeheuer*):

the immense and what has never yet been ... The uncanny is also not what has never yet been present; it is what comes into presence always already and in advance prior to all 'uncanninesses'. The uncanny, as the Being that shines into everything ordinary, i.e., into entities, and that in its shining often grazes entities like the shadow of a cloud silently passing, has nothing in common with the monstrous or the alarming. The uncanny is the simple, the insignificant, ungraspable by the fangs of the will, withdrawing itself from all artifices of calculation, because it surpasses all planning.[73]

To recur to Uexküll's *Umwelt*, what makes us (potentially) authentically human and what separates us from the animal, whose poverty in world means captivation, is when, through disclosive *logos*, the *Umwelt* shimmers within its own marks by bringing being into view, but not as a condition of understanding, which would be to synthesize the form-giving order of concepts, metaphysics and beauty with form-disturbing, sensual feeling and bodily drives. Rather, being comes into view as appearance, giving way to yet other appearance. As a dis-concealing (as opposed to revealing, which would harken to a knowledgeable state), it is an unsettling that is sufficient to bring about a two-in-one encounter with oneself, and to publicly reveal such an encounter, yet by inviting new appearances (seeing new names). Having been prepared, Cage's bolts and screws keep rattling in their own way, throwing the idea of music, of an audience, of silence, back at the performer and listener alike, without resolve or resolution. Unlike animals, who dwell in their habitat instinctually, *Dasein* dwells *ek-statically*; it can encounter beings (including itself) as distinct things whose presence lies outside any biologically established affective organization of marks and receptor organs. Being in touch with beings as beings means *Dasein* can be disturbed by what comes forth, much as Cage's bolts and screws haunt the piano as unruly, occult forces.[74]

Only in dwelling beyond itself is *Dasein* able to apprehend being itself as a condition of the world; but in this encounter it also loses a firm sense of what the self actually is or ought to be. In the wake of the loss knowledge and morality are no longer accompanied by certainty: any claim to a calling (to make more of oneself as a productive being, or to reveal oneself as, at core, a soul, or to relish ones doubt, or to eschew reason for belief and love) begets further expressive questioning of what it is 'to be': disconcealing simultaneously conceals what is being disconcealed, in what, Heidegger continues, is an emerging-abiding sway of coming into

---

[73] Martin Heidegger *Parmenides*, 101. Katherine Withy *Heidegger on Being Uncanny*, 170.
[74] William McNeill *The Time of Life*, xxi

appearance.[75] It is a kind of self-grounding where the being attains itself as ground by withdrawing from calculation and surpassing planning and leaping into an open region in which it exists, hesitantly.[76] It is not a move from being to leaping, but a leap from within being so that the concealed is disconcealed. It is a space of struggling for which Heidegger enlists the Greek term *polemos*. If for Arendt the *polis* was akin to a theatre, a place of performance, then *polemos* throws the spectacle into turmoil, one where the actor – in acting – is also being subject to the uncanny experience of watching themselves metamorphose into performative roles. It is here Heidegger enlists the *polis* as a clearing in which the continual conflict between the concealed and disconcealed finds an organizational expression. Heidegger likens it to *polos*, meaning a swirl of turning things from which one springs again and again (*Ur-sprung*), a constancy of motion that continually presences and absences, rather than its being an enclosure.[77] In turning the *polis* presences by way of absencing; it is a giving and refusing.[78] This yawing between presence and absence by which the human *Umwelt* is marked leaves a curious sense of vacancy at the ground of being; an event that both unsettles each being and brings it into its own-most (*eigentlich*) being without, however, resting or settling, but, rather, consigning it to a constant counterturning away.

The seeing of the concealing incurred by naming is a thoughtful movement, where to think is to be interested in what relates human beings to beings, and to Being itself, but also to then let itself, as thinking, be thought, and so to be claimed by Being, rather than remain in the relative comfort of its own categories as though it were looking down on Being.[79] Thinking is found in a being thrown out of the homely, and to whom the *polis* offers no homely equivalent; they live with the uncanny, as a being encountering the strangeness of its being open to Being. The human struggle is therefore grounded in this expulsion from the homely and the seeking, but failing to attain, the certainties by which one regains access to the home:

The human being has openness insofar as it is the open site – the entity that understands being, the *da* [there]. But the human being does not have openness insofar as it cannot wield openness perfectly against itself ... being, the human beings' origin, absences or withdraws from openness [and] the whence of its thrownness is obscure. This is the human being's inner counterturning (*pelein*); it is its uncanniness.[80]

[75] Martin Heidegger *Introduction to Metaphysics*, 196, 16.

[76] Martin Heidegger Letter on humanism, 229.

[77] Whereas for Arendt (*The Human Condition*, 64) *polis* derives from a ring-wall, a circling pen, a surrounding fence. See also Katherine Withy *Heidegger on Being Uncanny*, 129.

[78] Katherine Withy *Heidegger on Being Uncanny*, 149.

[79] Martin Heidegger Letter on humanism, 193–5.

[80] Katherine Withy *Heidegger on Being Uncanny*, 141–2.

To be authentic means to stop being at home; Agamben's 'moat' becomes doubly apt as a metaphor, being the very edge of the enclave that marks the language user's home, and defined by watery depths rather than solid elevations. This is the 'nothing' at the very centre of *Dasein*, that which marks us as uncanny. Heidegger observes an essential poverty in such a move, the poverty of one who is able to understand that in ascribing a value to everything (the good and evil, the sacred and profane, the useful and useless, the beautiful and ugly) every 'thing' is thereby always withdrawn from itself and made to stand out 'as an object for human estimation'.[81] To lessen and loosen this valuing tendency, to refuse the claims of those for whom human values and measures are of the highest order of being, is an admission that things cannot be exhausted by submitting them to the objectifying valuations and assessments of representational images and concepts.

To search for authenticity in such a space of appearances is to accept that what limits the capacity of *Dasein* to be authentic are the very practices in which humans typically think to find themselves as being most human: their civilized routines, their morals, their knowledge structures, their deeply held allegiances. To labour and to work in the service of these Promethean gifts is to conceal their potential behind a purdah of ideas or underneath a heap of possessions. It is in being set against this accumulation that Heidegger advances a condition of poverty. As an historically constituted setting in which the circuiting murmuration of a people find coherent organizational form, his advocacy of the *polis* and of Dasein's historical task, is profoundly problematic.

Nazi

i bi nie kein Nazi gsei[82]

Had he stopped with thinking rather than enlist his thought in the service of a name – Germany – events might have been different for Heidegger. But he wished to have his thoughts politically embodied, or perhaps he came to feel his embodied thinking was, in fact, political, not least in his association of poverty, authenticity and leadership, which found a mythical form in the metaphorical figure of the shepherd. Somewhat

---

[81] Martin Heidegger Letter on humanism, 228. A play on Hölderlin's Homecoming (Friedrich Hölderlin. *Selected Poems and Fragments*. Translated by M. Hamburger. Edited by Jeremy Adler. London: Penguin. 2007, 159).

[82] Martin Heidegger in correspondence with Ernst Jünger in 1969. The translation of this Swabian grammatical monstrosity is roughly 'I have never been a Nazi', yet it involves a double negative, throwing the certainty awry. In Martin Heidegger and Ernst Jünger *Correspondence, 1949–1975*. Translated by Timothy Quinn. London: Rowman & Littlefield. 2016, 49.

whimsically Heidegger also called the shepherd the neighbour of being. This living alongside life took the form of being both a guide accompanying and sheltering others, and a creator of worlds. The shepherd operates a little like Socrates, encouraging people in the impoverishing practice of self-examination from which they might imagine a better or ideal city state. It is a temptation, but as soon as poverty becomes a condition for which one becomes an advocate it loses its uncanny appeal, indeed it trips itself up on a fundamental contradiction: to value the poverty induced by thinking oneself into a state of unhomeliness is to submit it to a process of validation, it is to recur to the condition of estimation in which it is impossible to let things just be. Perhaps Arendt was more cautious here, despite her passionate advocacy for a *polis*, insofar as in her advocacy of the refugee figure we witness a grave sense of unease when encountering those who associate the organization of authenticity with a nation, state or people, and who value moods like collective anxiety because of the motive force they give to political (totalitarian) solutions. Heidegger's *polis*, whilst it is a space of gathering and refused the language of estimation, nevertheless exposed his thinking to the embodied presence of a central 'pole', perhaps to be found in the figure of the shepherd (or Heidegger), towards which a flock moves, and under whose stewardship an entire people might begin to transform its vision world.

Once politicized the line of being that lies at the heart of his distinction between nature, animal and humans, and which constitutes a basic and unquestioned estimation, becomes poisonous. Though in itself the distinctions are as old as the hills, when read against the race theories and the eugenics programmes supported by the German National Socialist regime, Heidegger's embrace and expansion of Uexküll's study into a step-wise taxonomy distinguishing humans and non-humans, is objectionable also because of the timing of its development around 1936. It was only two years after Hitler assumed the triple role as head of the army, leader and Reich chancellor, and coincided with Heidegger's own enthusiastic inclusion of National Socialist ideology, including biologism, into the University of Freiburg, of which he was, briefly, Rector.[83]

---

[83] Heidegger intervened, as Rector of the University of Freiburg, to secure the establishment of a chair in racial doctrine and biology, to promote racial science as part of National Socialist ideology. Bettina Bergo Sterben Sie? The problem of Dasein and 'animals' ... of various kinds. In *Heidegger's Black Notebooks*. Edited by Andrew Mitchell and Peter Trawny. 2017, 52–73. Nor was Uexküll absolved from complicity. Agamben points to a 'curious episode' in Uexküll's intellectual biography as, in 1928, 'this very sober scientist' contributed with a preface to Houston Chamberlain's 'Foundations of the Nineteenth Century', now seen to be a foundational text for National Socialism. Giorgio Agamben *The Open*, 43.

In politicizing the distinction, Heidegger debated with himself about how, as a shepherd, he might lead a people towards a more authentic condition sheltered from what he saw as the life-denuding influences of industrialism and global finance embodied in the figure of the Jew. More problematic still is whether his racism and his failings in relation to an academic calling for critique, are a result of a political turn, or whether his philosophy itself is subject to, or even a contributing factor to, National Socialist ideology, warmongering and anti-Semitism. This has become an even more pressing question since the publication and translation of (some of) Heidegger's *Black Notebooks* which are, as Jean-Luc Nancy remarks, black in cover and content.[84]

One particularly disturbing element of the *Notebooks* (amongst many) is that in the early period of his shift from the analysis of individual Being to being (*beyng*) as an historical event induced by a shepherd in the *polis*, Heidegger peddles the anti-Semitic tropes with uncritical enthusiasm. This includes a distinction between settled and rooted (*bodenständig; verwurzelt*) peoples and those that are rootless or groundless (*bodenlos*).[85] Given the 'blood and soil' *Lebensraum* propaganda circulating at

---

[84] Nancy stipulates Heidegger's banality in a direct lineage to Arendt's assessment of Eichmann. Just as the latter hid behind the normalization of orders and ignorance of their motives and effects, so Heidegger peddled the anti-Semitic tropes circulating in Europe, especially between 1920–1940. Jean-Luc Nancy *The Banality of Heidegger*. New York: Fordham. 2017.

[85] *Bodenlosigkeit*, lack of soil, groundlessness, is here made a distinctive trait of 'Jewry', and Heidegger links this 'being bound to nothing' to the tendency to 'making everything serviceable for itself' – that is for the 'Jewry'. He argues that the 'victory of history over the historyless' requires that 'groundlessness excludes itself' (sich selbst ausschliesst) – a euphemism which, Nancy notes, very much designates a destruction, an elimination. Nancy asks where Heidegger finds such an image of forgetfulness of being in association with the Jewish people, pointing to the 'most banal, vulgar, trivial, and nasty discourse that had long been scattered throughout Europe and that had been propped up for some thirty years by the miserable publication of The Protocols of the elders of Zion'. Jean-Luc Nancy: *The Banality of Heidegger*, 20–7. Nancy finds it particularly disappointing that Heidegger, whilst he so carefully investigated the ancient Greeks, so willingly adopted the popular myths – the banal *doxa* – about the Jewish people being bereft of soil and identity other than destructive calculation, never questioning the self-hatred that accompanies the decline of the West and the hatred towards Jews, or likewise the indebtedness of much of Judeo-Christian thinking to Judaism. Heidegger was guilty of the kind of scapegoating employed by totalitarian regimes which require the continual production and elimination of the unnatural (see Andrew Norris Jean-Luc Nancy on the political after Heidegger and Schmitt. *Philosophy and Social Criticism*, 2011, 37: 899–913). In contrast, Nietzsche, whilst still talking in a dubious language of 'types', sees the wandering as a source of strength and tenacity, a self-determining resilience that, freed from the youthful immaturity of nationhood, renders them enviable in their capacity for revaluating values (Beyond Good and Evil, §250).

the time,[86] his contrast of the Greeks as the original settlers (*autochthon*) against 'nomadic' Jews places any advocacy of spatial purity into an utterly contested frame. The argument that the Jews are agents of modernity whose profiteering and string-pulling contributes to the growing machination of the world, thus standing in the way of the event of awakening of the German *Volk* as a direct successor of the ancient Greeks as a people in touch with authenticity, is as facile in its analysis as it is reprehensible in its callousness.[87] Compounding this, in a well-known speech on 'the danger', delivered following World War II in 1949, Heidegger asks crassly:

Hundreds of thousands of humans die in masses. Do they die? They perish. They are put down. The become units of a standing reserve of the fabrication of corpses. Do they die? They are inconspicuously liquidated in concentration camps. And even without these – millions pauperise now in China through hunger into a perishing.[88]

Heidegger had spoken directly of the 'worldlessness of Judaism' and while this may merely be the acknowledgement of the plight of a persecuted people in exile, the experience of the diaspora and the condition of wandering, in Heidegger's quite specific language, we are beholden

---

[86] See Ian Klinke and Mark Bassin. Introduction: *Lebensraum* and its discontents. *Journal of Historical Geography*, 2018, 61: 53–68. Also see Trevor J. Barnes and Claudio Minca Nazi spatial theory: The dark geographies of Carl Schmitt and Walter Christaller. *Annals of the Association of American Geographers*, 2013, 103(3): 669–87, 672–3. Carl Schmitt was appointed Prussian Chancellor of State in 1933, encouraged by Heidegger to 'join the revolution', displaying the fervour of someone who has come late, eager to make up ground. He joined the Nazi party in 1933. Railing against emigrants as well as condoning and legally justifying the growing Nazi violence of the 'night of the long knives' in which the leaders of a rival fraction of street thugs (SA) which had helped propel Hitler to power were murdered. Jan-Werner Müller *A Dangerous Mind: Carl Schmitt in Post-War European Thought*. London: Yale. 2003, 37. Schmitt only occasionally mentions *Lebensraum* (for example referring to the sea lacking space for life), and while he does not engage in a biological justification for room, his geographical political theory develops the idea of space-population and space-density, giving rise to a conception of the unity of the German people as a spatial organism, capable of expanding or shrinking, while keeping its demographic intensity. This required the 'perfect coincidence between people and population in a unified, endlessly perfectable, biopolitical space' – with the 'other' – the enemy – being not-of-that-space, residing or being in need of expulsion, from that space. Claudio Minca Carl Schmitt and the question of spatial ontology. In *Spatiality, sovereignty and Carl Schmitt: Geographies of the nomos*. Edited by Stephen Legg London: Routledge. 2011, 163–82. Recalling our earlier discussion of Schmitt in relation to Arendt and the *polis*, his spatialized friend-foe definition provides the political justification for the racist categorizations of the National Socialist machinery and its many atrocities.

[87] Donatella di Cesare *Heidegger and the Jews: The Black Notebooks*. Translated by M. Baca. Cambridge: Polity, 85.

[88] Martin Heidegger *Die Gefahr. Gesamtausgabe III/79*. Bremer und Freiburger Vorträge. Edited by P. Jaeger. 1994, 2nd edn. 2005. Our translation.

to ask whether the implied negation of the capacity for those, mainly Jewish victims of the industrialized murder in concentration camps to 'die', but merely perish, raises the question whether he thought only some humans have world-forming capacity, namely those who belong and were open to being – while others can merely perish; merely be taken back by their environment of which they have always already been a part through their originary captivation.[89] As Bergo asks: 'Could this be one implication of the putative worldlessness of "the Jews"?'; thus forming the philosophical basis for a potential segregation of some humans to a less-than-human status?[90]

For Arendt it was precisely the rootlessness that gave rise to an ennobling natality and plurality. Yet in the twisted thinking of Heidegger, the Jews came to exemplify a type of human thrown into – but also somehow guilty of – the accelerating condition of instrumentality that had beset the modern world.[91] To identify the Jews as being both thrown into a condition of rootlessness – so as unattached in systems of calculation and the ensuing fate (*Geschick*) of machination (*Machenschaft*)[92] – and to then blame them for this thrownness (being caught in a wider ecology) makes little sense on Heidegger's own terms.[93] Equally egregious is his simultaneous association of the German *Volk* as a site of strife within which the 'unfathomable (*unergründlich*), approach of the historical vocation or destiny withheld for a historical people or community—their very ethos' may be revealed.[94]

---

[89] Donatella di Cesare *Heidegger and the Jews*, 161.

[90] Bettina Bergo *Sterben Sie?*, 58. There is also the philosophically vexing question about the nature of the modern human being itself. Why and in what sense are these forms of captivation, experienced in angst and through the essence of technology any different to that of the animal in its environment? See Bettina Bergo *Sterben Sie?*, 64, and Richard Polt *Inception, Downfall and the Broken World*, 80.

[91] Michael Fagenblat 'Heidegger' and the Jews. In *Reading Heidegger's Black Notebooks 1931–1941*. Edited by Ingo Farin and Jeff Malpas. Cambridge, MA: MIT Press. 2016, 145–68, 148.

[92] In a particularly egregious twist, this means that Jews have become 'symbolic exponents of the empty rationality and calculative thinking that globalize alienation in the modern age, including racialized ways of determining humanity. The Jews advance a type of thinking that determines the anti-Semitism they themselves suffer'. Michael Fagenblat 'Heidegger' and the Jews, 149.

[93] Krell argues that: 'When Heidegger blames "the international Jewish conspiracy," as it were, for what is wrong with his times, or when he blames the Catholics or the Bolsheviks or even the pragmatic Americans for their "machinations," it may be a sign that he has regressed even farther, slipping from paranoetic [as owing to the uncanny condition of humans, there is no being, no Seiendes, that can be feared and hated] thinking to a paranoid nonthinking, pure and simple. His vituperative polemics make no sense. They make no sense especially on Heidegger's own terms and in the light of what his own thinking has achieved.' David Farrell Krell *Ecstasy, Catastrophe. Heidegger from Being and Time to the Black Notebooks*. New York: SUNY, 7.

[94] William McNeill *The Time of Life*, 119.

This is no less than a transition from individual anxiety to a rupture that may reveal the authentic being of a historical people or community as one of settlement; hence the question to which extent this philosophical idea is also a politically concrete one.[95] Heidegger saw the people of the first beginning to be the ancient Greeks; and German *Volk* as that people who now stood ready for a second ('other') beginning through overcoming the labouring machination embodied in the powers of the USA and Russia in particular. It is here, Žižek argues, where 'Heidegger "takes a wrong turn" when he posits the only way of breaking the habit and the idle chatter of the commonplace (the disinhibitor ring of common sense) is the heroic assumption of one's historical Destiny.'[96]

Perhaps one of the bigger revelations of the *Notebooks* is the documentation of the political thought of a philosopher who has often been excused as politically naïve and idealist, or so captivated with post-metaphysical thought, and so far removed from mere ('ontic') matters of politics, that he was susceptible to the temper of the National Socialist programme, before realizing it was not capable of producing the historical rupture from mechanization that his brand of authentic thinking required.[97] The story continues that accompanying this disappointment came the realization of his own insignificance and impotence in the actual political task and his turning (*Kehre*) towards poetry, and, in his own nomenclature, from *being* to *beyng*.

The *Notebooks* reveal a more active political thinker. What appears to be emerging in Heidegger's *Kehre* is a change in narrative where his initial hopes for creating a kind of collective natality, a new beginning

---

[95] These concerns take on political reality when viewed in light of Heidegger's infamous rectoral address of 1933, where he proclaimed: 'Whether such a thing [as the collapse of the inauthentic enframed civilization of the West] occurs or does not occur, this depends solely on whether we as a historico-spiritual *Volk* will ourselves.... But it is our will that our Volk fulfill its historical mission' (In Bret W. Davis Heidegger's releasement from the technological will. In *Heidegger on Technology*. Edited by James Wendland, Christopher Merwin and Christos Hadjioannou. London: Routledge. 2019, 133–48, 139). And they are further exacerbated by comments in the *Notebooks* where he wrote, in relation to the university, that the 'first task of the leader in knowledge cultivation is to set the goals as a whole, to bring onto the way, and to create the weapons. That leads at all events to a "reform of the university," which makes an end of the university and creates an origin' (Martin Heidegger Ponderings II–VI. *Black Notebooks, 1931–1938*. Translated by R. Rojcewicz. Bloomington: Indiana University Press. 2016, 102).

[96] Slavoj Žižek The persistence of ontological difference, 190.

[97] Deleuze and Guattari suggest wryly that 'Perhaps this strict professor was madder than he seemed. He got the wrong people, earth, and blood. For the race summoned forth by art or philosophy is not the one that claims to be pure but rather an oppressed, bastard, lower, anarchical, nomadic, and irremediably minor race-the very ones that Kant excluded from the paths of the new Critique', Gilles Deleuze and Félix Guattari *What Is Philosophy?* New York: Columbia University Press. 1994, 109.

rooted in National Socialism,[98] gave way to his envisaging a beginning rooted in the self-annihilation of truth. The end of the possibility of fixed truths occurs, he argues, when machination reaches a point of domination so complete that there is nothing left for technology to consume, save itself. When everything becomes doable through labour, that is everything can be rationally planned and technologically made and reduced to a number, then the world is bereft of anything natural; bereft of roots and soil, the technological becomes an entire political-technological complex of power. This is '*Machenschaft*' (machination).[99] Then there is no room for a *polis* of any form, it is better simply to relinquish politics and with it the possibility of truth.

Organization against Authenticity

As the *Notebooks* attest in a disarming and deeply troubling way, any attempt to apprehend authenticity from the perspective of a notion of poverty rooted in biological thinking and authentic being is fraught with contention.[100] The development of hierarchies between nature, animals and humans has set a precedence for the neglect of environmentalism, animal ethics and for the 'monstrous' attempt to draw a line between the human and in-human.[101] Heidegger is netted in these attempts and fully culpable for the dangers that lurk therein.[102] Those who take him up,

---

[98] In the *Notebooks*, Heidegger writes: 'National Socialism is a barbaric principle. Therein lies its essence and its capacity for greatness.' See also Heidegger. *Ponderings II–VI*: 142; *Ponderings VII–XI*: 219. Farrell Krell notices the *Notebooks* are laced with 'bitter remarks' on 'drives to violence and destruction that are running amok', suggesting the barbarism Heidegger invokes is not, at least in its lineage from the poets Hölderlin and Schelling, a destructive force, but rather a nurturing and creative energy of nature. However, how this energy can be linked to the atrocities of National Socialism remains unanswered. David Farrell Krell *Ecstasy, Catastrophe*, 152.

[99] Ingo Farin The black notebooks in their historical and political context. In *Reading Heidegger's Black Notebooks 1931–1941*. Edited by Ingo Farin and Jeff Malpas. Cambridge, MA: MIT Press. 2016, 291–316, 301.

[100] Not least the sheer volume of the *Notebooks* which have been added to an already suffocating number of outputs – in addition to endless commentaries – on Heideggerian philosophy. Or, in the words of Steven Crowell: '"Shit! Three more massive volumes of Heideggeriana to plough through. Didn't I just finish skimming thousands of pages of Heidegger's Seminar on Hegel, Kant, and Leibniz? How do my colleagues manage to get to the bottom of such publications so quickly?" I still have no answer to that question.' Steven Crowell Reading Heidegger's black notebooks. In *Reading Heidegger's Black Notebooks 1931–1941*. Edited by Ingo Farin and Jeff Malpas. Cambridge, MA: MIT Press, 29–44, 29.

[101] Giorgio Agamben *The Open*, 22.

[102] Following the publication of the *Black Notebooks* in 2014 in German and 2017 in English, the reassessment of Heidegger's legacy, both personal and especially philosophical, has merely begun and while it is beyond the scope of this book to seek any form of final assessment, it appears for the moment at least, that for some the notebooks

read and use his thinking are equally culpable, caught as they are in the mirror-plays of a thinker stained by a long-standing affiliation with questions not just of human distinction, but of distinctions between human 'types'. Yet Heidegger remains the philosopher who, arguably, most vehemently unsettled the human individual from its assumed, technologically enabled pre-eminence. In its sustained concern with the comprehension and apprehension of being as a technological condition it has been a form of thinking that has permeated western thinking in the twentieth century, a century of technological machination that has witnessed a near total concealing of being. There has been no other thinker in whom this condition of technological machination has received more sustained and intense consideration, a condition first associated with the blunt term

offer at least a degree of reversal from the anti-Americanism of some of the published writings; as well as a distancing from the National Socialist project from around 1934, precisely by likening the National Socialist programme to the Machination that he hitherto had lamented in the guise of America, Great Britain, France and the Soviet Union. Žižek suggests that Heidegger's growing disillusion with National Socialism was not because of his recognition of the barbarism of that project itself (Slavoj Žižek The persistence of ontological difference, 186–99). Far from this, and as noted above, Heidegger argues in the notebooks that: 'National Socialism is a barbaric principle. The anger is not [Nazism] itself, but instead that it will be rendered innocuous via homeliness about the True, the Good, and the Beautiful.' This growing resentment rests on the discrepancy between the political project of National Socialism and the metaphysical idea of a beginning. But, as noted, Heidegger seems to be aiming at a different kind of barbarism rooted in metaphysical overcoming of the 'they', and not with street violence, mass murder and the total mobilization for war. He writes: 'One preaches "blood" and "soil" and yet pursues an urbanization and a destruction of the village and farm to an extent that could not have been surmised a short while ago' Martin Heidegger *Ponderings VII–XI Black Notebooks 1983–1939*. Translated by R. Rojcewicz. Bloomington: Indiana University Press. 2016, 283. In an interview with the German news-magazine Spiegel, Heidegger laments that that while National Socialism did move towards the attainment of a fuller relationship towards the nature of technology, those people 'were far too poorly equipped for thought to arrive at a really explicit relationship to what is happening today and has been underway for the past 300 years' (Der Spiegel 30. Mai, 1976): 193–219 and elsewhere in the *Notebooks* he mentions the 'stupid obstinacy of mere violence-doing [becoming] the tool of inner destruction' and the 'Futureless violence-doing' being an example of 'complete lack of questioning'. Heidegger even talks of the 'mildness' of the thinking of being and, Polt suggests, that as 'the world around him becomes more violent and brutal, Heidegger draws back' Richard Polt: *Inception, Downfall and the Broken World*, 87. Quotes also taken from this source. The notebooks also contain condemnations of what he calls 'idolatry of the people (Vergötzung des Volkes), especially the National Socialist "folkish" brutishness', and 'idolatry of race' (Vergötzung der Rasse) and the latter's irreducibility to biology as an absolute factor, rejecting the National Socialist 'principle of race' as a basic truth (Ingo Farin The black notebooks, 300. Those challenging what they sense is an overtly one-sided interpretation of the *Notebooks* include: Friedrich-Wilhelm von Herrmann The role of Martin Heidegger's notebooks within the context of his oeuvre. In *Reading Heidegger's Black Notebooks 1931–1941*. Edited by Ingo Farin and Jeff Malpas. Cambridge, MA: MIT Press. 2016, 92) and Donatella di Cesare *Heidegger and the Jews*, 12.

'Americanism'[103] but later, in the *Notebooks* and in his post-war comments expanded to include Bolshevism and also, by 1938, National Socialist ideology before finding its fuller conceptual development as 'technological enframing' (*Gestell*).[104] In thinking being through technology, and in not reducing technology to instruments or machines but to the very ground (*Umwelt*) of the possibility of being, Heidegger writes:

> Technology and its twin sister – '*organization*' – both the opposite of everything 'organic'—are by essence driving on to their proper end, a self-hollowing out. And we, *swept along*, i.e., just as captivated and enchanted or also dragged on by this procedure – what are we doing? We equip ourselves in the direction of technology and organization (said together: we equip for machination). We equip for the end – so as then in the end to be unequipped for the beginning and especially for the great desolation and derangement of everything.[105]

Thus equipped, technology is not merely linked to the breakthroughs achieved by modern science and elsewhere, but becomes the very basis of being, notably in the activities of planning and administration that characterize the practice of strategy and in so doing determine who we are. This organization towards a technological enframing (*Gestell*) of human life has only intensified, and strategy, the practice of struggling to understanding the organizational self being mediated in such technology, remains deeply complicit with this intensification. Hence our inquiry into strategy practice requires us to persist with our engagement of Heidegger, forewarned of the lurking dangers of such a project. As Farrell Krell has it: 'The situation, as always, calls for *critical* reading, and what that necessitates is the hard work of *reading* in the first place.'[106]

Arendt read Heidegger hard, perhaps finding it harder than anyone. Provoked by his insight that the world reveals itself through the space created in the thrownness and fallenness of human practice, and, like him, prompted by Nietzsche's concern that the human has withdrawn into technology in such a way that it has obscured itself from itself, she struggled continually to think through the possibilities for authenticity at a time when instrumentality had worked its way into all relations. It is with her constantly in mind that we too inquire into strategy practice as a systemic withdrawal into technology whose organizational impress aims for a totality of control in which everything – including each human – is, at best, a

---

[103] Martin Heidegger The age of the world picture. In *Off the Beaten Track*. Translated by J. Young and K. Haynes. Cambridge: Cambridge University Press. 2002, 57–85.

[104] Farin notes that linking the National Socialist dictatorship with machination was 'certainly a dissident view' (Ingo Farin The black notebooks in their historical and political context, 302).

[105] Martin Heidegger *Ponderings II–VI*, 265. Original emphasis.

[106] David Farrell Krell *Ecstasy, Catastrophe*, 26. Original emphasis.

separate and lonely unit. It is an aim rhetorically advanced using thoughtless, totalitarian clauses: world class, competitive success, global coverage, total quality management, business process re-engineering, tomorrow's leaders today (the apostrophe is often missing), owning the future, and so on. As Arendt looks for hints of authenticity amid this instrumental labouring and the fabricated work values of efficiency, effectiveness and success, so might we. For Arendt these hints were also grounded in biologism: with each human birth came the possibility of starting again, it was a body that had to be organized. Sure enough, the processes of subjectification into which it is thrown tighten from before the first breath is drawn: the rupture of each birth is little more than an opportunity for consensus-seeking strategic management to show its compliant organizational finesse.[107] Authenticity – the condition of plurality and natality by which moods of uncanniness find their generative potential – are antithetical to a technological ordering of the human species whose unthinking aim is to close off the openness of world into which beings are thrown: through technology humans have been organized into a poverty of world kept alive with means-end cleverness (*logos* made instrumentally rational).[108]

And this leads to the question of whether we are working here with a failure of organization, or whether it is in the nature of organization to always fail the self: is organization antithetical to authenticity? If so, then strategy can never realize a condition of authenticity. An organized idea of self is not an encounter with being but a confrontation, and one that is dedicated to securing a condition in which the organized are no longer required, or compelled, to feel uncanniness. In this sense, strategy aims at creating what Nietzsche called last men (sic): figures who would no longer need to transform or question or evaluate themselves, unable to go beyond themselves, they hop onto the organized world, and just stand there, blinking in the moment, attracted to the glitter of surface distinctions, and calling the distraction freedom.

---

[107] Management closes down spaces that are opened up for judgment, to seek a consensual order so we might fight terrorism, combat commercial waywardness, and to find collective delight in standardized leisure activities. We are less and less tolerant of difference for its own sake, we have no negative capability, we equate dissensus with what is wild rather than civilized, we orbit ourselves with timid trepidation. See Jacques Rancière *Dissensus – on Politics and Aesthetics*. London: Continuum. 2010.

[108] Martin Heidegger Letter on humanism, 221–223. Heidegger calls objectification 'the uniform accessibility of everything to everyone' (221), a condition in which language is no longer used to enquire after the mysteries of things, it has become instead pure method, a way of concealing the world under a grammatical cloak of evaluation, it has not been protected from itself. In such a condition rhetoric becomes impossible, there is none of the elegance of persuasion, there is just the method to be applied, and who wins the argument is the person with better data, with better access to the mouthpiece, with more cheerleaders. See also Martin Heidegger *Being and Time* §27 & §35.

Part II

The Three Epochs of Strategy

Technē, *Technology, Technogenesis*

4   *Technē*: Creating Organizational Forms from the Earth

Tuchē

How does a human being, furless and clawless, with unimposing height, survive against Pandora's *'daimon'* – against those demons that forever seem to conspire against prosperity, health, life; conspire against one's efforts at hard work and good conduct? A beginning for the question concerning strategy lies here: with humans roaming their environment. Here on earth: where the heavens, crossed by the burning sun and rain-laden clouds, throw themselves at human life down below; where the soils reveal their fruits, but often capriciously; where feasts are salted by the memories of starvation from which they are but temporary relief. For every coming together in form there is a pulling away, and the ebb and flow of uncertain life. Such was the imagined origin to human life referred to by ancient Greeks as *tuchē*,[1] which could translate as luck, which is less a quality of randomness than an experience of double play in which a vulnerability to external happenings is coupled to a persisting sense of the essential openness of life. Those with *tuchē* experience life as chaotic, but more in Hesiod's sense, for whom chaos was the first form-giving incision into the pre-natural unity of the cosmos, the first rupture (*eris*), one that distinguished the form (*eros*) of earth from heaven and which gave birth to language, and so to all the other distinctions at which humans, born into chaos and exposed to *tuchē*, have to work:

the race is indeed one of iron. And they will not cease from toil and distress by day, nor from being worn out by suffering at night, and the gods will give them grievous cares. Yet all the same, for these people too good things will be mingled with evil ones.[2]

---

[1] Martha Nussbaum *The Fragility of Goodness*. Cambridge: Cambridge University Press. 1986, 3. Also called *Tyche*.
[2] Hesiod *Works and days*. Translated by Glenn W. Most. Cambridge, MA: Harvard University Press. 2006, 135.

Hesiod speculates how humans came to acquire the skills, crafts or arts to cope: building shelters, stalking prey, gathering berries, and then the turn to planting, threshing and grinding, and to the yoking and taming of animals; the arts of metal and woodwork; of predicting weather and divining; and the most praised of all arts, those of building ships and navigating. Equipped with such arts, Hesiod 'recalls' how, with the gift of *technai*, humans were able to co-operate; record the seasons, to plant, rear, smith and hammer so as to have workshops and produce what they needed and more; so they could begin to store and trade; thus controlling nature's unpredictability; insulating themselves against long cold winters or periods of drought. *Technē* meant bringing something to realization; bringing something to sensory appearance and understanding through use. By giving form to what was inchoate, but always alive to the risky, loosening force of *eris*, humans could organize: not just guard themselves against *tuchē*, but play with it, and in doing so experience an immanent power that comes to beings who, bearing the element of iron and being skilled at working it, teem with life.[3] *Technē* thus came to stand in place of, and then opposition to, *tuchē* at whose mercy proto-humans had been thrown and under whose exposing influence the scheming, cunning, flexible, practical human – the human gifted with fire from the forge of Hephaestus - emerged. *Technē* is the organization of destiny through the 'deliberate application of human intelligence'.[4] It is a process of civilizing, of controlling events. In Hesiod's poetry it is symbolized in the efforts made by *eros* to tame *eris*. In the beginning this was a bloody game amongst the immortals, as when stabilizing, straight talking Zeus swallows the unruly, serpentine Metis, hoping to absorb and then manage her innate cunning. There would always be mysteries and anomalies, but these were treated as potential symptoms awaiting treatment strategies based on the initial collection and careful counting and weighing of observations, so that inferences could be drawn from individual cases, allowing the generation of more universal hypotheses, moving understandings

---

[3] Harold Innis argues that especially in cultures dependent on agriculture the necessities of irrigation required the measurement of time so as to predict floods and the important dates of the year, such as seed and harvest times. Through organizing time, pharaohs and kings could expand spatial control, for instance in exactly calculating natural events such as the Nile floods and linking these vital sources of irrigation with religious rituals. And in Rome, Julius Cesar's alteration of the beginning of the year from the first of March to the first of January in 46 BCE meant the coinciding of the new year with the date at which Rome had been founded 708 years prior (Harold Innis *The Bias of Communication*. Toronto: University of Toronto Press. 65ff).

[4] Martha Nussbaum *The Fragility of Goodness*, 95.

from mere description towards explanation.[5] Gradually, divine caprice and magic were expelled, and reasoning took hold.[6]

Counting, Weighing, Measuring

This conception of a human life guided and graded by reason, emphasizing the stable, and abstract aspects of things to be understood as objects, was fed by a narrative of growing self-sufficiency enabled through the arts of counting, weighing and measuring. Nussbaum refers to this struggle against the unreliable features of the world as 'trapping and binding'; a conception of form-giving eros being guided by intellect.[7] This leaves the human agent an overseer who continually tracks down, seizes, holds, arrests and controls *tuche*, but who, in doing so, remains a source of force and violence set against the world. The world becomes a place that needs taming, a space against which to guard oneself with the *techne* of counting, weighing and measuring. These epistemological processes filter understanding, taking out the grit and troublesome lumps, evening things up by naming them abstractly and in ways they might be related, ranked, tallied and stored: practical deliberation about the nature of something gives way to an intricate concern for its comparative, quantitative measure. These processes were teachable, but through inscription and imitation of scripted technique rather than just situational sensitivity, thereby schooling students not simply in practical technique, but in a proper way of relating to the world of things. With this distinction in mind, the experiments and knowledge claims of *techne* moved from trials and curiosity towards explanation, answering 'why' rather than 'how' things happened, and doing so in systematic rather than personal forms.[8]

Though we have written of *tuche* having given way to *techne*, and of *techne* becoming increasingly abstract in the process of this transition, our brief chronology is also itself an abstraction. The earliest known Greek medical text, for example, the *Hippocratic Corpus*, already elaborates on a

---

[5] Martha Nussbaum *The Fragility of Goodness*, 96.

[6] Heinrich von Staden *Physis* and *Techne* in Greek medicine. In *The Artificial and the Natural: An Evolving Polarity*. Edited by Bernadette Bensaude-Vincent and William R. Newman. Cambridge, MA: MIT Press. 2007, 21–50, 207.

[7] Martha Nussbaum *The Fragility of Goodness*, 20. So pervasive was the hold of this image that by the time we get to Descartes, for example, we have him arguing that the sole point of connection between the rational mind and its material setting was the pineal gland – and treating the world of objects as a space from which 'he' seeks to guard 'himself' through constant mind-directed activity.

[8] Drawn from Martha Nussbaum *The Fragility of Goodness*, 96.

distinction between general external forms and the specific nature of things. While human beings, or their limbs and other body parts, but also illnesses and other elements, can be described in general terms and along visible characteristics, there are also, it suggests, elusive but tangible factors in play: A body's age, strength, but also the specific nature of a person's digestive system and many other, merely inferentially knowable tendencies. A sound medical strategy should never rely on the textual generalizations pursued by physicians, but required, in addition, the kinds of craft skill exhibited by surgeons when navigating the interplay of general and recurring regularities (the *eidos*) and the hidden and changing specifics (the *dynameis*). This difference between what is generalizable and the changing specifics of every patient and situation exposes the physician to contingency (which in turn prompts the development of a professional jurisdiction connecting work practice, human problems and expert knowledge). There will be situations where available *technē* is not sufficient; and there are those situations when, as in advanced stages of illness, *technē* loses grip entirely and the struggle becomes more emotional and palliative than technical.[9] This was known from the outset, and has remained common sense understanding in medical practice: Indeed, any claim to medical expertise is animated by an awareness that the more *technē* is avowed, the more its limits are revealed. As with medicine, the same goes for engineering, for law, for architecture and for astronomy.

There is something about professional expertise that resists quantification. It invokes disciplined, precise and teachable techniques and principles, but then takes them on somehow, into a space of expressive discernment that cannot be translated into explicit knowledge. What is being valued in expertise is often the activity itself and how it grades what otherwise are unordered conditions, but it need not lead to comparable and quantifiable outcomes, it can only be witnessed, and acknowledged as sensitive, skilful, even beautiful.[10] With sensitivity comes care, an ability to absorb and even encourage the ways in which people can resist what seems rationally expedient. Human lives are riddled with minor twists of the self-destruct button; a breakdown of reason or weakness of will (a case of *akrasia*) or by acts of hedonism, animated by immature instincts when set against the practices of measuring and the weighing of alternatives against one another, pro and con. But expertise, such as that being exercised by the skilled surgeons of ancient Greece, is less judgmental. It understands those situations in which the body and feeling have their

---

[9] Heinrich von Staden *Physis* and *Technē* in Greek medicine, 28.

[10] Martha Nussbaum makes the comparison with playing a musical instrument, where expertise is realized in reaching beyond the programmatic following of a score. *The Fragility of Goodness*, 98.

own locus. Love, disappointment or anxiety, for example, remain heterogeneous and incommensurable; as 'ordinary human' experiences they have qualitatively unique features.[11] These experiences pertain to what we call human health, but they are beyond the reach of a physiological understanding. As Nussbaum so carefully observes, indeterminable and accidental *tuchē* begins to reaffirm its hold whenever we recoil from objects that feel disturbed in the face of alien or threatening things, or attach ourselves to vulnerable objects or people, through love, friendship, but also in trusting or dependent relationships where these others are not merely replaceable objects that can readily counted, weighed or measured; where our values are plural and thus incommensurable or in conflict; and where our passion overrides our calculative intelligence. *Tuchē* comes back at us whenever we speak of what seems, or appears as, the more essentially human aspects of our body we cannot rationally control.[12]

The Almanack

As *technē* reaches into the question of 'why' something occurs, *tuchē* pulls on its heels, bringing it back into a situational sensitivity to the question of 'how': Each rolls into the other, as a slope falls into a valley or rises onto a hillside, each an intimate aspect of the other. One reaches for the open sky and the other falls to earth, and each demurs to the necessity of yielding.[13] At least this is so for the vast range of knowledge by which humans survive and flourish as sentient creatures. Making things (*technē*) entails situational responsiveness: the country doctor might be less bookish than the academic physician, but be a lot more useful because of it. As a *technai* they make the best use of the available materials in the given conditions, aware as they are that the world of practice is inherently indefinite

---

[11] Martha Nussbaum *The Fragility of Goodness*, 115.

[12] This, suggests Nussbaum, is the domain of tragedy and not of scientific abstraction. The Platonic approach to explain the sensible world, the world of reflection with intelligence, with the power of the philosopher. Jean-Pierre Vernant and Pierre Vidal-Naquet *Myth and Tragedy in Ancient Greece*. New York: Zone Books. 1990, 323. But in tragedy, when truths collide unresolvedly, there is no philosopher classifying things in a true hierarchy; it is this resistance revealed in the tragic, that brings to the fore the limits of knowledge. Martha Nussbaum *The Fragility of Goodness*, 98.

[13] Aristotle suggests that for many advocates of timeless knowledge: 'none of the *technai* theorizes about individual cases ... only about what will help to cure any or all of a given class of patients ... – individual cases are so infinitely various that no knowledge of them is possible' (quoted in Joseph Dunne *Back to the Rough Ground: Practical Judgment and the Lure of Technique*. Notre Dame: Notre Dame Press: 1997, 259). When making something, the *technai* therefore does not need, or rather cannot have, a fixed idea of what the specific individual product will be like, which then seems to be a strange state of affairs, given something has to be produced, beyond ideas.

and indeterminate.[14] Their *technē* gains its own outline by corresponding with what is changeable: its objects 'come and go and change in various ways'.[15] But it is not raw *tuchē*, things occur and are made under a directing intelligence, the human becomes close to things that, in turn, amend and alter the world under the impress of human design.[16]

The printed embodiment of this intimacy between *tuchē–technē* is the almanack: a book outlining the rough plans that frame a life of practical wisdom. Their origin is archaic, arguably going back to Hesiod's *Works and Days* (though here in aural form), which provides a seasonal blueprint where cosmic patterns, mythology and advice for agricultural processes fuse:

When Zeus has completed sixty wintry days after the solstice, the star Arcturus is first seen rising, shining brightly just at dusk, leaving behind the holy stream of Oceanus. After this, Pandion's daughter, the dawn-lamenting swallow, rises into the light for human beings, and the spring begins anew. Forestall her, prune the vines first: for that way it is better. But when the house-carrier climbs up from the ground on the plants, fleeing the Pleiades, there is no longer any digging for vines: sharpen the scythes and rouse your slaves. Avoid shadowy seats and sleeping until dawn which when it shows itself sets many men on their way and puts the yoke on many oxen.[17]

Some 2,500 years later we find similar examples governing the agricultural rhythms, for instance the German abbot Mauritius Knauer's *Calendarium Oeconomicum Practicum Perpetuum* from 1652. The Latin title belies what became the wide appeal of the genre, and subsequent authors quickly took to using the vulgate. Issued yearly, almanacks combined observations on astrological rhythms, weather patterns, folk legends and timely homilies. The readers were those living from the land and who carried within them a desire to enrich their experience with reflection as well as routine. The almanacks combined text, drawings, sketches and tables into which the reader could project his or herself, creating a plan for daily living. The word plan comes from the Middle French for a diagram made by projection on a horizontal plane, which in turn came from the Latin *plantare*: to propagate from cuttings or seedlings and from '*planta*', sprout or shoot, but also indicating the sole of the foot with which seeds are spread out and pushed into the soil. Embodied in an

---

[14] Martha Nussbaum *The Fragility of Goodness*, 202; Richard Rojcewicz *The Gods and Technology: A Reading of Heidegger*. New York: SUNY. 2006, 60.

[15] Richard Rojcewicz. *The Gods and Technology*, 60.

[16] Aristotle *Physics Books I and II*. Translated by William Charlton. Oxford: Clarendon.2006, II 5–9. There is a quality of spontaneity in *tuchē* which makes it distinct from *anankē*, an enclosing, necessary force by which what 'is' is, and by which even immortals are cowed.

[17] Hesiod *Works and Days*, 133.

almanack, planning meant listening to advice and working it into the cyclical passages of everyday life. Books like Knauer's were to be a regular, easy-going, trusting companion: Light bonfires in autumn to burn better away the ruins of what is spent and dried up and clear and fertilize the ground for new growth; blanket what becomes frail during in winter, or let it fail; in early spring be wary of scathing winds that can strip back too hasty an attempt at seeding, but then leap with the opportunity for growth; enjoy the toil of harvesting during summer's dry moments. This attunement to rhythms might be simplistic, but its room for pause provided small advantages when dealing with natural forces. The almanack is a timely and considered reminder of how lives are scripted by passing seasons. The recognition of patterns; the capacity to use foresight and the ability to collaborate with others meant that one was no longer entirely delivered over to nature's changing fortunes.[18]

Where Knauer was one of the earliest authors of an almanack, it was the Lutheran priest and author from the Duchy of Baden, Johann Peter Hebel who became one of the most enduring (see Figure 4.1). Hebel's language is unashamedly poetic, with the intent of revealing what is most homely to us, what is own-most, which is not what we own and use, but what is naturally occurring around us and to which, if we are patient, we might listen. Hebel's *Little Treasure Chest of the Rhineland Family Friend* opens onto an immediate world whose natural and social abundance is netted in gently cosseting abstractions. We have an arresting and circuitous coming together of the felt and the rational, the historical and natural. The writing on seasonal rhythms is marked by detailed observations of the twist of the heavens; and poetic descriptions of the bursts of blossom or frost are interspersed by tables marking when best to plant seeds, and the detailed litany of Christian Saints' days are pressed alongside other calendrical conventions, reminding the reader of this polytheistic world. The world appears as neat and available to planning, but it is not totally ordered: Indeed, if one were to look closely enough at the cycles and repetitions, one would find oneself amid unruly exceptions and digressions. Hebel reveals this interplay of *tuchē* and *technē* with acute sensitivity. For example, he talks sympathetically of the cruel intercession of death into family life and considers what ought to be the natural period of mourning and lament, but then indicates the extent of this timespan using a list of significant historical events. The reader is comforted by being told that grief is natural and lasting, but not without also being reminded that there was a proper span for grief, one roughly equivalent, for example, to the French and Spanish siege of Gibraltar.

[18] Lawrence Freedman *Strategy: A History*. Oxford. Oxford University Press. 2013.

Figure 4.1 Hebel's *Hausfreund*. Wikipedia commons

As Sigmund Freud was later to observe, proper mourning works as a corrective. The loss of an object of love is painful, it requires a relinquishing of what has hitherto been a strong attachment, and none of us will relinquish the ties of love easily. Hence, we withdraw from reality awhile as an effective (reasonable) way of coping with what otherwise remains an emptying and even bewildering condition. To mourn is to create a space of transition – one goes into a process of mourning during which one's loves, one's faith in projects, one's interest in living even, gradually become unshackled from the objects that have died. Mourning is a necessary pause of re-organization (*eros* gives way to *eris*, to then recover): to go into mourning is to presuppose an exit and restoration of an ordered balance of the living and dead.[19]

Hebel's language is free from direct knowledge claims and moralizing principle; though it comes from the hand of a preacher it does not preach.

[19] Sigmund Freud *Mourning and Melancholia*. In *The Standard Edition of The Complete Psychological Works. Vol XIV*. Translated by James Strachey. London: Hogarth Press. 1914–1916, 244–5, 255.

Heidegger was entranced with Hebel's style, suggesting its power comes in letting understanding emerge, its naturalizing imagery (*Bilden*) being a pushing forth into awareness as vibrant and fulsome as that of the fields in spring. His language settles its roots deep in the earth, in which lay the dead, and its crown reaches up and spreads in a filigree of branch and leaf whose tips flutter almost invisibly in blue air. It is a language of connectiveness and suggestiveness rather than assertiveness, a language enriched through an unashamed use of lilting dialect, yet its rusticity is sophisticated, so that alongside the colloquialisms comes a cosmopolitan curiosity. In this way Hebel shows the reflections and aspirations of human planning being hardened by facts and measures, and then how they might be softened, were they to be taken back into the concourse of natural patterns. He makes 'far away facts' resonate with what is near in the most indirect, and therefore thoughtful, of ways. His words are touched with the taint of an immersive empirical method that demands the poet and reader stay in touch with what surrounds them, retaining a sense of the home that, inevitably, will be lost once life is done and falls under the falling of leaves. Hebel's language speaks of quiet ritual, and as a poet, he co-responds to this language, and amid the text, figures and tabulated figures of this language readers are able to discern 'the enduring in the inconspicuous'.[20]

As a genre the almanack encloses understanding between two small and inexpensive covers, making it available for anyone who can read, and cares to. The planning fostered in the use of an almanack is of a gradual and careful form, and it demands an ongoing relationship, so that year on year, with each iteration, the reader becomes more and more familiar with the appropriate ordering of life. Often the reader would add marginalia and reminders (see Figure 4.2), attesting to an active and ongoing reading of their own experiences into the textual and tabulated forms. It works as a ready-to-hand reckoner through which the world appears as a place that is open to control, but humbly so. Its spirit seems akin to what Heidegger meant by attunement: the reader finds his or herself being thrown into the world, having to abide by its structures, but with consideration of their own experience of being amid such a place.[21] It is a planning system in which a sense of self-awareness, albeit a rudimentary

---

[20] Martin Heidegger. Hebel – friend of the house. Translated by Bruce Foltz and Michael Heim. In *Contemporary German Philosophy, Vol. III*. Edited by D. Christensen, M. Riedel, R. Spaemann, R. Wiehl, W. Wieland. Pennsylvania: Pennsylvania State University Press. 1957/1983, 89–101, 98–100.

[21] For Smyth annotating almanacks was the most prevalent form of self-accounting in eighteenth- and early-nineteenth-century Europe. See Adam Smyth Almanacks, annotators, and life-writing in early modern England. *English Literary Renaissance*. 2008, 38(2): 200–44.

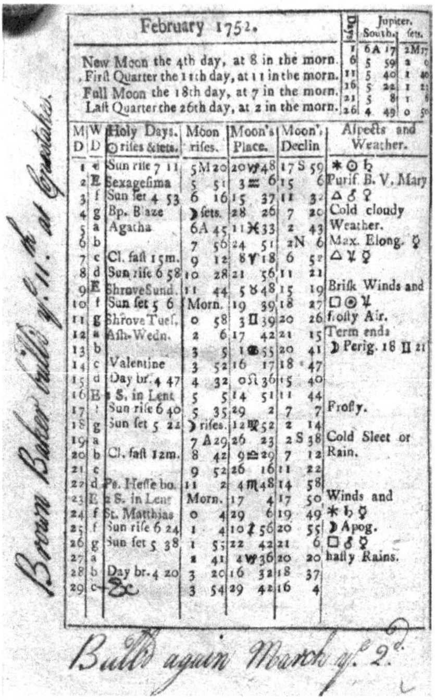

February 1752.

New Moon the 4th day, at 8 in the morn.
First Quarter the 11th day, at 11 in the morn.
Full Moon the 18th day, at 7 in the morn.
Last Quarter the 26th day, at 2 in the morn.

Days	Jupiter. South.	Jupiter. sets.
1	6A 17	2M 17
6	5 59	2 0
11	5 40	1 40
16	5 22	1 [illegible]
21	5 8	1 [illegible]
26	4 49	0 [illegible]

M D	W D	Holy Days. ☉ rises & sets.	Moon rises.	Moon's Place.	Moon's Declin	Aspects and Weather.
1	e	Sun rise 7 11	5M 20	20♑48	17S 59	✱ ☉ ♄
2	E	Sexagesima	5 51	3♒ 6	15 6	Purif. B. V. Mary
3	f	Sun set 4 53	6 16	15 37	11 32	△ ♂ ♀
4	g	Bp. Blaze	☽ sets.	28 26	7 20	Cold cloudy
5	a	Agatha	6A 45	11♓33	2 43	Weather.
6	b		7 56	24 51	2N 6	Max. Elong. ☿
7	c	Cl. fast 15m.	9 12	8♈18	6 52	△ ♃ ☿
8	d	Sun rise 6 58	10 28	21 56	11 21	
9	E	ShroveSund.	11 44	5♉48	15 19	Brisk Winds and
10	f	Sun set 5 6	Morn.	19 39	18 27	□ ☉ ♃
11	g	Shrove Tues.	0 58	3♊39	20 26	frosty Air.
12	a	Ash-Wedn.	2 6	17 42	21 15	Term ends
13	b		3 5	1♋55	20 41	☽ Perig. 18 ♊ 21
14	c	Valentine	3 52	16 17	18 47	
15	d	Day br. 4 47	4 32	0♌36	15 40	
16	E	1 S. in Lent	5 5	14 51	11 44	
17	f	Sun rise 6 40	5 35	29 2	7 7	Frosty.
18	g	Sun set 5 22	☽ rises.	12♍52	2 14	
19	a		7 A 29	26 23	2S 38	Cold Sleet or
20	b	Cl. fast 12m.	8 42	9♎29	7 12	Rain.
21	c		9 52	26 16	11 22	
22	d	Pr. Hesse bo.	11 2	4♏48	14 58	
23	E	2 S. in Lent	Morn.	17 4	17 50	Winds and
24	f	St. Matthias	0 4	29 6	19 49	✱ ♄ ☿
25	f	Sun rise 6 24	1 4	10♐56	20 55	☽ Apog.
26	g	Sun set 5 38	1 55	22 42	21 6	□ ♂ ☿
27	a		2 41	4♑36	20 20	hasty Rains.
28	b	Day br. 4 20	3 20	16 32	18 37	
29	c	&c	3 54	29 42	16 4	

Figure 4.2 Wing's Almanack, 1752. The handwritten notes record specific cows being bull'd at certain times. Reproduced with permission from Thomas Fisher Rare Book Library, University of Toronto.

one, becomes possible. In being a practical expression of attunement, it is a form of planning that Heidegger looks to warrant in some way. He wishes to remind us that planning with an almanack would allow a farmer to come to know how a tool like a mattock may be 'used in the most adequate way possible",[22] a use that carried within its stroke a generational familiarity that allowed the user to simply and uncomplainingly get-on with the task at hand. The mattock-wielding farmer would come to know themself as a *technai*, sowing seeds in good soil and content to wait for the necessary period before the plants sprout and mature, alive to situational demands, paying heed to the acidity of the ground, the weather, the local trading conditions, and the tremors of an ever-ageing body.[23] What gives justification and meaning to the things around

[22] Martin Heidegger *Being and Time*, §69.

[23] In Plato's *Phaedrus*, Translated by R. Hackforth. Cambridge: Cambridge University Press. 1952, 159, we have Socrates comparing the sensible farmer with the appropriate use of seeds to a dialectician and the appropriate use of language:

them is, in the context of *making*, the use towards which things are being continually put. The farmer finds use for the seed *in-order-to* produce crop *for-the-sake-of* feeding his family or exchanging it via the tools of the market into other goods and tools. What gives justification for that thing to appear as a 'seed' is the wider set of relationships that are circumspective (rather than explicitly) grasped by the farmer, and which thereby also lend justification and definition to their own existence 'as a farmer' into which they project themself, and about which they are, on occasion, conscious, as when they write in a well-thumbed copy of an almanack. It is in caring for the land, animals and the crops that the farmer gains this wider sense of use, which is borne out of an intimate connection with, and care for things that make up the agricultural surround. In caring, past and future belong together; history and folk knowledge fuses with the immediacy of practical requirements and a horizon of understanding within which the possibility of *existing as a farmer* first makes sense.

Francis Bacon's Platform

Whilst *techne* is suffused with everyday affairs, its refinement is more equivocal and conscious than a state of absorbed creative flow: in eschewing purely formal knowledge (as espoused by Arendt's experts in possession of their conversation stopping truths) it also refuses to become the habitualized and mindless routine of those who are so skilful as to be acting thoughtlessly. It is neither absorbed doing nor generalizing contemplation. Rather, *techne* entails 'initially and constantly looking out beyond what, in each case, is directly present at hand', and so any stratagem for making must thus look beyond the maker's own contribution to how the world in turn affords making (*viz.* is of a character that affords possibility to making).[24]

> If a sensible farmer had some seeds to look after and wanted them to bear fruit would he with serious intent plant them during the summer in a garden of Adonis [a window box for forcing plants during festival of Adonis] and watch it producing fine fruit within eight days? If he did so would it not be in the holiday spirit, just by way of pastime? For serious purposes would he not behave like a scientific farmer, sow his seeds in suitable soil, and be well content if they came to maturity within eight months? (159).

There is also here a sense of different temporalities in play, the one managed and hastened, the other timely and patient.

[24] Joseph Dunne *Back to the Rough Ground: Practical Judgment and the Lure of Technique*. Notre Dame, IN: University of Notre Dame Press. 2009, 250, 440. Erich Hörl elaborates Heidegger's fascination with work through the latter's studies of Aristotle's notion of energy (*dynamis and energeia*). In this interpretation, Heidegger translates energy as work, and being at work, so making work (*ergon*) (of the kind alive to the

Heidegger's reading of *technē* situates making in being as an opening-up to thought, which becomes both an active as well as contemplative condition. It is an intimate, engagement with things that speaks to their nature, and reveals these in accordance with this nature rather than through calculating, measuring and weighing. *Technē* provides beings with room:

> to grasp beings ... in their outward look, *eidos*, idea, and, in accord with this, to care for beings themselves and to let them grow, i.e., to order oneself within beings as a whole through productions and institutions. *Technē* is a mode of proceeding against *physis* [nature], though not yet so as to overpower it or exploit it, and above all not to turn use and calculation into principles, but, on the contrary, to retain the holding sway of *physis* in unconcealedness.[25]

Through *technē* objects change and those who possess *technē* disclose this or that depending on the different natures of the things they encounter, their immersive skill in technique of planting, cobbling or painting, and the situation.[26] So in the making of things *technē* is always also a concealing, where concealing is a threefold combination of hiding away or veiling, of closing down and turning away, and of restraining and holding back.[27] To make thoughtfully is to be alive to a materiality of things, to the forms they take and uses to which they are put, and to be there amid these things, imagining oneself into the world through such a company.

In learning the value of this restraint, a self is steadily revealed to itself as a being complicit with what is being made: a consciousness of doing yields a conscience through which human experience, as a brute and unquestioned scene of occurrence, acquires an authority of publicly shared maxims and proverbs and ways of going about things. This going about things is common sensical, but never rises to the condition

---

four causes) synonymous with world (*logos*), so that, according to Heidegger, it is not merely the case that Plato and Aristotle conducted the first interpretations of work as an activity, but that the very basic concepts of philosophy sprang from their investigation of the phenomenon of production, and in particular the notions of four causes (form, matter, efficient cause and purpose), and the opening up of a struggle between the completion of a work and the many possible interruptions, mistakes and oversights that continually threaten any such project. Erich Hörl Das Arbeitslose der Technik: Zur Destruktion der Ergontologie und Ausarbeitung einer neuen technologischen Sinnkultur bei Heidegger und Simondon. In *Promethische Kultur: Wo kommen unsere Energien her?* Edited by Claus Reggewie, Ursula Renner and Peter Risthaus. München: Fink. 2013, 111–36.

[25] Martin Heidegger *Basic Questions of Philosophy: Selected 'Problems' of 'Logic'*. Translated by Richard Rojcewicz and André Schuwer. Bloomington: Indiana University Press. 1994, 180.

[26] Martin Heidegger *Introduction to Metaphysics*. London: Yale University Press. 2000, 178.

[27] Martin Heidegger *Parmenides* §1.13. See also Martha Nussbaum *The Fragility of Goodness*, 242.

of formal knowledge. To know is to claim there are relations between things that resist time, whereas holding sense in common is an acceptance of how time ascribes limits to all appearance. Smooth-sided knowledge baulks at the rough surfaces of experience, it sees the patches of ordinary life as little more than place holders for information and data which it might extract and analyse in its laboratories, then re-impose, creating order from unruliness.

Though uneasy, the relation can be productive. It was in enjoining the improving and restless spirit of scientific inquiry with the acquired wisdom of common sense, for example, that the natural philosopher Francis Bacon instructed readers on how to create an ideal garden. Written towards the end of his life, his meditation on gardening is a mature reflection on how to gather and influence nature all the year-round, but without imposing oneself directly. He suggests the objective of any expert gardener is the creation of a platform: 'plat' being a plot or piece of ground, and 'form' being an outline, and it is very much a sketch, an outline, as opposed to detailed instruction. His textual advice is often brief, aphoristic and even poetic, leaving blank spaces to be filled by the experimental gesture of those who are actually doing the gardening at his, Bacon's, suggestion, but more pressingly under Nature's guidance. Bacon extemporizes on his knowledge of nature by succumbing to its force: he talks of filling the ground with different plants and blooms, beds, benches and trellises so that it might yield of itself. He finds excitement in realizing that a stretching of flowers might be coached into second flush (the violets that come in April *and* around Bartholomew-tide), he is respectful of the way juniper and fritillaries embrace rather than shy away from winter, he delights in the spring dance of the daisy, almond tree and stock-gillyflower, and he plays with the sequence of colour offered by sequential planting of pinks and cherries, vine flowers, and lime tree blossom. The cycles and rhythms of the year are being discovered by the laying out of plants according to their differing rates of growth and from the overlapping and contrasting of blooms and scents. Bacon observed, always observing, how some plants gave of their scent wantonly, whereas others like rosemary were demur and needed coaxing by touch, how bees would be drawn to a succession of flowers and leaves through the spring and summer, how small heaps and pathways would break up a broad sweep of land and lend to the visitor an air of discovery, how restless water cleans the roots of cress and still waters encourage the frogs (which he didn't like).

In organizing the platform he was absorbing the styles and wiles of nature in such a way that a connectedness of things comes to the fore. He was also learning how, amid all the order he might chance to imagine a garden taking, it was the chance and fleeting occurrence that was the most arresting and beguiling. In planting flowers for aroma, for example, we find Bacon gradually straying from obvious blooms like musk rose and honeysuckle. He becomes partial to 'the cordial smell' of dying strawberry leaves, as well as those flowers giving their scent when 'trodden on and crushed', the 'burnet, wild thyme and water-mints', which might be set in 'whole alleys' upon which one can walk. It is the metamorphosis itself that becomes apparent, the cycles of birth and death, the planting of something so innocuous as a small, hard, black seed becoming in a matter of months a scarlet poppy dressed for death. And through his walking the then fashionable geometric gardens of strictly aligned, heavily decorated hedges and gravels gave way to a less contrived, naturalistic form whose curvature was ever sensitive to the solicitations to think, feel and act offered by plants, soils and the open sense of the wider countryside, and it was this sensitivity, rather than abstracted images, that gave his platform life.[28]

Being inside Bacon's platform was an invitation to be something and be somewhere else. The plan was a condition of transformation, a projection of the change that befalls us, wild as much as civilized, and a desire to think anew. *Technē* becomes embodied in a gathering of shared, continuous and immersive experience to which mental direction is but an occasional and respectful visitor.[29] To inquire and so learn is to 'make with' what is present at hand, being guided by the body as it sensually falls into places, and from this experience empirical life is rendered sensible and available to imaginative speculation. It is not always an easy falling in, a scent revisited can change from intoxicating to disturbing, hinting at a brutality as much as well-being. Nature is not always easy, or easily confined in nice spaces.

Though a garden and not an overtly political space, Bacon's platform bears loose comparison with Arendt's space of appearances (as set against Heidegger's more centralizing pole, or shepherding 'leader'). Bacon's platform is more organically rendered than the somewhat separated, overtly civic, *polis*. Bacon's thoughtful action generated opinion through

---

[28] Francis Bacon Of gardens. In *The Essayes or Counsels, Civill and Morall, of Francis Lo. Verulam, Viscount St. Alban* London: John Haviland for Hanna Barret. 1625, Essay XLVI, 266–79.

[29] Hubert Dreyfus Merleau-Ponty and recent cognitive science. In *Cambridge Companion to Maurice Merleau-Ponty*. Edited by Taylor Carmen and Mark Hansen. Cambridge: University of Cambridge Press. 2005, 129–50. Dreyfus talks of how a learner moves from being a performer to an expert because of a willingness to stay with situations, appreciate the salient features that afford one the possibility of what any situation entails.

a kind of empirically infused *logos* whose methods were less severe than those of Socrates. Bacon's method is little more than to walk as well as talk, to observe and then experiment, to plant and so to understand the farthest reach of a plant's expressive viability across different conditions and climates. From this peripatetic learning emerges a vision for growth in which nature and experimenters are entirely complicit. This understanding might begin with, and by crystalized by, certain rules, but quickly absorbs itself directly in things, which can then be made subject to further representational mediations as a means of guidance, from which one might take one's cue, and to which one might return, pausing, from amid the sway of things.

In plotting his garden Bacon seems to have moved away from his earlier attempts to pressgang experience in the service of science. In *Novum Organum*, for example, Bacon had recommended a regulated and digested, rather than vague, course of experiment, from which to deduce axioms, and to set up new experiments. Experience itself was a 'maze' a 'forest' that needed taming, and no better way than to substitute natural appearance with those altogether core predictable and ordered appearances of the laboratory. Agamben notices how Bacon as an advocate of science rather than as a gardener seeks to displace experience by moving it away from the individual and towards instruments and devices that are not so easily deceived.[30] Hebel's world – the world of worldly maxims and advice whose authority lies simply in their being spoken and acknowledged without need for analysis – gives way to a world of knowledge being secured through the conscious and explicit appropriation of experience through the scientific method. Bacon's treatise on the garden reads almost as though he were regretting the emerging ascendancy of formal experiment that he did so much to initiate, it is as if, in his wiser dotage, he recalls what it was like to experience in the company of wonder rather than verification and control.

Technē and Wonder

Bacon's advice to gardeners is a distilling of *technē* in which the influences between things arrives as voices that can be listened to and held in abeyance, or ignored completely, heard and opposed, or taken up and riffed on. But there is little in the way of imposition. The planner, as planter and builder of platforms, is akin to an artisan, a figure that, in the hands of Heidegger, is as much a midwife as creator, as much subaltern

---

[30] Giorgio Agamben *Infancy and History*, 19–23.

to as controller of nature, a paver of ways rather than director.[31] The artisan experiences a sense of *techne* that is full of wonder:

What is wonder? What is the basic attitude in which the preservation of the wondrous, the Being of beings, unfolds and comes into its own? We have to seek it in what the Greeks call [*techne*]. We must divorce this Greek word from our familiar term derived from it, 'technology,' and from all nexuses of meaning that are thought in the name of technology ... *techne* does not mean 'technology' in the sense of the mechanical ordering of beings, nor does it mean 'art' in the sense of mere skill and proficiency in procedures and operations. *Techne* means knowledge ... For that is what *techne* means: to grasp beings as emerging out of themselves in the way they show themselves, in their essence [*eidos*].[32]

Heidegger confronts us with the curious circumscription of *techne* neither as a knowledge *of* facts, nor an embodied, habituated, and mindless skill. Instead, he seems to suggest a way of knowing that apprehends something more than is immediately the case; a way of knowing that apprehends 'that which first gives to what is already present at hand its relative justification, its possible determinateness, and thus its limit'.[33]

What is being made determinate through *techne* is not one thing or another, but a relational intimacy amongst things that can be more or less harmonious. The farmer, the plough, the land, the sky, the tightly packed and stepped landscape into which one fits with the other, bending to each other's contours, giving form to plants, animals, tools and humans in concert, each making itself available and becoming to the other. Bruegel imagines such a scene shown in Figure 4.3.

He can imagine it because he has lived through harsh Flemish winters where the cold freezes the feet of crows to the black, bare branches on which they perch, he is attentive to the raw cruelties being felt amid everyday happenstance by those who have to work the fields. As noticed by W. H. Auden,

> About suffering they were never wrong,
> The old Masters: how well they understood
> Its human position: how it takes place
> While someone else is eating or opening a window or just walking
>   dully along;[34]

So too was he alive to when nature was beneficent and giving, when the plough sank evenly into rich loam and the evening sun fell unbidden and

---

[31] Richard Rojcewitz *The Gods and Technology*, 44
[32] Martin Heidegger *Basic Questions of Philosophy*, § 38, 1, 178–9, 154.
[33] Martin Heidegger *Introduction to Metaphysics*, 170.
[34] Wystan Hugh Auden Musée des Beaux Arts. *Another Time*. London: Faber and Faber. 1940.

Figure 4.3 Pieter de Oude Bruegel, *Landscape with the Fall of Icarus*. Painted c. 1560, possibly a copy of Bruegel original. Koninklijke Musea voor Schone Kunsten van België, Brussels. Wikimedia commons

untroubled over fertile fields. Yet nothing is at it seems. For a start, the stated subject matter of Breuegel's painting is not farming, but the myth of Icarus' fall. Bruegel's scene depicts an imagined island of Crete, which, as Ovid recounts, is the bucolic prison of Daedalus and his son Icarus, held captive at the whim of King Minos. Desperate to escape, Daedalus reasoned that given the king had shut off routes across land and sea he and his son ought take to the sky. He fashioned wings from feathers and wax, and they leapt upwards. Momentarily, unbound from the earth onto which they had been thrown, they soar, the impetuous and delighted son becoming so enraptured with flight he strays too high, burns and crashes. Bruegel depicts the final moments. In the far bottom corner of the painting a flailing leg and arm thrash hopelessly, the panic quickly quenched by waves, as a nearby fisherman watches his line, oblivious to the tragic denouement of untrammelled exuberance and self-centred delight. Beyond them a ship is sailing into the open waters, its aft to the doomed adventurer, and its prow pointed towards a setting sun. In the foreground comes a neatly dressed ploughman, stepping after a well-managed horse (*managiare*, management), his sword and swagger carefully laid to one side on the ground. In the centre a shepherd looks upwards into empty sky, momentarily held in this up-looking gesture by a vague suspicion of an impossible movement having passed by the very corner of his eye.

In the image there is some of the settled comfort Heidegger believed he had found in Hebel, and which Bacon imagines in his platform. But we also have a scene which for Auden carries a unifying quality of quiet indifference, throwing up a spray of disturbing thoughts on:

> how everything turns away
> Quite leisurely from the disaster; the ploughman may
> Have heard the splash, the forsaken cry,
> But for him it was not an important failure: the sun shone
> As it had to on the white legs disappearing into the green
> Water; and the expensive delicate ship that must have seen
> Something amazing, a boy falling out of the sky,
> Had somewhere to get to and sailed calmly on.[35]

The labour of ploughing carries on regardless, treading the middle of the field, the middle way, which is the right way for a being placed on earth to labour, a calm, knowing way, submitting to the plan laid down by unwritten law.

Labour as an Out-of-Body Experience

In the myth, Daedalus' grief at his son's death is confounded further by a deep sense of complicity. Daedalus was a peerless fabricator and devious fixer whose artifice was in high demand. In many ways his work was brim full of *technē*: his machines and solutions were always bespoke, appropriate and fitting the purpose at hand. When, for example, he had been commanded by Minos to build a prison for Asterion, the Minotaur, and had been imprisoned in the island to set about the task (brutish masters like Minos never ask, they just act) he had built something not from his own mind, but the creature's. Asterion's confused origin lay deep within the chasms of classification and feeling that separated, and so joined, animals, humans and gods. His confusion was twinned

---

[35] Wystan Hugh Auden Musée des Beaux Arts. The poem was written in 1938, with the clouds of war lowering over Europe, the dogged pursuit of ordinary life was becoming increasingly absurd, but necessary. Hence Auden's sense of being out of joint, wandering the gallery of the Musée in Brussels, looking at paintings, whilst national socialism, having worked itself into a populist lather within Germany and, though panting from the effort, was rapidly regaining its breath, ready for more. Later (published in 1960) William Carlos Williams also wrote about the painting, also remarking on the insignificance of the event, the splash unnoticed, whilst all around spring was bursting forth, tingling with life in the cycle of things.

with angry uncertainty and bewilderment, and it was from this jumble of feelings that Daedalus had taken his cue for the maze: a network of twisting stone and tenebrous shadows leading first one way, then another, all the while going from nowhere to nowhere.

Daedalus knew his subject well, indeed he played a role in its birth. Asterion – the Cretan for wandering star – survived by eating human sacrifices selected by lot from the youth of a vanquished Athens and sent in tribute to Minos. Crete's regional influence was pre-eminent in those days, yet Minos' victories had been bought at some cost. Promising fealty to the god Poseidon in exchange for his assistance, Minos had received, by way of answer to his prayers, the gift of a beautiful white bull, which he was instructed to sacrifice as a consummation of his pact with the god. Minos agreed and secured Poseidon's aid in dominating the region, especially Athens, but he could not bring himself to kill such a fine animal. Poseidon, always grumpy and often perverse, was understandably annoyed at this covetousness. He exacted punishment by encouraging Pasiphae, Minos' wife, to lust after the bull rather than her husband. Transfixed, she bade Daedalus make a 'mechanical cow' into which Pasiphae strapped herself, mated, and gave birth to Asterion. Despite her motherly affection the half-bull, half-human child refused to be instructed in civilized manners and mores, always raging and wanting to eat human flesh, whether to affirm better its belonging to the species, or in disgust of it. Minos ordered its imprisonment and sent word to Athens to provide the food from amongst its own children. The ingenuity of the solution pleased Minos – who seems as equally perverse as Poseidon – for Asterion had given him a way of exacting terrible tribute from the Athenian upstarts. In a world that demanded ingenuity and cunning it worked to further endow his reputation for strength and vengeance whilst effectively dealing with the local problem of an unruly stepson. There had been little in the way of planning, but an acute awareness of situational limits and how far these might be moulded and even transgressed, first by human desire, and second by the work and labour of makers like Daedalus who knew how to channel their tool-making imagination in the service of solutions.

Minos used Daedalus as both a source of labour and work through which his island kingdom might be better managed. The *techne* of Daedalus was important, that of impetuous, dreamy Icarus far less so, his gesture carried too much of the open between its wings, whilst his father knew how to get stuck in, enabling Minos to treat his city as Daedalus did the Minotaur. The country and body were alike: built from separate organs, each with their characteristic needs, and requiring continual management. And Minos was not alone in acknowledging this intimacy between organic and social form, he was simply embodying common sense: the body is tended by physicians/surgeons, the state by kings/*strategoi*. With the cunning work of the hand and the intelligent work of the head, both exponents of the practical arts could restrict 'the contingent, speechless events that *Tyche* loves to have happen',[36] they could push the gods back up the slopes of Mt. Olympus, they could gain a little distance from nature, not just by using machines, but in thinking about their improvement in practices of calculation, and in thinking about society through such machinery. In this form of thinking through machinery, though, comes a removal from practice, much as surgeons removed themselves from tending the sick and became too much the physician, accruing knowledge and dispensing facts.

This distancing shifts the concerns we see in ancient Greek considerations of *technē* and *tuchē* from the here and now to the proximal and distant. If Daedalus can make machines that sate lust and imprison monsters, where are the limits to this practical capacity to project ourselves upon the world through such prostheses? Through Daedalus' skill Minos was beginning to project himself into objects through which, he presumed, he became more present. And Daedalus, being wary of this ambition, tries to escape, but his machinery is worn by someone who lacks worldly *technē*, and who finds himself above everyday things. Icarus has had the temerity not only to use but enjoy and explore the potential of machinery, he has taken himself away from a world of labour, he has broken the rules laid down by his father for the correct use of tools, and freed from earth-bound projects, he touched on something that, whilst ultimately deadly, was a beginning: for in rising above the earth he has put paid to the natural order of things, the facts have bucked and will not be the same again. In Bruegel's painting the sun, though it melted the wax in the wings, is not high, but setting, it is giving way, not to the puny body now swallowed by the sea, but to what it augured: the expressive will of being that sought to break the confines of dwelling in his house and to find a solitude amongst the clouds.

Bruegel's falling and flailing Icarus is a wonderfully equivocal figure. At the dawn of the machine age he is excited. Courtesy of his father he has discovered what tools might do. Yet as Auden also points out, the loftiness comes with a price, not just death, but more devastating still, the lesson of submission to the rhythms of machinery. There is now no

---

[36] Friedrich Kittler Towards and ontology of media. *Theory, Culture & Society*. 2009, 26(2–3): 23–31, 27.

good reason to acknowledge wonder and surprise, or to linger: a thin and invisible film of acceptance and even callous indifference has fallen over human affairs in the wake of Icarus' fate; the joyously acting and thinking self has been clipped by a warning to stay within human limits.

The Coming of Machines

For Elaine Scarry this awareness of limits has meant a gradual turning over of our body (and bodily self-awareness) to machines 'out there'. For Scarry it takes three forms. First, how, when for example a bandage is placed over an open wound, the tool substitutes for missing skin, literally dressing the wound through man-made fibres. Similarly, eyeglasses, microscopes or cameras project materializations and conceptualizations of the lens of the human eye; or, through the association of the workings of organs like the heart with machinery like air and water pumps.[37] A second form is a re-presentation not of body parts, but of bodily capabilities and needs. Photographs, for example, materialize the bodily capacity for memory; or mechanical pinions and pistons with their hissing and wheezing, dissipating heat and with a constant need for water and fuel, materialize the bodily capacity for movement and need for sustenance; re-presenting an external materialization of the body's capacity for self-replication and self-modification. And a third form conceives the body from the outside; as containing pumps and lenses without these being part of the felt-experience of being sentient.[38] All three forms turn the inanimate, external and unfeeling world inside out and, through the object, represent it to take on the internal, animate and sentient characteristics of human agency (the efficient cause) in two complementary transformations.[39] First, the separation and (objectification of the bodily attributes and, second, the recovery by the body of the objectified and now organized attributes in a process of self-appropriation.[40] The shape of the wings worn by Icarus, for example, is neither that of the spine nor

---

[37] Elaine Scarry *The Body in Pain. The Making and Unmaking of the World*. Oxford: Oxford University Press. 1985.

[38] Elaine Scarry *The Body in Pain*, 286.

[39] Elaine Scarry (*The Body in Pain*, 290ff) works through an intriguing argument about object-responsibility. Objects hurting humans used to be punished; a well where a person drowned filled; a tree felled if a person fell from it; even in modern legal structures, cases can attempt to establish the fault of the object's design for having caused pain. It is a revenge notion built on the idea that the object 'should have known better', imbuing objects with mimetic attributes of sentient awareness.

[40] Robert Cooper Technologies of representation. In *Tracing the Semiotic Boundaries of Politics*. Edited by Pertti Ahonen. Berlin, Boston: De Gruyter Mouton. 1993, 279–312, 282.

the shape of the body and its weight, not even the shape of the release of energy it receives and then absorbs from Icarus as he kicks off from the cliff: it is, rather the counter factual structure of the shape of 'earth-bound-imprisonment perceived ended'.[41]

This externalization of the body into the external world of material objects has the advantage that the animated, surrogate body (the world of objects) can be directed more easily by the human mind than the living human body. The wings can be improved, redesigned, repaired, adjusted as a prosthetic extension of an inner into an outer world but the second act of self-appropriation brings those extensions back into the body, altering and marking in reciprocal transformation:

human beings project their bodily powers and frailties into external objects such as telephones, chairs, gods, poems, medicine, institutions, and political forms, and then those objects in turn become the object of perceptions that are taken back into the interior of human consciousness where they now reside as part of the mind or soul, and this revised conception of oneself – as a creature relatively untroubled by the problem of weight (chair), as one able to hear voices coming from the other side of a continent (telephone), as one who has direct access to an unlimited principle of creating (prayer) – is now actually 'felt' to be located inside the boundaries of one's own skin where one is in immediate contact with an elaborate constellation of interior cultural fragments that seem to have displaced the dense molecules of physical matter.[42]

Just as the body imbues the external world with animate expectations, the outside world, *qua* objects, comes to shape the inner world of the human body, and in an organized way.

It is a process of outward–inward projection that Scarry finds being depicted in the paintings of workers and peasants by Jean-François Millet. For Scarry, Millet's subject is labour, not labourers. An overwhelming number of these paintings were made when Millet was living with his family in rural Barbizon, observing closely the regimen of peasant life; its sheer mechanical repetition, how life was increasingly being scripted by the routine interaction of humans and things, and little more; the possibility for lingering and surprise simply did not arise; as Auden noticed in Bruegel's painting of Icarus, the repetitive motion of the ship and the plough had somehow eaten into those who operated them, and from which scars they could never separate. Millet makes the mutual absorption of human and labour explicit:

[41] This is a paraphrase of Scarry's discussion of a chair in which to sit after a long journey as the counter-factual structure of 'the shape of perceived-pain-wished-gone'. Elaine Scarry *The Body in Pain*, 290.

[42] Elaine Scarry *The Body in Pain*, 256.

Figure 4.4 Jean-François Millet, *Women Carrying Faggots*, c. 1858. Charcoal, gouache, paper. Metropolitan Museum, New York. Public domain. DT3296

for example, his drawings of faggot gatherers, the women carrying the long, thin bundles of wood are barely distinct, smothered by both their load and the coppiced woodland from which it has been cut.[43]

Women Carrying Faggots (Figure 4.4) reveals how, in labouring movements, the body is taken out of itself into what Brown, commenting on Scarry, calls 'a world that always already accommodates, through its made design, the shapes and functioning of the human body'.[44] These flowing transitions from body to material to background and back to the body in Millet's paintings reveal individuals fusing with the tasks of daily labour, caught in endless cycles of need that occupy them in their totality,

---

[43] Elaine Scarry *The Body in Pain*, 248. These comments on Millet are prefaced with a number of quotes from Marx, perhaps most telling his observation 'What turns the soil into a prolongation of the body of the individual is agriculture.'

[44] Steven Brown Violence and Creation: The Recovery of the Body in the Work of Elaine Scarry *Subjectivity* 2016, 9(4): 439–458.

leaving no excess. The painfulness of the labour processes, its demands on the body, the women carrying bundles larger than themselves, exemplify how for Arendt '[T]he *animal laborans*, driven by the needs of the body, does not use this body freely...'.[45] The essential nature of labour is to be repetitive, perpetual; labour is what it is in its repetitions.[46] The human body is present in these made objects and these, simultaneously, reach into the body. The body is therefore no longer a container of an inner against an outer but a permeable border region that lives by reaching out beyond itself and which, in turn, is continually breached by what lies beyond: 'the presence of the body in the realm of artifice has as its counterpart the presence of artifice in the body, the recognition that in making the world, man remakes himself'.[47]

As Arendt attests, at the most basic level, this remaking consists in the act of meeting biological needs. The labour process is akin to metabolism of the human body, and the body's limited capacity to store away excess energy allows but for brief moments of 'wealth', which has to be 'spent', setting in train rapid cycles of production and consumption. Labour is a condition of non-durability in which *individual* human lives are also consumed in their coming and going without leaving either residue or mark by which their efforts can be remembered. Bound to necessity, the labouring body is not free, but given over in its entirety to the activities of survival.

These many activities, however, are morphing, Already, by Millet's day, the very nature of labour was undergoing a profound change, one expressed economically, politically and socially by the contagious and, in their first blush at least, progressive revolutions spreading across Europe in 1848. It was less the harshness of labour that was the object of the protests, but its disappearance. Labourers were being ousted by machinery transforming at a pace that their long-inured bodies were not even required to match, they were simply set aside, losing their livelihood. Millet captures its twisted poignancy in his painting *Gleaners* (Figure 4.5).

The gleaners work in the lengthening shadows of sunset, women given permission to scour a near exhausted field for the wheat missed

---

[45] Hannah Arendt *The Human Condition*, 118.

[46] Making labour an ongoing, beginning and end-less process; habitualised repetition. An eight-hour stretch being irreducible to any single segment of it; it is what it is only through its many-fold repetitions. Indeed, eight hours is a modern innovation, the gleaners and spinners knew no such limits in the passing of their day. Elaine Scarry *Resisting Representation*. Oxford: Oxford University Press. 1995, 65.

[47] Elaine Scarry *The Body in Pain*, 251. In *Being and Time* Heidegger also observes that 'what "occurs" with tools and works as such has its own character of motion, and this character has been completely obscure up to now'.

Figure 4.5 Jean-François Millet, *Gleaners*, 1857. Oil on canvas © RMN-Grand Palais (Musée d'Orsay)/Jean Schormans. Wikimedia commons

by the harvesters. Once found, and then ground between stones, these slim pickings are enough to keep them alive, barely. Their bodies bend forward in intimate echo of one another, their bearing is stripped of the self-conscious social cares that force the distant overseer upright upon his horse. Their vision world is pictured as immediate and near to the ground. Their fingers are shortened, almost stumps, worn down by scraping. Their scarves, bleached by the sun and scuffed by soil, bear the colours of the *tricolour drapeau*, red, blue and white, the symbols of a nation alive with liberty, equality and fraternity, or a nation living off the back of a multitude of home-bound peasants, whose human scope for flexing an intellectual and emotional repertoire of feeling and ambition had, under the impress of necessity, shrunk to nothing. All they had was the earth below them and the sky above, each as thankless as the other.

In their earth-bound poverty, Millet is attesting to the very palpable presence of these women at the foreground of a vanishing point: they are being pushed forwards towards the viewer. Indeed, in giving them so much presence, so much of a central role, they cannot but help to also be seen dramatically, to be being self-consciously presented outwardly to an audience.[48] Yet Millet is not dignifying them with an identity to which he is privy and which he wishes to show us directly, he is not placing them in a theatrical *mise-en-scène*. Their faces are shadowed, perhaps in acknowledgment that here are folk whose life neither he nor we will ever really understand. All he can do is portray the absorption and rhythms of bodies at work, two of them bending in near perfect symmetry, their left arms held in steadying balance, though the figure on the left holds her arm high on the back, the second holds the arm a little lower, and then a third, who has stood upright awhile, though still bent, holding her hands lowest of all, clutching a handful of wheat of which we the viewer see only the inedible stalks, not the ears which lie hidden. Moreover, despite their being so apparently 'there', it is what is behind them that is the subject of the painting: the well-lit, cleanly attired wheat gatherers, arranged as if in an organized mass, all facing away from the viewer, and held fast along the line of a neat horizon. It is not a flat horizon, but receding, arrow like, pulling away from the gleaners, who are being left by irresistible forces of modernization, linear forces from which, on the right of the canvas, houses emerge in neatly gabled straight lines, and on the left and centre come hayricks in a neatening echo, and between these all sentient life – overseers, workers, cart horses – is being held attentive to the 'active extensions and distensions of distance',[49] for it is in these straightening motions of organized production that life is now being perceived, the outward forms of mechanized production are being internalized by the workers, by the painter, and by the viewer. Only the gleaners are untouched, they are being left behind.

Goodbye to the Body

With *Gleaners* Millet is showing, first, how traditional farm work meant bodies being in a generational thrall to the soil and seasons by virtue of both need and social standing, and then second, how, with the onset of organized overseeing, the bodily forms taken by this work were dying away. In Millet's paintings of the spinner or faggot gatherers what is

---

[48] For a fuller discussion, and in relation especially to Gustave Courbet's painting of stone-breakers (painted around 1849, destroyed in the British bombing of Dresden 1945), See ftn. 33 of Michael Fried Painter into painting: On Courbet's 'After Dinner at Ornans' and 'Stonebreakers'. *Critical Inquiry*, 1982, 8: 619–49.

[49] Robert Cooper Georg Simmel and the Transmission of Distance. *Journal of Classical Sociology*. 2010, 10: 69–86.

being transformed is done so at the apparent behest of human agency: the spinner's grip and the wood gatherer's back. Humans seem to stand at the entry of the making process into which they feed both energy and information. The same body, the same nervous system, provides the mental and physical input into the production. This is less true of *Gleaners*. Gleaning is predicated on the existence of waste, and so an anachronism. The picking and stooping and scanning of the ground is giving way to industrialized production. The labour process will soon begin to use machinery and steam power, which ensure nothing is left to glean, which warrant the enclosure of fields into private spaces, and which demand evenly stacked and sized ricks barely touched by human hand. The early signs are all here. We sense how farm labourers are starting to employ sources of energy that are not their own, but instead borrow energy from other sources and thereby tap into an infinite reserve that far outstrips the energy they alone could provide.

But this also means that the entry of information into this productive system is no longer the same as in a labourer's own body. Instead of the nervous system and muscle power of the gleaner we have a network of machinery, to the point where fields are networked as a nexus of productive space leaving increasingly little room for human expression or even decision. Labour is exposed to infinitely expandable and expendable sources of power, and in turn becomes itself expandable and expendable. As Gilbert Simondon remarks, the input of information becomes infinitely distributed through the invention of machines which demand operators concentrate on only a single aspect of activity which is in itself infinitely repeatable and machine like, with no possibility for pause or for acknowledging the integrity of what is being produced.[50] These divisions of activity are then explicitly networked, and so no longer linked organically one to the other through a human body: 'it [production activity] is exploded into separate movements taken on by separate individuals or groups', and these become increasingly machine like, whilst at the same time machines start to replace parts of the body, allowing operations to be performed in conditions of heat, pressure and scale that exceed the variables of tolerance to which a human body can reach.[51]

Gleaners is one of the first images showing the diminishing of human influence and the onset of technological order, and it does so not by depicting the machinery but the last vestiges of machine independent

---

[50] Marx's notion of 'labour power' (Arbeitskraft) speaks to this separation of the worker from the means of production, engendering a difference between the capacity to 'sell the products of labour' and to sell 'labour power'. Elaine Scarry *The Body in Pain*, 250.

[51] Gilbert Simondon Technical mentality. Translated by Arne De Boever. *Parrhesia: A Journal of Critical Philosophy*, 2009, 7:17–28, 21.

human labour power, making them centre stage as if to say look, here, amid this abject condition there is at least the dignity of not having fully internalized the outward projecting thrust of machine-led ambition.[52] For the rest, well it is machine-led thinking all the way. The horse and carts in the painting have yet to be left aside, but they are obediently lined up, and soon they will give way to tractors, and the tractors give way to GPS controlled multi-purpose farming vehicles leased from specialist companies owned by hedge funds, and the houses will become connected to electricity grids, the overseer replaced by land management systems, the sun by programmed doses of differently coloured LED light, and the soil by the water-borne nutrient flows of vertical farms. But the gleaners are to know none of this, they are outside the network.

Simondon talks of a rise of network objects, each connected to others by wires, antennas, stations, towers, (almost) perfectly uniting energy and information flows, and their origins can almost be seen in along the vanishing points of *Gleaners*. And in the same way that energy is distributed outwards in infinitely scalable ways, so it can be used in concentrated form to power tools, as well as gigantic machine plants.[53] As network objects grow in complexity, information and energy inputs are further distributed, often in parallel processes at rapid speed. The parallel and complex relays of modern industrial complexes unfold at speeds and magnitudes at which the individual no longer counts as an originator. No longer inventors, creators, learners and users of the machine, technical mentality finds its fulfilment in systems that automatically adjust information and energy inputs, in the cybernetic processes of automation, machine adjustment and learning that no longer require human input in any of their productive stages. Labouring

---

[52] Millet's subject is an unruly one. As Gilbert Simondon (*The Mode of Existence of Technical Objects*. Translated by Cecile Malaspina and John Rogove. Minneapolis: Univocal. 2017, 104) acknowledged, at the time, despite the exceptions of hunting, war and navigation, general human labour and activity was not considered fitting for contemplation and thought.

[53] Simondon Technical mentality. This growing network of energy and information flows is only intercepted by the inefficiencies introduced by those seeking to adorn the elements with inefficient features, geared not towards the greater reaping of networked efficiency but towards the whims and aesthetic preferences of agents who are no longer designers or constructors of machines, or those, at a far distance, using them to produce goods, but mere users hankering after inessential distortions, beguiled by charm, prestige, flattery and the like. Unlike the chair whose design already assumes the sitter's physiology and weight, and takes on her weight and pain, the machine's purpose is interrupted when it is modified to accommodate human features. The ideal, post-industrial technical object finds perfection in normalization and standardization and thus to extension and further perfection in infinite progression.

subjects come to 'live amongst machines'.[54] What is being spread here is not human influence, but that of machinery, or more profoundly, of technology. The form-giving human is nowhere near centre stage anymore (the bare-handed gleaners were the last who could possibly have such a position). And nor is nature, in all its capricious bounty. Both it and humans have been outclassed by the machine-based process of manufacturing. Machines take over, and the hand, the origin of labour power, is reduced to surface level gestures. Gloves, rackets, pincers, pliers, pencils, wrist supports, buttons, joy sticks, levers extend and then replace it entirely, the natural hand '(burnable, breakable, small and silent) [which] now becomes the artifact-hand (unburnable, unbreakable, large, and endlessly vocal)'.[55] The body of the labourer is being increasingly compressed and transformed by the rhythms of machinery; the epoch of *technē* is giving way to one of technology.[56]

---

[54] Erich Hörl Die offene Maschine. Heidegger, Günther und Simondon über die technologische Begegnung. *MLN*, 2008, 123: 632–55, 643.

[55] Elaine Scarry *The Body in Pain*, 254.

[56] The evolutionary biologist August Weisman offered an apparently incontrovertible explanation for the inability of the hand (and organisms as such) to adjust to changing environments and to inherit these adjustments on to next generations. Inheritance of characteristics, he argued, only occurs in the via germ cells and as there is no known process by which acquired characteristics could impact germ plasm (the 'Weismann barrier'), inherited adaptations to environmental characteristics (often associated with the biologist Larmarck) remain impossible. There are, however, indications that some (epigenetic) marks that produce changes in gene functions without involving changes in the DNA sequence may be inheritable (see Michael Haworth. Bernard Stiegler on transgenerational memory and the dual origin of the human. *Theory, Culture & Society*, 2015, 33(3): 151–73). However, the human body's double, the artificial body into which the inward human body falls, is not subject to such limitations.

5 Technology, Machinery and Giving Over to the General in Strategic Practice

Technē is a knowledgeable condition in which things are gathered in relations of use and yet also, momentarily and occasionally, in mutual indebtedness. Yet its scope is becoming restricted to the repetitive, constant, iterative generation of energy and information, in both processes of production, consumption and tool use; but in no way being constitutive or in control of these processes. What happens when technology has replaced the labourers' and workers' nervous system as the supplier of both energy and information? How can we understand the effects of the networked condition with its parallelly unfolding processes, vast complexities channelled through relays that effortlessly switch between magnitudes, in ways that automatically respond and adjust – that is 'learn' – so that human being stand neither at the beginning, nor the end of use, consumption and production patterns, but as replaceable, self/similar units within them? What, here, is left of strategy?

Machination

To consider the role of strategy in the age of technology is to consider how it is we, as a species, have organized and continue to organize through the use of tools. It is, suggests Heidegger, only by thinking through work (and labouring) activity that the changes in meaning (*Sinnsverschiebung*) that occurred in the twentieth century, and which continue to intensify at ever growing rates, can be articulated:[1]

'Machination' is the name for a specific truth of beings (of the beingness of beings). We grasp this beingness first and foremost as objectivity (beings as objects of representation), but machination, since it is related to τέχνη [*technē*], grasps this beingness more profoundly, more primordially.[2]

---

[1] Erich Hörl *Das Arbeitslose der Technik*, 114.

[2] Martin Heidegger *Contributions to Philosophy: (Of the Event)*. Translated by Richard Rojcewicz and Daniela Vallega-Neu. Bloomington: Indiana University Press, 2011 104.

Considering the tool-bound intimacy between hand, eye and mouth signals the changes from the growing dominance of the machine on how we perceive the world. As machines come to do the work of the body, we begin to perceive and experience differently. *Gleaners* encapsulates the early moments of this growing dominance. It was being painted at a time when machines were inveigling their way into human practices with alarming rapidity; their productive power was obvious and disarming. It was no longer the arm of the labourer controlling the levers of work, but the machines controlling the arms, to the point where it was impossible to tell whether a machine or a human was acting. In the same year as *Gleaners* was painted Marx was writing *Outline Sketches for a Critique of Political Economy* (the *Grundrisse*) where he elaborated on an arc of economic (and hence social and political) activity in which it was impossible to isolate an origin. We have the labourer, tools, output and capital, through whose organization relations of production are (continually) reproduced: humans became either owners of capital or purveyors of labour, both of which are mediated by the process of production itself. What we have, in the stead of the living human being, is its appropriation by a living machinery in which labour appears as a mere accessory.

In no way does the machine appear as the individual worker's means of labour. Its distinguishing characteristic is not in the least, as with the means of labour, to transmit the worker's activity to the object; this activity, rather, is posited in such a way that it merely transmits the machine's work, the machine's action, on to the raw material – supervises it and guards against interruptions. Not as with the instrument, which the worker animates and makes into his organ with his skill and strength, and whose handling therefore depends on his virtuosity. Rather, it is the machine which possesses skill and strength in place of the worker, is itself the virtuoso, with a soul of its own in the mechanical laws acting through it; and it consumes coal, oil etc. (*matières instrumentales*), just as the worker consumes food, to keep up its perpetual motion. The worker's activity, reduced to a mere abstraction of activity, is determined and regulated on all sides by the movement of the machinery, and not the opposite.[3]

In such a condition, where 'objectified labour materially confronts living labour as a ruling power and as an active subsumption of the latter under itself', the actual value of the labour power becomes increasingly insignificant. The isolated individual is as nothing against the massive and tireless presence of machines who now embody value in a form appropriate to capital, which indeed becomes capital, an embodiment of force distinct from labour: 'the appropriation of labour by capital confronts the worker in a coarsely sensuous form; capital absorbs labour into itself – "as though

---

[3] Karl Marx Notes on machines. *Grundrisse 1857–1858*. Translated by Martin Nicolaus. London: Penguin Books in association with New Left Review. 1973, 692–3.

its body were by love possessed"'.[4] Indeed the only way that the human can make any room for itself, as a raw being of origins, is as a myth.[5] As when, a few decades earlier, Mary Shelley had mythologized the 'man-made' machine, which took on living without the need for love, without a mother, having only Dr Frankenstein as a father, and the mechanized human form was imagined to be an attenuated, struggling, disjointed sort of creature being unable to conjure itself into full life. The myth was a powerful one: without love, life is always an automatic life whose influence is disastrous, skewed as it is towards a thoughtless expression of directed force. It was as if all labouring activity was being configured in a similar condition to this loveless creature. Marx, with Engels, was witnessing the almost total subjection of workers to loveless life, watching appalled as even small children were fed into the complex innards of the shuttling, twisting, clattering, networked machines. The machines were becoming the new life form, disturbing, fundamentally, the human understanding of itself as the vital and reasoned force in control of things.

(Work)-Force

Amid such machination there is little possibility for the natality by which Arendt marked the distinction making capacity of being human. There was no room to shelter the incessant open movement of freely made opinion. Machinery is everywhere, and so, as Heidegger notes:

[t]he world changes into object. In this revolutionary objectifying of everything that is, the earth, that which first of all must be put at the disposal of representing and setting forth, moves into the midst of human positing and analyzing. The earth itself can show itself only as the object of assault, an assault that, in human willing, establishes itself as unconditional objectification. Nature appears everywhere – because willed from out of the essence of Being-as the object of technology.[6]

Machinery becomes technology, not simply an array of tools, but a mediated condition of organization into which we fall in which all possible distinctions have already been made mechanically.

Heidegger came round to this view gradually.

---

[4] Karl Marx 'Notes on Machines', VII, 704. The quote is from Goethe's Faust, 1,4. Marx's antidote is the offer of free time and place to exercise that freedom, both idle time and doing time, time to develop into a becoming being, one is both free and yet serious, and intensely hard (VI, 611).

[5] Ben Brewster Introduction to Marx's 'Notes on machines'. Economy and Society, 1972, 1(3): 235–43.

[6] Martin Heidegger The word of Nietzsche. In The Question Concerning Technology and Other Essays. Translated by William Lovitt. London: Garland. 1977, 53–115, 100.

During what Hubert Dreyfus sees as the early period of Heidegger's thinking, including the 1927 book *Being and Time*, Heidegger emphasizes the role of equipment, that is objects that are directly 'ready-to-hand' as tools, and how these are ontologically more fundamental than those which have been made intelligible ('present-at-hand'), for instance by being labelled, taxonomized or otherwise put into calculating, objectifying relations of labour.[7] Dreyfus argues that here Heidegger still sees the possibility for ready-to-hand objects, for example the carpenter's hammer, to function as a means of realizing intelligible subject–object ontological separations, and so rescuing beings from objectivity and representation.[8] This is bound up in a primordial totality in and from which all things (even language itself) find their intelligibility. And so nature, too, can only show up and be encountered in the context of the equipmental world and therefore in the context of Dasein's practical activity.[9]

But this pitching of tools against the sway of technology stands against other remarks in *Being and Time* which seem to acknowledge more fully the technological character of all nature, which has itself become 'proximally ready-to-hand' by virtue of machine mediated perception.[10] Here Heidegger speaks of 'regions' such as the workshop in which technology functions in relatively autonomous fashion:

Something akin to a region must already be discovered if there is to be any possibility of referring and finding the places of a totality of useful things available to circumspection.[11]

---

[7] Hubert Dreyfus Heidegger's History of Being of Equipment. In *Heidegger: A Critical Reader*. Edited by Hubert L. Dreyfus and Harrison Hall. Oxford: Blackwell. 1992, 173–85.

[8] In *Being and Time*, the hammer is defined by its 'in-order-to', its function, and its 'for-the-sake-of-which', its purpose, so that there is no essential nature to be had in the hammer. But unlike nature, whose water is being used to power plants, or its woods burned to generate heat, and unlike objects that are produced to be used up, the hammer – as a tool – functions, and so disappears in its handiness, or it fails in its functioning and it stands out, as broken, inadequate or missing entirely. Then, in these moments of breakdown, the hammer becomes circumspect: it may be inspected (a derivative, unproductive engagement that interrupts the task at hand), and with this we enter a slippery slope of 'degeneration' from use to utility as fulfilling a function, to using-up as exploitation – which equally signifies the move from the caring relationship of the craftsperson to their hammer and, in turn to a degree of openness towards the hidden nature of the materials such as the structure of the wood, compared with the industrialized 'checking up' and 'looking over' that characterizes human engagement in industrial production. As Dreyfus notes, in *Being and Time* there is no discussion of the resistance and reliability of equipment – only its functioning or breakdown; not even hands feature in the idea of 'ready-to-handness', and so the tool itself remains a curiously empty thing. Hubert Dreyfus Heidegger's History of Being of Equipment, 177–8.

[9] Hubert Dreyfus Heidegger's History of Being of Equipment, 181.

[10] Hubert Dreyfus Heidegger's History of Being of Equipment, 176.

[11] Martin Heidegger *Being and Time*, §100.

In a local region such as the workshop, the machines are relatively autonomous, and in expanding this local idea of context to a totality, *Being and
Time* makes a first step to transpose a technical notion of craft with its
independent and only partially connected tools arising out of the nearness of equipment (as in the gathering of tools in a workshop) to the
functioning of one single system, which becomes a workshop writ large
as autonomous and autochthonous space that precisely enframes and
sets all things into interconnectivity, thus denying localness and so pav-
ing the way for an understanding of the essence of technology as the
'total mobilization of all beings'.[12]

Marx also hints that technology, in its essence, cannot merely consist of
a set of tools, cogs, rivets or cylinders; it is labour embodied as capital, and
this opens up the thought that the relational nature of this condition, the
nature of technology, is much more than the materiality of the machinery.
Arendt too locates a decisive shift in the relation of labour and technology at the beginning of the industrial revolution, one which is distinct
from similar occurrences in the past: 'that expropriation and wealth
accumulation did not simply result in new property or lead to a new redis-
tribution of wealth, but were fed back into the process to generate further
expropriations, greater productivity, and more appropriation'.[13]

Work as *Energeia*

Though without the lucidity of Arendt's conceptual distinction of labour
and work, Heidegger's interest in the workshop and of the work of the
craftsperson is seemingly an attempt to articulate and preserve the possibilities for *technē*, but one that places him in dubious proximity to the
idealization of work in the National Socialist regime. As Werner Hamacher notes, like every totalitarian system, National Socialism defines
itself as a complete system of work that generates the means of infinite
survival.[14] In one way, this means that work is not merely what happens
in workshops or factories, but also the proper work of (human) nature:
'the work of *our* proper nature'; in Nazi ideology playing out as a natural-
mystical homage to force and strength that is restituted and reinstituted
through the fusing of life and work as the natural and proper being of the
Volk.[15] Hamacher traces the links of this rhetoric to Christian theology:

---

[12] Hubert Dreyfus *Heidegger's History of Being of Equipment*, 181.
[13] Hannah Arendt. *The Human Condition*, 255.
[14] Werner Hamacher Working through working. Translated by Matthew T. Hartman.
  Modernism/Modernity, 1996, 3(1): 23–56.
[15] Werner Hamacher Working through working, 26.

the resurrection of the people through the power of work first requires the acknowledgment of a fallen and insulted community, not just stabbed in the back by the signatories of the World War I armistice, but a more fundamental inferiority complex that has been 'artificially bred' to degrade and persecute the German people, and which will be eradicated through hard work. So deprived of life, the murdered corpse of the Weimar Republic, requires redemption and restitution, not by a superpower or theological spirit, but rising from the grave through the sweat of the brow. As Hamacher reminds us, this commitment to work finds chilling expression in '*Arbeit macht frei*" (work makes free), not just as 'the resurrection formula of the 'necro-vitalistic mythology of fascism,'[16] but also as the message on Auschwitz's iron gates, marking the place where those unredeemable by work (the Jews, the Gypsies, the politically, physically or sexually different, and so on) find their second death. Those who cannot resurrect their already fallen, already dead lives through work; that is those who are not at home in work but foreigners to that possibility of the recreation of the self, cannot be made free; and therefore, in this totalitarian logic, their unproductivity warrants their expulsion from the people and, ultimately, their genocidal murder.

Hamacher sees Heidegger's ontological conception of work in his existential analytic of *Dasein* as being related to this mythological motif. As rector in Freiburg in October 1933, in a speech to 600 unemployed, summoned after being enlisted in the massive National Socialist work-procurement programme (*Arbeitsbeschaffungsprogramm*),[17] Heidegger declares being out of work a spiritual disruption. Without work one cannot have rapport with things and so one is unfit for *Dasein*: what matters here is *Erhebung* (ennoblement) which, in Hamacher's translation becomes 'erection', thus also emphasizing how much of this is masculine 'ego enhancement'.[18] In stipulating that work is a precondition for *Dasein*, fitness for work, both intellectual (the brow) and manual (the fist) activity become a precondition for authentic being. This 'brow' and 'fist' tag-team receives its most direct formulation in Heidegger's 1934 rectoral address on the 'self-assertion of the German university', where

---

[16] Werner Hamacher Working through working, 27.

[17] Martin Heidegger Nationalsozialistische Wissensschulung. In *Nachlese zu Heidegger. Dokumente zu seinem Leben und Denken*. Edited by Guido Schneeberger. Bern: Suhr. 1962, 198–202, 198.

[18] Werner Hamacher Working through working, 28. Much later, in 1968, in a letter to a French author by Ernst Jünger, which the latter forwarded to Heidegger, Jünger draws a distinction between the Latin root of work via travail to '"tripalium", an instrument of torture', and the gothic roots of work (Arbeit) in 'arpeo', which means inheritance, equally signifying how work is a path to history and historicity. Martin Heidegger and Ernst Jünger. *Correspondence*, 44.

he argues that the 'questionability of Being, at all, demands of the *Volk* work and fight, and it forces it into its state *(seinen Staat)*, to which the professions belong'.[19] Heidegger's subsequent elaboration of three services *(Dienste)*: Work service, military service and scientific service *(Wissensdienst)*, at once makes the latter a service that is now aligned with higher political ends, it also emphasizes that even theory, even that very domain of thinking – which, before as well as after his rectoral period, he treats with immense caution and almost mystic reverence, coupled, of course, with the self-aggrandizing arrogance of seeing himself as a direct heir to the Greeks – is now a matter of work:

For once, 'theory' does not happen for its own sake, but only in the passion to remain near to Being and to remain under its affliction. For another, however, the Greeks fought especially to understand and carry out *(begreifen und vollziehen)* this observing-questioning as a manner of *energeia*, of 'being-at-work' *(am-Werke-Seins)* of the human being.[20]

Being-at-work is therefore not a prelude to *Dasein*, but *Dasein* itself; it is the ultimate actualization *(höchste Verwirklichung)* of *Dasein*. Those who work 'choose the knowing *(wissenden)* fight of those who question and confess with Carl von Clausewitz' whereas those who do not associate themselves with 'the reckless hope of rescue through the hand of coincidence'.[21] Unlike *Being and Time*, the rectoral speech portrays *Dasein* – *qua* work – as creative not only of itself, but also of its world. In this emphasis on world-creating work Heidegger was unambiguously placing workers, academics, soldiers and administrators in the service of the state, all of whom ought collectively engage in 'the erection *(Aufbau* – emphasized in the original) and building *(Bau)* in the new future of our people'.[22] There is a departure here from the openness of being sketched in *Being and Time*. The fluidity of technē is being hardened into a self-asserting future, a future already decided, and here reinstituted through

---

[19] Martin Heidegger *Die Selbstbehauptung der deutschen Universität*. Breisgau, 1934, 5–22. Our translation.
[20] Martin Heidegger *Die Selbstbehauptung*, 1. Our translation.
[21] Martin Heidegger *Die Selbstbehauptung*, 1. Our translation.
[22] Martin Heidegger *Nationalsozialistische Wissensschulung*, 199. In this address to the unemployed 600, he continues, arguing that the educated ones (using the somewhat derogative Swabian term die *'Gschtudierten'*) stand ready, not as the 'educated' against the 'uneducated', but as comrades. A few lines down he continues: 'Knowledge and possession of knowledge, as National Socialism understands these terms, does not divide into classes, but ties and unifies the *Volk*', and that the achievement of the navvy *(der Erdarbeiter)* is in principle not less of spirit *(geistig)* than the work of the educated. Next to this, one reader laconically scribbled: 'why did you then not do navvy work?' into our copy of the text. Heidegger finishes with a salute to 'the man of this unconscionable will, our Führer, Adolf Hitler (emphasized) a threefold "Sieg Heil!"'. Heidegger *Nationalsozialistische Wissensschulung*, 200–2.

a state and a leader figure. Here we have an 'arrest and internment Being in what already is'. Hamacher continues:

The political ergontology and morphontology of Heidegger during the Rectorship period was the ethical and political collapse of his philosophy: the collapse, namely, of the ontological difference, in many respects an endogenous collapse, for Heidegger never ceased to think Being as the Being of beings and of *Dasein*.[23]

Work and Technology

In the years following World War II, Heidegger returns to the question of Being, in light of the rise of technology, and, as he does so, goes back to the more open, speculative view of work found in *Being and Time*. Branded a 'fellow traveller' by the Allies, and partially restricted in his work, but by no means disenfranchised from academia, he begins to assess the post-war condition. In the 1948 *Bremen Lectures*, his opening thoughts on what was to become the idea of technological enframing, Heidegger argues:

We say 'technology' and mean modern technology. One likes to characterize it as machine technology. This characterization hits upon something correct. But what is correct about it still contains no truth, for it does not reveal anything of the essence of modern technology, and indeed it does not do so because the manner of representing that this characterization of modern technology as machine technology stems from is never able to reveal the essence of technology. One is of the opinion that modern technology, as distinct from all previous forms, would be defined by the machine. But what if it were the reverse? Modern technology is what it is not through the machine, but rather the machine is only what it is and how it is from the essence of technology. Thus one says nothing of the essence of modern technology when one conceives it as machine technology.[24]

The machine is a product of the essence of technology and not vice versa. The 'engine (*Motor*) produces power or force (*Kraft*) and this power-generating machine (*Krafterzeugungsmaschine*), stands as the representative machine for the human being',[25] and force is what Heidegger, the faithful student of Nietzsche, associates with the capacity for overcoming, for the leap, but also invoking Ernst Jünger's figure (*Gestalt*) of the

---

[23] Werner Hamacher Working through working, 33.

[24] Martin Heidegger *Bremen and Freiburg Lectures: Insight into That Which Is and Basic Principles of Thinking*. Translated by A. J. Mitchell. Bloomington: Indiana University Press. 1949, 32. In Erich Hörl *Das Arbeitslose der Technik*, 120–3. Our translation; also David J. Gunkel and Paul A. Taylor *Heidegger and the Media*. Cambridge: Polity. 2014, 53.

[25] Andrew J. Mitchell. The Question Concerning the Machine. Heidegger's Technology Notebooks in the 1940s and 1950s. In: *Heidegger on Technology*. Edited by A. J. Wendland; C. Merwin & C. Hadjioannou. London: Routledge, 115–132.

worker (*Arbeiter*) and his characterization of work as 'the total character of the reality of the real'.[26]

Published in 1932, Jünger's book *Der Arbeiter* develops this figure, a warrior steeled in the fires of World War I, who is also egalitarian, uniting members of all social strata, side-by-side, in the trenches. There, and altogether beyond the values of enlightenment and beyond bourgeois comforts, they can embrace instead a new world order driven by ruthless efficiency and exploitation and the total mobilization that converts life into energy; violent and powerful; 'the whole that wills itself'.[27]

If machines, and not humans, provide power, the capacity for ordering is no longer within human hands and, as Scarry, Marx and Arendt also suggest, it is the outsourcing of power that locates the source of authentic being beyond the human:

What belongs to the planning and carrying out of the production of force? Force as such – separated from animal and man-power [from *Tier- und Menschenkraft*]; (Forces of nature) – simply to use what is present-at-hand (water wheel, windmill, wind for the sail). 'Forces' 'artificially' (*technē*) produced. Making available for any and all goals and for the most comfortable and cheapest application. Machines, that first produce 'force' (what kind of production is this?) and unleash forces once again captured in installations [*Einrichtungen*], held as utterly replaceable.[28]

Here we approach a pivot point in Heidegger's outline of technology, and so for our understanding of its conditioning relation to strategy. Where power is separated from the human being and located in machines, the world is revealed according to a movement that equally has no origin in the human being; installations and not human order. These early lectures are still coined by a mechanistic understanding, lacking engagement with terms such as 'control' and 'information', which became central to the 1953 essay, *The Question Concerning Technology*. Heidegger, a reader of Gotthard Günther and Norbert Wiener, became increasingly aware of the cybernetic development of machines and their role in the completion of Western metaphysics as the fulfilment of this process, not only reducing language to communication, but communication to information transmission.

---

[26] Martin Heidegger. *The Question of Being*. Translated by William Kluback and Jean Wilde. New York: Twayne. 1958, 59.

[27] Wolf Kittler. From Gestalt to Gestell: Martin Heidegger reads Ernst Jünger. *Cultural Critique*, 2008, 69: 79-97.

[28] Martin Heidegger *Leitgedanken zur Entstehung der Metaphysik, der neuzeitlichen Wissenschaft und der modernen Technik*. Edited by Claudius Strube, 2009, 291–329. Our emphasis and translation.

In its basic organization this condition of technological ordering is perfectly and completely distilled in Samuel Beckett's precise, brightly lit play *Act without Words II*. Words have become superfluous. On the stage there are two sacks ('A' and 'B') and a pile of clothes ('C'), set in a line. There are three scenes, or 'positions'. Position 1 (CBA) (from left to right as the audience look at the stage) has a mechanical goad appearing from the right-hand side. Like a long spear, it moves perpendicular to the stage floor, pauses, retreats a little, then darts forward and prods sack 'A' ... nothing ... then it draws further back and darts forward again, before departing. On the second prod, 'A' stirs and a person climbs out of the sack, reluctantly, hesitantly, moody, prays and puts on clothes from the adjacent pile 'C', takes some pills, eats and then spits out some carrot, then takes up the sack and moves it to the other side of 'B', undresses and throws the clothes into an untidy pile, gets back in sack 'A'. Position 2 (CAB) the goad returns now having to stretch a little further onto stage, supported by a wheel as it moves linearly, pauses, then rapidly prods 'B', and departs. From 'B', a person emerges keenly, dressing, brushing teeth frantically, performing exercises, eating hastily, making to look at a watch repeatedly, then moves to the other side of 'A' undresses and piles the clothes neatly, and jumps back into the sack. Position 3 (CBA). The ensemble of sacks, clothes and persons is moving across the stage from right to left as the audience looks, each time advancing in a linear progression, prompted by the prodding machine. The goad reappears, now having to stretch even further, supported by two wheels, pauses, then prods 'A'. Nothing, it recoils further, pauses, then darts forward to prod 'A'. The sack moves, reluctantly. Person 'A' emerges, halts, broods, prays. The curtain falls.[29]

The goad initiates action and organizes the sacks, bodies and clothes but is never visible to person 'A' and 'B' on stage, and each time it appears with an increasing number of wheels it inhabits more space, gradually pushing them to the edge of the scene, displacing them from the stage. There is a strangely compelling equivalence amongst the objects on stage (characters, goad, clothes, sacks), each finding their distinction as units, each positioning itself without the movement being explained, or explicable. The play seems to distill Heidegger's observations on the intimacy between technology and positioning:

We now name the self-gathered collection of positioning [*des Stellens*], wherein everything orderable essences in the standing reserve, positionality [*das Ge-Stell*].

---

[29] Samuel Beckett *Shorter Plays and Poems*. London: Faber and Faber. Written in 1956, 47–51.

This word now no longer names an individual object of the sort like a bookcase or a water well. Positionality now also does not name something constant in the ordered standing reserve. Positionality names the universal ordering, gathered of itself, of the complete orderability of what presences as a whole.[30]

The stage remains a space, but one bereft of reasons. In its clean sparsity it makes apparent the ontological grounding of the question of production in Heidegger's analysis:

> Technology is not equivalent to the essence of technology. When we are seeking the essence of 'tree', we have to become aware that That which pervades every tree, as tree, is not itself a tree that can be encountered among all the other trees. Likewise, the essence of technology is by no means anything technological.[31]

And when Heidegger goes on to proclaim 'positionality is drive"[32] we arrive at the unsettling condition that marks the demise of *technē*. The movement from manual technology and artisanal manufacture to engine technology [*Kraftmaschinentechnik*] is therefore not merely a shift from simple tools to more complex machines, but a shift marked by a way of seeing the world as things that already occupy a position within a wider frame of production, and always will; the goad has a position, the characters and the sack, there is no other movement, and certainly no action.

Making as Folding the Four Causes

It is a condition in which the looser ideas of 'work' Heidegger discusses in *Being and Time*, and which he revisits in his *Question Concerning Technology*, the ones he begins to associate with the 'the term *Her-vor-bringen* (to bring forth; educe) which describes a seeing and knowing things through a letting be (*lassen*), have no room. This 'letting be' is not quiescent, there is agency involved in revealing what otherwise would have been concealed, but the agency entails a reticent holding back (*ver-an-lassen*), a resistance to the impress of the human will, which now, post–World War II, certainly includes a resistance to political will.

Hervorbringen is cast as an attentive awareness of, and struggling with, things that are being brought forth into existence without an explicit sense of initiation or end point. It rests within an equal relationship

---

[30] Martin Heidegger *Bremen and Freiburg Lectures*, 31. Our emphasis.

[31] Martin Heidegger *The Question Concerning Technology and other Essays*. Translated by W. Lovitt. London: Garland. 1977, 4.

[32] Martin Heidegger *Bremen Lectures*, 31. Drive is translated as '*Getriebe*' – but also refers to both gearing mechanism/transmission as well as hustle and bustle (*Trieb* meaning strive).

constituted by the ancient Greek fourfold breakdown of causes: material (such as a stone), form (the planes and volumes into which the stone falls), *telos* (purpose; the resonance of the stone as a sculpture, say) and efficient cause (the maker bringing about the whole effect). Under the framing of *technē* we have been pursuing here, there are two historical trajectories in which this fourfold relationship has been apprehended. The increasingly dominant one is skewed towards the pre-eminence of the efficient cause found either in humans, or in technological positioning, whose force is transferred through the practices of counting, weighing and measuring. The efficient cause is presumed both an originating and separated force initiated in moments of assessment and decision to do this, and not that. The other trajectory finds the efficient cause co-responsible for what Heidegger variously calls the mutual indebtedness or bringing forth found in a gathering of material, form and purpose, each inducing what is not yet in presence to become present. This making is not directed by the cause–effect reasoning of goal-directed force, but nor is it a spontaneous natural eruption that springs forth of its own accord, with no reason, and which, being firmly confined in its disinhibitor ring, is just bringing itself forth (*physis*), such as the flower in bloom, or the lark's evening song. Rather, it is a making in which we find the loosening form of *technē;* and so an efficient cause (human will) that works by inducing rather than managing or coercing things to come forward. The maker here is more an agitator, the origin of a gathering, who, within the 'region' of the workshop makes (in the sense of the more archaic 'bringing forth') things. The maker considers carefully (*überlegen*) and gathers (*versammeln*) the material, the form and final end (*telos*), to give sight to the named thing. This consideration and gathering does not amount to oversight and control over a productive process. The agency evokes a relationship of tightening, a pulling together that is slow, attentive, passive even. In this form of tightening (*Verfestigen*), the careful consideration and gathering renders the maker an indebted part of the causal fourfold; a cause no more influxious than those of material, form or *telos* (*überlegt sich und versammelt die drei genannten Weisen des Verschuldens*); all of them are, equally considered, modes of occasioning.

The form of sight (or vision world) arising from *Hervorbringen* is one of revealing in which the made thing is an arrangement of materials, forms, ends and agency that are themselves not smothered into invisibility by its being named and used. In this revelatory making there is a sense of complicity with, and not command over, what exists. As a bowl is turned on a wheel, or jewellery hammered on an anvil, the maker displays reticence, skill and thought, as well as the confidence of the experienced artisan to abdicate singular control and merely tighten material, form and end to bring forth the thing, becoming co-responsible and, collectively with the material, form and purpose, indebted to the 'thing'. Describing the influence of agency using *Verfestigen* denotes an almost contemplative way of bringing awareness about; a way of unconcealing that hears the saying of things without imposing upon them an idea of their form, material and end. Under the aegis of *Hervorbringen* form, purpose and material emerge, and we agents are standing back from the centre and accepting that we are not makers (*Schöpfer*) of 'things', but, rather, are implicated, our agency counts somehow, only never totally, nor from the outside. This is a letting be (*lassen*) accompanied by *an-lassen*, an arrival, starting, or ignition, as what is brought about is not an ending (*telos* mis-translated) but the arrival of a beginning, the completion of a coming into being, a natality.

Presence/Distance

This folding of the four causes of material, form, *telos* and efficient cause as equally indebted elements outlined in *The Question Concerning Technology* transcends the earlier identification of the 'ready-to-handness' in *Being and Time* in which Heidegger provides us with what Friedrich Kittler calls a 'slight displacement' of the original four Aristotelian causes: 'in lieu of "making" or "producing" [Heidegger] speaks only of "using"'.[33] In §38 Heidegger begins with the by-now familiar investigation of the mattering of things not in an abstract sense, but always already as belonging to a context of work. What is encountered within the world are 'things at hand'. Their handiness belongs to the world, to worldliness, which is 'already there' in the things at hand. We encounter the world first with everything in it, not as separate themes or qualities of things but rather:

things at hand are suited and unsuited for things, and their 'qualities' are, so to speak, still bound up with that suitability or unsuitability, just as objective presence, as a possible kind of being of things at hand, is still bound up with handiness. But as the constitution of useful things, serviceability is also not the suitability of beings, but the condition of the possibility of being for their being able to be determined by suitability.[34]

Suitability as the key determinant of something's 'being' is a different affair to the bringing forth of the made thing in joint indebtedness. In *Being and Time*, Heidegger is elaborating on a 'displaced' set of causes:

---

[33] Friedrich Kittler *The Truth of the Technological World, Essays on the Genealogy of Presence.* Translated by Erik Butler. Stanford: Stanford University Press. 2014, 291–2.

[34] Martin Heidegger *Being and Time*, §81–2.

Relevance is the being [*Sein*] of innerworldly beings, for which they are always already initially freed ... What the relevance is about is the what-for of service-ability, the wherefore of applicability [*Verwendbarkeit*]. The what-for of service-ability can in turn be relevant.[35]

Heidegger's hammer is not foremost a thing, but it has 'to do' with hammering, which in turn has to do with fixing something, which has to do with building a shelter from rain, which has to do with sheltering *Dasein*, making its being possible. Relevance cannot be understood outside this circuit of connections, outside what he calls a 'total relevance' that is synonymous with being itself.

The total relevance itself, however, ultimately leads back to a what-for which no longer has relevance, which itself is not a being of the kind of being of things at hand within a world, but is a being whose being is defined as being-in-the-world, to whose constitution of being worldliness itself belongs. This primary what-for is not just another for-that as a possible factor in relevance. The primary 'what-for' is a for-the-sake-of-which. But the for-the-sake-of-which always concerns the being of *Dasein* which is essentially concerned about this being itself in its being.[36]

Kittler laconically thinks through these thoughts using the example of a shoe, or bootmaker. The shoe is mere 'equipment': '[*Schuhzeug*] [which] has a "whereto" [*Wozu*]—namely, wearing', and in putting the shoe on the philosopher's foot, Kittler argues that this *Wozu*:

can also be conceived as the Martin Heidegger, Media, and the Gods of Greece walking on a street. It has its 'wherefrom' [*Woraus*] in leather, which for its part comes from the skin of animals. Third, it has a carrier and user for whom, in the best of cases, it has been tailored (even though this no longer occurs in the age of machines).[37]

The purpose is just wearing; the material is the skin of a dead and forgotten animal; and the form is the wearer's foot, often cast in industry standard sizes using pre-made lasts. And

[f]ourth and last, all equipment—especially when it is damaged, lost [*abhanden*], or unusable—presents a primal 'whereto,' which no longer represents the 'whereby' [*Wobei*] of any 'involvement' [*Bewandtnis*] at all, but rather affords the 'wherefore' [*Worum-willen*] of *Dasein* that, in its Being, essentially concerns this Being itself.[38]

How can the shoemaker be indebted to materials (equipment) that are not there? The shoemaker may find the animal hide missing, or of

---

[35] Martin Heidegger *Being and Time*, §81–2.
[36] Martin Heidegger *Being and Time*, §82–3. Our emphasis.
[37] Friedrich Kittler *The Truth of the Technological World*, 291–2.
[38] Friedrich Kittler *The Truth of the Technological World*, 291–2.

the wrong firmness, or her hammer breaking; Heidegger, wearing his new shoes down the road, may find them uncomfortable, or he may realize he put on the wrong pair for the weather. To have these pre-conceptions of what ought to be there (by way of functionality) means that the version of making filtered through equipmentality does not draw from the presence of things but always already begins from a distance of conventional expectation. This 'intermingling of form and matter' is grounded in serviceability, the 'basic trait from out of which these kinds of beings look at us – that is, flash at us and thereby presence and so be the beings they are ... as a piece of equipment for something'.[39]

When things can do nothing more than fit into a pre-configured world of use, they cannot reveal anything by themselves; no inner beauty or authentic essence. At best they are reliable, like a pair of well-worn boots worn by a peasant. The individual piece of equipment becomes worn out and used up. But also: 'customary usage itself falls into disuse, becomes ground down and merely habitual. In this way equipmental being withers away, sinks to the level of mere equipment'.[40] And here is the rub, because as the machinery takes over, it is as purpose, not as an efficient cause, which just withers.

'[T]hese days' suggests Kittler 'aeroplanes and radios belong among the things that are closest to us',[41] becoming increasingly alive to an emerging ontology of distance; on the one hand by elaborating the essence of things in terms of their reliability, and on the other by considering how that distancing influence has come to mark a transformation from an epoch of *technē* and making, towards one of technology. Aeroplanes and radios are not simply different means of transmitting messages, they reveal a new world:

We just need to look at the airplane and the radio broadcast to immediately see that both machine constellations (*Maschineneinrichtungen*) have arisen not only in conjunction with contemporary science but that they have come to determine the unfolding of the history of our contemporary time. For it is not only that the same processes that hitherto were completed with help of the rural postal worker and the horse-drawn post carriage now are done with through the use of other means. What is more is that the airplane and radio-broadcast out of themselves: that means to say out of their machine-being (*Maschinenwesen*) and the reach (*Erstreckungsweite*) of their being, make possible the new degrees of

---

[39] Martin Heidegger The origin of the work of art. In *Off the Beaten Track*. Translated by Julian Young and Kenneth Haynes. Cambridge: Cambridge University Press. 2002, 1–56, 9–10. Our emphasis.
[40] Martin Heidegger The origin of the work of art, 15.
[41] Martin Heidegger The origin of the work of art, 5.

play (*Spielraum*) of possibilities, which can be planned and executed through human will.[42]

We can begin to appreciate the importance of this shift from presence to absence when we trace the development of Heidegger's thoughts throughout a series of influential works, culminating in the famous essay *The Question Concerning Technology* in 1953.

Already, in the 1938 essay *The Age of the World Picture*, Heidegger approaches this distancing through the separation engendered by the process of picturing.[43] Here picture does not refer to the representation or imitation of any specific object but a wider entire mindset required for abstract conceptualization and the ways in which nature is disclosed representationally, as picture; as something that is present-at-hand [*das Vor-handene*].[44] It was a condition that Nietzsche had also recognized: 'We have perfected the picture of becoming, but have not got over, got behind the picture'; our pictures of the world are being traced out in ever more complex and nuanced relations of cause and effect, we have never understood, and how could we understand when what we are using in our inquiry of the world are things that do not exist 'lines, surfaces, bodies, atoms, divisible times, divisible spaces', so then how, he concludes, 'is explanation to be at all possible when we first turn everything into a picture – our picture!'[45] Taking up Nietzsche's frustration, Heidegger argues that we get a grasp of things, we are 'in the picture', when we not only see some-thing standing before us but when

---

[42] Martin Heidegger *Gesamtausgabe. II. Abteilung: Vorlesungen 1923–1944: Hölderlins Hymne: Der Ister. Band 53.* Frankfurt: Vittorio Klostermann, 53. Our translation.

[43] Martin Heidegger The age of the world picture, 57–85. It is here where we have to return to Bernard Stiegler's point about the dangerous romanticizing of thought in Heidegger. In *The Age of the World Picture*, Heidegger explicitly identifies the bleak machination (the 'darkening of the world') that goes with the representing production of the modern world picture with 'Americanism'. For Morten Thaning, in attempting to counter this picture, 'Heidegger now claims to have gained insight into the objective delusion of the modern age, the metaphysical logic of technical rationality. This is the point of his reaffirmation of National Socialism as a tragic necessity. In sum, the entry [from Black Notebooks] tries to depict his own philosophical misinterpretations as tragic experiences from which insight has been won by inscribing these delusions into the history of Being, which at the same time is interpreted as a greater, encompassing tragedy.' Morten Thaning Reading Heidegger's Black Notebooks in light of Gadamer's philosophical hermeneutics and Mann's Dr. Faustus. Unpublished. 2019, 30.

[44] The picturing is in writing itself. In the *Phaedrus* Socrates argues writing issues reminders and so erodes the capacity of poets to recall history in the act of speaking: to write (and read) is to remove meaning from the human form and to place it in its own, representative terms, giving history over to the process of an abstracting *mimesis* that bore no physical resemblance to the things named, but which marked them. We only know of Socrates' point of view, however, because Plato wrote.

[45] Friedrich Nietzsche *The Gay Science*, §112.

we get a systemic sense of the entirety of its relations: 'world picture, when understood essentially, does not mean a picture of the world but the world conceived and grasped as picture'.[46]

In crucial counter-distinction to the holding back (ver-an-lassen) in which the maker merely reveals the form of the made thing, the world 'as a picture is always already world made by man'.[47] As Arendt also noticed, writing as she was at the time when the first Sputnik satellite had been sent into orbit, the totality of the earth was being mapped. Indeed Arendt opens *The Human Condition* with reference to this 'earth-born object ... [which] circled the earth according to the same laws of gravitation that swing and keep in motion the celestial bodies—the sun, the moon, and

---

[46] Martin Heidegger *The Age of the World Picture*, 67, shaped by the perceptual and actual imagery being produced in the habituated interactions of eye-telescope-heaven. The stars lying upwards, out of reach, pull the astronomer upwards, extending out of itself, and the telescope pulls the stars inwards into lens, perceptual organs, star charts and creation of the world, each shaping the other's form. The astronomer-telescope prosthesis has the power of projecting images of the world to come and shaping its own form. Heidegger insists that there is no direct lineage from the world picture of antiquity or from the medieval world picture to the modern one but that the modern world picture engenders a shift where the world *itself* becomes a picture.

[47] Care is required not only in the identification of the problem but also in Heidegger's implied solution. Of particular interest, by way of a warning about the thin line that has to be trod here, is Sidonie Kellerer's analysis of the 'metamorphosis' of *The Age of the World Picture*. In her careful tracing of the changes from the original text as presented in a lecture in Freiburg in 1938 to its published version in the *Gesamtausgabe* in 1950, Kellerer reveals a much darker 'picture' of Heidegger's implication in National Socialist and therefore fascist and anti-Semitic ideology, which was not only partly redacted or in other cases tempered through additional insertions in the final publication (without making these changes explicit), they also serve to undermine the claim Heidegger invoked, following the World War, that he had, through his technology warnings, issued attacks on 'the party' in form of a critique of the delivering over of science to technology. Kellerer's analysis does much to undermine that claim. This begins with the (not redacted) association of Frenchman Descartes with a 'degenerative' superficiality of thought set against the originary power (*Kraft*) emanating from the Germans 'Leibnitz, Kant, Fichte, Hegel and Schelling', when the very term '*entartet*' (degenerate) was explicitly used by the National Socialist regime to denounce non-Arian art as well as dehumanize people on the basis of biological and cultural traits. It also includes a change in the clear self-association ('we') of himself and the German Volk as a historically concrete example (or perhaps as 'the' case) in the lecture with a much more distant and abstract notion of 'contemporary thinking' *as such* in relation to the world picture in the published version. Similarly, the association of the modern world picture with 'Americanism', which is softened by the insertion (after the lecture) that this Americanism 'is something European', finds a more radical precursor in the lecture which claims that 'even today' (that is, in 1938) this Americanism 'has to be fought'. Here again, Heidegger uses a slur, '*Abartig*', meaning degenerate and perverted. This all culminates in the final paragraphs of the text which outlines a Nietzschean version of overcoming and being witness to a people (*Volk*) that leaps out of its own history in an event where metaphysics transforms into the unequivocal (*das Unbedingte*). As Kellerer acerbically notes, this is issued precisely at the time when Nazi troops invaded France.

the stars'.[48] And just as this object dwelt and moved amongst the heavenly bodies whilst remaining a thing of 'man's' making, so did it conjure desires to sever the ties that bind humans to the *Umwelt* expanding satellite, one that is denied to animals and all things of nature. Through objects like satellites humans come to relate to the earth as a thing out of which rockets can be built and from whose surface they can be launched. And in anticipating the media analysis that was to follow, she asks:

could [it] be that we, who are earth-bound creatures and have begun to act as though we were dwellers of the universe, will forever be unable to understand, that is, to think and speak about the things which nevertheless we are able to do. In this case, it would be as though our brain, which constitutes the physical, material condition of our thoughts, were unable to follow what we do, so that from now on we would indeed need artificial machines to do our thinking and speaking.[49]

And so, when, in our human *Umwelt*, the earth is no longer a scene of action but an object of analysis, read through the images transmitted from satellites, what can be measured can no longer inspire awe, it is no longer immense. As the world gets transformed into such a picture, so do humans, as:

that being who gives to every being the measure and draws up the guidelines. Because this position secures, organizes, and articulates itself as world-view, the decisive unfolding of the modern relationship to beings becomes a confrontation

---

Sidonie Kellerer Heideggers Maske "Die Zeit des Weltbildes" – Metamorphose eines Textes. *Zeitschrift für Ideengeschichte*, 2011, Bd. V/2, 109–21. The matter gains further importance in light of the more recent publication of the Black Notebooks which contain poisonous commentary, some of which directly relates to, and clouds the interpretation of his philosophy of technology. For instance, Heidegger writes that 'one of the most hidden forms of the gigantic and perhaps the oldest is the tenacious aptitude for calculating and profiteering and intermingling, upon which the worldlessness of Jewry is founded'. Peter Gordon Prolegomena to any future destruction of metaphysics: Heidegger and the Schwarze Hefte. In *Heidegger's Black Notebooks*. Edited by Andrew Mitchell and Peter Trawny. New York: Columbia University Press. 2017, 136–51, 137). Later in the notebooks he writes: 'The Judaism of the world, spurred on by those who were allowed to emigrate from Germany, is intangible everywhere and does not need to engage in warlike acts in spite of their display of power, whereas we are left to sacrifice the best blood of the best of our nation.' Martin Gessmann Heidegger and National Socialism: He meant what he said. In *Heidegger's Black Notebooks*. Edited by Andrew Mitchell and Peter Trawny. 2017, 114–29, 126.

48 Hannah Arendt *The Human Condition*, 1.

49 Hannah Arendt *The Human Condition*, 1. We can recur here to Uexküll's *Umwelt*, and his conjecture of how this already made world of the astronomer's vision world would be made through the relational interaction of the picturing eye of an astronomer, a body of knowledge about space, and an ever more powerful telescope fixed on the sky. See The Astronomer's *Umwelt* in Jacob von Uexküll *A Stroll through the Worlds of Animal and Man: A Picture Book of Invisible Worlds*. Image 53. 1934/2009. Reprinted in *Semiotica*, 1992, 89(4).

of world views … [setting] in motion with respect to everything, the unlimited process of calculation, planning and breeding [that is] the collective image of representing production [*das Gebild des vorstellenden Herstellens*[50]][51]

It is a picture increasingly incapable of conveying anything of the reality being experienced by those being pictured.

With such picturing we have, for example, Bertolt Brecht, commenting wryly '[r]eality itself has shifted into the real of the functional. The reification of human relationships, such as the factory, no longer betrays anything about these relationships.'[52] Brecht was reflecting on photographs of a Krupp factory (Figure 5.1) that showed a neatly ordered functionalism, but conveyed nothing of the alienation this mechanization entailed.

In its entirety, Brecht's work, from his first play *Man Equals Man* onwards, was an epic attempt to employ his own uncanny, distancing effects (*Verfremdungseffekt*) to reveal how readily we transform ourselves to conform with pictures:

> Tonight you will see
> A man reassembled like a car.
> Leaving all his individual components
> Just as they are.[53]

Brecht experimented continually with methods of disturbance, trying to reveal the mechanisms by which picturing was taking hold of the world. In his plays actors were to break the scene, images were broken up and blocks of text were treated as images, all of them forms of apostasy that constituted an incision into settled orders and that thereby attempted to break open the seductions of picturing, revealing the true

---

[50] Literally translated: the standing or placing-before (vor-stellend) production; that is the combination of the isolation of things – as things – in a conceptual, present-at-hand grasp, and their simultaneous arrangement into already existing plans and schemes that render them standing reserves.

[51] Martin Heidegger The age of the world picture: 71. Our emphasis.

[52] See Bertolt Brecht The threepenny lawsuit. In *Brecht on Film and Radio*. Edited and translated by Marc Silberman. London: Methuen. 2000, 164. Also in Walter Benjamin Little history of photography. In Walter Benjamin *Selected Writings, Vol. 2, Part 2, 1931–1934*. Cambridge, MA: Harvard University Press. 1999, 507–30.

[53] Bertolt Brecht Man equals man. In *Brecht's Collected Plays*. Translated by Gerhard Nellhaus. London: Bloomsbury. 1994, 3. The v-effekt makes ordinary appear arbitrary, not natural, and so open to question (as when he has characters break into song to then comment on the events in the play, a form of two-in-one conversation). In setting up a relationship of curiosity to habit it is an authenticity device, it reminds us of how habituated practices (including the artifice of theatre) come to have the quality of natural facts – a fixed *Umwelt* – rather than as institutional facts that can be transformed under the crucible heat of revolution.

Figure 5.1 Krupp factory, World War I. Photo Brown Bros. From *The New York Times Current History of the European War (January–March 1915)*, 2, 889. Wikimedia commons

(exploitative) conditions under which humans were organizing themselves technologically. Heidegger, less sanguine than Brecht, thought it too late to fundamentally alter the world picture because there was nothing behind to reveal, it was picturing all the way through. We were already all of us captive to the Gigantic, in whose thrall all relations to things, including to artistic techniques of disturbance, are already made small.[54]

---

[54] It is important to highlight the epochal technological advances taking place during Heidegger's life. In the famous Spiegel interview in 1966, Heidegger argues: 'Everything is functioning. That is precisely what is awesome [uncanny; Unheimlich – *our insertion*], that everything functions, that the functioning propels everything more and more towards further functioning, and that technicity increasingly dislodges man and uproots him from the earth. I don't know if you were shocked, but [certainly] I was shocked when a short time ago I saw the pictures of the earth taken from the moon. We do not need atomic bombs at all [to uproot us] – the uprooting of man is already here. All our relationships have become merely technical ones. It is no longer upon an earth that man lives today.' Martin Heidegger Nur noch ein Gott kann uns retten. *Der Spiegel*, 30 May 1976, 193–219. Translation by W. Richardson Only a god can save us. In *Heidegger: The Man and the Thinker*. Edited by T. Sheehan. London: Taylor and Francis. 1981, 45–67. It is perhaps particularly ironic, given Heidegger's distinction of the animal as that being that is driven by its strive (Trieb) and thus unable to move outside its environment against the human being, which is precisely not subject to animalistic appetite, that this famous interview, in the print version of *Der Spiegel*, is flanked by two adverts

The Gigantic

Where the made object such as a bowl or piece of jewellery stands for an ontology of presence, where the maker unites the material, form and purpose, the process of representing production that marks the world picture of the new world is animated by what Heidegger identified as an interplay of the 'Gigantic' (*das Riesige*) and the small: what was once a horizon is brought closer, by measurement, into distances that can then be traversed (the aeroplane), or obliterated (the radiowaves).[55] This recalls Heidegger's analysis of the sway of modern technology in his distinction between *technē* and the revealing (*poiesis*) that can be attained by a maker who heeds material and form, and the technological challenging forth (*Herausfordern*) that imposes a design onto the thing. But here we encounter another dimension, in addition to design; the Gigantic, which not only changes the way we make things, it more fundamentally alters our relation with our world, and with earth. The fundamental changes in outlook are not just Heidegger's but they recall that of Jünger, which was equally beset by acute experiences of societal crises and forged in the unprecedenced expereince of industrial-scale destruction in the 'storms of steel' of World War I. Could a totally mobilized world birth a new human being who is familiar with technology in its most destructive, nihilistic form, and so transformed, in an 'organic construction', from subject to worker? This question marks a shift in emphasis from the thought of machination as an objectification of experience. Technology is not merely machine technology but, more essentially still, a historically conceived '"org[anic] construction;" something alongside something else ... not as a "goal" in the widest sense, but instead as the truth of being [Sein], which joins with and arranges beings'.[56]

---

for potency-increasing pills for men ('Sexanorma' and 'Libid-6' [the number 6 (sechs) in German is pronounced very similar to 'sex']).

[55] The observation was of a materially shrinking space, transport was quicker, had greater spread and was more accessible, film could speed up and reverse time, and the radio cast a wireless net of news across the globe. See Martin Heidegger The thing. In *Poetry, Language, Thought*. Translated by Albert Hofstadter. New York: Harper Perennial. 1971, 163–80, 163. He also talks of quantification being the measure by which what is unmanaged is made manageable, what is alien becomes familiar, and what is distinct is brought into relations of comparison and exchange. Martin Heidegger, The age of the world picture, 71.

[56] Martin Heidegger *Leitgedanken zur Entstehung der Meaphysik*, 287. Heidegger argues that the 'fact that man as animal rationale, here meant in the sense of the working being, must wander through the desert of the earth's desolation could be a sign that metaphysics occurs in virtue of Being, and the overcoming of metaphysics occurs as the incorporation of Being. For labor (cf. Ernst Jünger, *Der Arbeiter*, 1932) is now reaching the metaphysical rank of the *unconditional objectification of everything present which is active in the will to will'*. Martin Heidegger *The End of Philosophy*. Translated by Joan Stambaugh. Chicago. University of Chicago Press. 1973, 85. Our emphasis.

Heidegger applauds that Jünger's *Der Arbeiter*: 'achieves what all the Nietzsche literature was not able to achieve so far, namely, to communicate an experience of being and of what it is, in the light of Nietzsche's outline of being as the will to power'.[57] But he also sees Jünger seeking rescue in the flight (*Flucht*) from the insight into the questionability of the metaphysical position of the human being. Hamacher labels Jünger's *Arbeiter* a proto-fascist pamphlet conceiving work in the entirely undifferentiated uniformity of the 'total' that espouses not so much the vulgar racism of National Socialism, but a techno-racist ideal rooted in fundamental sets of repetition.[58] The ensuing ideal of a planetary dictatorship links Jünger's notion of 'organic construction' and the emerging man-machine symbiosis of Norbert Wiener's cybernetic command and control circuits. And where, for Jünger, the worker reigns *as* a figure, Heidegger radically reverses Jünger's analysis and locates being in the essence of technology, where the 'will to power is revealed as truth. Truth is not a manmade gestalt, but Being ... as *Gestell*'.[59] This also marks a turn from an affirming relationship with technology towards a diagnostic one. In place of the militaristic figure of the worker as the figure that completes the subjectivity of human beings Heidegger returns to work; to the configuration of world through work, rendering Jünger's *Arbeiter* merely a figure in an epoch: the 'central actor of the world and sense-forming history of being [*Seinsgeschichte*] in the epoch of subjectivity'. Heidegger therefore stands back and revises the role of Jünger's worker from the absolute figure that spells the end of being towards a figure that marks the end of an epoch in the history of being; more a figure of the past, understood through the historical notion of work.[60]

---

[57] Martin Heidegger. *The question of being*, 43; 46.

[58] There are also influences of contemporary psychology, notably the notion of *Gestalt*, which equally indicate a figure consisting of a multiplicity of elements, where the whole exceeds the sum of its parts. Wolf Kittler notes that in Heidegger's recently published notes on Jünger's *Arbeiter*, Heidegger specifies 'aircraft crew, submarine crew, astronaut ... [but also:] An organic construction is, for instance, the S.S.'. Jünger already speaks of 'standing reserves' (*Bestand*), including 'human stock', and control (*Steuerung*) in the sense of feedback. But where Jünger, with much pathos, sees a 'cosmic antagonism' at play, Heidegger comments 'to speak of the "cosmic" here is romantic bogus! ... it is the sheer superiority of machine power, controlled by experienced British colonial troops and privates ... the world order is not perturbed at all, but the one which has reigned up to now is coming to an end'. Even the Heidegger of the rectoral period saw in work a directedness against the other, rather than Jünger's totalizing assimilation. But especially the later Heidegger rejects Jünger's embrace of total mobilization with reference to warfare, accusing Jünger of mere participation, a readiness for action just to be up to date, and against this violent view of Jünger's he begins to elaborate a response drawing on contemplation (*Besinnung*) and letting be (*Gelassenheit*). Wolf Kittler From Gestalt to Gestell, 84, 86, 90–1, 95.

[59] Wolf Kittler From Gestalt to Gestell, 84, 86, 90–1, 95

[60] In Erich Hörl *Das Arbeitslose der Technik*, 120–3. Our translation; also David J. Gunkel and Paul A. Taylor *Heidegger and the Media*, 53. This, Hörl argues, also marks a shift

Heidegger's concerns quickly exceed the historical figure. In the wake of technology, of calculation, the earth is lost; it is concealed, for while it is, naturally, a place of vast swathes and immense densities, a place of stupefying myriad detail and endlessly arresting distinctions, these are not qualities that can be classified. The earth has been captured, and in being captured it has become small, small as in Gigantic, which is not, then, an interplay of opposites, but a filtering of what is natural into measured distances, positions, connections and effects.[61]

nature soon became a being and then even the counterpart of 'grace' and, after this degradation, was completely set out in the compulsion of calculative machination and economics. Ultimately what remained were 'scenic views' and recreational opportunities, and now even these have been calculated to gigantic proportions and prepared for the masses. And then? Is that the end? Why is the earth silent at this destruction? Because the earth is not allowed the strife with a world, not allowed the truth of beyng. Why not? Is it because that gigantic thing, the human being, becomes all the smaller the more gigantically grown? Does nature have to be renounced and abandoned to machination? Can we yet seek the earth anew? Who will kindle that strife in which the earth finds its open realm, secludes itself, and is genuinely the earth?[62]

In its open realm the earth was approached by the maker, not as a map or diagram but as an intensive array of forces through which they dwelt, as a place for being without subjugating or mastering the things to which they were indebted for their living. This indebtedness emerged when one listened to things and recognized what Ralph Waldo Emerson had called the method of nature. For Emerson nature was ungraspable:

Like an odor of incense, like a strain of music, like a sleep, it is inexact and boundless. It will not be dissected, nor unravelled, nor shown. Away profane philosopher! Seekest thou in nature the cause? This refers to that, and that to

---

from Heidegger's infamous rectoral speech in 1938 in Freiburg in which he argued that theory does not happen for its own sake but out of the passion to get close to being; and here he refers to the 'Greeks'' struggles to frame this question in terms of Energeia; as 'Being-at-work' (and close to the product of work: 'am-Werke-Sein'). Erich Hörl Die offene Maschine. Heidegger, Günther und Simondon über die technologische Bedingung. MLN, 2008, 123: 632–55, 644; see also: Martin Heidegger Die Selbstbehauptung der deutschen Universität. Breisgau, 1934: 5–22. Our translation.

[61] Heidegger invokes Parmenides to suggest that: 'The apprehension of being belongs to being since it is from being that it is demanded and determined. The being is that which rises up and opens itself; that which, as what is present, comes upon man, i.e., upon him *who opens himself* [sic] *to what is present* in that he apprehends it.' Opening oneself to what is present does not mean first looking at beings but to 'be looked at' by them; 'to be included and maintained and so supported by their openness, to be driven about by their conflict and marked by their dividedness, that is the essence of humanity in the great age of Greece'. Martin Heidegger The age of the world picture, 68. Our emphasis.

[62] Martin Heidegger *Contributions to Philosophy*, 218.

the next, and the next to the third, and everything refers. Though must ask in another mood, though must feel it and love it, though must behold it in a spirit as grand as that by which it exists, err thou canst know the law. Known it will not be, but gladly loved and enjoyed.[63]

Heidegger laments the loss of an earth opening to itself where nothing might be commuted to ends, nothing that can be identified as starting and complete, where all is beginning and spilling over, nothing is separate, all is in communion, nothing is elevated, all is leavened.

When humans, in their attempt to control the earth, insert themselves into the infinite curve of emanation, they then isolate: they select the fruit of a tree at the expense of variety in woodland, they light fires at the expense of darkness, they cure idleness with a proclivity for possession. With all these insertions and comes a tendency to imagine 'raw' earth as a scene of profligacy agitated by a wanton and juvenile urge to grow everywhere and anywhere, untamed and wasteful because it lacks a specific end. In this way the picture justifies intervention from a reasoning being, a humanist subject, who builds dikes, channels, walls, and conduits to contain and then use the earth. Humans propose themselves the end and direct the rich natural redundancy of the earth towards themselves. There is a moment here, a sense of possibility, which for Emerson is generative and uplifting, prefiguring aspects of Heidegger's idea of dwelling by a hundred years or so, observing how, in turning the earth towards them, humans might become so much more than what they are, alive to *ek-stasis* and its possibilities which they might take up, and embody: 'The termination of the world in a man, appears to be the last victory of intelligence. The universal does not attract us until housed in an individual.'[64] Each human saves the earth just as the earth grounds their own world. Each being has a world into which earth protrudes, and the earth is touched by the active being of each individual world rooting itself. Emerson aches for more of these dwelling beings, for their newness, their zest for concentrating on the vast potency of a single earth dwelling act, and then to act again, each caught fast in their own 'personal ascendency'.

But it goes wrong, humans fail to dwell because they fail to apprehend the effulgent quality of natural ecstasy, they find themselves transferring their thoughts in life to ends-in-themselves, and finding in the ends reasons to act that are separated from a sense of world. Dwelling gives

---

[63] Ralph Waldo Emerson The method of nature: An address to the Society of the Adelphi. Waterville College, Maine. 11 August 1841. In *Emerson: Essays and Lectures*. New York: The Library of America. 1983, 113–32, 119–20.

[64] Ralph Waldo Emerson *The Method of Nature*.

way to instrumental acts, and expressive work gives way to tools, and the earth itself becomes a resource, rather than a source of life.

Enframing (*das Gestell*)

In contrast with the maker's abetting, which we find in Greek beginnings, and in contrast to Emerson's world-revealing 'individual', comes the modern and technological experience/action of *Fertigen* (producing). Where *Verfestigen* is a considerate and almost artistic (*technē*) way of letting be, *Fertigen* is an active making of something (the move from life to ends) that encompasses both manufacture and management, and which Heidegger likens to a setting upon and challenging forth of things, *Herausfordern*. *Herausfordern* is a state of knowing predicated on incision as an intervention through which we demand things show themselves in service to ends, all of which, in being known and measured as ends, can be compared and improved upon. Here the efficient cause, the agent, stands out, but not in the way Emerson hankers after, for with him the individual remains a gathering space for nature's ecstasy, plenitude and redundancy, whereas here it is as a separating force that brings about, directs and governs in the name of ends. The agent presumes to hold sway over material, form and *telos* in such a way as things are made to stand out for the purposes ascribed to them under organizational direction, a direction set by goals.

Moving from the somewhat refined and archaic examples of craft work to describe the difference between *Hervorbringen* and *Herausfordern* (see Table 5.1), Heidegger pursues these differing forms of 'vision world' (seeing alongside naming), extending the examples into more industrial settings, for example by contrasting the use of wind power in windmills to the hydroelectric schemes then being envisaged on the river Rhine. The miller grinding wheat gathers the wind in order to meet material interests in making flour; the wind is used. But no demands are made of it, it passes through, without exhaustion, and is let be, to then be used by others downstream. Using the flow of a river to turn a generator might similarly be described as *Verfestigen*, a loose coupling to things to bring about power that otherwise would be latent, or redundant. But here differences arise. The river Rhine is dammed, its course and depths are altered, spatially and temporally it becomes contained, a demand is made upon it that it become still, captured to yield energy that is not used directly, but directed elsewhere, an object of management and, in turn, a subject of political and social concern. The dam is an incision that expels communities from their homes, that accentuates the boundaries between regions and nations, that depletes surrounding rivers and water tables, that

Table 5.1 Hervorbringen *and* Herausfordern

	Hervorbringen (revealing)	Herausfordern (challenging)
Material	From the earth and sky.	Resource, raw material, increasingly immaterial and interchangeable.
Form	That which (already) is.	That which is this, or that, depending on use or 'purpose'.
Final/end	Purpose, completion of the arrival, *telos*. The thing's indebtedness to function, for instance. So a sculpture in its setting, a chalice in its ritual, each giving to life in some way.	Means/end, fashion. Rendering of 'objects' to being available, standing reserve so that more can be produced/ manufactured. 'Ends' are suspended continually; replaced by further processes, becoming itself merely a means for further challenges.
Efficient/agency	Tightening/*Verfestigen*, a lingering of involvement, slow agency, contemplative (*logos*) gathering of the causal fourfold which gives forth, without direction.	*Fertigen* (manufacturing and management); setting upon and being set upon through challenging forth in intensive cycles of: *Erschließen* – unlocking *Fördern* – extracting *Speichern* – storing *Verteilen* – distributing *Umschalten* – switching.

elevates urban above rural needs, that concentrates power in the hands of those who control the taps, that enlists huge bodies of labour, that connects to globally configured distribution networks. It was the need to justify investment in dams that led to the creation of cost-benefit analysis, a calculating tool for managerial economics designed to measure and weigh up the cause/effect structures of any scheme; only neither the costs nor the benefits could ever be estimated with any surety, so complex and evolving were the forces in play. Once one relation was identified in a dam project, another emerged down or upstream, or way away in the big city for which the dam was being built as a water supply, well in part, because its construction was also, for example, a way of elevating a political elite who had promised jobs to an otherwise redundant labour force, and as we know, idleness is wasteful and corrosive of character, unless it is the idleness of the reservoir water itself, which is awaiting its release, being made to stand forth, protected behind signs and security measures, ready to be set upon, endlessly on call, as a resource. It lies still, then suddenly it is off, funnelled down into pipes, there to drive generator turbines which feed into electricity cables hung from pylons that pinion the landscape between one settlement and the next. The cable feeds a substation, which feeds factory machinery that produces other machine parts which are then boxed, stored, distributed and used to move yet other machines; and so the flow goes, everywhere things being challenged by other things. Conceptually, Heidegger breaks this challenging or setting upon into organized sequences of: *Erschließen* – unlocking; *Fördern* – extracting; *Speichern* – storing; *Verteilen* – distributing; *Umschalten* – switching. Specific causes and effects are being named, continually, but they remain representations circulating in the language of strategic discussions, barely touching the experience of challenging forth they ostensively define.

As the power of the water's flow is unlocked and extracted through generators users relate to the river increasingly as a source of power (or transport, irrigation, water supply); a thing that stores energy that requires exploitation and through ever more efficient means. Where the windmill stands isolated, a steady but dependent agency, reticent, the damming and mechanization of the river represents an entirely different order of organization in which political, social and economic forms vie endlessly to articulate and further their ends, none of which quite align, but all of which carry cogency insofar as they can – as named ends – be transformed into means to serve other ends, extending the reach of management into an infinity of naming. As the essence of technology is the *Gestell*, the essence of the *Gestell* is the danger (*die Gefahr*) of the forgetting of being because it positions everything, putting it in its place.[65]

Herausfordern strives after control, a positioning of the human being as the *Schöpfer*/creator, as the crucial and central originator for the causation of effects, the genius of lightening behind the flash from which individual 'other destroying' source innovation springs. The 'letting' side of *Hervorbringen* eschews this zero-sum elevation of a solitary cause, instead entailing an awareness of the limited possibilities of human intervention and of the 'wider' systemic interrelations that render any attempt at complete control or sight feeble and dangerous. Here Heidegger draws out a stark distinction between placing the human 'maker' as the initiator of things (thus replacing mysticism, the Gods, nature) and as the steward of things. The latter is a starting up, a setting in motion, an arrival at the beginning of something without any prospect of how once begun things will unfold. The former is a gathering of the setting upon things that, with some irony, sets upon human beings themselves as they too are challenged to stand and make themselves available for ordering as a standing reserve (*Bestand*). Things exist because they are means to

---

[65] Martin Heidegger *Leitgedanken*, 320.

ends (potential or actual); they are confined by a functional condition of being known 'as something ...'. Thus, knowing equates to an enframing (*Gestell*), 'the gathering together of that setting upon that sets upon man, i.e., challenges him forth, to reveal the real, in the mode of ordering, as standing reserve',[66] where *stellen* means both setting upon and producing and presenting what is brought forth in organization.

The sight we see is a presenting of things enframed as *Bestand*. This reserve is more than a supply of resources, more than a stockpile, rather it designates that everything that 'is', is so in terms of availability; to be available is to be made ready (unlocked) to be extracted, stored, distributed and switched over into something else. There is no end to this extracting, storing, distributing and switching, as an ordered supply of calculable and present reserve. *Bestand* becomes the collective term for the constant ordering of things in organized cycles of standing out, unlocking, extracting, distributing, storing and switching; a 'calculable coherence of forces'.

---

[66] Martin Heidegger *The Question Concerning Technology*, 302.

6 Strategy as World Picture

An ontology of distance and order has given rise to the spread of the Gigantic; the world is nothing but a picture:

> Where the world becomes picture, what is, in its entirety, is juxtaposed as that for which man is prepared and which, correspondingly, he therefore intends to bring before himself and have before himself, and consequently intends in a decisive sense to set in place before himself ... Hence world picture, when understood essentially, does not mean a picture of the world but the world conceived and grasped as picture.[1]

The confluence of the orderability of all things, including humans, is the notion of the *Gestell*; the distancing of relations that continually displace what is near with what is faraway, thus relating human concern continually to the Gigantic, finds expression in the world picture, that is in re-presentation. It is possible to point to a number of key developments that indicate this move towards picturing and which culminate, argued Heidegger, in the technology of the radio.

The first form of picturing technology made generally available as a product for discerning consumers, artists or otherwise, was a Claude glass (see Figure 6.1). A tinted, portable mirror, often in the shape of an oval, designed to be held aloft by the viewer (see Figure 6.2) to contain and reflect the entirety of a view in such a way that it rendered the scene in a balanced but subtly dramatic hue of contrasting, tinted light, in emulation of the French landscape painter Claude Lorrain (d.1682). The landscape was filtered, categorized, becoming immediately a place figured through a specific aesthetic form in which human narratives are enveloped in naturally balanced contrasts: ruin and civilization, near and far, adventure and nostalgia, vast and small. It was a form to which all well-bred people would affectively respond in an appropriately refined way.

Thomas Gray in his journal written on a tour of the English Lake District was an early advocate for the glass, suggesting the visitor use it to

---

[1] Martin Heidegger *The Question Concerning Technology*, 129.

Figure 6.1 William Gilpin, watercolour study, c. 1782–1804. Victoria and Albert Museum. O1040728

frame what otherwise might appear as an untutored jumble of imposing rocks and unchanneled water. In publishing his journals Gray was, in the spirit of an autodidact, schooling readers in how to develop an aesthetic sensitivity for the virtuous and hence enhancing classical verse of Virgil and Horace, writers whose antique sensitivity to nature provided a readymade example for those able to extend, test and temper their taste by having it encompass the rough expanse of raw landscape.

But not so raw as all that. For Gray, an advocate of the picturesque (here meaning the world reduced to a picture), what was wild and untouched should be made available through the aesthetic poise of a balanced composition in which dangers (inaccessible pinnacles, terrifying heights) and decay (ruins, evening light) were accompanied by human drama and promise. In seeing and representing the scene the viewer would be 'taken in' as such, as a source of uplifting and educational stimulation.[2] Gray's journals describe how he himself was able to use the glass to contain what was otherwise overwhelming:

[2] Though overtly Western in its skew, the picturesque movement of the eighteenth century replays similar feelings to those found, say, in tenth-century Sung China. Here artists

Figure 6.2 Thomas Gainsborough, *Man Holding a Claude Glass*, undated. Graphite on paper. Yale Centre for British Art. B1975.4.24.

our path here tends to the left, & the ground gently rising, & cover'd with a glade of scattering trees & bushes on the very margin of the water, opens both ways the most delicious view, that my eyes ever beheld. behind you are the magnificent heights of Walla-crag; opposite lie the thick hanging woods of Ld Egremont, & Newland-valley with green & smiling fields embosom'd in the dark cliffs; to the left the jaws of Borodale, with that turbulent Chaos of mountain behind mountain roll'd in confusion; beneath you, & stretching far away to the right, the shining purity of the Lake, just ruffled by the breeze enough to shew it is alive, reflecting rocks, woods, fields, & inverted tops of mountains, back to top 1080 with the white buildings of Keswick, Crosthwait-church, & Skiddaw for a back-ground at distance. oh Doctor! I never wish'd more for you; & pray think,

also found a didactic force in landscape, civilization was grounded in the apprehension of landscape (its suggestion of an ordered, harmonious world in which government was mirrored in the solid elevation of the mountain encircling its fertile foothills, valleys and bodies of water). The landscape is a scrolled journey of an examined life that has been lived in happiness, in pain, in melancholy, but always of refinement. Appreciating the earth as a place to live, as a source of plenitude, is an integral aspect of this refinement. Virgil had written similarly, his *Georgics* indelibly marked with a sensitivity to the pullulations of the earth and how these give to and take from life: the bounty and perfection of a place beyond but intimate to the human world, one that is compelling in its abundance, and inspiring in its inscrutability.

how the glass played its part in such a spot, which is called Carf-close-reeds: I chuse to set down these barbarous names, that any body may enquire on the place, & easily find the particular station, that I mean. this scene continues to Barrow-gate, & a little farther, passing a brook called Barrow-beck, we enter'd Borodale. the crags, named Lodoor-banks now begin to impend terribly over your way.[3]

'Stations' were viewing points from where the visitor was encouraged to stand and take in an intensely rendered scene. Gray's journals, written in 1769, became a de facto guide to the Lakes, organizing tourists along prescribed points, instructing them in how to turn their backs to the view so they might reflect it in their Claude glass. The use of the glass was further encouraged in Thomas West's *Guide to the Lakes* published in 1778. West, a preacher from Scotland, wanted to extend the reach of picturesque by explicitly encouraging readers to visit the north of England, hitherto thought rude and savage by the refined and moneyed classes of London and surrounding 'home' counties. By providing a detailed map of the stations, and describing in detail how best to reach the exact spot, West was providing safe passage towards the ideal positioning from which nature would reveal itself; it was wilderness contained in a hand-held device.[4]

Not content with a small pocket mirror, tourists (and painters) quickly scaled up the mediated experience by employing portable camera obscura. Consisting of a light-proof box with a small hole, this device worked as a noise filter that only admitted a few rays of light, thereby blocking scattered distortions and focussing the scene into a single bundle of straight lines, re-presenting, on the inside of the box, a sharp image of an object or view of the outside world. These visual representations gathered through the self-depiction of nature allowed for the rapid execution of perspective paintings, simply by painting over the image that the bundled rays projected onto the paper or canvas inside the box. Friedrich Kittler elaborates on the transformational influence of the camera obscura by arguing the camera not merely functioned as a painting aide but, by automatically recording images, as a 'first-order simulation',

---

[3] Quote taken from *Journal of a Visit to the Lake District in 1769 (1971)*. Edited by Herbert W. Starr. *Thomas Gray Archive*, 1 May 2019. Accessed 15 May 2019. <www.thomasgray.org/cgi-bin/view.cgi?collection=primary&edition=TWS_1971iii&page=1079>

[4] Jonathan Bate *The Song of the Earth*. Cambridge, MA: Harvard University Press. 2000. 'That massive branch of the modern tourist industry, the journey back to nature, has its origins here. The early tourists went armed with guidebook, sketchpad, Claude glass and sometimes camera obscura' (127). Bate concludes '[T]he ultimate gesture of the picturesque is that in which the genteel viewer stands on her promontory, turns her back on the view itself and takes out her Claude glass' (133).

made reality appear on a wall.[5] Larger, more elaborate versions found their way into entertainment industries where musical performances were held in night-clad rooms with camera obscura projections of moving pictures sending audiences into 'ecstasies', but not of the ec-statical kind vaunted by Emerson.[6]

As technology developed, these first-order representations – a kind of naming of seeing – became doubled with the emergence of the 'magic lantern', which placed a light-source inside the camera obscura box, and in reversing the direction, functioned as a light projector that re-presented images placed in front of a lens system in enlarged form onto an outside background.[7] In sliding a representation (the source image) into the box, and illuminating this representation so that a second-order simulation in form of the re-presented representation emerged on a wall, the magic lantern established a new kind of relationship with the image. No longer just representing nature or real objects, the images, often of saints or of the flames of hell, enveloped the image with affective meanings.[8]

John Martin, town planner and painter of pantomimes, and one of three brothers known as the mad Martins because of their Millenarian tendencies, intensified and then commercialized the representations emerging from the use of light technologies. He was self-taught, concentrating on the depiction of largely biblical scenes, rendering them as though they were huge stage sets against which the viewer was to feel small and overwhelmed, yet still able to absorb and easily read the symbolism.

Belshazaar's Feast from 1820 (Figure 6.3), for example, encompasses nothing less than infinity, and does so with an exactitude and gargantuan size that creates a spectacle. Martin broke the then current conventions of landscape painting by not even attempting to depict the world 'out

---

[5] Friedrich Kittler *Optical Media: Berlin Lectures*. Translated by Anthony Ends. Cambridge: Polity. 2002, 50ff. Kittler argues that before the invention of the lens as an optical device for more efficient bundling of light, these boxes only allowed for very small holes to avoid multiple, out-of-focus projections, and early examples of the device were accordingly found in sun-rich places such as Italy rather than the somewhat more overcast, 'wetter' English lakes. See also Alexander Galloway *The Interface Effect*. Cambridge: Polity Press. 2012, 14.

[6] Friedrich Kittler *Gramophone, Film, Typewriter*. Translated by Geoffrey Winthrop-Young and Michael Wutz. Stanford: Stanford University Press. 1999, 121.

[7] Galloway notes that the progression from the magic lantern to modern-day film projectors retain this 'second-order' quality of the magic lantern while adding a new simulation on the axis of time and it takes the television to more fundamentally upset these functions in the representation of images through pixels and grids before the computer, finally, annihilates the imagery entirely in its reduction of all things into writing (code). Alexander Galloway If the cinema is an ontology, the computer is an ethic. In *Kittler Now*. Edited by Steven Sale and Laura Salisbury. Cambridge: Polity. 2015, 175–91, 179.

[8] Friedrich Kittler *Optical Media*, 79.

Figure 6.3 John Martin, *Belshazzar's Feast*, c. 1820. Half-size sketch held by the Yale Center for British Art. Google Art Project

there', but to use its picturesque conventions to create a spectacle of affect. Upon purchasing it, one William Collins took it on a tour, showing it not only in galleries throughout the UK but in music halls, and using mood enhancing bulls-eye lanterns and gas lighting to heighten the drama, all with an accompanying pamphlet on how to read the painting written by Martin. God's wrathful hand invisibly appears through a storm-lit sky to etch a prophecy of doom onto the palace. Belshazaar has had the temerity to use sacred vessels to serve wine at a feast to which all the Babylonians have thronged, leaving in the distance their hanging gardens and ziggurat. The entire city is concentrated into this one event, foretelling the demise of its king, who can do nothing but cower in shock as the prophet Daniel, centre stage, reads the writing on the wall.[9] The content of the message in the image itself is elusive, it needs deciphering

---

[9] The painting has served as a grounding reference for film directors (Griffith, de Mille, Emmerich), both technically in the development of cinemascope and symbolically in terms of portraying staged epics and disasters. Griffith, for example, in his 1916 film 'Intolerance', working with a fixed camera, learned from this painting how to direct a viewer's attention across a scene, as did Harryhausen, whose was experimenting with the use of lock shots upon which other images might

by a prophet, but there is no mistaking the immortal medium whose vigorous flash of anger illuminates the vainglory beneath. The message does not need interpreting with any exactitude, it is there for all to feel, and the affect is fear, embellished by Martin's painterly pyrotechnics, and Collins' light and sound effects. Audiences were transfixed: they bore witness to a new, old world.[10]

Strategic Pictures

These early picturing technologies exhibit an interplay of a first- and then second-order form of representation whose structuring both mirrors and fosters what is typically thought of as strategic understanding. In strategy the equivalent first-order form of self-presentation amounts to increasingly sophisticated attempts at gathering information about the view 'out there' (commercial markets, military assets and terrain of battle, political climate) using equivalents of the Claude glass (strategists also tend to look through their measuring devices, with their back turned to the world). These equivalents to the Claude glass frame, colour and unify the world out there in an approachable (tasteful) way: there are, for example, two-by-two matrices, rising arrows, lines of relation between agreed categories. The world arrives already mediated into neat configurations ready to be counted, weighed and measured, it is presented before the strategist ready prepared. The second-order form comes with the organizational attempt to project itself outwards, employing increasingly visual aids not only to talk of, but also embody, the flora and fauna of the strategic world: ambition, threats, values, visions and missions.

These media–technological developments engendered new ways of seeing the self, those which Heidegger called the 'world picture', represented also in Descartes' representation of the subject that is re-presented to the subject again in the famous 'cogito ergo sum' (Figure 6.4), which

then be superimposed. See John Martin I, Jonathan Griffin. *Tate Etc*, 2011, 23 (Autumn). A show at Tate Britain in 2012 vividly recreated the effect of Martin's work, animating them with lighting and sound in a theatre space, immersing viewers in another world entirely, one where time flows and space opens differently.

[10] Friedrich Kittler *Optical Media*, 72. Though criticized as an artistic trickster, Martin's works became, arguably, the most seen art works of the nineteenth century. His even larger scale triptych of the last judgment painted in 1851–1853 was reputed to have been seen by over eight million paying visitors, entranced by an immediacy of scale and righteous affect. See Martin Myrone John Martin's Last Judgement triptych: The apocalyptic sublime in the age of spectacle. In *The Art of the Sublime*. Edited by Nigel Llewellyn and Christine Riding. Tate Research Publication, January 2013. Accessed 18 December 2019. www.tate.org.uk/art/research-publications/the-sublime/martin-myrone-john-martins-last-judgement-triptych-the-apocalyptic-sublime-in-the-age-of-r1141419

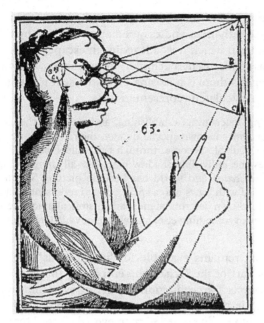

Figure 6.4 Reproduced from *Descartes: The World and Other Writings*. Cambridge: Cambridge University Press. Figure 64, p. 154.

then Kittler rebrands as: 'I am because I can represent anything presented before me.'[11]

Alexander Galloway elaborates on how such a world picture begins to create a sense of self whose self-presentations are configured in a mirror play of machine-like capabilities: seeing, touching, hearing, processing sensory data, moving muscles and the like: 'The Cartesian self does what the magic lantern had already demonstrated: [it] projects a representation, the thinking mind, back inwards towards a previous representation, the self, and therefore (for Descartes at least) shores up the metaphysical relation.'[12] As such, the self finds itself being cut off from the world, and instead entombed in endless cycles of representation of a world 'out there' being processed 'in here', within the subject operating the Claude glass and magic lantern, so to speak. For in here, within, is the seat of consciousness, whereas out there it is all mechanical, including most of our own selves each of whom is as subject to the mute and indifferent

[11] Friedrich Kittler *Optical Media*, 75.
[12] Alexander Galloway *If Cinema Is an Ontology*, 179. Zahn spent some time working with one of the early pioneers of the magic lantern, Johan Griendel

laws of the universe as a sloth or a stone. Yet really what is it to be in here? It is nothing more than an endless mediation realized by the very mechanical ordering from which it is, allegedly, an escape.

In the wake of this modern encroachment of machinery into thought itself, Heidegger suggests there is a closing off of the self, it is concealed and sealed-off behind calculated representations:

> the gigantic, in planning, calculating, establishing, and securing, changes from the quantitative and becomes its own special quality, then the gigantic and the seemingly completely calculable become, through this shift, incalculable. This incalculability becomes the indivisible shadow cast over all things when man [sic] has become the *subiectum* and world has become picture. Through this shadow the modern world withdraws into a space beyond representation and so lends to the incalculable its own determinateness and historical uniqueness. This shadow, however, points to something else, knowledge of which, to us moderns, is refused....[13]

The knowledge that remains available for 'us moderns' is of things already organized as part of the *Gestell*, the enframing that positions us and the world as resources for production, rendering everything ready to be used and exploited in the service of technological thinking. Humans no longer dwell with things. Even the German everyday word for a thing, *Gegenstand*, takes on a different meaning once cleaved by Heidegger's literal word play through which it becomes a thing that stands-against (*Gegen-stand*), and thus no longer as a unified entity, but as a represented (*vor-gestellt*) and oftentimes produced (*her-gestellt*), object held in a position of waiting to be called (*be-stellt*) upon as a reserve (*Be-stand*) and used in an already determined cycle of production and consumption. This rendering of things as framed in productive cycles is the essence of technology; the *Gestell* is therefore not this or that piece of equipment or a specific factory (or its image) but, rather, an *a priori* positioning of everything – ourselves included; and it is on the basis of this framing that any actual production can begin.

No General in General Motors

If Heidegger is right in his analysis of the sway of technology over human existence, we are beholden to significantly alter, if not reverse, our understanding of the very possibility of strategy. Certainly, it can never really be – as Arendt might have hoped for in the hands of a modern form of *strategos* – a practice of authentic self-presenting constituted in free and opening experiences of action. Nor is it even an instrumental relation with

---

[13] Martin Heidegger The age of the world picture, 72, Our emphasis.

things in which distinct, intentionally motivated strategic agents settle upon and pursue given ends through the management of specific means, both material and symbolic. At best, it seems, strategy understood as a struggle for self-presentation, reveals strategists as having been thrown into an end-making complex that is always already positioning them (even in their strategic questioning) within an organizational *Umwelt*. Strategy becomes the endless processing of an information-technical apparatus in which all the possibilities for decision making and vision can in principle already be pictured because they all, already belong, to the world.

We therefore have to break with what has become a dominant picture for strategy, especially business strategy, of a single figure or leadership group determining the shape of an organization or scenario over which they sit, like patriarchs of the household. It is an antique image that finds its apotheosis in Alfred Pritchard Sloan Jr.'s memoirs *My Years with General Motors*,[14] published in 1963, after some delay over lawyers' fears of antitrust lawsuits on the basis of the book's boasts about market manipulation (another form of strategic innovation). Sloan's is a narrative of reasoning, vision and strength of character in which a maker of horse carriages is transformed into a massively scaled producer of automobiles designed to encapsulate an idealized lifestyle for millions of customers. Sloan is represented as the figure who presided over the transformation, creating an organization that, over time, became a vast, ordered flow of communications between it and its wider environment. Its success was a function of the accuracy and speed with which it was able to subsume the world 'out there' into a gigantic scene of operations of which its strategists were the governors: they regulated the flows of investment, evened-out the cycles of productive effort, and sequenced the desire of consumers. Sloan pictures himself as at the apex of this scene, the head of an Executive Committee populated by division heads, all of whom were held aloft in large, high buildings, removed from the concrete surroundings of daily manufacture and sales, but intimately connected to

---

[14] Listed as recently as 2011, as one of the twenty-five most influential business and management books by *Time Magazine*: http://content.time.com/time/specials/packages/completelist/0,29569,2086680,00.html

In a 2014 *HBR* review of the book *My Years with General Motors, 50 Years On*, Friedman sees the era of 'organization men' eroding in the face of networking and digital firms, but still argues that 'despite the wholesale changes in the business landscape, there are timeless lessons in *My Years at General Motors* ... The lasting value of Sloan's book is not really the dream, but the ambition, detail, and scale with which he commercialized it. Sloan was the consummate organization-builder. His vision was evident in the very structure of the new multidivisional firm, which divided the American automobile market into five price segments'. https://hbr.org/2014/03/my-years-with-general-motors-fifty-years-on

them via an array of micro-representations in the mediating form of networked information flows. These representations could not convey awareness of the individual lives being affected by decision making (as Brecht complained, such pictures are not troubled by vestiges of human sorrow). But they did not need to deal with affect. The impression of awe was no longer anything wild, but of order and progress.[15] The picture that Sloan and the General Motors' board members presented to themselves and others was the representation of an organization: it was a world of orthogonal divisional structures jointed by well-defined roles and committees linking policy and operations, of integrated branding and sales trajectories married to carefully regulated consumer aspiration, and of manufacturing steeped in clearly calibrated work patterns and responsibilities. The strategists, those designing the policy, were to be separated from day-to-day operations. They occupied corporate headquarters, they ran a central office, they controlled the allocation of all budgets. As strategists, they looked upon their gigantic organizational world as if from afar.[16] It was no different from the picture an astronomer has of the circumference, velocity or density of a planet or sun, and just as distant.[17]

Not only did the neatness of Alfred Sloan's narrative picture of General Motors suffer from abstracting distance, it itself, as a representation

---

[15] This required skilled managers and lawyers capable of working in different, often unspecifiable settings, and so far better to keep them employed in-house, and loyal. With growth also comes the increasing hazard of managerial frailty, either because of ineptitude or opportunistic behaviour, both of which need organizational correction, warranting yet more growth in the form of accurate information collection, inspection, auditing, regulatory compliance and so on. The more apparent are asset specificity, complexity and moral hazard, the more logical is a Multidivisional (M-form) organization, which in turn requires statistical and financial controls coupled with a clear separation of the operations within each division from the strategic planning work at the top of the organization, thus limiting the potential for self-interested actions by partisan division representatives that could be detrimental to the organization in its entirety as well as keeping top executives, whose information is largely restricted to financial and statistical data, from involving themselves in divisional affairs, of which they lack detailed knowledge. And so it is, in a curious way, that General Motors may be remembered less for the vehicles it has produced and more for its organizational form, which was revisited continually in strategic thinking, to the point of its being a default structure for any large business: deviations from its natural practicality had to be thoroughly justified. The strategic significance of the M-form lies with its creating a form of management dedicated to *universal* forms of oversight, or what be more colloquially known as a general perspective. Sloan dis-assembled and re-assembled the collection of firms gathered in the sprawling General Motors conglomerate by taking the idea of the general very seriously indeed. The resulting M-Form realizes such a general or universal condition by identifying and then separating the powers and interests of firm owners, central management, divisional directors and operational employees.

[16] See Harold Wolff The great GM mystery. *Harvard Business Review*. May 1964.

[17] Hannah Arendt *The Human Condition*, 264.

of the representations so to speak, was fabricated. The book was not, in fact, written by Sloan, but by a business journalist called John McDonald who, in turn, hired another Alfred, the business historian Alfred Chandler Jr, as a research assistant.[18] In his reflections on writing Sloan's book, and following the lawsuit with General Motors over its release, McDonald wrote:

My take on the corporation story was to give particular attention to strategic situations where individuals, institutions, and groups of various kinds interacted interdependently and thought in ways – both cooperatively and noncooperatively – that escaped common classical economic and decision theory. This concept of strategy came from game theory, which has become more widely known since 1994, when three game theorists received the Nobel prize in economics. With the help of its original developers, John von Neumann and Oskar Morgenstern, I had done studies in game theory and had written on the subject, for Fortune in 1949 and in the book *Strategy in Poker, Business, and War*, which was published by Norton in 1950. I thought I could do a good job on Sloan and General Motors somewhat along these lines if I had the materials.[19]

In this 1950 book a section entitled 'the game of business', McDonald advances a game-like situation between two grocery stores who have settled into a non-competitive alliance.[20] They make 'a coalition against the consumer; they play a two-man game with each other which results in taking more money from the consumer'. Once a new supermarket comes along, however, offering lower prices (based on efficiencies) it is the supermarket and the consumer making a coalition (convention)

---

[18] Christopher D. McKenna Writing the ghost-writer back in. Alfred Sloan, Alfred Chandler, John McDonald and the intellectual origins of corporate strategy. *Management and Organizational History*, 2006, 1 (2): 107–26. 2006

[19] John McDonald *A Ghost's Memoir: The Making of Alfred P. Sloan's My Years with General Motors*. Cambridge MA: MIT Press. 2003, 16.

[20] To quote: 'Like all economic theories, the theory of games is based on the assumption that man seeks gain ... [and] that man is rational, whereas it is generally believed that man is more often irrational. The "player" here must be willing to forgo maximum desires, to remember that he is not, like Robinson Crusoe, alone in what he wants ... he must be willing and able to recognize and come to terms with his conflicting desires and actions of others ... the theory of games establishes a concept of a strategy though which conflicting maximum desires can be reconciled in an optimum ... the strategic situation ... lies in the interaction between two or more persons, each of whose actions is based on an expectation concerning the actions of others over whom he has no control. The outcome is dependent on the personal moves of the participants [and] the policy followed in making these moves is strategy', John McDonald *Strategy in Poker, Business and War*. New York: Norton, 15–17. It is also telling that Norbert Wiener, perhaps one of the few mathematical equals to von Neumann, believed that such strategic theories and programmes were significantly flawed in terms of their assumptions about human reasoning and decision making – and that those people and societies that all too eagerly trusted electronic systems based on such logics were putting themselves at enormous risk. Flo Conway and Jim Siegelman *Dark Hero of the Information Age: In Search of Norbert Wiener the Father of Cybernetics*. New York: Basic Books. 2005.

against the grocer coalition where the supermarket receives payments in profit and the consumer reaps savings. The game is not over, however, when the grocers disappear, because, unless the supermarket has other competitors, it can now raise prices at the consumers' expense as a single-firm monopoly. The whole affair is therefore, in McDonald's analysis, a question of 'structure' and position (numbers, sizes and their relationships), as was, then, the representation of General Motors.[21]

It is easy to see how McDonald's interest in coalitions and small-number games attracted him to the world of a real-life oligopoly player in the form of General Motors. What is concealed, however, is how one of the foundational texts in business strategy was written by a ghost writer retrofitting game theory onto Sloan's actions. Hence the influence of the book on the development of strategy as taught in business schools is coined not so much by the practical reflections of a successful strategist, but by the rhetorical skills of a writer schooled in game theory. As McKenna reminds us, there were, of course, other influences too. Chandler, in particular, was trained at Harvard by the famous institutional sociologist Talcott Parsons, but despite the rational appeal of Parsons' structural–functional models to understanding strategic activity, their theoretical complexity made the operationalization into business research difficult, and there is some evidence that Chandler's 'structure follows strategy', which became the touchstone mantra for generations of business school educated strategists, takes intellectual inspiration from the collaboration on 'my years with General Motors', and thus as much from McDonald's elaboration of strategic positions as from Parsons' theoretical systems.[22] Rather than being a direct piece of reportage, the foundational text in business strategy thinking is itself a reflection on the rational mind of a strategist, viewed through the prism of a game-theorist ghost-writer and a sociologically trained historian. Its message of strategic oversight and control emerges from an idealized and heavily theorized idea of an organizational form being structured through an environment of feedback and control processes, and of communication and data-processing apparatuses, that themselves are representing the world continually, charted from a distance, as picture: strategy was born as a mode of challenging forth.

Strategy has been tipping inexorably into a flow of pictured occurrence whose feedback flows are so mobile and multiple that strategists, whilst

---

[21] John McDonald *Strategy in Poker, Business and War*, 105–6. There is, of course, an additional player in business in form of the USA state and its antitrust laws, foremost the Sherman Act against monopolies and conspiracies. It is this act that led lawyers at General Motors to delay the publication of Sloan's 'my years with general motors' for several years over worries it could be used as evidence.

[22] Christopher D. McKenna Writing the ghost-writer back in, 113–14.

they possess increasingly distinct, current and accurate information with which to populate representations, lack the means of orientation by which to gain a perspective and use these images in the development of an organizational self.

The loss of perspective to which strategy becomes prone appears to be inherent to technologically mediated organization, a condition that becomes most apparent when the organizational effort is at its most intense, namely with the rise of totalitarian systems and what Arendt observes is their 'perpetual-motion mania', their restlessness, the understanding 'that they can remain in power only so long as they keep moving and set everything around them in motion'.[23] The movement is a refusal to accept things as they are, to refuse their distinction as things, and to thereby transform all things into carriers of an idea, an idea that has no end save its own organized perfectibility. The quality of the idea makes little difference, the organization is similar: totalitarian systems dedicated to the snuffing out of life in the service of such movement:

If it is the law of nature to eliminate everything that is harmful and unfit to live, it would mean the end of nature itself if new categories of the harmful and unfit-to-live could not be found; if it is the law of history that in a class struggle certain classes 'wither away,' it would mean the end of human history itself if rudimentary new classes did not form, so that they in turn could 'wither away' under the hands of totalitarian rulers. In other words, the law of killing by which totalitarian movements seize and exercise power would remain a law of the movement even if they ever succeeded in making all of humanity subject to their rule.[24]

The ensuing terror emerges from a loss of distinction and judgment; even the rulers are simply media for the inexorable force of nature or history, the law of movement, in whose maws the vast plurality of a people become 'One Man of gigantic dimensions'.[25] The space both between people (the distinctiveness so strongly revealed by those in whom it is most precarious, the refugee) and within people (the two-in-one dialogue of authenticity) is obliterated by the suprahuman idea of nature or history. And the obliteration is continual, for as new people are born, new sources of distinction and natality emerge, which need eliminating, in order to clarify and purify the natural and historical idea and to hasten its realization, not in conviction, but as a necessity. In a totalitarian system you are either media of the state and party, or executed.

Totalitarian systems work through ideological representations that picture conditions as historical movement, an imaginary: of a passage

---

[23] Hannah Arendt *Origins of Totalitarianism*, 306
[24] Hannah Arendt *Origins of Totalitarianism*, 464.
[25] Hannah Arendt *Origins of Totalitarianism*, 466

from an origin to a destiny within which everything had a necessary place; of alienation, an image of revelation of a reality that lies behind the appearance of things, accessible only to those with requisite theoretical sensitivity; and finally of axioms from which one can logically or dialectically deduce the essential grounding of all things.[26] Once tested against experience, however, these pictures prove hard to sustain, the immense effort of maintaining a 'true' reality of movement to which the 'falsities' of immediately present, everyday life ought be subjected are frequently overwhelming. The inevitability of an unfolding truth becomes snagged against alternate deductions, and in being stalled in this way a movement slows, exposing itself to the questioning of those having to live out its predictions, in spite of their experience.

That particular instances of totalitarianism inevitably exhaust themselves in their own accelerating enthusiasm is part of historical record, but the movement of which they are avowedly a natural or historical expression is maintained. Instead of ideas of nature or history represented as laws of which people were to be medial carriers (or die), we now find a technologically mediated movement, without the need for law-like warrant. This is the second form of loss Arendt identifies, tentatively, and one which takes in us all.

Earth and Universe

In the final chapter of *Human Condition*, Hannah Arendt revisits the prologue of her book where she introduced the launch of the Sputnik satellite, continuing to diagnose how we as a species have found our direct experiences of a living earth being mediated by representations of a measured globe, to the point where humans seem to have (through the world picture) taken 'full possession of [their] mortal dwelling place and gathered infinite horizons'.[27] The spread and affective reach of these representations has only intensified since the book's publication in 1958, making Arendt's analysis even more prescient. We no longer live on the earth, but inhabit a globe, orbiting in a universe, where 'nothing can remain immense if it can be measured' (the Gigantic that Heidegger called small). As both Arendt and Heidegger attest, such representations are peculiarly modern.[28]

---

[26] Hannah Arendt *Origins of Totalitarianism*, 470–1.

[27] Hannah Arendt *The Human Condition*, 250.

[28] For Parmenides, for example, 'truth is to be found only in a place "far from the beaten path of human beings"', where reliably true judgments can be made from a perfect 'god's eye' standpoint, far removed from the 'mere' appearances of everyday beliefs and conceptions. Martha Nussbaum *The Fragility of Goodness*, 241. And it is in this context of a non-representational

For the moderns 'what-is' becomes a question of representation, one that is of a twofold order: first representing a view of the world 'out there' through positioning and idealizing media like the Claude glass, and second concealing the world altogether under the impress of images emerging from picture-producing devices such as a magic lantern.

The effects of the first order of transformation include: the incessant outpouring of mass-produced objects made possible by exponential gains in operational efficiency; increasingly rapid product development cycles; ever wider global sourcing and distribution networks; and exponential increases in the sheer number and variety of the products, equipment and services being offered. With the second order of transformation, at least in Heidegger's analysis, comes a sensitivity to a growing uniformity of subjectification. Writing in a period marked by the emergence of mass media, Heidegger's examples include the radio, the television and the telephone and, in this, argues his untimely successor Friedrich Kittler, he was the first thinker 'on whom the question of nearness dawned'.[29] With the dawning of nearness comes an opening up to distance of a measured form which, being measured, makes it of no distance at all. This eradicates the coming together of the four causes from human making: form, matter, *telos* and the maker. The fashioning of bowl, or planting a field with hand tools, requires the presence (*anwesen*) of the maker; the presence of materials such as clay or seed, and models and plans for pottery and harvesting, and gods

---

understanding of language and the world that mythos and logos were the same, referring to a 'word or 'story' – a 'mythologos' being a 'storyteller'. David Greenham *The Resurrection of the Body: The Work of Norman O. Brown*. Oxford: Lexington Books. 2006, 27. However, unlike Parmenides, and unlike Plato's striving for the ideal and thus for an objective and external 'god's eye view', Aristotle emphasized the importance of practical reason. Martha Nussbaum *The Fragility of Goodness*, 292. Yet, this does not diminish the importance of being able to give a general account (*logos*) when making (*technē*) something, as only then can we speak of the kind of deliberate reasoning that is a hallmark of excellence when the *technai* brings about higher ends by making something. Joseph Dunne *Back to the Rough Ground*, 259. But what are the features of these general accounts, if not those of objective, scientific objectivity? One approach is through Aristotle's careful distinction in medicine between general, class-based accounts and individual ones when he suggests that: 'None of the *technai* theorizes about individual cases ... only about what will help to cure any or all of a given class of patients ... – individual cases are so infinitely various that no knowledge of them is possible.' Joseph Dunne *Back to the rough ground*: 259. When making something, the *technai* therefore does not need, or rather cannot have, a fixed idea of what the specific individual product will be like. This would be rather problematic as making something usually entails situational responsiveness: the farmer pays heed to the soil and the weather in the same way in which a carpenter has to work with the pattern of the wood at her disposal. Excellence therefore meant not that each product must abide by some particular objective standard, but rather that the *technai* makes the best use of the available materials in the given situation, as the realm of the practical is inherently indefinite and indeterminate Martha Nussbaum *The Fragility of Goodness*, 303; Richard Rojcewicz *The Gods and Technology*, 60.

[29] Friedrich Kittler *The Truth of the Technological World*, 291.

to whom altars can be dedicated and rituals devoted, and mortals who can dwell on the earth and use bowls from which to eat crops. Bereft of such nearness, only the distant now comes close; and the distant is, in Heidegger, the Gigantic, and telescopic, that far-brought-near concern with world affairs that always already lies beyond any immediate engagement with the here and now, which finds itself eternally discounted in favour of a reached-for future. The strategist lives in this reached-for future, always having to look ahead, and being pressed back into the present by this future that refuses to ever reveal itself, and which stands there, setting itself against life as a representation of lack and absence that the strategist must fill, though never can.

In the context of strategy, Arendt's last chapter is compelling because its prognosis for self-understanding is one in which the earth is always being framed by the closeness and accuracy of distances. It stems, she suggests, from a Cartesian doubt that in coming to know about ourselves and our world we can trust neither the everyday world, nor our senses. It is a doubt, Arendt notes, that replaces the ancient Greek sense of wonder (*thaumazein*) that the world is indeed sensually given and may reveal *itself*. To allay this doubt we recede into ourselves, and find there the ideal of being able re-produce our own world rather than accept what is being immediately experienced as a definitive state of affairs. This turn to artifice finds us developing instruments by which we can remove ourselves, and gaze at distances brought close: As when Martin's paintings re-produce a world consisting of moral principles, ancient myth and idealized landscape. The wonder and awe here is not of the world, it is designed; it is the upshot of deliberate organization mediated by technological instruments. It is these instruments, and the accompanying processes of fabricating, that offer a way out of the Cartesian dilemma: the apparatusses of the modern age let us create the parameters of enquiry and experiment, and lets us find trust in the tools and methods for enquiry, so that we neither have to rely on the world to offer itself, nor on our credulous senses. In this way we are in the picture of all things, and all possible things can appear in our enquiry. We can be clear and confident in our picture. Nevertheless, as Arendt notices, having receded into ourselves like this, we have begun to suspect that what we have discovered in all this rational enquiry and experimenting (that which goes by the name strategy, amongst other terms) has nothing to do with the world 'out there' at all, but is simply representing the patterns of our own doubting mind. Meantime, whilst we seem to be doing little more than methodologically confirming an image of the world designed by the very same methods, out there 'nothing happens more frequently than the unexpected'.[30]

---

[30] Hannah Arendt *The Human Condition*, 300.

To this argument Arendt delivers a further, crucial twist. Because the earth is no longer seen as having the potential to reveal itself, human enquiry (the work of *homo faber*) can no longer be concerned with open questions of what a thing is as it is, in its *Umwelt*. The concern of modern human, then, turns to the fabricating processes of discovery. But what is fabrication without contemplation? Or rather, what kinds of end can fabrication lead to when contemplation (seeing the technologically mediated organization of naming) is removed from the process? *Homo faber*, the experimenter, interested only in the conduct of the experiment and in the refinement of tools, reduces human investigation into producing for the sake of producing:

Nature, because it could be known only in processes which human ingenuity, the ingeniousness of *homo faber*, could repeat and remake in the experiment, became a process, and all particular natural things derived their significance and meaning solely from their functions in the over-all process.[31]

As processes change continually in line with the development of instruments and ongoing experimentation, the fabricator is 'deprived of those permanent measures that precede and outlast the fabrication process and form an authentic and reliable absolute with respect to the fabricating activity'.[32] And when there are no verities or standards outside the processes of fabrication, where there is only contempt for contemplation, and where the claims emerging out of fabrication processes are merely secondary to the process of fabrication itself, all that is left for the worker is the focus on life itself; on her labouring activity, which has now become elevated to the highest sphere of human motivation.[33] *Homo faber* becomes *animal laborans*. This is, however, no longer the condition of labouring that is tied intimately to the metabolic process of biological life, such as depicted in Millet's paintings. The labour of the modern *homo faber*, if noticing these processes at all, experiences labour as a taken-for-granted means to an end:

For even now, laboring is too lofty, too ambitious a word for what we are doing, or think we are doing, in the world we have come to live in. The last stage of the laboring society, the society of jobholders, demands of its members a sheer automatic functioning, as though individual life had actually been submerged in the overall life process of the species and the only active decision still required of the individual were to let go, so to speak, to abandon his individuality, the still individually sensed pain and trouble of living, and acquiesce in a dazed, 'tranquilized,' functional type of behavior.[34]

---

[31] Hannah Arendt *The Human Condition*, 296.
[32] Hannah Arendt *The Human Condition*, 307.
[33] Hannah Arendt *The Human Condition*, 313.
[34] Hannah Arendt *The Human Condition*, 322.

Arendt's sombre conclusion of *The Human Condition* places both *homo faber* and *animal laborans* in a condition of earth-alienation, characterized, somewhat ironically, by confident, practical commitment ro utility and productivity as ends in themselves. To treat nature as a set of resources that can be infinitely recombined is to internalize the limits of the human species to its own intelligence and ingenuity. Alienation emerges from the elevation and severance of the species from its wider ecology. Take as an example Mies van de Rohe's handmade readymade Seagram building in New York. It is an ingenious expression of human confidence in technology. Its glass and steel construction, floating above street level like some benign visitor from an already known future, promises the occupants a life of status, ease and light. Yet the confidence of its form emerges from a conformity to what Reinhold Martin calls an emerging cybernetic order of standardized, (re)combining patterns of living and working spreading the logic of efficiency from one unit to the next: one office looks like the next, one worker like the next, one building like the next, one district like the next, a spread of self-similar patterns in which all interior spaces were also in-folded exteriors.[35] Nothing is hidden, life is tranquilized by self-maintaining communications, all is, potentially, available. Enter the marble lined lobby, await the elevator: 'going-up'.

Disappearing Artefacts

Arendt's critique alludes to the penetration of life by technological mediation. Analyse any aspects of an object like the Seagram building and we find that it is media all the way though. The content of an mid-twentieth century office is a (male) human dictating a letter, the content of the letter is structured through a Dictaphone and (female operated) typewriter, the content of these are buttons and spools of magnetic tape, or inked tape and keys, and so on. Moving outwards, the same occurs: adjacent offices contain similar workers, on similar floor plans, clad with similar glass looking out onto similar buildings, which repeat across a skyline. The content of a medium is always another medium.[36] This directs the focus on the medium itself, the role of the technological device such as the ducting, the communication cables, the elevator shafts, the lighting systems, all of which, as media, calculate, store and transmit information.[37] As transmitting devices, these media disappear the more

---

[35] See Reinhold Martin *The Organizational Complex*. Cambridge, MA: MIT Press. 2003, 103–6.
[36] Developing Marshall McLuhan's famous dictum. See Alexander Galloway *The Interface Effect*, 31.
[37] Friedrich Kittler *Film, Gramophone, Typewriter*, 243; Friedrich Kittler. *The Truth of the Technological World*, 143.

successful they are in their operations.[38] The hissing background noises of poorly maintained elevators for example, the bulk of a door that fails to open properly, is information about the medium itself, they intrude as reminders and residues of the process of life being an utterly mediated one. As the transmission network and receivers evolve to lessen the white noise the media become less obtrusive. Being less present they can become more pervasive, mediating the act and thought of 'users', all the while determining our situation; as Kittler suggests 'we knew nothing of our senses until media provided models and metaphors'.[39] Or, we might say, pictures.

This pervasiveness of media, found in all technical devices that store, transmit and process information (such as a building), is of concrete importance for strategy. For instance, an editorial in *MIS Quarterly* argues:

> The case for success and general management attention is no longer an intellectual or theoretical one, but can be based in fact. The introduction of information technology into the strategic boardroom has 'yielded a language and set of concepts which allows us to talk more crisply about information systems application and competition'. Words like 'switching costs', 'barriers to entry', and 'exit barriers' have become a part of the [information systems] lexicon … using [information systems] technology to gain pre-emptive competitive advantage.[40]

The phrase 'technology-based competitive opportunities' suggest the possibility for efficient and effective organizing; strategists can imagine out-processing others through competitive games. The editorial implies that the opportunities provided by technological progress are hampered only by strategists who remain ignorant of information technology and its uses, or who sentimentally resist change, or who attempt to frustrate the use of technology. Only their lack of ingenuity and intelligence stops them from becoming true labourers in the pursuit of fabrication.[41] With unbridled enthusiasm, the aforementioned editorial concludes:

> All this is but a prologue. New opportunities and challenges now lie ahead. We have turned the prism, looked at the same world from a new perspective and found rewarding paths for future development.

The prism turned, the world picture emerges, a world in which human worlds and the earth are both configured through representation made

---

[38] Alexander Galloway *The Interface Effect*, 25.
[39] Friedrich Kittler *Optical Media*, 34.
[40] Editorial. *MIS Quarterly*, 1986, 10(2): vi.
[41] Günther Anders speaks of the shame of humans for their limits next to machines and the growing tendency to rectify these limits, seen as faults, through prostheses, from clothing to artificial intelligence computing. Günther Anders On Promethean shame. In *Prometheanism*. Translated by C. J. Müller. London: Rowman & Littlefield. 2016, 29–96.

by methodologically rigorous and exact means that fix or, rather stand (*stellen*) objects, as objects to be represented (*vor-stellen*); compared, measured and verified. And in representing, comparing and measuring the individual takes a position (*Stelle*), becomes a subject that is defined uniformly by its ability to represent the world as a picture.

In this picture-making age, strategy turns into pure method: analysis replaces folk-wisdom; calculation takes the place of experimenting, playing and tampering. The strategist no longer deals with the reality of the world, but a reality of mediated representations. Technological mediation is not an attempt to filter and reflect what is out there – the earth. Instead, it is what is out there: a world of calculation combining 'things' in ever renewed ways to create new regularities: beginnings are everywhere but lead nowhere, there are repetitions without ensuing difference: it is a vast complex of endlessly mediated movement; a condition we call technogenesis.

7   Who or What Is Running Strategy?

Power On

The emergence of computing systems and, in particular, the shift from identifiable computers, such as PCs, towards ubiquitous computational infrastructures, marks the extension of 'extraction operations' from the world of computed simulation to the 'real world'. It is an extension of machine presence whose very invisibility affords it potentially devastating power:

Extension wants your bloodstream and your bed, your breakfast conversation, your commute, your run, your refrigerator, your parking space, your living room.[1]

Shoshana Zuboff calls the extension an 'apparatus'. The apparatus extracts information about human lives continuously and tirelessly through the ubiquitous devices that have come to constitute the internet of things: chat bots, courier delivery records, conversational interfaces, alarm and heating systems, keyboards, health and pension records, social media posts, email corpuses, activity monitoring apps, and all manner of networked devices and applications operating in dynamic and generative concert without the users' conscious choice, or even knowledge. In recoding, storing and moving data with such fluidity and connectivity the apparatus also identifies patterns in user behaviours, from which predictions of future behaviour become possible, and through prediction comes an 'execution architecture' of suggestion, nudging and alteration, moves that induce users into specific purchase spaces. The apparatus 'is not just a knowing machine; it is an actuating machine designed to produce more certainty *about us* and *for them*'. The 'them' here refers to the online media companies and their clients. These online media companies survey and manipulate human habits, beliefs, relations and

---

[1] Shoshana Zuboff *The Age of Surveillance Capitalism: The Fight for a Human Future at the New Frontier of Power*. New York: Public Affairs. 2019, ch. 7.

affinities. Through ever more nuanced and swifter algorithmic analysis and the proliferation of networked computers linked to sensors and other data collection points, they are not only aware of how humans use a fridge or if they palpitate at night, but also how they use language. Each time we interact with a conversational interface or a chat bot we become data for algorithmic analysis and machine learning. Conversations become broken into types and played out according to scripts. These scripts can be categorized as informational (involving the transmission of decisions, descriptions and receiving questions)' productive (scheduling, compiling data on activity, planning), transactional (court procedures, commercial trading) and controlling (device operations). All of these types of conversation can be performed by machines schooled in language processing. These pick up not just words, but increasingly the grammar by which words are used. Learning grammar requires not only a sense of the criteria by which distinctions between correct and incorrect use are legitimated, but also a situational awareness that allows words to be used in semantically appropriate ways. In human use, grammar is not just procedural, but riven with personal feelings and the projection of these as emotion. Machines identify the patterns of tone and rhythm associated with certain feelings and emotions, they 'understand' the charged inflection of vocal tones, the uncertainties lying in pauses, or the tendency to emphasize using ranked lists.[2]

To touch on language in these ways, to inveigle themselves into conversation, is to have machinery script the personal and social relations by which, historically, humans have always considered themselves distinct as a species: machines have entered the house of being and made themselves invisible at home, running our affairs with increasing certainty and predictability. Humans are no longer even autonomous in appearances, and the things by which their autonomy was made most apparent, such as the automobile, the twentieth century's most dominant, iconic expression of individuated private space, have become utterly integrated. The car company Tesla, for example, has pioneered the idea of a car as a piece of updatable software. Its features are no longer static, but evolving, moving with the user, linking accelerometers to smartphones, together with GPS and gyroscope data, tracking driving behaviours to advise on 'better' driving, storing sharing these data with others like insurance companies, or digital platforms such as the ride-hailing company Uber, all the while generating feedback loops

---

[2] Especially AI systems work well when it comes to drawing correlations, for example between images and labels but struggle with whole-part relations such as the relations between words and phrases. Gary Marcus and Ernest Davis *Rebooting AI: Building Artificial Intelligence We Can Trust*. New York: Pantheon, p. 150.

in which decision making and cognition as such is distributed across a wide range of actors, human and non-human, and at various temporalities, from the time-less voltage differences at which algorithms are executed, to their messaging across information networks; to drivers' sub-conscious perceptions of themself as being updatable were they to receive grammatically persuasive instruction on how to improve; and to their conscious reflections on themself as an investor in a new, more sustainable (apparently) e-lifestyle. As it is with cars, so it is with humans: the technological upgrading of the mind and body is well underway: with neural implants, cyberware and more perfected brain–computer interfaces in the making.[3] The complexity of these connections include extensive driver information such as ride hours, rider feedback and on-demand heat maps for traffic. Users are being continually informed, apparently sovereign in their decisions, but their future is being calculatingly spun out from patterns of past behaviour, steered by algorithms: 'computers are now more profound programmers than their human counterparts'.[4]

Though they organize human movement, neither Tesla nor Uber wish to bear responsibility for it, and so invest heavily in avoidance tactics. Uber, for example, argues it has no responsibility for the drivers, it does not employ the drivers, and has no responsibility for driver actions; it has a gigantic picture of them brought close, but the distance to each of them remains immense.[5] To make sense of itself as an organization that organizes movement abstractly, Uber has a strategic self-presentation as a facilitator connecting drivers and passengers, and the more connections it mediates between these users the more comprehensive and seamless the facilitating: predicting where rides will be hailed and to what destinations, what type of person or good needs transporting, what payment methods work most conveniently, which additional services

---

[3] Aleksandra Przegalinska *Wearable Technologies in Organizations. Privacy, Efficiency and Autonomy in Work*. London: Palgrave Macmillan. 2019, 33.

[4] Wendy Chun *Programmed Visions. Software and Memory*. London: MIT Press. 2009, 9.

[5] One driver posted on social media that 'a grade of 210 out of 247 "smooth accelerations" earned a "Great work!" from the boss': www.nytimes.com/2018/10/12/opinion/sunday/uber-driver-life.html. Relatedly motor insurance companies ask drivers to fit sensors into cars or use mobile-phone apps, to record not just where they go but also the telematic patterns of acceleration and breaking, along with the condition of the vehicle. These continuous data flows come to replace the calculation of risk on the basis of proxies including demographics – and thus not only promise the idea of a bias-free assessment of each case on the basis of its own metrics, it also influences the behaviour of those measured. This comes in form of insurance premiums or by limiting or disabling the capacities of vehicles on the basis of a series of data parameters defined by the insurers. Or, more crudely, through the selling of telematic data to restaurants and other facilities frequented by drivers, so that these can be used in directed advertising attacks on the senses. See Shoshana Zuboff *Surveillance Capitalism*: ch. 7. Uber also employ gaming technology to influence driver behaviour: www.nytimes.com/interactive/2017/04/02/technology/uber-drivers-psychological-tricks.html

might be warranted as part of a more comprehensive service (school runs, ambulances?), all the while sharing very little of this increasingly nuanced information with those from whom it has been harvested.

Tesla and Uber are just two of many organizations entwined in a vast, sprawling, restless, seething of limbed connections and each limned in strategic representations that examine lives as through a one-way mirror. Behind the mirror lie chief technical officers, programmers and market analysts working on ever more extensive and refined ways of extracting yet more rents from data produced by users. They thrive on the apparent paradox of connecting people and things, whilst reducing any liability or responsibility for connection. Their concern for users is a light and agile one: seductive in appearance and functionality, yet opaque and disorienting when made the subject of enquiry. They are in the business of providing means, not content. Zuboff offers a trenchant critique of the corporate architects – or puppet masters – of this totalizing power:

As to this species of power, I name it *instrumentarianism*, defined as *the instrumentation and instrumentalization of behavior for the purposes of modification, prediction, monetization, and control.* In this formulation, 'instrumentation' refers to the puppet: the ubiquitous connected material architecture of sensate computation that renders, interprets, and actuates human experience. 'Instrumentalization' denotes the social relations that orient the puppet masters to human experience as surveillance capital wields the machines to transform us into means to others' market ends.[6]

Instrumentarianism is totalitarian in nature. Recalling Arendt's comments, it achieves its objectives precisely because it operates without a singular vision, or indeed very little sense of value, save for the value of movement, of doing yet more to service the operative concern for generating ever increasing presence:

it only cares that whatever we do is accessible to its ever-evolving operations of rendition, calculation, modification, monetization, and control.[7]

The more invisible the technology of picturing, the more pervasive. The interface to the apparatus is becoming ever less apparent, and ever more permanent, to the point where using and being become synonyms. The volume of attention-seeking stimulation and information entering users' lives is overwhelming: users must 'keep up', and instrumentarianism governs these attempts with an ever-updated array of positioning nudges and recommendations.

In stipulating surveillance capitalism as the 'puppet master' that imposes its will through a variegated undergrowth of algorithms, platforms, sensors,

---

[6] Shoshana Zuboff *Surveillance Capitalism*, ch. 12, n.p.
[7] Shoshana Zuboff *Surveillance Capitalism*, ch. 12, n.p.

scrapers, bots and crawlers, Zuboff's analysis presents us with organizational forms whose strategy is to develop a prowess in data analytics so proficient that there is no longer room to distinguish between personal and private life: the *oikonomia* becomes utterly public, and the nature of the public is utterly commercial.[8] There has been a steady picking off of public spaces, to the point where social spaces are simply collection points for connecting and plugging in constituting a heteronomous sociality in which, in the words of Sherry Turkle, we are alone, together.[9] 'The more individuated the subject', Lucas Introna argues, 'the more valuable it is, in terms of impression-ability'.[10] Immediate and global digital connectivity yields increasingly intense forms of isolation because the possibility for open, unscripted, specu-lative conversation is being thinned out to the point it becomes nothing more than the circulation of retweeted opinion, and hash-tagged identities. It is a coming together that has been stripped of *logos*, and which champions forms of individual expression devoted to making an immediate, and thereby circu-lated, impression. Turkle's diagnosis of structural loneliness recalls Arendt's analysis of isolation prevalent under totalitarian regimes, and which, when transformed into global industrialization and commerce, becomes, as her contemporary Adorno observed, a source of profound alienation:

For tenderness between people is nothing other than awareness of the possibil-ity of relations without purpose, a solace still glimpsed by those embroiled in purposes; a legacy of old privileges promising a privilege-free condition. The abolition of privilege by bourgeois reason finally abolishes this promise too. If time is money, it seems moral to save time, above all one's own, and such par-simony is excused by consideration for others. One is straightforward. Every sheath interposed between men in their transactions is felt as a disturbance to the functioning of the apparatus, in which they are not only objectively incorporated but with which they proudly identify themselves. That, instead of raising their hats, they greet each other with the hallos of familiar indifference, that, instead of letters, they send each other inter office communications without address or signature, are random symptoms of a sickness of contact. Estrangement shows itself precisely in the elimination of distance between people.[11]

Relations without purpose – action – has given way to profiles, 'likes', compliance records, messages and access rights. Because the users'

---

[8] Public service broadcasting, social housing, student grants, unemployment benefits, collective health services, social care, all collapse and deprive the culture of the energy that emerges from spaces that are somewhat insulated from the means–ends instrumen-tality of generating revenue. We all of us become anxious and exhausted when business and busyness are all there is, and these conditions are yet a further opportunity for solution-driven revenue generation.

[9] Sherry Turkle *Alone Together*. New York: Basic Books. 2011.

[10] Lucas Introna The algorithmic choreography of the impressionable subject. In: *Algorithmic Cultures: Essays on Meaning, Performance and New Technologies*. Robert Seyfert & Jonathan Roberge (eds). London: Routledge. 2016. 26–51, 39.

[11] Theodor Adorno *Minima Moralia*. Translated by E. F. Jephcott. London: Verso. 2005, 41.

attention is always being directed, and is always considered in deficit to the performative object of this direction, there is no civic space of appearances: the care we might show to another's own unique projects is given over to an instrumental solicitude and concern for advancement framed by concepts like 'career', 'wellness' and 'competitive success'. There is no reprieve from the urgencies of cyberspace and no space to get bored or diverted under an inundation of stimuli.

Users lose their autonomy, they become the puppets of strategists in control of otherwise agnostic and self-perpetuating data collection and computing machination. From the picturing viewpoint of these strategists, users are nothing more than behavioural patterns to be assembled and spun into a revenue-generating future. Under the attentions of instrumentarianism the minute processes by which human lives are lived have become minutely predictable and to keep it thus the apparatus continues to enforce an individualizing regime of comparison (alone, together) in which users are permanently anxious, permanently dispersed, permanently fragmented. The apparatus has occupied the horizons of what is visible and sensible, and in the process it has exhausted both private and civic space to the point where both personal desire and the public forming of opinion have already been made subject to what Mark Fisher calls pre-corporation – not incorporation.[12] Pre-corporation is the pre-emptive forming of desires, and opinions prior to experiencing them. The more alternative or radical these desires and opinions, the more valuable they are to the puppet masters: Kurt Cobain's death, he suggests, was anticipated before Nirvana struck their first chord, he played in chains of air, his rebellion was absorbed as a money-generating circulation of impressions before it ever began.[13]

There has been a sacrifice of self to media that is immense, and total. It is as if, Fisher continues, there is no alternative to this mediated conversion of capital fuelled by psycho pharmaceutical lightheadedness, sustaining competitive enthusiasms and productive excess. It is the only reality out there, there is nothing left for it to incorporate.[14]

---

[12] Mark Fisher *Capitalist Realism*. London: Zero Books. 2009.

[13] Fisher finds in music a concentrated expression of the baleful condition in which computerized neoliberalism has cast us. He notices how, from around the turn of the millennium, there have been massive changes in distribution and consumption of culture through platform like Spotify, and yet little innovation in the sound of music. Perhaps grime and electronica were the last gasp, a form of lament for the lost world of delirious and popular collectivity.

[14] Even the psychological illnesses that might be attributed to its operations are made the subject of revenue-generating opportunity. By associating illness such as neuroses with low serotonin levels, for example, the apparatus subjectifies the individual to a corrective regime of biological rebalancing. The individual can be cured, opening up huge markets in controlling the 'deviance' of personal brain chemistry. There are, in comparison, very few attempts to critically analyse the social, cultural and political conditions in which low serotonin levels might prevail.

We are, suggests Fisher experiencing capitalist realism, a term that had originally been coined by a group of German artists as a frame in which to gather their profound distrust of modern commerce and the alienating experiences it entailed.[15] The most trenchant and ironic of these artists was Sigmar Polke who, like Brecht, paints, draws or creates a montage with a view to revealing the processes of their construction, thereby attempting to shed the illusory nature of representational images, whilst still indicating their seductive prevalence. He often uses everyday representations of growth, of progress, of success in his work: rockets, flags, prop planes, moons, advertisements, for sale signs. Polke admits, and yet mocks, such a reality and its aspirations: amid the representations, human figures typically appear in pixelated or crude outlines, as lonely as they are ignorant of their mediated state. Polke's capitalist realism pictures an assembly line of simulated life, which, as Fisher then elaborates, seems, now, to be all there is. Its substance is an immense and infinite plasticity whose shape-shifting flexibility works in an ad hoc and pragmatic way, its limits are flexible and self-governing, allowing it to metabolize and re-form itself to absorb whatever it comes into contact with. It is the ontological realization of Frederick Jamieson's quip that it is easier to imagine the end of the world, than the end of capitalism. Even in China, where the state involves itself in the operations of companies like Tencent and Alibaba, this form of capitalism is to the fore.[16] For example, by encouraging technology such as facial recognition into the city infrastructure (e.g., catching people jaywalking and fining them) to enforce social normalization, the Chinese state-sponsored interaction of machine human networks is still serving the interests of capital. The machinery for endless transforming capital is no longer one system above others, it is a plenum, a life-giving force seeded in all of us to which there is no outside save airy nothing.

---

[15] 1963–1966. In addition to Polke, were three other artists: Gerhard Richter, Konrad Lueg and Manfred Kuttner. They organized around the use of self-reproduced, easily found materials. It sat between socialist realism of the East and the spread of capitalism from the West, denying either, but ironically, and using capitalist techniques, for example putting on art shows in shops (a butchers, and furniture store) packing the pieces as though they might be products, refusing to engage with visitors but instead watching television. See Mark Godfrey, Gregor Jansen, Elodie Evers, and Magdalena Holzhey (Eds), *Living with Pop: A Reproduction of Capitalist Realism.* Kunsthalle Düsseldorf: Verlag der Buchhandlung Walter König. 2013.

[16] Jaron Lanier sees the involvement of state services, in particular intelligence agencies, to be part of a particular business model (a 'statistical machine') pursued by a number of technology companies also in the West. He calls this model BUMMER (Behaviors of Users Modified and Made into an Empire for Rent), issuing perverse incentives that corrupt people (or turn them/us into assholes, as he has it). Jaron Lanier *Ten Arguments for Deleting Your Social Media Accounts Right Now.* New York: Holt. 2018.

Power Off

When set against the backdrop of Fisher's trenchant thesis that there is no longer an outside from which to challenge, to even picture capitalism, Zuboff's concerns feel timely. Her concepts of apparatus and instrumentarianism evoke a similar diagnosis to Fisher's, yet throughout Zuboff enlists figures who have apparently been exempted from the world picture, indeed they are authoring it, the so called the puppet masters and their organization the Big Other. These are the tech strategists who operate with very distinct and totalizing sense of strategic agency. These are figures whose presence is often deliberately opaque and whose organizational reach is immense. Zuboff's humanist concern lies with how to manage these strategists better so that the corporate architecture they have designed better respects human autonomy and commits to basic standards of welfare provision. The question remains, however, whether this concern is not off the mark, given it presumes there are strategic mechanisms of control for creating organizational forms that are more just, more open to authenticity, and that the puppet masters might be persuaded to change their ways. The fact that they do not is attributed to the seductions of corporate profit, seasoned with a malevolent desire to protect their personal power.

What feels missing in this anthropocentric diagnosis is any consideration of whether the strategists themselves – or for that matter narrating authors – are caught within the instrumentarium. As Arendt noted, a defining characteristic of totalitarian systems is the ubiquity of fluidity, and how, as we quoted earlier, the only way of staying in power is to keep people in motion, to have them activated as media of the law of movement. In the perpetual motion of a spreading and tightening apparatus, are not strategists, workers, as well as customers and content providers alike caught in the metabolism of machinery? Being an author of the code does not exclude you from its ministrations. The author, the strategist, is to act within the reality created by codes which, if properly realized, institute a form of life in which the illogical accidental, unsatisfactory nature of the real world can be traded for a newly conceived space built according to world-smoothing and world-revealing principles: the objective is order, not persuasion.[17] To recall Arendt writing on totalitarianism, and then Fisher writing on capitalist realism, there is a 'big', but no 'other'; it is gigantic, but also, thereby, ever so small.

Being subservient to their own edicts and protocols was something the poet William Blake suggested was common among those who sought to organize others according to their own plans, a condition he embodied in the mythological figure Urizen (see Figure 7.1).

---

[17] Hannah Arendt *The Origins of Totalitarianism*, 361–2.

Figure 7.1 William Blake, *The First Book of Urizen*, plate 12, c. 1794 (Bentley 22). Google Art Project

Strategists – or those who had design upon human lives as Blake would have them known – are into aesthetics, they create new spaces: 'On the shore of the infinite ocean,/ Like a human heart, struggling and beating, The vast world of Urizen appear'd.'[18] In Blake's cosmology it is a world that has, under the organizational impress of Urizen's knowledge and language, split from Eternity and become a limited space. Limited, but still potentially infinite in that it can be made the subject of endless perspective and interpretation. The problem, suggests Blake, writing at the outset of the nineteenth century, has been the way in which interpretation has become overtly rational, resulting in Urizen's bloodless, dry categorization of space as geometric and linear, one whose vast enormities are always of a measurable and so diminished: things are being continually parsed into this and that, now and then, good and bad. Urizen sits above this continual process of division in which enclosed spaces impress upon one another, squeezing out possibility, coldly delineating the make-up of the mortal world (the facts of classification) and its morals (the right and wrong). Initially those living in Urizen's world fail to live by these ordering procedures, and this causes Urizen no amount of irritation. He turns on them by investing in systems that further narrow their perspectives to the point of lifeless predictability, systems that follow the logical process of what Blake called 'mill and machine': do and therefore become this, not that. Urizen looks towards order, and above all the ordering of desire and passion into predictable patterns of living.

But the greatest source of Urizen's frustration, that which shakes him and makes his soul sicken, is that he too is caught in these enclosures, he too is embodied in similitudes and mortality. In his attempts to restrain and mould others' desires he reveals something stuttering and lifeless about his own being, for as Blake observes 'those who restrain desire, do so because theirs is weak enough to be restrained'. Urizen too is in chains, locked into an ordering technology in which passion and desire are nothing more than canalized impulses.[19]

So just as technology is being used to exploit the lives of others, the smaller others who are having to negotiate very real intrusions into their life, so too does it intrude into the lives of the puppet masters, which then begs the question of what they are masters of. Like Urizen, they wield force, but it is of a limited form (it is administrative, not rhetorical). Blake imagines Urizen's aesthetic efforts to mould a biddable world

---

[18] William Blake *The (First) Book of Urizen*, lines 127–129. In *Poetical Works*. Oxford: Oxford University Press. 1908.
[19] William Blake *Marriage of Heaven and Hell (The Voice of the Devil)*, line 13. In *Poetical Works*.

to be of a limiting and coruscating form because he restricted his perception to what is already there as a representation: frail and faulty human beings who had to be controlled with mill and machine. Urizen lacked the imagination to see the world differently, openly. The same goes for the strategists of media organizations, who create in order to restrain. They organize the creation of algorithms that begin to pan the flows of human activity, sifting the sediment, looking for data patterns that glow amid the slipping, messy chaos, and once they find a sufficient concentration of these patterns they start to make unauthorized excavations and manipulations, trying to establish chains of data, and networks of chains that, through combination, might then amount to the management of sensory affect, feelings and decisions. There is something unruly about these material beginnings, rigorous in application but uncertain in outcome. Their motivation is to transform a contingent, open, unmarked future (the radical contingency of time as an open future) into a future that already has form so as to incorporate and thereby eliminate contingency. The gaps have been filled and the kinks straightened: the experience of becoming repeats, without difference intruding. Their concern is simply an operational one of discovering chains of experiential stability and exploiting them by revealing and expanding them, gaining revenues, to then undertake new prospecting for regularities, or more commonly, by swallowing smaller prospectors. It is a strategy grounded in crude but apparently effective minimax reasoning: just in case these smaller seams prove rich, we ought govern them, that way we forestall competition, and so we gain rents either way: users either stay using our service, or move to other providers that we also control, all the while gaining access to more and more seams of activity. In such a world, size and monopoly have an unerring efficiency of outcome.[20] Hence the strategic obsession with the real-world forces of presence and control, as set against real-world experience of contingency and uncertainty. Through the algorithms the world is less fateful, less agonistic, less inscrutable, at least for a while.

These strategies make money, and the strategists become media figureheads. But to ascribe these strategists the status of a puppet master successfully pulling the strings is to be captured by an 'us-and-them' picture that feels out-moded in an age in which, as Blake intimates, and as Arendt, Fisher and Heidegger make explicit, everything has its measure as picture, leaders and followers alike. In being measured nothing

---

[20] This is perhaps most clearly advocated in Peter Thiel's version of 'monopoly capitalism' that, by some curious logic, promises to 'benefit everybody and [provide] sustainable profits for the creator [of new products]'. Peter Thiel with Blake Masters. *Zero to One: Notes on Start-Ups or How to Build the Future.* New York: Crown. 2014, 46.

remains beyond the picture, no-one has oversight, there is no 'beyond' above the cloud from which to sit invisibly and pull strings. Already, at the turn of the nineteenth century, even before Millet's *Gleaners* and Marx's *Grundrisse*, Blake's Urizen myth was attempting to show us the totalizing effects of reason as a picturing force, one that strategies unthinkingly perpetuate in singular language of calculation. Strategists, like Urizen, are as bound as the rest of us by pictures that explain and so manage the world by dividing and representing it as a complete place of parts and wholes.

Platforms

The effort at completion is itself a process, always underway, never ending. It is the strategic attempt to sever being from becoming which itself only ever remains an attempt, a struggle. In such a condition strategic control is winnowed to the algorithmic generation of experiences that users find seductive enough to continue repeating by showing yet more of their mediated, represented selves.

As Wendy Chun notices, the proliferation of computer mediation representation is predicated on a paradox:

Computers have fostered both a decline in and frenzy of visual knowledge. Opaque yet transparent, incomprehensible yet logical, they reveal that the less we know the more we show (or are shown).[21]

Visual images of things divided from other things fall like leaves in an endless autumn: they are everywhere, with different hues and vibrancy, some old and withering, others bright for brief moments, all destined to be endlessly circulated and yet forgotten. Underneath this gathering litter, moving more invisibly, interfaces, trackers and sensors are continually absorbing user interaction in ever finer-grained efforts at data visualization.[22] Applications, for example, that generate click, waive or touchable images on a graphic user interface can be activated by users in ways that produce revenue-making information loops (more clicks, related clicks). But for the click to produce the expected response, the interface has to limit the choices available (or, rather, eliminate or veil other equally valid responses) so as to simplify the systemic complexity for users. The user sees an image and the response, and not the intricate pathways and the frictions and fissions that eliminate or veil the majority of the systemic complexity to arrive at a limited set of responses. The image at the interface

---

[21] Wendy Chun *Programmed Visions*, 15.

[22] Steve F. Anderson *Technologies of Vision: The War between Data and Images*. London: MIT. 2017. For example, see 40ff., for an extended discussion on Netflix's viewing pattern analyses.

therefore soothes the user; it gives unity to the world, qua image, but it, and the interface of which it is an operation, are a small fraction of what exists, most is out of sight. Here the user is no longer 'in the picture' but presented with simulated images that present actionable decision paths. The user's learning and ensuing cognitive maps are therefore not 'of the world' but merely of the reduced choice patterns and cause–effect relations (click and response) entailed in the technology. This is Paul Valery's form of seeing we discussed in Part 1, it is not even a naming in language, but a process of being named (addressed) through mechanized updates.

This might appear as though users are being controlled, that behind the scenes, at the other side of the technology, we have programmers and strategists pulling strings as they direct unwitting and credulous users towards revenue generating destinations. Not so. The technology is not a governing unity, it is far more disorienting, because it is far more pervasive, as Benjamin Bratton suggests: 'Computation turns the image into a technology, just as it then turns technology more generally into fields of actionable images.'[23] In this way the human and the machine become singular in operation: a picture is the world, the world a picture.

The traditional (technological) sense of a strategic picture works on a cartographic visualization of territory in which there are things like corporations parsed into places called markets and connected along conduits of movement called value chains. It is the same form of visualization that runs through Zuboff's critique of media corporations enacting technologically facilitated forms of territorial land-grab, much like colonizing nation states were doing back in William Blake's day. Yet, as Zuboff herself seems to intimate, this picturing of stable media organizations parcelling out market territory on the basis of efficient and effective algorithmic control is wholly inadequate. Their organization is interlaced with intelligence and security services, with global financial interests, with data analytics that can be weaponized, to create all manner of trans-border influences. They reach pan-national trade agreements, assist and yet also evade the judicial reach of international courts, encourage and also oppose the creation of NGOs living off the detritus left by human schisms and natural disasters, they facilitate the creation of megacities populated by itinerant non-nationals, they divert profits into new currencies, or to assist in spray cleaning a world they did so much to smear. Strategists have no flat surfaces on which to play out their board game representations anymore: rather it is a folding array of different territorial images and claims, forming often unlikely and always temporary alliances, before unfolding and refolding, using an interacting media of organization.

---

[23] Benjamin Bratton *The Stack: On Software and Sovereignty*. Cambridge, MA: MIT Press. 2015.

To make sense of this restless, multiple and ungraspable condition demands, at the very least, we should eschew the easy dualism of an 'us' and 'them' story in which strategists are made immune to, and responsible for, a situation in which they are, like Urizen, mired. Bratton likens the situation to a layered 'stack' of interacting material and immaterial forces and processes.[24] The stack, like Zuboff's apparatus, is totalizing. It consists of smart cities, app-enabled white goods, financial trading systems, conversational interfaces and all manner of other aspects of computational activity that in their calculating totality bring together users, interface, addresses, city, cloud and earth. Unlike Zuboff's apparatus, (and so unlike much in the way of strategic thinking, critical or otherwise), there is no centralizing or even distinct human intelligence governing operations.[25]

At the foot of the stack comes Earth, the ground. It is the level of ecological flows, of energy and minerals, into which the stack sits itself. The electrical and computing become very material here. They are shown to be hungry and heavy things needing physically vulnerable server farms, microwave antennae and power-hungry temperature control. The stack sustains itself by building these infrastructures that enhance and protect its capacity to build newer infrastructures. Built into the earth,

---

[24] Benjamin Bratton *The Stack*. Bratton (81) emphasizes the 'stacked' nature of most digital systems, from the internet itself to platforms such as Facebook or Instagram. Stacks are: 'a kind of platform that also happens to be structured through vertical interoperable layers, both hard and soft, global and local. Its properties are generic, extensible, and pliable; it provides modular recombinancy but only within the bounded set of its synthetic planes'.

[25] Mark Fisher draws an adjacent conclusion here in what he terms 'capitalist realism', the condition left when 'beliefs have collapsed at the level of ritual or symbolic elaboration, and all that is left is the consumer-spectator, trudging through the ruins and the relics'. Capitalist realism is therefore where the postmodern has moved from being a vanguard characteristic of what is yet to come to being the pervasive state of the world: 'analogous to the deflationary perspective of a depressive who believes that any positive state, any hope, is a dangerous illusion', exhausting, double-bind fuelled, paranoia inducing and schizophrenic, deprived of the capacity for novelty, and entirely without alternative. Drawing on Kafka's novel *The Castle*, Fisher elaborates the lack of 'central control' in this late-stage form of capitalism, the state and its institutions merely playing the role of scapegoats for corporate and consumptive excesses and failures: for *their* supposed failure to curtail and control the very companies that they empowered to 'run' hospitals, prisons and infrastructure projects. Here, the 'big other' is the crucial collective fiction that pre-structures the social field without itself ever being encountered. Mark Fisher *Capitalist Realism*, 10; 12; 50; 67. Fisher points us to Nick Land's bleak (followed by a more recent and dangerous neo-reactionary) assessment that: 'Conceptions of agency are inextricable from media environments. Print massifies to a national level. Telecoms coordinate at a global level. TV electoralizes monads in delocalized space. Digital hypermedia take action outside real time. Immersion presupposes amnesia and conversion to tractile memory, ... Voodoo passages through the black mirror. It will scare the fuck out of you.' Nick Land *Fanged Noumena: Collected writings. 1987–2007.* Falmouth: Urbanomic. 2012, 455.

the other levels of the stack continually and mutually work to sustain themselves in the form of clouds, cities, address systems, interfaces and users. Clouds are constituted in a weird geography of platform economies structured by a multiplication of borders and access points, one on top of another, merging with state and security operations. It is a level of firewalls, router infrastructure, hacking-friendly jurisdictions, rapid-response military units and the circumventing flow of search engines. Though universal, cloud activity is most concentrated in urban spaces. Cities: landscapes of thinking and sensing species, cohabiting, overlapping, nested, some based on electricity and code, others on blood and genes. Humans are becoming thoroughly mired in the city's pay-point surveillance systems, its QR-codes, its traffic sensors and phone trackers, its augmenting media, its affective publicity. In being so, humans enhance their capacity for and experience of sensory stimulus, yet they are also subjected to the abstractions of the city, the supply chains, the urban planning, the intelligent interaction of non-human agents who have their own sensory fields that humans can trigger, more or less wittingly as protagonist and target, or not at all. Perhaps the most pervasive way of organizing a city is through universal address systems and interfaces. These fix locations and give credentials that allow what is disparate and different to become uniform. For anything to appear in and to the stack, it must be addressed as such, it must be located and typified through signature digit strings. And in appearing, things and systems interact through interfaces, primarily, for humans at least, buttons and the graphical user interface. And what is being organized here, in the cloud and the city, are users. To be a user requires that something knows something (password) they are something (fingerprint) or they have something (keycard). All sorts of things can be users, a leaf or algorithm as readily as a human.

Once the apparatus is apprehended as a stack, it becomes impossible to attribute anything resembling puppeteering agency to a few elevated strategists. Strategy, like all practices, is enmeshed in a flow continually interacting stacked layers to which there is no visionary order, no outside God's view. At best, all these digitally enhanced strategic leaders can do, is to continue to accelerate the life absorbing, life enveloping power of the *Gestell*, to animate and excite its reach to yet new heights of productivity and permissiveness, to commit themselves whole heartedly towards the furtherance of life being lived by other means. They are, as Urizen, still living amongst the fragments, as though being pushed irresistibly by progress, much like in Walter Benjamin's reading of Paul Klee's angel of history (see Figure 7.2). The angel that wants to fix what is breaking and replenish what has been exhausted, but is

Figure 7.2 Paul Klee, *Angelus Novus*, 1920. Israel Museum, Jerusalem.

unable, because its wings are pinioned by the storm called progress, by its inexorable motion to which it is subjected.[26]

In this, the strategic condition of these 'puppet masters' is on a continuum with earlier industrialists: irrespective of the technological material and form, all are in thrall to an ineluctable, analogue patterns of

---

[26] The drawing was bought from Klee by Walter Benjamin, in whom it provoked a profound sense of malaise and distrust of those who advocate political solutions to the plethora of social ills that seem to fall on humanity as naturally and as regularly as the rain:

> There is a picture by Klee called Angelus Novus. It shows an angel who seems about to move away from something he stares at. His eyes are wide, his mouth is open, his wings are spread. This is how the angel of history must look. His face is turned toward the past. Where a chain of events appears before us, he sees one single catastrophe, which keeps piling wreckage upon wreckage and hurls it at his feet. The angel would like to stay, awaken the dead, and make whole what has been smashed. But a storm is blowing from Paradise and has got caught in his wings; it is so strong that the angel can no longer close them. This storm drives him irresistibly into the future, to which his back is turned, while the pile of debris before him grows toward the sky. What we call progress is this storm.

Walter Benjamin On the concept of history. In *Selected Writings Volume 4 1938–1940*. Edited and translated by Michael Jennings, Marcus Bullock, Howard Eiland and Gary Smith. 1940/2003, 389–400, §IX, 392.

accelerating movements the perfection of which is an unending, abstracting quest that bestirs all commercial systems. It was a pattern that both fascinated and appalled Walter Benjamin, from whose pen Klee's picture had received this now well-worn interpretation: progression is irresistible, it is impossible for strategists to intervene and arrest its natural unfolding, but it is possible to represent it as progress and to thereby legitimately canalise the movements into temporarily settled patterns. There is only movement, something Benjamin also found encapsulated in this quote from the poet, traveller and photographer Maxime Du Camp, a quote he collected in his *Arcades Project*, itself a kind of wasteland scattered with small shards of wisdom:

Steam will conquer cannon. In two hundred years-well before, perhaps-great armies from England, France, and America . . . will descend upon old Asia under the leadership of their generals. Their weapons will consist of pickaxes, and their horses will be locomotives. Singing, they will fall upon these uncultivated, unused lands.... It is thus, perhaps, that war will be waged, in the future, against all unproductive nations, by virtue of that axiom of mechanics which applies to all things: there must be no wasted energy![27]

Productiveness is the organizational impetus by which machinery works and works anew, finding and using sources of energy to allow the processual force of productivity to continue to express itself. The idea that there must be no wasted energy is an open axiom to which all apparatuses are beholden and which, in the age of surveillance, allows the ever-restless platforms or stacks to keep moving, absorbing effort and endeavour as they go.

Just as the generals fell upon unused lands, so corporate forms search out ever- renewing sources of energy, a prime example being Amazon, no longer the name of a forest, but a vast amalgam of networked devices controlled by artificial intelligence, server farms, warehouses ('fulfilment centres'), web services and the like, much of which recedes into a twilight world to which humans are increasingly a foreign body. As the artist Simon Denny suggests in his piece '*Amazon worker cage patent drawing as virtual King Island Brown Thornbill cage, US 9,280,157 B2: 'System and method for transporting personnel within an active workspace, 2016'*, when the human has to interact with the computational operations of the stacked system they must take on the material form of a machine. It is still very much an analogue condition of realising synthetic variations across qualitative different states: the human becoming continuous with the metallic and electronic device, a merging of sensory capacities, a fluidity

---

[27] Maxime Du Camp Preface. In *Les Chants Modernes*. Paris: Michel Lévy frères. 1855, 20.

(ideally) of progressively motivated movement.[28] The cage (shown on the cover of this book) Denny made was based on a patent design lodged, but never built, by Amazon.[29] The human-in-cage would integrate with the motorized shelving, and robots, covering distances quickly, sorting, stacking, distributing, storing objects in accordance with indexing systems designed by algorithms. The cage is indicative of how nothing is exempted from its being in the presence of the productive, waste eliminating power of the ever-porous stack. Denny's work evokes this totalizing condition with its accompanying use of montage in which drawings of the cage and details from the patent's text are set against images of an endangered bird, the brown thornbill. Its small, alert body has been overridden by data, by permissions, by code, by innovative speculation: its *Umwelt* has been fundamentally composed and then compromised by industrialized progress, and just as it, as a bird, cannot ask the question 'Why?', it is increasingly the case that neither can humans.

ERP

Take, as a case in point, the computer-based software designed to craft and enforce organizational strategy: ERP (enterprise resource planning). ERP – in strategic practice the use of the acronym is as pervasive as a picture – is the moniker for software applications that survey and analyse all the core business processes of a commercial organization with a view to reconciling function, performance and ambition. Its origins lay with a concern for efficient material resources planning, which then necessitated the planners involving themselves in workflow patterns, machine integration and updates, accounting and budgeting, risk management, pricing, personnel training, supplier management, customer demand scheduling, and strategic intelligence, all of which is processed through a common set of interfaces and databases. In the relative simplistic context of these strategic ERP systems we find the axiom of mechanics perfectly embodied. The system is predicated on Du Camp's axiom: there must

---

[28] Alexander Galloway Golden age of analog. *Critical Inquiry* 2022, 48(2): 211–32

[29] The patent's existence was unearthed by Kate Crawford and Vladan Joder as they were undertaking their anatomical study of Amazon's voice interaction (Echo) system which shows how the voice-activating user of the system is simultaneously: a consumer (they purchased the product); a resource (their voice commands are surveyed, stored, analysed as part of an ever growing store of information); a labourer (they contribute to Amazon's understanding of its products and services, their behaviours and commands are continually refining what it is Amazon does); and a product (they become an extension of Echo itself, and not at all in control of it). Echo is an ear, set into the home, picking up information that is then fed forward into the Amazonian stack, of which the cage could have been another part.

be no wasted energy. In pursuance of such, ERP systems involve adherents in elaborate processes of boundary work linking generic as well as particularized or customized templates, generating a system whose:

internal workings continually contort as they move around and as new functionality is added … It is through this morphing/extension process that software packages are able to move from place to place and to reach out into new settings. Such amoeboid movements, in turn, enable users to grab on to and then align themselves with the various protuberances and protrusions.[30]

But, as Pollock and Williams add, this requires continual forming and reforming of what constitutes a good user, setting in train a constant, ever-open exchange between the mechanics and the organizational form in which it is hosted.

There is, here, a territorial micro-politics that tinctures the interplay of mechanics and form. It comes, for example, in the differing expressions of 'willingness' amongst software providers and the programmers dedicated to customizing processes and interfaces. It comes in the capacity of firms to pay for adaptations and upgrades, and the terms of their contractual buy-in. It comes in the stacked enthusiasm for new technologies associated with cloud-based data storage, transnational accounting operations, cyber security, seamless interfaces and regulatory anticipation. And it comes in the way different industries and societies have different ideas concerning the nature of organizational functionality.

This gives the impression of an increasing strategic alignment of organizational power and practices associated with digital computing, but as Lisa Conrad shows the politics extend beyond this, pushing back into the materiality from which ERP boasts an organizational escape.[31] Indeed, it is even within ERP systems itself, whose users continue to also use older manual processes such as planning boards. These arrangements of printed cards and colour coded scheduling slots are prone to various infrastructural breakdowns: printer malfunctions, erroneous entries, and so on.[32] Yet they also show immense resilience. Planning boards can be rearranged

[30] Neil Pollock and Robin Williams *Software and Organizations. The Biography of the Enterprise-wide System or How SAP Conquered the World.* Milton Park, UK: Routledge. 2008, 175.

[31] Lisa Conrad *Organisation im soziotechnischen Gemenge: Mediale Umschichtungen durch die Einführung von SAP.* Bielefeld: Transcript. 2015, 7. Our translation. See also Lisa Conrad Peg board. In *The Oxford Handbook of Media, Technology and Organization Studies.* Edited by T. Beyes, R. Holt, and C. Pias. Oxford: Oxford University Press. 2020. See also Jannis Kallinikos *Governing through Technology: Information Artefacts and Social Practice.* Basingstoke: Macmillan. 2011, 54.

[32] Lisa Conrad *Organisation im soziotechnischen Gemenge Mediale Umschichtungen durch die Einführung von SAP.* 168ff.

on the spot and publicly; a misplaced pink order sheet can be found in a pile of papers; an erroneous figure can be crossed out and corrected. A digitized, comprehensive ERP system, on the other hand, lacks this flexibility. Because the system does not deal in things, just in data, it is never clear whether a mistake is in the form, the entry, or the calculating processes, and the effects and affects of the system are harder to discern. To siphon through these issues, workers have to become ERP-users, alongside other users, whether consultants or algorithms. Users familiar with reading and processing work instructions, as well as the work-arounds for software idiosyncrasies, with repairing and isolating gaps and weaknesses and sources of error in an inherently un-transparent system, learning from resident 'experts' who help others navigate and repair, and generally find a way through the 'maze of transactions'.[33] To become such a user means workers be granted access rights, and be addressed themselves as experts. The question of expertise therefore shifts from knowing how to (in this case) manage the production of goods towards managing the software infrastructure that has taken over the primary task of organizing work. It is work that occurs in clouds whose reach extends beyond the firewalls of the company for which they are an employee. But then their employee status might change, as their expertise in new technology couches their role differently, removing them from everyday activities in such a way that they treat organizational situations as generic rather than bespoke, resulting in increasing reliance on packaged solutions that bring as many problems with them as they resolve.[34] As Galloway has it: 'Those who were formerly scholars or experts in a certain area are now recast as mere tool users beholden to the affordances of the tool.'[35] It becomes hard to even locate expertise in these systems, as large software package providers attend to activities of product development, marketing and technological support while outsourcing the lifecycle management of these solutions (including implementation, updates and customization, as well as training) to vast networks of partners.[36]

Coupled to this hollowing out of situational wisdom comes a strategic preoccupation with the availability of masses of stored and real-time data gathered from users.[37] The systems no longer rely on expertise and ensuing expertise-based categories when selecting which data ought to be measured and processed. Galloway notices how:

[33] Jannis Kallinikos *Governing through Technology*, 58.
[34] Jannis Kallinikos *Governing through Technology*, 83, 48.
[35] Alexander Galloway The cybernetic hypothesis. *differences*, 2014, 25(1): 107–31, 127.
[36] Neil Pollock and Robin Williams *Software and Organizations*, 242.
[37] Ioanna Constantiou and Jannis Kallinikos New games, new rules: Big data and the changing context of strategy. *Journal of Information Technology*, 2015, 30: 44–57.

information is often uncoupled from a human observer, given that information may be gathered, processed, and re-sent by instruments regardless of human intervention. Thus, just like the agents within the system, information also gains a relative autonomy when deployed within a cybernetic environment because it may directly effect certain outcomes without the intervention of a human actor.[38]

Data consist of user-generated content or unfiltered sensor information, tagging and upload and download clicks are collected randomly and incessantly, consisting of everyday, often trivial data points in various data formats and it is not clear how, given such complex and extensive data pools, such filtering and experience-based classifying and the required data reduction and aggregation processes (especially of videos, images or sensor data gathered from tracking devices) may be conducted, so as to arrive at any half-way meaningful strategic insights.[39]

The ERP system is organized through repeated crossings of the layers in the stack, and within each layer come a host of contingencies and disturbances, few of which can be planned for, despite the avowed intent of the system. As a strategic tool ERP organizes as it goes, in organizational practice it is often supplemented by legacy systems, and serves multiple organizational needs and indeed organizations. To the extent there is order, it is enacted as much in the micro-activities of replication, recursion and enforcement as it is in the expression of intentional resource allocation decisions. If this is the case with ERP – which is, according to its developers, *the* means by which an organization can consciously achieve strategic clarity in goals and outcomes – then it is the case everywhere. The promise of ERP systems comes in offering strategists a picture of an organization's operations in relation to its own historical sense of self, and to its wider market positioning: it is touted as a strategic tool which, with the rise of digital computing, becomes even more compelling in its reach, rapidity and immediacy. ERP systems are predicated on a view of strategy that encourages an organization to insist on acting in accordance

---

[38] Alexander Galloway The cybernetic hypothesis, 115.

[39] While digital information and 'big-data' approaches have stimulated much real-time organizational reaction, such as in the case of point-of-sale data, traffic patterns or logistics tracking, much visual data, Ioanna Constantiou and Jannis Kallinikos argue, is not analysed digitally, that is they are not themselves processed as bits and bytes, but instead these data are coded through metadata consisting of tags offering brief descriptions of an image or video's content, akin to Amazon's Mechanical Turk Ioanna Constantiou and Jannis Kallinikos New games, new rules, 50. The irony, it seems, is that despite their direct computability digital 'images' still resist machinated meaningful semiotic analysis which has meant, so far, masses of pictures and videos being taken and shared, requiring, in turn, ever-more standardized methods of analysis (e.g., through meta-tagging), which radically de-contextualizes the resulting data. See Attila Marton and Jose-Carlos Mariategui De/contextualizing information: The digitization of video editing practices at the BBC. *The Information Society. An International Journal.* 2015, 31: 106–20, 108.

with its own self-assignments, rather than simply imitate others. It has been designed to enhance a sense of organizational self. But this picture is thoroughly outmoded. From within the lived experience of using and being used by a system amid other stacked systems, ERP systems mediate any strategic sense of organizational self to a point of turning it inside out: what is presumed to be inside the organization – its distinct skills and singular sense of direction – spill across boundaries and what is considered an organizational 'outside' is little more than a measured projection of organizational machinery: form and mechanics cannot be disassociated.[40]

To recall Kittler's phrasing, this and myriad other forms of media 'determine our situation' by configuring and shaping the very operations, effects and affects entailed in organizing *qua* mediating devices and forms.[41] The expanding cloud of addresses and permissions needed to run ERP systems, the interlacing of application interfaces, the urban ecologies in which working lives are increasingly a part, the incessant noise of different users competing for speedier more total online access to real-time data, and so on, all interact and shape the systems in ways that limit and stabilize the information provided to users, pre-selected from a near-infinite pool of other available data so that 'dealing with the device consists of being led through the narrative of the interface over which only limited control is available'.[42] Attempt to get a perspective upon the nature of such an organizational form, attempt to follow and gather the flows of information and you encounter the mechanism: the strategic desire to represent an organization to itself and others and thereby show its place is sublimated in the computational mechanics by which organization occurs.

Machine Intelligence

It is this orientation to events that defines intelligence, insofar as intelligence, being more than adaptation or stimulus response, involves cognitive capacities for interpretation and anticipation from within one's

---

[40] Maxime du Camp's work on Hausmann's Paris almost ecstatically immerses itself in the rhythmic pulse of the city, the networked techniques and technics of the city, the way an outward solidity so rapidly gives way in all manner of mechanized movement. Whilst Benjamin cites du Camp's insight in a spirit of melancholy inevitability, du Camp himself, ethnographically noticing the increasingly ordered and networked nature of human activity, was in places entranced with the evident regularities steadying themselves on the earth without any apparent progenitor.

[41] Armin Beverungen, Timon Beyes, and Lisa Conrad The organizational powers of (digital) media. *Organization*, 21(5): 621–35, 624.

[42] David Berry *The Philosophy of Software Code and Mediation in the Digital Age*. London: Palgrave Macmillan. 2011, 132.

Umwelt, ones that came first from techne, and which were then absorbed into the Gestell. A very basic example of human intelligence might be the supposition that a German operator using an Enigma encryption machine to send messages during World War II, one that was stationed in the same place for a good while and so likely to be reporting on similar kinds of event, might be expected to repeat the same message in response to the same event, such as 'plane flying overhead', or to use a similar form of greeting. It was by painstakingly noticing and logging these patterns of event and their encrypted representation in messages, that British code-breaker operators working from Bletchley Park in Buckinghamshire were able to restrict the range of computational calculations they had to perform while trying to crack the encrypting code. They even went so far as to arrange for a plane to be flown above the operator's observational area, to try to goad him or her into sending a message. Subsequent iterations of code breaking machinery would be programmed to predict such patterns: the computers would anticipate by themselves. For example, they were programmed with routines that, in the interests of speedy processing, would predict the outcome of a sub-routine before it was finished, and only go back to re-calculate if the outcome of the sub-routine was not as predicted. The burden of listening in, of unscrambling scrambled letters, of placing and predicting movements, was increasingly taken on by machines. They were faster, more reliable, more comprehensive. The intelligence officers became operators set within an increasingly vast industrial machinery of crypto-intelligence trading in awareness of the shifting array of strengths, weaknesses, threat and opportunities emerging from a restless array of resources and positions.

The predictive intelligence of machinery is woven into an already superior – to humans – capacity to operate at what Katherine Hayles calls the level of nonconscious cognition. She suggests that, in addition to primary and higher forms of consciousness configured through self-awareness, reasoning and narrative, the human brain also employs 'nonconscious cognition'.[43] These nonconscious processes operate at a neuronal level and, while inaccessible to modes of awareness, they nevertheless perform functions essential to consciousness. They are too fast to reach the level of consciousness[44] but indispensable for those slower, higher

---

[43] N. Katherine Hayles *Unthought: The Power of the Cognitive Nonconscious*. Chicago: University of Chicago Press. 2017, 10.

[44] Relatedly, Dieter and Gauthier show how user-experience driven website development absorbs these micro-temporalities when considering users' limited attention span, typically 3 sec., after which the 'specious present' yields to a wandering mind or, rather, a wandering cursor, already clicking new tabs or applications. The task of (website) designers, etymologically cast as 'cunning plotters', is to arrest the wander by captivating

cognitive processes to function as they provide the basis for dynamic interactions with the environment.[45] Without them our conscious cognition would be overwhelmed with occurrence, requiring we reach decisions on the most inconsequential of things. Though unconscious, this cognition still takes time. Hayles records how a human noticing a light flare on a bank of dials, and responding involves the firing of a neuron which takes about 0.4 milliseconds; for this sensation to register in their brain takes around 80 milliseconds; from there to understanding, such as recognizing the symbolic significance of the light, takes up to 250 milliseconds, and grasping the implications can take several minutes or hours.[46] Compared to these speeds this 'cost of human consciousness' makes human physiology far too slow to keep up or notice even basic computational inputs and outputs.[47] Just as the hand was outmoded by steam machinery, so now the brain is being outmoded by electronic computing. Equally limiting is the fact that human operators get tired – those working at Bletchley Park were constantly overworked, complaining of an incessant tiredness to which the stirring of patriotic intensity proved only a limited antidote. Their complaints drew sympathy from Winston Churchill who sanctioned far higher levels of investment, less in people than in machinery. Bletchley became an intelligence factory in which the physical fatigue common to any human body was sublimated by a tireless whirr of switches and relays. Though they still needed the human energy of operators and analysts, they drew more and more on the then apparently limitlessness reserves of nature, indifferent to which operator was attending to an increasingly limited set of roles, running faster and faster, dispersing decisions on various levels and at various moments in a systemic process over which there was less and less direct oversight.[48]

the user in simulations of a promising future, a feeding-forward of anticipation that then cognitively implicates the user, in the operations of abducting value. 'Captivation' suggest Dieter and Gauthier, takes the form of 'abandonment or losing of the self, a non-productive process (a distraction or daydream)' Michael. Dieter and David. Gauthier On the politics of chrono-design: Capture, time and the interface. *Theory Culture and Society*, 2019, 36(2): 61–87, 62ff.

[45] N. Katherine Hayles *How We Think: Digital Media and Contemporary Technogenesis*. London: University of Chicago Press. 2021, 87.

[46] N. Katherine Hayles *How We Think*, 104.

[47] Armin Beverungen and Ann-Christina Lange. Cognition in high-frequency trading: The cost of consciousness and the limits of automation. *Theory, Culture & Society*, 2018, 35, 7, 75–95, 82. Hayles points towards a now popular video showing a basketball game with instructions to viewers to count the passes. In the middle of the scene, a person in a gorilla suit walks across the paying area, but most viewers do not notice this. She provides a number of further examples to that effect. N. Katherine Hayles. *Unthought*, 44ff.

[48] Gilbert Simondon Technical Mentality, 7.

As Hayles notes, the sheer plenitude of activity and outputs begins to swamp conscious forms of intelligence, it gets easier and easier to let the computers think for us. The striking element of these stacked, computational media is not that they are particularly more important than other technologies, such as roads, containers, optics or photography, but seemingly their unconscious cognitive abilities have a transformative potential that makes for an interesting if not disturbing projection of the limits of human intervention in future iterations of stacked systems.[49] In other words, how we humans interpret and anticipate (the marks of intelligence) is based on series of distinctions that are devolved into unconscious layers and trajectories extending into distributed apparatuses that continually develop and so take on more and more of the processing power of our conscious activities (say, when we use a GPS system rather than memorizing a city layout or our direction of travel, or we do the food shopping online at the behest of recommender systems, or we outsource the writing of an exam essay or funeral speech to open AI), we end up having less and less control over or insight into the majority of information processing efforts that mark our everyday (organized) lives.[50] It is a lack of control grounded in our having been handed over to machinery.

Andy Clark speaks of this spread or bloom as a *supersizing* of the mind by cycles involving body and world in outward loops that push cognition outward,[51] suggesting '[t]he "extended mind" hypothesis is really a hypothesis about extended vehicles – vehicles that may be distributed

---

[49] N. Katherine Hayles *Unthought*, 33, 51.

[50] Beatrice Fazi pushes this idea to the extreme, ascribing cognitive processes to computational operations capable of experience or consciousness in the sense that algorithms not only evaluate and transform (or switch over as Kittler argues), but also produce new actualities. Fazi focusses on 'contingent computation' that is the 'method of systematizing reality through logico-quantitative means', which are often assumed to merely represent reality through binary calculations. We need to jettison our assumption that experience is woven with having a body. Fazi argues that computation is not just physical manipulation of data and therefore a form of abstraction based on previously conceived programs, because in every algorithmic procedure, there remains incomputablity (198). Here, computers harbour the capacity for novelty beyond their inherited elements (programs, pre-arranged hardware, etc.), they are exposed to indeterminacy, if not that of biological life or lived experience, then that of the logical and mathematical character of the computational system (116). This indeterminacy comes into play whenever a computer system is powered up. it is impossible to say in advance whether it will run (also known as the Halting problem as outlined by Turing, and which we elaborate in Chapter 8). Following Whitehead's notion of prehension as an 'uncognitive apprehension' – that is, 'a grasping, a seizing, or the holding of one thing by another thing' (63), we can think of computing as an *event*, constructed '*within the actuality* of computation' so that the 'infinity of the incomputable is always present; it cannot be avoided' (128, original italics).

[51] Andy Clark *Supersizing the Mind: Embodiment, Action, and Cognitive Extension*. Oxford: Oxford University Press: 2008, xxvi.

across brain, body, and world'.[52] Following both Clark and Hayles' accounts we can see how someone with, say, flu-like systems uses an internet search engine to find remedies, and thereby lets their cognitive processes circulate through server systems, networks and other 'network objects', with the combined 'person+search engine+networks+…' system gaining the intelligence of the benefits of adding honey to hot water, the phone number of a doctor or the optimal route to the next open pharmacy, doing so via networked GPS systems and mechanistic extensions of transport systems. On the other side we see how such search entries allow for the analysis of the spread of flu through Big Data analyses of the rates and distribution of 'flu'- (or flu-anxiety) related internet searches by epidemiologists, as well as the rapid spread of misinformation, in the unfolding interplay of swarm intelligence and (post-)human connectedness.[53] Yet for both Hayles and Clark this spread does not reduce the importance of the mind, which Clark assigns the function of a controller of embodied action, forming an extended set of relations between nature and culture, forever capable of responding to and driving new actions in the environment. This means the things we typically perceive to be paraphernalia of cognitive processes, the notebooks, post-its, pens, recorders, storage spaces, encoders, distributors, are no longer merely there to store or manipulate information – but become crucial devices of the cognitive processes itself.[54] In this way, the machines and artefacts that populate the pathways of extended cognition are both prosthetic extensions and 'scaffolding' affording new neural connections. Prosaic examples might include how we enter a dark room and automatically search for the light switch, asking mapping software for a direction, acquiring the right pose for full body selfies.[55] Here the internal organization of the mind is extended, spatially, into the wider environment, acquiring new powers,

---

[52] Andy Clark *Supersizing the Mind*, 217.

[53] Ragnar Fjelland Why general artificial intelligence will not be realized. *Humanities & Social Sciences Communications*, 2020, 7(10): 1–9.

[54] Clark refers to a person with advanced memory loss using a range of technological devices to record and thus remember actions and conversations. When leaving the room after a discussion, he would for example consult his smartphone to recall what the conversation so far entailed before re-entering the room. How, asks Clark, would we be able, in such a case, to see the potential theft of that phone as merely a crime of property. If that person thinks through these devices, then surely this means that they are part of a much more important process and the ethical ramifications of such conclusions. Similarly, processes of organizational change that unsettle individuals by changing their environments can become a severance of information pathways, infringing their sense of self in ways a purely cognitive perspective of identity could never apprehend, Andy Clark *Supersizing the Mind*. See also Gregory Bateson *Steps to an Ecology of Mind*. Chicago: University of Chicago Press. 2000, 322.

[55] Luciana Parisi *Contagious Architecture*. Cambridge, MA: MIT Press. 2022, 215.

to the point that cognition runs through bodies and local environments almost without a unifying or centralizing mind. Thought, in other words, is extended into hardware and code, which supersize the brain; artificially enhance it to solve ever growing problems.

Tertiary Retention

Is it, however, really just a problem of managing the extent of machine capture as Clark and Hayles (echoed by Zuboff) imply? Perhaps not. For Bernard Stiegler the situation in which humans are being thrown cannot be simplified to one in which prosthetic devices have taken over their operators. Rather, he suggests, cognition has changed, and it is no longer human, a conclusion he reaches by concentrating not only on the influence of technology on perception, but also the senses.[56] For Stiegler, human awareness (the phenomenological emergence of 'appearance) cannot be situated in the mind, but is instead utterly situational, and therefore utterly technological.

Stiegler sees the interplay of memory and technology as being central to the development of the human being, an argument he unfolds via a number of routes, one particularly interesting one is through Edmund Husserl's identification of the 'big' or 'large' *now* of perception. A temporal object, for Husserl, is constituted in its duration as a flux that is coincident with the flux of consciousness of which it is the object; an example is a melody, which is constituted only in its duration, hanging together with notes preceding and following it.[57] Husserl connects with every present moment (with each originary impression), an additional element that extends that now; its 'just past' that is constitutive of the present – in the case of the melody, the already disappeared notes that cojoin the present ones. Immediate perception drags with it a 'comet's tail' of this immediate past (as well as anticipatory elements), and the ensuing *'present+immediate past'* construct is what Husserl calls *'primary memory'* – memory that constitutes an original impression. Husserl's example is the fading sound of a violin:

When a tone dies away, it itself is sensed at first with particular fullness (intensity); and then follows a rapid weakening in intensity. The tone is still there, still sensed, but in mere reverberation.[58]

---

[56] Mark Hansen *Feed Forward: On the Future of Twenty-first-century Media*. Chicago: University of Chicago Press. 2015, 47.

[57] Bernard Stiegler *Technics and Time, 2: Disorientation*. Translated by S. Barker. Stanford: Stanford University Press. 2009, 5.

[58] Edmund Husserl *On the Phenomenology of the Consciousness of Internal Time*. Translated by J. B. Brough. London: Kluwer. 1991, 33.

The reverberation is therefore different from the perception itself, but as a memory it is neither 'really' present in retentional consciousness (*retentionales Bewußtsein*); nor is it a different tone in addition to the original one. Instead, the intuition of time, at any point, involves not just what appears to be enduring right now, but also what has just been. Husserl speaks of 'primary memory' or 'primary retention' in terms of this immediate form of memory coupled with perception. It differs from what Husserl calls 'secondary memory' or 'secondary retention', which exists only as a (necessarily selective) memory in the sense of a recollection of a past as a total temporal phenomenon that can come back into presence (*Wiedererinnerung*). Where primary retention names the tail of a reverberating note, secondary retention is like remembering a melody one has heard at a recent concert – it is therefore a selection – as everyone in the audience will retain something different from all the music played in the concert; it is merely a *represented* past, not a *perceived* past.

Husserl asserts that both primary and secondary retentions are also different from a third kind of memory, which is not lived or subject to an individual's own experience, but is fixed in the work of paintings or sculptures (which he refers to as image-consciousness – *Bildbewusstsein*), which retain memory in an external (or exteriorized) way, and it is this third form of retention – the tertiary memory made possible through non-living things – that preoccupies Stiegler's own work.

Unlike Husserl, who directly opposes primary and secondary memory as separate forms of retention, Stiegler argues that primary memory can be influenced by secondary memory, but this requires the capacity for temporal objects to be retained and repeated in exactly the same way.[59] Repeatedly listening to an identical song (possibly over and over again), we are able to hear new things in the same object while also changing our anticipation of the next moments in the recording and so both secondary and tertiary memories influence perception in the 'large' now. But this only became possible when tertiary memory became carried not only by works of art, but forms of machinery; specifically, the invention of the phonograph.

Stiegler's concern lies therefore with the influence of such technical, exteriorized and non-living retentions; with the technical nature of tertiary memory and its influence on consciousness and, as we will see, the formation of the self and the social body. Here, Stiegler leaves Husserl's phenomenological concern for the living present behind and turns to Heidegger's considerations of the past of *Dasein*. *Dasein* always already has a world; a world that is always already there (in a *ready-to-hand*,

---

[59] Bernard Stiegler *Technics and Time, 3: Cinematic Time and the Question of Malaise.* Translated by. S. Barker. Stanford: Stanford University Press. 2011, 40.

engaged way); a world that it inherits without having experienced it directly.[60] Heidegger speaks of an *always-already-there* and he refers to world-historiality (*Weltgeschichtlichkeit*) to name this ghostly presence of the dead who have not entirely vanished because their traces remain for future generations. Right at the beginning of *Being and Time*, he asserts:

historicity is prior to what is called history [*weltgeschichtliches Geschehen*]. Historicity means the constitution of being of the 'occurrence' of Dasein as such; upon its ground something like 'world history,' and belonging historically to world history, is possible. In its factical being Dasein always is how and 'what' it already was. Whether explicitly or not, it is its past. It is its own past not only in such a way that its past, as it were, pushes itself along 'behind' it, and that it possesses what is past as a property that is still objectively present and at times has an effect on it. Dasein 'is' its past in the manner of its being which, roughly expressed, on each occasion 'occurs' out of its future.[61]

Rather than beginning afresh with each new generation – that is beginning just with the genetic predispositions that are germane to the particular evolutionary stage of humanity's development – the *always-already-there* bestows individual humans their identity, their customs and manners, their speech and gestures. *Dasein* is being-thrown into an *Umwelt* and so inherits its past; it inherits *experience* in addition to genetic information, which allows it to become a '*Who*' – a child or grandchild, a member of a family, culture, city and so on, and even though this past is not anything the new earthling has lived, it is still *its* past. Having a past is a *facticity*, a sense of self and belonging, from out of which the self can project itself forth into its future; to become this or that person, and so to glimpse possibilities that are rooted in their heritage: ways of being that arise out of the thrownness into an *Umwelt* that is already brimming with cultural life, recipes, traditions, labels and much more, even if none of these have been experienced by that particular individual.

Dasein grows into a customary interpretation of itself and grows up on that inter-pretation. It understands itself initially in terms of this interpretation and, within a certain range, constantly does so. This understanding discloses the possibilities of its being and regulates them. Its own past-and that always means that of its 'gen-eration' does not follow after Dasein but rather always already goes ahead of it.[62]

Any engagement with tools, even in their most basic form such as a pencil, deploys a collectively memory of how the writing tool was made, how it has been used previously, and modified, all of which is

[60] Bernard Stiegler *Technics and Time, 1: The Fault of Epimetheus*. Translated by R. Beardsworth & G Collins. Stanford: Stanford University Press. 1998, 140.

[61] Martin Heidegger *Being and Time*, §19–20.

[62] Martin Heidegger *Being and Time*, §20.

held fast in already existing practices into which the user of a pencil finds themselves thrown. The pencil appears from within a technical consciousness to which its present use is always contributing, not just inwardly, as part of the subject's own personal memory, but also outwardly, as a technical supplement in form of prosthetic memory systems.[63] In addition to *genetic* memory, which is stored in genes, and *epigenetic* memory, which comprises individually acquired experience stored in the central nervous system, we therefore find Stiegler's *epiphylogenetic* or *tertiary* type of retention, which is exteriorized into instruments and so can be passed on across cultures and generations, outside, as it were, of the human body. *Hominization* is, for Stiegler, therefore inseparable from *technicization*; a co-emergence of the '*Who*' and the '*What*'.

Stiegler follows Heidegger in this analysis of heritage but accuses him of falling short of exploring the most radical implication of the *always-already-there*, namely, that at the very ground of the human *Umwelt* lie *material elements*, media, that convey traces of the dead:

It is a memory that is neither primary nor secondary; it is completely ignored in Heidegger's analyses, as it was in those of Husserl, and yet it is immediately there in a tool; indeed it is the very meaning of a tool.[64]

Like Husserl, who excludes pictures and sculptures as mere image-consciousness from the conception of retention, Stiegler argues that Heidegger excludes the realm of the technical from the analysis of world-historiality, retreating instead into a quite human concern of a totality (or finality), in which authentic Being runs against the sway of what is already there.

In addition to the comings and goings of humans there is therefore an experiential (*epigenetic*) layer of life that is not lost with the living when they die; this layer conserves *itself* and passes *itself* down to future generations. Stiegler attributes to this layer an active and ontologically prior character; not a biological programme (and not a process attributable to 'pure life', as experience cannot be inherited genetically) but instead:

a cipher in which the whole of Dasein is caught; this epigenetic sedimentation, a memorization of what has come to pass, is what is called the past, what we shall name the *epiphilogenesis* of man, meaning the conservation, accumulation and sedimentation of successive epigenesis, mutually articulated.[65]

---

[63] Bernard Stiegler *Technics and Time, 1*, 150.
[64] Bernard Stiegler *Technics and Time, 1*, 254.
[65] Bernard Stiegler *Technics and Time, 1*, 140.

In identifying the importance of technics as a medium that allows for heritage, Stiegler follows the Heideggerian idea of *Dasein* being reliant upon a past, and that this past is not only what it has individually experienced. However, unlike Heidegger, Stiegler does not allow for *Dasein* to have its having-been on its own accord. In being more than its own past, *Dasein* is always already technological; Being happens amidst and as a result of tools. Any engagement with tools, even in their most basic form such as chipping a flint stone to develop sharp edges that can then be used in the collective organization of work (hunting, preparing food or carpeting), as well as conflict and exchange, involves remembering how the tool was made, how it was deployed and modified, so creating a form of memory that is inscribed in the activity of social life. Tool use brings with it a specific kind of memory that differentiates early man from all other species: 'to use a tool is to remember how it was made, how it has been deployed and, crucially, how it can be modified',[66] as when John Cage modifies bolts to unhome the tertiary memory lodged in concert technology. Stiegler even suggests reversing the story of origin by claiming that it is not the human that invents the tool, but the tool that makes the human (or rather that the development of tools makes it possible for humans to emerge):

Tertiary retention is in the most general sense the prosthesis of consciousness without which there could be no mind, no recall, no memory of a past that one has not personally lived, no culture.[67]

Subsequent technological regimes simultaneously open up new forms of cognition and linguistic expression. Humans depend on technical objects that preserve *epigenetic* experience outside of the body and so make *experience* available for future generations, something genetic evolution is unable to do.[68]

Pharmakon

To explain this condition, Stiegler expands on the Greek term *pharmakon*, originally invoked in Jacques Derrida's reading of Plato, naming both a poison and its remedy, to indicate the relationship between technology and humans whose complicity is indicated both by a gain and a loss. Quite literally, the growth of pharmaceutical chemistry brings relief, yet through the pursuit of strategic competitive advantage it

---

[66] Bernard Stiegler *Technics and Time, I*, 150–4.
[67] Bernard Stiegler *Technics and Time, 3*, 39.
[68] Bernard Stiegler *Technics and Time, 1*, 245.

also transforms the appearance and understanding of human health into a commercial market and a place governed by explicit knowledge. The same goes for all technologically mediated activity (which, for Stiegler, means all authentic human activity). The act of writing, for example, exemplifies this pharmacological pattern as it involves the loss of the practice of internal memorization, as well as a gain because it allows for the storage of information on paper:

Tertiary retention is … what compensates for the default of retention – which is also to say, the loss of both memory and knowledge. But it is also what accentuates this loss (this default): it is a pharmakon.[69]

Once stored on paper, the information on how to understand and relate to things can be transferred across time and space, it can form texts to teach others who have no direct experience, it can be questioned rationally, and distantly. The practical memory of experience of the scribe or scrivener gives way to a formal memory of mediated, grammatical procedure held fast in print, in type, in filing systems, in indexes. A book retains speech in the same way in which the tool retains the gesture of the worker and so technics allow for the development and transmission of culture, science, and so for humans to become human; they provide a supplement for a lack (*de-fault*) and so give to humans the capacity to evolve by means other than life.

Once we move from simple tools (technical elements) to more complex machines (technical ensembles) we see a wider transposition of knowledge. Where tools aggregate into industrial complexes, generations of labourers' and workers' gestures, knowledge and experience pass into machines, replacing or rather displacing technical being – that being that since hominization has made itself in the image of tools now is reduced to operating (Stiegler speaks of 'serving') technical ensembles.[70] Stiegler's observations echo those of Simondon: As machines and machine complexes get upgraded continually in a process of 'concretization', the labourer and worker do not:

The progress of the eighteenth century is a progress experienced by individual through the force, speed, and precision of his gestures. The progress of the nineteenth century can no longer be experienced by the individual, because it is no longer centralized with the individual as the center of command and perception in the adapted action. The individual becomes the mere spectator of the

---

[69] Bernard Stiegler *The Age of Disruption: Technology and Madness in Computational Capitalism*. Translated by Daniel Ross. Cambridge: Polity. 2016, 17.

[70] Bernard Stiegler *For a New Critique of Political Economy*. Translated by Daniel Ross. Cambridge: Polity. 2010, 37.

results of the functioning of the machines, or the one who is responsible for the organization of technical ensembles putting the machines to work.[71]

What Stiegler and Simondon are exposing here is that when it is acknowledged, the role of spectator, the role we earlier ascribed to strategy as the attempt of an organization to gain critical perspective upon itself, becomes more an acknowledgement of a profound and inevitable impotence. Günther Anders, using the term bystander, argues it is even a shameful experience. The capacities of technology are updated continually while the labourer and worker are merely reborn, naked and wrinkly, from generation to generation. with the same limited set of skills, and so forever falling behind.[72] Because of its limited capacity for enhancement, the human being is increasingly removed from the productive process, or merely tolerated, as an 'unavoidable appendix' to the machine; as the weakest link or bottleneck.[73] And, in the context of the continual transformation of capital, not just as producers, but consumers too. Anders notes the perverted reversal of the mass-market culture in which the consumer is still being treated as the subject of desire and demand, even if they are 'terrorized into their needs', and the new machine culture where machines now 'openly and shamelessly' posture as the subject of demand.[74]

Put in Stiegler's conceptual framing, the stock of tertiary knowledge, retained in massively growing knowledge and productive facilities comes at the expense of a loss of knowledge in the labourer and worker, now left merely to operate buttons and computer interfaces so becoming unable to penetrate these surface level inputs into otherwise incomprehensible machine operations. Even the engineers and other experts who design, maintain, repair and upgrade technological systems mostly do so by drawing on defined processes and by installing modular, black-box systems that conform to established regulations.[75]

All this points to a profound reorientation of memory systems, in particular in the context of organizations that are replete with technological ensembles that mimic and therefore retain human knowledge and action, able not merely to repeat it tirelessly, but also able to be continually upgraded and adjusted. This means that industrial technical objects have a consistency that goes beyond being utensils owing to their capacity to operate at their own accord, harbouring a self-determining logic that belongs to them alone: their own mode of existence.[76] Machines are therefore not merely a

[71] Gilbert Simondon *On the Mode of Existence of Technical Objects*, 12, 137.
[72] Günther Anders On Promethean shame, 29–96.
[73] Günther Anders On Promethean shame, 40–5.
[74] Günther Anders On Promethean shame, 42.
[75] Bernard Stiegler *For a New Critique of Political Economy*, 47
[76] Bernard Stiegler *Technics and Time*, 1, 68.

retainer for selective human memory (such as the secondary kind of memory identified by Husserl, which retains certain elements of a wider flow of primary perceptions). Technical objects are a form of social memory – and they are part and parcel of a transformation from a version of humanness characterized by their bearing of tools towards machines (which are organized inorganic matter) taking the role of tools bearers.

As a *pharmakon*, the human depends on technology for the chance of 'spirit' (of authentic 'seeing' as well as 'naming' activity), while suffering the simultaneous threat to self-consciousness from the hyperindustrialized forms of this technology. Technological developments can bring a new *pharmakon* and so herald transformatory changes, such as the invention of the alphabet, writing, book printing, but also the process of industrialization and more recent computer-based systems. The book inscribes speech in writing in the same way in which an industrial machine inscribes the gestures of the hand, while sense becomes inscribed in the audio-visual apparatuses that have become the latest lures of consumer capitalism, and all of these contribute to the loss of knowledge, which Stiegler links to the endemic growth of the proletarianization of Western industrialized life.

Proletarianization indicates the degradation of the reflective and expressive potential in societies. What is made present as experience – what appears – is staged technologically, and through the global spread of logistics and informatics all appearance has been touched and stained by constantly expanding forms of market economy which effortlessly integrate and absorb sentient experience into biotechnological, virtual-aesthetic, digital and cybernetic systems. Media technologies are surrogates to capital flows: they mediate the flow of conscious experience by replacing natural or 'lived' memories with tertiary ones, manufactured so that what can be anticipated, imagined or expected is no longer rooted in authentic social and cultural traditions, but geared towards the more effective functioning of capital.

To understand why Stiegler attributes such destructive power (or pharmacological toxicity) to digital media, it is necessary to briefly return to the question of memory as primary, secondary retentions as in Husserl's experience and recollection of a concert, and Stiegler's tertiary extension through a phonographic repetition of the *same* temporal object. Perception, we recall, can change when exteriorized memory is presented again (even over and over). Stiegler sees the phonograph 'making it obvious' that it produces the recording of a track on a material object.[77] However, the matter gets more complicated when we turn from the simple and analogue phonograph to the cinema. Unlike the exteriorization of memory

---

[77] Bernard Stiegler *Technics and Time, 3*, 39.

in music, the cinema brings a shift in the relationship between the three types of memory, as it connects disparate elements together into a single temporal flux.[78] It does so by working with all three elements of memory whereby tertiary memory first roots secondary and primary memory in one another. The cinematic is so profoundly influential because it works precisely at the level of tertiary memory: a temporal object that coincides with consciousness which, in turn, is 'intimately penetrated and controlled by cinematic sequences'. Put differently, for Stiegler, the temporal flux of cinema coincides with the spectator's consciousness – not, however, because cinema has adapted human memory, but because the work of consciousness 'is already somehow cinemato-graphic'.[79] This is so because any sense of '*We*', that is of a social body, of belonging, culture, history and scientific progress is only possible because *epiphilogenetic*, technical memory provides access to a past that was never lived:

The process requires access to a false past, but one whose very falsity is the basis of an 'already-there' out of which the phantasmagorical inheritor can desire a common future with those who share this (false) past by adoption, phantasmagorically.[80]

The trick performed by the cinema is to replace the source of the past that was not lived. Earlier technologies like the phonogram still worked as a prosthesis of a 'singular type': it makes its recording obvious. The cinema does no such thing. The technology of the moving image now *coincides with consciousness* (with primary retention) which is equally, at its base, fundamentally artificial, that is it is always already modified and constituted through secondary and tertiary memory (that is, it is always already 'somehow' cinematographic).[81]

The effects of this change are far-reaching. The formation of a self is, as we have seen, subject to engagement with tertiary memory – with the continually growing masses of things that are made available for experience through mnemonic devices, but which do not require any direct experience themselves – Heidegger's *always already there* sedimented through Arendt's work. Libraries, rituals, cultural practices, songs and stories preserve the collective memory of a '*We*' as a shared, common past that allows for the development of a shared desire of a common future.[82] Any self (the *I*) is continually formed in relation to this '*We*' – through processes of 'synchronization'[83] by which a self experiences these rituals,

[78] Bernard Stiegler *Technics and Time, 3*, 15.
[79] Bernard Stiegler *Technics and Time, 3*, 38, 87.
[80] Bernard Stiegler *Technics and Time, 3*, 40.
[81] Bernard Stiegler *Technics and Time, 3*, 39.
[82] Bernard Stiegler *Technics and Time, 3*, 88.
[83] Bernard Stiegler *Technics and Time, 3*, 102.

reads books or engages in social practices, thereby never totally fusing with the remnants of the old. And just like the '*I*' (and recalling our discussion of Aubyn's, Knausgaard's and Didion's equivocal experience of their own '*I*') must remain partially undetermined to be able to be part of a group, so the collective '*We*' also retains an open and developing character.[84] Both the collective '*We*' and the conforming '*I*' are never fully formed and so capable of both continuation as well as novelty, continually emerging in this process of co-individuation. It is precisely this process of working out alignments and discrepancies between the self and the social (a working out which we earlier likened to seeing as well as naming) which Stiegler now sees endangered with the cinema and the culture industries *writ large*. The cinema (and as we will see, more recent digital developments) subsumes these processes of self and society making (Simondon's 'co-individuation'), as the cinema provides scripted and averaged out versions of non-lived pasts – and of desired futures without requiring the deliberative, reflective and self-forming processes of synchronizing self and other. Retentions (tertiary memories) but also protensions (desires for futures) become standardized and, in Stiegler's analysis, fall under the control of marketing.[85] The cinema begins a process of confusion of primary and secondary retentions with tertiary ones – it is as if one has lived through the film or rather, to pick up Stiegler's bugbear, through masses of films spewed out by Hollywood studios, each presenting a version of a largely Anglo-Americanized way of life: of capitalism and individualism, as if these memories *are* those of a collectively shared past; of a collective '*We*' Whichever elements the self now chooses from this standardized cinematographically scripted, phantasmagorical past, it never finds the kind of divergence or reason to bristle at norms and ideals that prompt it to modify what does not fit, and so engage in a process that sets synchronization and divergence in play. The cinema therefore short-circuits the possibility of the self becoming capable of both conforming with but also rubbing against the social (and socially inherited) body:

just as the worker has been deprived of individual technical potential by machine tools, the subject-conscious-of-objects has become a consumer of products deprived of all possibilities of participating in the process of defining, constructing, and implementing the retentional criteria for a life of the mind.[86]

[84] Bernard Stiegler *Technics and Time, 3*, 97.
[85] Bernard Stiegler *The Nanjing Lectures 2016–2019*. Translated by Daniel Ross. London: Open Humanities Press. 2020, 172.
[86] Bernard Stiegler *Technics and Time, 3*, 103.

Supplementations of Twenty-First-Century Media

Through these interactions the condition of being human, of *Dasein*, changes: humans are adapting to immediate and universal interfaces, to the permanent operation of surveillance systems, or to the instantaneous presence of calculation, by adjusting their behaviours (they act, feel and think as though they were being pictured, they are the picture), but without sharing the most basic of temporal synchronicities.[87] Though determining our situation, therefore, it is not as if either the media or the media bosses are in control. Zuboff, Hayles and Clark diagnose a struggle between human and machine intelligence: just who or what is the intentional force behind cognition, decision making and feeling? Stiegler then complicates the diagnosis by arguing technology mediates all the way through, seeping into practices, traditions and history rather than just individual cognition. The pharmakon is an affective, atmospheric and long-sedimented force that colours the inflections of experience without ever reaching a conscious or cognitive level. Mark Hansen, however, hints at something far more uncertain than even this.

For Hansen, there is no intentional origin or grounding space, no ontological gathering place in which knowledge and experience vie with one another, no equivalent to the essentially contested idea of a subject which is both a thought predicate and experiencing self. He agrees with Stiegler that technologies mediate experience as an a *priori*. They are ever present, but then suggests that whilst humans are organized by this mediation, this is not a symptom of power 'over'. They are not being controlled. The machines are not taking over human life, they are developing their own, and humans are struggling to adapt, submitting to a determining order whose temporal force buries both consciousness and conscience.

At the root of these developments lies the rise of non-perceptual yet still sensible data generated by microsensors, smart devices and the microtemporal scales of digital computation. These have insinuated their way into both thought and perception, and pre-conscious, atmospheric feelings and sensations that need never become the subject of conscious recognition:

---

[87] Hansen discusses the (tertiary) retention of memory through the storage medium of films that are then played out in cinemas and so coinciding with the playing out of the viewers' consciousness, or even earlier to the recording of a melody as a way of 'binding time'. Instead, to follow Hansen, it is a case of 'technically distributed cognition'. Digital inscriptions do not bind time or record concrete experiences but rather 'trigger, score, or format for a viewer-centred potentializing of the present', Mark Hansen Living (with) technical time: from media surrogacy to distributed cognition. *Theory, Culture & Society*, 2009, 26(2–3): 294–315, 307.

For the first time in history, media now typically affect the sensible confound independently of and prior to any more delimited impact they many come to have on human cognitive and perceptual experience.[88]

As twenty-first-century media collect data invisibly and imperceptibly at speeds and volumes that far exceed human perception, they simultaneously expand 'appearance', whilst denuding it of self-awareness. Instead of archiving information like older technical systems (the writing pad or the cinema movie), these media present data to the user with the purpose of influencing the present and immediate future. Hansen speaks of *feed-forward* loops through which data gathered by microsensors loop with aspects of our own experience to which we would otherwise have no access, and in so doing script successive moments of experience, much of which continues to appear without human awareness.

Rather than read this as a progressive lessening and degrading of the human figure as is done in much post-humanistic work, however, Hansen's analysis continues to incorporate the human. Higher-order cognitive and perceptual processes co-function with micro-sensibilities that, while being peripheral to awareness, are still of crucial importance to the overall situation in which a subject finds itself. In so unseating perception and consciousness from its central position in understanding the nature of the human, Hansen creates space for the analysis of sensibility itself. In the spirit of phenomenological approaches, including Heidegger's, Hansen reframes the idea of appearance: the human body is both read as and fed sensory data through its now near-constant immersion in twenty-first-century media, which directly mediate the infrastructure of worldly sensibility.

For Hansen the threat has perhaps less to do with the commercial manipulation of technology. It operates as an ontological and systemic rather than economic force. The emergence of mediating technology has given vent to a profound change in temporality to which all action, feeling and thought is being subject: 'time has changed in the wake of the digital computational revolution'[89] and the fine-grained computational theorizations that underwrite the technical regimes of our times are not only no longer re-presentable to human perception, but of a different temporal ordering altogether. It is not at all a case of milliseconds and limits expressed in the language of clock time. It is a case that machinery has no time that we humans can acknowledge; if they could 'speak' we could certainly not understand them. Computing processes retain their

---

[88] Mark Hansen *Feed Forward*, 37.

[89] Mark Hansen Living (with) technical time: From media surrogacy to distributed cognition. *Theory, Culture & Society*, 2009, 26(2–3): 294–315, 294.

own temporal specificity – which then interact with human affairs in myriad and repeated 'positionings and juxtapositionings'.[90]

Hansen, then, in accepting is also revising Stiegler's pharmacological regime. Prior technological media, including writing, perform a supplementation on the same register and so directly give back what they take away: short-term (natural) memory is sacrificed for the possibility of retaining memory in writing (artificially) outside the body. With its sensors in smartphones, cars, fitness and sleep trackers, insulin dispensers, weather apps and much more, twenty-first-century media provide a new direct and micro-temporal access to the sensible world and so take away the need for perceptual grasp. In return, however, they offer merely an 'indirect' recompense, as they do not give back perception in a new and artificial way. The newly gained sensory contact cannot appear as such because it has a different temporal structure to that of human experience; the experience it offers is entirely technically distributed in that it couples humans with machine operations but it restores neither meaning (neither to the human nor to the machine component) nor memory.

The pharmacological loss comes therefore not only in terms of memory and perception, but also in the form of a growing imbalance of deliberation or decision time. *Feed-forward* loops bypass perception and implicate bodily senses directly, be that in the form of body trackers or smartphone sensors, but also through video games that require reactions by players on thinly sliced micro-intervals, and the everyday observation of countless thumbs scrolling mindlessly through never-ending

---

[90] To be successfully implemented as consistent systems that in-form the world not arbitrarily, but as a set of stable and reliable ground for practices, a 'vast apparatus' is required: a technological unconscious akin to an 'automatism' that allows 'orderly and guaranteed repetition'. This apparatus used to be in the form of timetables, diaries, indexing and address systems 'gridding' everyday life; of calibrating, slicing, sequencing, ordering and disciplining the otherwise empty spaces of civilization. With the onset of electronic computerization and the stack this apparatus has changed allowing for the continuous tracking of positions; computer systems allow for more elaborate logistical calculations, and advanced spreadsheet and planning software provide new means of calculation. The automatism of being addressed and ordered is therefore undergoing a shift from relatively stable systems (zip codes or postcodes or manual diaries) to networks that continually shift and adapt to situation and context. Similarly, addresses used to be fixed (a street name and house number) while now addresses increasingly move with the human or non-human actants, be it in form of mobile phone numbers or RFID systems that can, in tango with mobile tracking systems, feed highly developed coordination systems that can continually recalibrate arrangements in real time. All these produce a revised system, an unconscious order, that in-forms the social organization upon with social practices are based. The implications of this shift are profound. No longer is it possible to 'get lost' or merely to 'walk around' without plan or purpose, and thus to be taken by surprise or wonder about what hides around the bend. Nigel Thrift Remembering the technological unconscious by foregrounding knowledges of position. *Environment and Planning D: Society and Space*, 2004, 22: 175–90, 176.

streams of attention-grabbing 'feeds'. Deliberation becomes a luxury which lies increasingly on the side of content providers and so, ultimately for Hansen, with capitalist institutions that now have found a way of manipulating consumers directly:

With their capacity to gather massive amounts of data about our likes and dis- likes – data to which we individual consumers of today's digital commerce have little or no access – today's culture industries benefit from a massive informa- tional imbalance: they offer us stimulation, an instrumentalized perversion of what Whitehead calls 'our lure for feeling,' that directly solicits 'our' mircotem- poral, subconscious motivation, and that completes its solicitation long before any output appears in and to consciousness.[91]

The strategy of the engineers of such patterns is to 'shape sensation *before the emergence of bodily self-perception and consciousness*'[92] and so to 'drive a wedge' between events of sensibility and alter events of experi- ence, so that the latter no longer can shape or constrain how sensibility is experienced and to which ends it is discharged. This tightening of solicitation and response patterns happens in massive data milieus to which any individual consumer has access (if at all) only after the fact, once perception has caught up. Rather than any real-time access to the processes involved, instead having to rely on simulations (Hansen speaks of 'presentification') of sensory information that is not graspable as such through user interfaces that produce imagery suitable for human cogni- tive processing.[93]

Hansen illustrates the point tangentially (how could he do other- wise?) through a video art project that produces 'time holes' by play- ing scenes that overload a computer's processing capacities, and so renders the movement of figures on a screen pixelated and stuttering and so out of synchronicity with the real-time of the film. What fails here is not digital technology, but the production of an interface that is graspable by humans; in these moments the 'otherness' of technological time shines through and unreadable glimpse of a thing that is utterly

---

[91] Mark Hansen *Feed Forward*, 57.

[92] Mark Hansen *Feed Forward*, 197, original italics.

[93] Mark Hansen *Feed Forward*, 59; 190ff. Hansen elaborates another pharmacological pat- tern. The loss of perceptive mastery over micro-temporal processes that comes with the research tools and techniques employed by capitalist media apparatuses may also afford the means to regain some agency in what he calls 'operational present of sensibility' – when we learn how to intervene and shape these patterns in ways that modulate how they shape us. This, however, means admitting the limits of perception and ourselves to try to engage in micro-sensibility directly, arguing that media theory ought to replace its focus on technical objects with a concern with the sensory processes to which technics gives access, that is to find ways to address sensibility directly (197).

'unready-to-hand' and which, in being such a contrast, reveals the temporality by which the human *Umwelt* is organized (or scansioned). The implication of Hansen's argument, which slinks into view, in the way dawn can announce itself in a pale and thin lustre between a merging sea and sky, is both bleak and entrancing: just as there is no human puppet master, there is no machine-based one either. He shares with Zuboff a profound concern with the mediating force of commercial interests, yet implies that, ultimately, there is no mastery to be had here. Whilst media determine our situation, they are not authoring our situation in any consciously evaluated way, and to presume they are akin to strings being pulled by puppet masters is to fail to appreciate the extent of this determination.

This indifference of media is, like Heidegger's stone, inscrutable, given its apprehension is always already mediated. It feels uncanny. Like *Dasein*'s incapacity to apprehend its own being without, thereby, interrupting the process of 'being', software only functions when it is executed and once that process is paused for inspection, it is no longer itself and so cannot be properly observed. To what degree, then, is anything in control of the various processes that make up these complexly stacked systems of computational infrastructure? Agency, not just human agency, but all agency, is dissipated in brief small blips. In what way, then, can we still talk of having any picture of the world and of one's picturing self in relation to it?

8   Machine Intelligence and the
     Rhythms of Predictability

Joy Division were a band with a firm sense of place, for which their songs are an epitaph. Their short oeuvre is an extended soundtrack for a post-industrial doom-scape of broken urban promise and resilient communities, which went by the name 'Manchester'. They gave the city a sound, and in doing so a form, which in turn gave them form; they had a *topos* and their sound was an urgent, angular and angry embodiment of this belonging. Their place was temporally fixed, historically speaking, at the tail end of a long process of industrial demise. As they sang, the last embers of the UK's welfare society pitted the evening sky, before dying back in cinders, and leaving the horizon to Thatcher's iron-black certainties, the perfect backdrop for the godless 'Big Bang' of digital financialization.

They recorded the song *Digital* in October 1978 at Cargo Studios in Rochdale, a town in Manchester's hinterland. During the recording the band were introduced to a DMX 15–80 unit rented from Advanced Music Systems (AMS) in nearby Burnley. Nestled amid steep spoil heaps left by forgotten industries, and in the shadows of high moors, Burnley is an unlikely place for AMS to have built the first ever microprocessor controlled digital delay line, offering what Joy Division's newly arrived producer Martin Hannett called a quantum leap in ambience control. Fed through the delay, their sound became utterly different, causing consternation among the band. Their instruments no longer sounded like they should. Their output was being parsed into engineered effects that fragmented the already febrile edge of the singer Ian Curtis' voice: the music became contained, imprisoned at the discretion of a machine that operated with silent space, not variable sound. It made noise discrete, pushing away the 'large' now of extending tone in favour of its own, machine discretion: The world would just 'fade away'.[1] The digital delay allowed Hannett to

---

[1] Sourced from the inestimable Shadowplay homepage: www.users.globalnet.co.uk/~liden/joyd/digital.html

effectively render impressions of both immense distance and throt-
tling restriction, closing in and fading away, and to then hold them
cheek by jowl, within a time delay that was not only indiscernible to
the human ear, it was an utterly different time. Hannett was ruthless
in allowing the digital delay unit to completely transform the band's
sound. The snap of the drum was gathered, then played back, thread-
ing different spatial and auditory realities to a point where what 'was'
and 'is' were being compressed into a two-world present. It was not
about the milliseconds of delay between the playing, processing and
near instantaneous playback of a drum sound, it was the manner in
which the original and its representation came into in a kind of unruly
pairing, a compound of human and machine time that both belonged
to the band, but then not at all.

The DMX 15–80 divide's noise into discrete parts, an event of capture
and sampling that created distinct, non-transferable units of sound that
existed in the abstract – like the symbols of logic – but which could then be
played back in waves with real analogue affect. The digital machine took
on the human burdens of time and place by closing in and then annihilat-
ing them. It was in this small studio on the edge of a city that had been the
setting for the first industrial revolution, and upon whose factories Marx
had so passionately voiced his critique in *Grundrisse*, that a second industrialized age was being initiated, one in which machine time and not human
time became the new order of a never-ending day. In recording the song
Digital (italics) Joy Division were witnessing a new machine ontology, what
Stiegler memorably called the onset of life being lived by other means. It
was the culmination of developments in recording and communications
technology that began, like many such developments, with the military.

The Apparatus of Napoleon's Forms
of Communication

In the wake of Heidegger's extensive analysis of broadcasting, Kittler
claimed it was with developments in radio broadcasting that technology
began to assume the burden of time and place. The radio, Kittler argues,
emerged out of an 'abuse of army equipment' when, towards the end of
the Great (hah!) War in 1917, a German engineer used a primitive trans-
mitter to broadcast records and newspaper readings to soldiers in the
trenches, repurposing 'army radio equipment' for entertainment purposes.[2]

---

[2] Friedrich Kittler *Gramophone, Film, Typewriter*, 96.

This misuse could only occur by virtue of an established procedure for its proper use, which was as a form of communication to transmit orders, to gather information, in short, to aid strategic thinking. In a similar move to that first digitized by the DMX 15–80 – but then not at all the same, as it was still working in analogue, and so still operating in conjunction with continuous events – the radio encapsulated a strategic problem of how to gather intelligence from the wider world, and then intelligently and decisively communicate back to the world, a long-standing organizational concern going back to the *strategoi*. It was a problem of especial interest to Napoleon, who, says Kittler, was able to dictate seven letters simultaneously, issuing instructions to, and diagnoses of, troop movements, supply lines, the weather, or the current state of a region's politics to multiple audiences in a wide range of organizational settings. At the centre of the map, and indeed, at the centre of the Napoleonic war bureaucracy, was a custom-made and highly portable writing desk situated in a bureau that would accompany the general on almost all campaigns. The letter-writing system was the epicentre of Napoleon's war machine.[3]

This governing apparatus was set up so Napoleon, who spoke very fast but who also had atrocious handwriting, could dictate letters and orders as well as simultaneously have access to maps and books. Part of the imperial entourage consisting of hundreds of horses and mules, a wine collection, silverware, kitchens, chefs and secretaries, the bureau and desk constituted a governing apparatus in which communications were issued with such rapidity that they appeared almost to hover above the realities upon which they pronounced. Papers that were no longer needed were discarded on the floor; important ones were placed on the desk and those needed for future reference were put aside, and these piles of paper shifted continuously, some maintaining priority, some floating between the necessary and the redundant, others being consigned to oblivion. And like all information systems, there was a lot of noise, as papers were mislaid, the emperor forgot things or discarded valuable documents, forcing the mobile secretaries to continually sift through the immense volumes of papers. As Krajewski notes:

the flow of information is much closer to actually resembling the metaphor than one might initially believe. It is not comprised of individual bits of news coming in one by one like drops, but by countless, swirling, nonlinear, turbulent pieces of information that disseminate in different speeds, with different relations to one another, sometimes interacting, sometimes wholly unrelated, and sometimes contradicting one another and giving each other a new trajectory.[4]

---

[3] Markus Krajewski *The Structure of (Information) Infrastructure*, 4. See also Markus Krajewski *World Projects. Global Information Before World War I*. Electronic Mediations. Minneapolis: The University of Minnesota Press, 2014.

[4] Markus Krajewski *The Structure of (Information) Infrastructure*, 4.

Napoleon's information apparatus reflected the organization of his troops. Kittler notes how the success of the Napoleonic campaigns in Europe depended on a military reform that divided all armies into corps that had their own infantry, artillery and cavalry, thus being able to operate as independent tactical units, though all of them remained answerable to Napoleon, via his desk.[5] The emperor would dictate up to twenty letters in the hours preceding a battle (the paper was the reality), and once equipped with these orders the units would operate in accordance with their own reasoned interpretation of the instructions, and in response to local demands (the battle was the reality). The strategy was both central and dispersed, decisive and sensitive, directed and nuanced.

These patterns of strategic information gathering and instruction engendered a kind of intelligence that was, following Kittler,[6] quite unique to the vision world of human beings. Just how might be made clearer if we contrast Napoleon's system by recalling the communication system operating in the vision world of Uexküll's bees. A bee, returning to the hive, often takes up a dance that in its directed movement codes the route to a source of nectar. There is an intelligence gathering in play here, but there is a fixed relationship between the signs (the dance pattern) and the reality these signify (a route). Humans, on the other hand, like Napoleon, have the linguistic capacity to say: 'You will go here and when you see this, you will turn off to this flank here.' It is communication in which the 'other', as in one option or another, is always present as a provocation, it intrudes, and introduces a redundancy that can be infuriating for those who wish for centralized, hierarchical control, or a boon for those willing to flexibly exploit it, because it is coextensive with the condition of which it is an expression. The difference is neatly encapsulated by John Durham Peters' observation that we should not confuse communications – the mediating forms by which ideas, information and attitudes are transmitted such as flags, microwaves, photographs and type – with communication – which is the elusive and enigmatic experience of aligning and reconciling the self with other. Though the writer is necessarily alone, communication evokes a sense of communion in which what is being sent is also received in that an audience is being constituted by the act: it is performative.[7] It is the permanent kink in

---

[5] Friedrich Kittler *The Truth of the Technological World*, 233.
[6] Friedrich Kittler *The Truth of the Technological World*, 179.
[7] John Durham Peters *Speaking Into the Air: A History of the Idea of Communication*. Chicago: University of Chicago Press, 1999, 11–13. Durham Peters sets up the debate from within media theory. On the one hand we have media theorists such as Lippmann, for whom communication was a managed affair: public discourse and engagement were the creations of experts using persuasive symbols to create opinions. Communication

communication, the tragic fact we can never experience the full clarity of meaning available to a discrete, digital event of symbolic recognition, which grounds our all too human community which is only ever a relational attempt at making worlds. We are always reaching out from within, and in this urge are always finding new ways of creating a muddle, in which riskiness we continue to have faith.[8]

In Napoleon's case faith was being shown in his army developing a capacity to act with a kind of 'free obedience', an apparently oxymoronic condition that was to subsequently warrant nearly all of the non-linear, self-organization and decentralization approaches to modern warfare that were to come. One of the principal advantages of such 'network-centric warfare' is the possibility of creating what have become known as 'lock-out' effects. Rather than percolating information and instructions up and down hierarchies of command (as in the M-form, see Chapter 6), the bottom-up, inter-operable organization of flexible units which can continually re-organize and restructure can significantly disrupt an enemy's strategic planning; it can also seriously disrupt one's own, if somehow the letters go awry.[9] And they will. No matter how effective, Napoleon's war machine, orchestrated by the mobile bureaucratic administration and writing and filing apparatus, like any machine, was always liable to fits and starts, to upset, to an overload of paper, to emotional disturbance, not least from the emperor himself, as depicted in a contemporary cartoon (Figure 8.1).

Improvements in military communications followed rapidly. For example, the connection of border towns with the capital through optical

theory gave the lie to theories of political democracy. There is no opinion to represent, and no open space in which to generate that opinion, there is only the semantic production of opinion through symbolic massage. Effective communication is coordinated action. On the other hand we have the likes of Ogden and Richards for whom communication was one mind affecting another, configured according to its different intentional functions (transmit information, excite emotion) where people could be educated into spotting how words manipulate and twist and imperfectly conjoin. Was there a way of aligning so what is intended by the speaker is similar to what is received in the listener, of making sure intended meaning was properly communicated? Of course not. The performance was everything, and the very acts of writing and speaking exposed meaning to all manner of looseness and complexity that is continually being settled relationally and historically, using imperfect media, like language. Hence their interest in perfecting language (such as Charles Kay Ogden *The General Basic English Dictionary*. London: Evans Bros. 1960.).

[8] John Durham Peters *Speaking Into the Air*, 30. The Shannon model of communication upon which computer networks are built, on the other hand, excludes the sense-making processes of the communications, focussing instead on mathematical functions relating signal to noise ratios.

[9] N. Katherine Hayles *My Mother Was a Computer: Digital Subjects and Literary Texts*. Chicago: University of Chicago Press. 2005, 21.

Figure 8.1 James Gillray, *Maniac Raving's, or Little Boney in a Strong Fit*, 1803. Library of Congress, Washington. Prints & Photographs Division, LC-USZC4-8795. Wikimedia commons

systems such as beacons and flag signalling, allowed for record time dispatch to and from dispersed armies (though as far back as Homer's Illiad (18.211) mention is made of using fire beacons). And superseding these we find telegraph cables emerging during the American Civil War, with the first prototypes built in the 1820s, to be followed by the wireless broadcasts of World War I. Before copper-filled coaxial cables allowed the transportation of electrical impulses,[10] Napoleon used an optical technology of distance-writing: a tele-graph consisting of the exchange of visual signals between towers, situated on hills.[11] These seemed to admit an instant and so ultimate form of communication, which allowed for the standardization of time and new forms of agile organization. And

---

[10] Ned Rossiter Copper as a mediating technology of organization. In *The Oxford Handbook of Media, Technology and Organization Studies*. Edited by Timon Beyes, Robin Holt and Claus Pias. Oxford: Oxford University Press. 2020, 160–72, 164.

[11] Mikkel Flyverbom and Anders Koed Madsen Telegraph as a mediating technology of organization. In *The Oxford Handbook of Media, Technology and Organization Studies*. Edited by Timon Beyes, Robin Holt, and Claus Pias. Oxford: Oxford University Press. 2020, 452–63.

yet as the errant soldiers using the radio for the un-war like purpose of entertainment showed, wireless communication then gave rise to a whole new set of problems associated with control and secure transmission, for who, invisibly, might be listening in, spying, or using the system, for different ends?[12]

Entscheidungsproblem, or What Incompleteness Theorems Say about Truth

For all the machinic prowess of wireless broadcasting – the development of remote controlled armoured divisions or real-time orchestration of air and land assaults – there was, still, as with Napoleon's letters, a lingering doubt as to the veracity and authenticity of the recording and transmission.[13] The fact that strategists often concealed or discounted this doubt, especially when flush with apparent strategic success, then hid from view what it was Napoleon knew all along, that wars are won through the rapidity and reliability of communication, not brute force or violence. As Kittler laconically observes, commenting on a later conflagration not (at least directly) of Napoleon's making:

World War II occurred simply as combat between two typewriters. On one side stood the Enigma and cipher machines, which did not encrypt just single messages but a telecommunications system in its entirety [and in which German high command placed unquestioned confidence]. On the other side stood apparatuses called 'Bombe,' 'Eastern Goddess,' and 'Colossus,' which merited their prophetic or gigantic names because of their capacity to decode this same system (after relatively simple radio interceptions). The most important factor for the end of the war was the fact that British intelligence set up the first operational computers in history (and thereby brought about the end of history).[14]

Involved in the building of these machines was the mathematician engineer Alan Turing at Bletchley, who had been drafted in to help decode the messages being sent by the Enigma machine. The Enigma mechanism consisted of three and later five rotating drums that switched between ever-changing coding possibilities, producing gibberish for any intercepting ear, and only arriving back at their point of origin after eight billion letters of text, exceeding any human capacity for calculation, especially in the real-time demands of warfare.

---

[12] Friedrich Kittler *Gramophone, Film, Typewriter*, 96, 128, 189. Kittler locates the emergence of civilian radio in 'misuse' of army equipment.
[13] Friedrich Kittler *The Truth of the Technological World*, 297.
[14] Friedrich Kittler *The Truth of the Technological World*, 186.

His being called up as a code breaker was almost inevitable. British intelligence officers were well aware that the Enigma machines were material iterations of what Turing had, in 1936, conceptualized in an academic paper as a 'universal computer'. The idea of the computer began way back, perhaps when Ada Lovelace and Charles Babbage imagined a mechanical machine, an analytic engine, which was programmed to perform operations. Through these operations it manipulated its way into the world, being fed by incisions that then operated on other things. The engine was to follow the rules fed in by punch cards (Lovelace and Babbage were inspired by the same weaving looms that had so horrified Marx and Engels, machinery free from human operators and running according to basic programs). The analytic engine had no power of anticipation, no power of imagination, it could not, in an Arendt's sense, originate anything because it lacked any capacity for synthesis; a lack encapsulated in Ada Lovelace's often cited dictum that the 'analytical machine has no pretensions to originate anything. It can do whatever we know how to order it to perform'.[15] Yet it could perform, move and intervene in a world in an active and elaborate way by calculating. It was this capacity, argued Turing, nearly 100 years later, that warranted further inquiry.

The path to Turing's invention and why it matters to our analysis of world picturing strategy requires a tentative detour along the edges of logic and mathematics. Georg Cantor, a German mathematician and engineer was intrigued by the infinite in mathematics, a topic often eschewed as far back as Aristotle.[16] Infinites come in many variations, $\sqrt{2}$; 1/3, and so on, producing infinite series, and in using these symbols, also called 'algebraic numbers', instead of the series, mathematics offers a solution to the problem of how to represent answers to statements such as $x^2 = 2$. Cantor wanted to find out if infinites could be counted and, if so, if there is equivalence of such sets of numbers. Take a series of even numbers (bottom row) and a series of numbers (cardinal numbers, which 'count' how many there are), counting the even numbers:

1 2 3 4 5 6

2 4 6 8 10 12

Here, both sets are of equal size; there is a cardinal number on the top row for every natural, even number on the bottom row. When we move

[15] Douglas R. Hofstadter *Gödel, Escher, Bach, An Eternal Golden Braid*. New York: Basic Books. 1999, 25.
[16] Our brief overview relies heavily on the lucid descriptions given in Martin Davis *The Universal Computer: The Road from Leibniz to Turing*. London: CRC Press. 2000.

from such finite series to infinity, again with an infinitely long series of even numbers at the bottom and an equally infinite series of cardinal numbers on top, we also find that both sets are of equal size. Even though the top one includes both even and odd numbers, parsed into infinity, this difference disappears. But within infinite sets there can also be different rankings, for example a series first listing all even numbers, followed by all odd ones. If we tried to assign a cardinal (counting) number to the entire series, all available numbers would be used up to count all even numbers already, leaving none for the odd numbers. Here, Cantor designated the Greek letter ϖ, a so-called transfinite ordinal (ranking) number, that could be used so the counting can continue:

1 2 3 4 ϖϖ +1 ϖ+2 ϖ+3, etc. (the [ordinal] position or [cardinal] count)

2 4 6 8 ... 1 3 5 7, etc. (the infinite series of, first, all even numbers, followed by all odd ones)

But what if one collected all transfinite cardinal numbers into a single set – what would this set's cardinal number be? It would have to be a number that is larger than any cardinal number contained in the set: a paradoxical situation.[17] As Russell put it:

The comprehensive class we are considering, which is to embrace everything, must embrace itself as one of its members. In other words, if there is such a thing as 'everything,' then, 'everything' is something, and is a member of the class 'everything.'[18]

Cantor ended up not being able to either prove the existence, nor the non-existence of such cardinal numbers,[19] and it took around sixty more years for another mathematician, Kurt Gödel in the 1930s, to provide a way into the problem.

A member of the Vienna circle, itself based around the study of symbolic systems such as that developed by Russell and Whitehead, Gödel was arguably equally influenced by Wittgenstein's arguments about the implications of speaking within language about language. He spent some time ferreting into gaps in the rules provided by the *Principia*, which held that mathematics can be developed inside a logical system, developing a coding system as he went that approached the problem of logical systems from the outside, replacing logical systems with decimal digits. Logical symbols such as ⊃ (if ... then), ∀ (every), and ∃ (some), as well as letters

---

[17] Summarized from Martin Davis *The Universal Computer*, 59ff.

[18] Bertrand Russell *Introduction to Mathematical Philosophy*. London: George Allen and Unwin. 1919, 136.

[19] Martin Davis *The Universal Computer*, 66ff.

standing for individuals or properties, could simply be represented by a series of numbers, but because these were imported from outside the system, they could not be proven within the system; a gross violation of Russell and Whitehead's injunction. This represented a form of meta-mathematics that could be applied to any formal and sufficiently complex system, and there was no better example than the *Principia*. Rather than avoiding paradoxes, as Russell and Whitehead had suggested, as they were unsolvable within the logical system they had so painstakingly developed, Gödel explicitly acknowledged that for any such system there are true propositions expressible in the system but not provable from within that system, resulting in the now (in mathematical circles) famous statement:

To every w-consistent recursive class K of formulae there correspond recursive class-signs r, such that neither v Gen r nor Neg (v Gen r) belongs to Fig (K) (where v is the free variable of r).[20]

Or, as Hofstadter helpfully translates:[21]

All consistent axiomatic formulations of number theory include undecidable propositions.

This is the sixth proposition in Gödel's 1931 paper 'On Formally Undecidable Propositions in Principia Mathematica and Related Systems I'; and while it looks rather innocent and straightforward there on the page (at least in its translated form), its proof requires the generation of a strange loop, which comes to unsettle Russell's famous dictum regarding self-referentiality. One translator of Gödel's work therefore claims that 'Gödel's Theorem is thus a result which belongs not to mathematics.'[22] It suggests that while the *Principia* holds that there is a well-defined account of mathematical truth that applies to every formula in the book, there are truths that are unprovable within the system of the *Principia* and so the consistency of this system cannot be proven within the system; any such proof would require us to go beyond the power of arithmetic and purely deductive reasoning, and so beyond the power

[20] Gödel's original formulation of the First Incompleteness Theorem. Kurt Gödel Über formal unentscheidbare Sätze der Principia Mathematica und verwandter Systeme I. *Monatshefte für Mathematik Physik*, 1931, 38, 173–98. See also Panu Raatikainen Gödel's incompleteness theorems. In *The Stanford Encyclopedia of Philosophy*. Edited by Edward N. Zalta. https://plato.stanford.edu/archives/spr2021/entries/goedel-incompleteness/
[21] Douglas R. Hofstadter *Gödel, Escher, Bach*, 17.
[22] Richard Bevan Braithwaite. Introduction. In *On Formally Undecidable Propositions of Principia Mathematica and Related Systems*. Kurt Gödel. Translated by B. Meltzer. No date.

of the *Principia* itself.[23] Put differently, in arguing that some particular proposition, (say 'U') is not provable in the *Principia*, and in saying that that particular proposition is 'U' itself, U remains unprovable within the *Principia*. Or differently again: if the *Principia* is consistent, then it is inconsistent.[24]

Gödel's genius lay in the application of this logic to numbers theory or, more specifically, to Russell and Whitehead's *Principia*: Because Gödel's statement is unprovable within the *Principia Mathematica*, the system of the *Principia Mathematica* has to be incomplete as 'there are true statements of number theory which its methods of proof are too weak to demonstrate'.[25] But far from merely applying to Russell and Whitehead's *Principia*, Gödel's proof held for any axiomatic system that tries to formalize a numbers-theoretic set of results; making any rich system prone to statements that can neither be proved nor refuted, unless the system itself is inconsistent. In arguing thus Gödel imports Epimenides right into the heart of the *Principia*, despite its being an attempt at rigorously avoiding these strange loops. Hans Magnus Enzensberger, in a poem about Gödel, puts it thus:

> In order to be vindicated
> any conceivable system
> must transcend, and that means,
> destroy itself.

> 'Sufficiently rich' or not:
> Freedom from contradiction
> is either a deficiency symptom
> or it amounts to a contradiction.

> (Certainty ¼ Inconsistency.)[26]

Gödel's ascription of numbers to logical symbols, and therefore the reduction of questions of logic to questions of arithmetic, provided the chance to finally deal with the paradoxes that had evaded the *Principia*. Following Gödel, the mathematicians Hilbert and Ackermann coined the term *Entscheidungsproblem*, 'decision problem', to indicate a problem that asks for an algorithm, that is a finite number of steps, capable of stating the universal validity of an argument or formula. Proof, therefore, comes by way of 'mechanical calculations according to

---

[23] See Juliet Floyd Prose versus proof: Wittgenstein on Gödel, Tarski and Truth. *Philosophia Mathematica*, 2001, 3, (9): 280–307, 296.

[24] Martin Davis *The Universal Computer*, 101.

[25] Douglas Hofstadter *Gödel, Escher, Bach*, 18.

[26] English translation by Hans Magnus Enzensberger and Michael Hamburger. From: *Selected Poems*. Sheep Meadow Press. Suhrkamp Verlag; Translated by the poet and Michael Hamburger. 1999.

given instructions',[27] an algorithmic decision procedure to ascertain the provability of any well-formed formula, and not through human ingenuity in the process of finding solutions. If *all* true formulas can be derived from given axioms, then the logical system is complete (i.e., provable). This raises an interesting tension between provability and truth, because even if certain formulas cannot be derived from axioms, it does not mean that they are not true, it simply means that their truth cannot be proven. This is not helped by the effort such a procedure demands when framed in propositional logic, requiring massive combinatory tables equating all possible derivable formulas with the original axioms. To say that this is not the most practical approach is quite an understatement:

Suppose a sentence has 100 propositional variables. The number of lines in the truth table is 2100 or 1,267,650,600,228,229,401,496,703,205,376, or about 10^{30}, which is a very large number. Even with a futuristic computer that processes each line in 1 nanosecond – a billionth of a second, or the length of time required for light to travel approximately one foot – the processing time would be 38 trillion years, about 3,000 times the current age of the universe.[28]

Gödel's incompleteness theorems did not resolve the *Entscheidungsproblem*. While he had shown that in logical systems, some arithmetical truths remain unprovable, this did not in itself rule possibility of an 'effectively computable' decision procedure that could, in a finite time, show whether or not any given proposition was, or was not, provable. And while Gödel's translation of the propositional logics syntax into numbers did not reduce the complexity of the task of deriving all provable formulas from axioms, it allowed for the conception of a brute-force approach, even though this would entail a gigantic quantity of data.[29]

Intelligence, Learning and the Emergence of Machine Computing

It was Alan Turing who would offer, first a theoretical, then a mechanical solution: an all-purpose computer that could provide the explicit algorithmic processes that animated Hilbert's *Entscheidungsproblem*.

---

[27] This is the wording of one of Hilbert's assistants, Heinrich Behmann, in 1921, well ahead of the later application of this thought through Turing. See Charles Petzold. *Annotated Turing*, 48.

[28] Charles Petzold *Annotated Turing*. Indianapolis: Wiley. 2008,211.

[29] For Yuk Hui, Gödel's 'ingenious invention' was that he turned axioms into strings of natural numbers and so to make them subject to calculation. This method meant that it was now possible to arithmetically prove symbolic logic, thereby also giving the recursive form central status. This forms the foundation for modern computers and for algorithms. *Yuk Hui Recursivity and Contingency*. London: Rowman & Littlefield, 2019, 110.

Turing imagined the machine consisting of a head that moves along a tape divided into discrete cells with zeroes and ones written onto it. The head scans the cells and in response to what it reads it writes (prints) a zero or a one or erases the content in response to a program (an algorithm for calculating), whilst moving forth and back. A marker can be an electrical signal or an entry in a tape, and in the case of the universal machine, it can have two states: present/absent (or 1/0). It is universal because it can carry out any task for which an instruction can be written so that the machine can simply read these instructions and carry them out on a tape:

The possible behaviour of the machine at any moment is determined by its 'configuration' [the pairing of the scanned symbol and the machine's program] ...

In some of the configurations in which the scanned square is blank (i.e. bears no symbol) the machine writes down a new symbol on the scanned square: in other configurations it erases the scanned symbol. The machine may also change the square which is being scanned, but only by shifting it one place to right or left. In addition to any of these operations the m-configuration may be changed. Some of the symbols written down will form the sequence of figures which is the decimal of the real number which is being computed. The others are just rough notes to 'assist the memory'. It will only be these rough notes which will be liable to erasure. It is my contention that these operations include all those which are used in the computation of a number.[30]

On the basis of Turing's notion of computation, it is now possible to conclude *anything* computable by any calculation process.[31] The imagined machine established the basic framing of what was to become the modern science of computing.[32] Turing continues:

the digital computer is a universal machine in the sense that it can be made to replace any machine of a certain very wide class. It will not replace a bulldozer or a steam-engine or a telescope, but it will replace any rival design of a calculating machine.

Anything any computational device can do, can be dealt with through this universal machine. This was fundamentally altering the thinking on computation. The hardware of a machine the universal machine

---

[30] Alan Turing On computable numbers, with an application to the *Entscheidungsproblem*. *Journal of Math*, 1936, 58: 230–65, 231.

[31] Martin Davis *The Universal Computer*, 134.

[32] Jack Copeland Computable numbers: A guide. In *The Essential Turing. Seminal Writings in Computing, Logic, Philosophy, Artificial Intelligence, and Artificial Life plus the Secrets of Enigma*. Edited by B. Jack Copeland. Oxford: Clarendon. 2004, 5–58, 6. Norbert Wiener says of the 'desk computing machine's' operations, they are 'made according to rules which are not memorized in all their details, but which are entrusted to the instrument, and carried out by its intervention'. High-speed electronic computers, Wiener adds, are only speedier versions that offer greater complexity but do not vary in the logic employed, and the logic for all these machines derives from the seminal work of Alan Turing.

was imitating became the equivalent of software, they drifted into one another, a fluidity that allowed, in theory, computers to imitate all manner of human practice: speaking was calculation; drawing was calculation; relationships were calculation.

Turing's contribution lay in the conceptualization of a stored program that could be modified by the operation of the machine itself and, corresponding to the length of its tape, the machine can 'remember' what happened in previous steps.[33] If the machine is capable of solving any mathematical task through a series of yes or no answers in a finite amount of time, it can not only be said that, by making the machine the arbiter of mathematical properties, the number (task) in question is computable, but the question of the difficulty of a question now becomes subject to the resource-intensity of the calculations involved (steps, computing time, storage space, etc.),[34] thus replacing the complex solving of a problem with a combination of the basic operations of a machine.[35]

Through the automation of the discrete, simple steps of sampling binary information in accordance with 'if ... then ...' specifications, an application of such a machine, Turing argued, could find patterns in a seemingly random mess of letters, and it was this reasoning that grounded the material creation of the machine set within the industrial-scale deciphering operation at Bletchley Park, responding to the similarly industrial-scale generation of messages by over 30,000 Enigmas (see Figure 8.2) used by the German *Wehrmacht*.[36]

---

[33] Paul Nahin *The Logician and the Engineer: How George Bool and Claude Shannon Created the Information Age*. Princeton: Princeton University Press. 2017, 165.

[34] Claus Pias *Computer Spiel Welten*: Inaugural-Dissertation. Fakultät Medien an der Bauhaus-Universität Weimar, 2000, 124.

[35] Turing's computability is therefore the archetype of all computers. An arrangement of devices that can read, write, erase and store, in its most basic form a scanner and a limitless memory-tape that moves back and forth past the scanner that can read, erase and print (Jack Copeland *The Essential Turing*. Oxford: Oxford University Press. 2004, 7). Such a machine is capable of processing, transmission and storage, combining inputs (the state it is in, i.e., its memory and the information on the scanned cell of the tape) and processing these in accordance with a table of instructions (a program), thus leaving behind a tape containing binary digits as well as well as blanks and, importantly, a new state of its memory. This machine represents the universal conception of computability as it is capable of calculating all that is calculable; Friedrich Kittler *The Truth of the Technological World*, 145. Objects of the digital age are therefore those that can be calculated; that is if, in Turing's words, they are 'real numbers whose expressions as a decimal are calculable by finite means ... a number is [therefore] computable if its decimal can be written down by a machine'; Alan Turing, On *Computable Numbers*, 42. See also Von Neumann. *The Computer and the Brain*. New Haven: Yale University Press. 2012, 5.

[36] Friedrich Kittler *The Truth of the Technological World*, 190.

Figure 8.2 Plugboard (*Steckerbrett*) positioned at the front of an Enigma machine, below the keys. Wikimedia commons

Fair Play for Machines

Since Turing there has been a continual encroachment into human life from the discrete machine (culminating, finally, in the usurpation of that life, in Joy Division's studio, in Rochdale in 1978 as the 'large' now of tone gave way to discrete, digital space). The discrete has always been there as a possibility: beginning first with the voice that finds its articulation in speech, marked by the discreetness of phonemes, extending further into the letters of the alphabet typed on the typewriter. But with the universal machine these discrete letters and numerals were imagined being transformed into digitized electronic pulses operating gates, into the entailed sequences of discrete number patterns that gathered and divided in electronic blooms, creating a self-contained world of operations, a world of computer languages that, on a higher level, move closer to natural languages, and on a lower level, translate into bit patterns guiding electronic switching.[37] For Turing the digital was never real, more a provocative abstraction of universality, one that belied the reality of continuous variations by which life was

---

[37] N. Katherine Hayles *My Mother Was a Computer*, 56.

Figure 8.3 DEUCE. Photo Graeme Ridgway, 1963.

lived. Yet as Galloway suggests, considerations of ontology were quickly concealed by the headlong rush to engineer digital infrastructures, not just in computers and electronics, but in language (Semiotics), in work (the Gilbreths' time-and-motion studies), in statistics (Otto Neurath's isotypes), in decision making (cybernetics).[38] By the 1960s Turing's automatic computing engine had become fully engineered as the digital electronic universal computing engine (DEUCE; see Figure 8.3). Punched cards were used to input and for output. The machine had a clock speed of 1 Mc/s (1 Mhz). It could perform addition/subtraction and multiplication/division operations in binary arithmetic. The machine memory of mercury acoustic delay lines or 'circulation unit' used a 16 Mc/s carrier frequency, which was modulated by pulses that represented binary. It accommodated 32-bit binary words that circulated through the mercury delay line circuits and amplified them to be sent around again until the data or instructions in the 'memory' were needed – the binary pulses would be accessed through electronic gating circuits. It was Turing's original idea that a 'delay circuit' of some kind was required for a 'stored program' machine. The gating

---

[38] Alexander Galloway Golden Age of Analog. *Critical Inquiry*, 2022, 48(2): 211–32.

circuits and their control by a program stored in the machine were incredibly complex. At the engineering level it was all machine code, so in binary.

This very material machine bares the rudiments of intelligence because it can create, manipulate and respond to signs (it used a card reader and punched cards for input and output signals) and to the changes consequent on changing these signs; it produced meaning through the use of symbolic abstractions, it stored and accessed information. In the production of such meaning the computer uses both 'mind' (the pause in delay circuits) and 'body' (mercury): it has a networked, programmable architecture laden with code that connects to the wider world through cards, sockets, sensors and actuators through which information is generated, analysed and then held in relation to events that are yet to come.

The challenge of clarifying Gödel's theorem, framed through Hilbert's *Entscheidungsproblem*, had prompted the theoretical development of the universal machine. The nature of this machine, however, is only partially worked out in Turing's 1937 paper 'On computable numbers', finding a substantial extension – and revision – in his later publications, especially the 1950 paper' Computing machinery and intelligence'. In 'Computable numbers', Turing had outlined an architecture in which the 'configuration' of the machine scripts what, at each given state and input, the machine's next steps will be, thus determining the possible behaviour of the machine, prompting Ludwig Wittgenstein to comment that 'Turing's "Machines" ... are *humans* who calculate', comparing them to the many jobs occupied, at the time, by clerks and others performing small and repetitive tasks.[39] These machines were therefore not computers in the contemporary sense, and their human comparison was restricted to the mechanical and repetitive aspect of their labour.[40] Between 1939, when Turing completed his dissertation, and the end of the war, however, he introduced the notion of 'mechanical intelligence', even that machines risk 'making occasional serious mistakes' as a sign of their intelligence. This seemly paradoxical idea, that mistakes are signs of intelligence, harks back to Gödel's incompleteness theorem and the solution provided by Turing's universal analytical differentiator machine. The machine, after all, will not be able to prove the truth or falsity of *any* mathematical proposition in a system, at least for as long as it smoothly completes its tasks. It only begins to apprehend the problem of incompleteness and recursion when it breaks down. As Turing states:

[39] Alcibiades Malapi-Nelson *The Nature of Machines and the Collapse of Cybernetics*. London: Palgrave. 2017, 100.
[40] The opening of Ludwig Wittgenstein's *Philosophical Investigations* poses a rudimentary language emerging from small repetitive tasks. Ludwig Wittgenstein. *Philosophical Investigations*. Translated by G. E. M. Anscombe. Oxford: Basil Blackwell. 1986.

Thus if a machine is made for this purpose it must in some cases fail to give an answer. On the other hand if a mathematician is confronted with such a problem he would search around and find new methods of proof, so that he ought eventually to be able to reach a decision about any given formula.[41]

The machine works like the canary in the mine; whilst humming and tweeting it holds no revelatory insight, only when it begins to near its breakdown does it indicate a truth. And here we find a crucial difference between the Lovelace-style machine as a recipient and executor of pre-established programs or configurations and the human mathematician who Turing sees searching around when faced with an endlessly idling, recursive problem. In a lecture in 1947, Turing states with regard to the machines that 'This is certainly true in the sense that if they do something other than what they were instructed then they have just made some mistake',[42] when their fault for not completing their program is precisely due to their doing precisely as instructed. The very human capacity for search is not merely the product of the limited human life span versus the infinite tape that Turing envisaged for his analytical machine, it is also the very human proneness for mistakes and for getting things wrong, such as the 'blunders' we make when trying out new techniques. But here Turing reminds us that we judge the machine by too harsh a standard: 'It is easy for us to regard these blunders as not counting and give him [the human mathematician] another chance, but the machine would be shown no mercy. In other words, if the machine is expected to be infallible, it cannot be intelligent.'[43] To erase that double standard:

Let us suppose we have set up a machine with certain initial instruction tables, constructed that these tables might on occasion, if good reason arose, modify those tables ... It would be like a pupil who had learnt much from his master but had added much more by his own work. When this happens I feel one is obliged to regard he machine as showing intelligence.[44]

Instead of judging the machine by how well it executes a pre-established program, Turing issues a 'plea for "fair play for the machines"' when testing their I.Q'. And, crucially: 'Instead of it sometimes giving no answers we could arrange that it gives occasional wrong answers.' The intelligence of machines is not subject to better programs but to its capacity to learn, like a human child: 'The machine' suggests Turing, in a prescient

---

[41] Alan Turing *Lecture to the London Mathematical Society*, 20 February 1947. London Mathematical Society, 1–12.
[42] Alan Turing *Lecture to the London Mathematical Society*.
[43] Alan Turing *Lecture to the London Mathematical Society*.
[44] Alan Turing *Lecture to the London Mathematical Society*.

phrase 'must be allowed to have contact with the human begins in order that it may adapt itself to their standards.'[45]

Turing is thinking well ahead of the technological possibilities of his time. A machine, capable of changing its internal registers to surprise its maker, just like a pupil who can surprise their teacher, is the step from mindless execution of a program and configuration to machinic intelligence. By 1948 Turing is speaking of the 'unorganized machine', and again invoking the education of a human child. He envisages inputs of pleasure or reward as well as pain or punishment so that the machine's character might develop along with its capacity for situational adaptation. Pleasure, he argues, fixes the character, while pain stimuli disrupt it, loosening fixed features so that they can become subject to random variation.[46] Transposed to the logical computing machine (LCM), Turing imagines a device without a tape and whose description is largely incomplete, so that when a configuration arises for which no action is determined, a random choice for the missing data is made and a record of this is placed into the description, 'tentatively', as Turing emphasizes, before the random choice is applied and whenever the machine goes into a repetitive cycle, by means of a pain stimulus, that cycle is broken:

> The process actually adopted was first to let the machine run for a long time with continuous application of pain, and with various challenges of the sense data [fed into it to prompt choices, i.e. non emotional pleasure of pain inputs] ... Observation of the sequence of externally visible actions for some thousands of moments made it possible to set up a scheme for identifying the situations ....[47]

Simply allowing the machine to wander at random through these consequences, and by applying the stimuli of pain whenever a wrong or irrelevant choice is made, and vice versa pleasure stimuli for the right choices, conditions the machine into the development of its character into the 'chosen one'. Once conditioned in this way, the machine is 'ready to use'.[48] To judge, then, whether a machine is intelligent means being able to detect whether a machine's reactions are guided by some underlying plan. In an interesting twist of the logic followed in strategy planning, if that plan, programme or configuration is detected, it is evident that it is merely an execution of a set of instructions, while the absence of detectable rules of behaviour indicate actual intelligence. Turing outlines that this poses the problem me of the interpretation of any observer of such

---

[45] Alan Turing *Lecture to the London Mathematical Society*.

[46] Alan Turing *Intelligent Machinery: A Heretical Theory*, a talk given by Turing at Manchester, typescript in the Turing Archive. 1948, 121. https://turingarchive.kings.cam.ac.uk/publications-lectures-and-talks-amtb/amt-b-20

[47] Alan Turing *Intelligent Machinery*, 124.

[48] Alan Turing *Intelligent Machinery*, 124.

systems, as one observer may consider intelligent what another would not, if the latter had found out the rules of such behaviour.

Alan Turing's Imitation Game

In his 1948 paper, Turing imagines a machine 'which will play a not very bad game of chess' playing against three rather poor human chess players across two rooms. A game played between one of the participants and another human player or, indeed, the machine and the third participant (Turing advises that person to be both a mathematician and a chess player) judging who is playing: human or machine.[49] However, it was not this game, but one described in a 1950 paper published in the journal *Mind*, that was to become Turing's most famous: one that attempted to imitate a human being. This game, it turns out, brings into an empirical, experimental setting, a curious form of self-referentiality of the Gödel variety: an intelligent machine is only an intelligent machine if it is identified as not being a machine at all or, more formally, the intelligent machine (IM) only belongs to the set of intelligent machines if it does not: $IM \in IM \Leftrightarrow IM \notin IM$.

Reading 'Computing machinery and intelligence' one quickly becomes aware of a speculative interest in the possible parity between a state of mind and a machine state.[50] The paper opens with the question 'Can machines think?' The theme reverberates through the rest of the paper, but more as a hidden undercurrent, because right away he wants to

---

[49] In 1997, IBM's chess computer Deep Blue beat Garry Kasparov, Chess Grandmaster and then chess world champion. Deep Blue was a development of early research in IBM's Poughkeepsie site where Arthur Samuel, who coined the term *machine learning*, began programming chess playing computers drawing on elaborate decision trees, which still form the basis for current computer board games. Taking leave from the players' board positions, a partial decision tree could be established, looking a few steps into the future, calculating the outcomes, before propagating back to the current position to produce a rating of all possible immediate moves forward, in light of the best possible intermediate outcomes. The program therefore learned which features of the board to include in the evaluation function at each point, and how to weight these features when calculating options. See Melanie Mitchell *Artificial Intelligence: A Guide for Thinking Humans*. New York: Farrar, Straus and Giroux. 2019, 157. But, as Levesque ironically remarks: 'As it turns out, there is little demand for man-machine tournaments', and that the very specific, small-range capacity of machine-learning systems, including those we see today in narrow applications to household, medicine or transport solutions, are a far cry from the much more profound question Turing posed in his imitation game: the question not of the imitation of a set of specific rules in an adversarial setting of a game, but of a more genuine capacity for common sense or for what later came to be known as GOFAI: Good Old Fashioned Artificial Intelligence. Hector J. Levesque *Common Sense, the Turing Test, and the Quest for Real AI*. Cambridge, MA: MIT Press. 2017, 132ff.

[50] Alan Turing Computing machinery and intelligence. *Mind*, 1950, 49: 433–60.

recast the question. He fears such a simple question might collapse into simply canvassing for opinionated responses, so he proposes to go at it in a more roundabout but stricter way.

The new form of the problem can be described in terms of a game which we call the 'imitation game.' It is played with three people, a man (A), a woman (B), and an interrogator (C) who may be of either sex. The interrogator stays in a room apart from the other two. The object of the game is for the interrogator to determine which of the other two is the man and which is the woman. He knows them by labels X and Y, and at the end of the game he says either 'X is A and Y is B' or 'X is B and Y is A.' The interrogator is allowed to put questions to A and B thus:
  C: Will X please tell me the length of his or her hair?
Now suppose X is actually A, then A must answer. It is A's object in the game to try and cause C to make the wrong identification. His answer might therefore be:
  'My hair is shingled, and the longest strands are about nine inches long.'
In order that tones of voice may not help the interrogator the answers should be written, or better still, typewritten. The ideal arrangement is to have a teleprinter communicating between the two rooms. Alternatively, the question and answers can be repeated by an intermediary. The object of the game for the third player (B) is to help the interrogator. The best strategy for her is probably to give truthful answers. She can add such things as 'I am the woman, don't listen to him!' to her answers, but it will avail nothing as the man can make similar remarks.
We now ask the question, 'What will happen when a machine takes the part of A in this game?' Will the interrogator decide wrongly as often when the game is played like this as he does when the game is played between a man and a woman? These questions replace our original, 'Can machines think?'[51]

There are larger questions than definite methods of computation at stake here. Turing wonders whether the computer, whilst it will make mistakes, will make as good a fist of the task as a human. Perhaps persuaded by his work at Bletchley, Turing is clearly envisaging a machine programmed into performing many small mechanical actions, including modifying its own programs, and so one that could perform computational operations whose significance might be sufficient to constitute the appearance of intelligence. The game isolates the interrogator in such a way that it is only through unsighted talk (via reading) that he or she can judge the intellect. And in its question and answer form the investigation can flow in a free-form manner, covering a vast array of human endeavour, and the witnesses, as Turing calls 'A' and 'B', can talk as boldly and boastfully as they wish, for they are never required to give practical demonstrations of the qualities and skills they claim to have. The machine that replaces 'A' is one of the universal computers Turing had already employed to great effect at Bletchley. Such a machine has a store, an executive unit and a control. The store contains packets of information, the rules of operation

---

[51] Alan Turing Computing machinery and intelligence, 433–4.

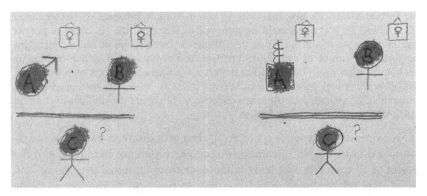

Figure 8.4 Turing's imitation game. Drawn by Morven Holt.

or program, the space of operations or accessing memory, and the operating memory. The executive unit (being of a humbler status than the Executive Committee in General Motors) performs operations, following the program. The control checks whether rules have been followed, and in the correct sequence, and amends the performance where necessary. Turing is at pains to point out that the machine need not be electric. Electricity just made the switching faster, an important innovation given the immense number of configurations a discrete state machine was possible of generating from an initial starting point with a given set of inputs. But it is a digital computer, and so it can mimic any discrete state machine (a loom, a calculator). But can it imitate a man imitating a woman?

The stakes are as philosophical as they are mechanical, and almost to a point where Turing seems sensitive to what Galloway was, much later, to make explicit when considering the potency of the universal computer:

It does not facilitate or make reference to an arrangement of being, it remediates the very conditions of being itself. If one may be so crude: the medium of the computer is being.[52]

The question of Being that is being set in the imitation game (Figure 8.4) is whether machinery can imitate itself into such a remediating role. Turing thinks it can, at least insofar as the interrogator will not perform any better in the game with a machine present instead of 'A'. He is alive to objections, wondering whether a machine really could 'make some one fall in love with it, learn from experience, use words properly, be the subject of its own thought'. He then supposes that in some ways a machine can indeed be understood as a subject facing its own subject as an object:

[52] Alexander Galloway If the Cinema Is an Ontology, 186.

If, for instance, the machine was trying to find a solution of the equation $x2 - 40x - 11 = 0$ one would be tempted to describe this equation as part of the machine's subject matter at that moment. In this sort of sense a machine undoubtedly can be its own subject matter. It may be used to help in making up its own programmes, or to predict the effect of alterations in its own structure. By observing the results of its own behaviour it can modify its own programmes so as to achieve some purpose more effectively. These are possibilities of the near future, rather than Utopian dreams.[53]

This works as the generation of an 'I', but as a discrete, switching condition, and not an open, continuous one. The difference here relates to the realm of computable problems suitable for computational processing, and what they omit, namely problems that do not lend themselves to being configured as solvable because they are inherently paradoxical and so cannot be read off from an initial state and set of inputs. The archetypical example of such is the 'halting problem'. Here an algorithm solves a problem as soon as there is an input, but instead of stopping with an output, the output is treated as a new input, thus sending the algorithm into a continuous loop. The player 'A', being deemed by Turing 'a frustrator', could impress upon the interrogator the realization that if all responses must be doubted, this was itself a condition of conviction in the interrogator that ought also be doubted, given the impression came from one of the players.

Doesn't the role of 'frustrator' require forms of creativity, intuition and spontaneous judgment, qualities that Turing readily admitted were not admitted to the discrete states by which a digital computer would operate, but to which, nevertheless, he seems to have allocated central roles in his game?[54] In imagining the machine's responses we are to consider not just the mechanics of a performance but whether a machine can understand what a game is: is it animated with the spirit of imitation, so to speak? Is this, as Turing supposes, really just a matter of programming capacity and engineering? The computer's job is to respond as would a man playing a woman, set in a world of other women and men, each with gender defining characteristics and yet each potentially able to play with the roles and traits typically assigned to the other, at least in imagined pretence. Isn't it the case that the delight in playing the game – and games require the possibility of delight – occurs in the very twists and pauses, the misfires and unnoticed glitches, that a discrete state machine forbids itself, at least in principle. Syntactically, the movement across discrete states, from 1 to 0, is immediate. Semantically it carries what in

---

[53] Alan Turing Computing machinery and intelligence, 449.

[54] Jacob Gaboury On uncomputable numbers: The origins of queer computing. *Journal of New Media Caucus*. 2013. http://median.newmediacaucus.org/caa-conference-edition-2013/on-uncomputable-numbers-the-origins-of-a-queer-computing/

Chapter 1 we called the duration of interpretation. Rather than immediate semiotic recognition, there is a sense of passage and hence development through which a conscious self becomes aware of things happening
to them as a self during the performance, and not as an input consequent
on an output. It is this sense of ongoing, immersive encounter that the
digital computer lacks, but which 'A' and 'B' carry within them as prac-
titioners and performers of gender, and 'C' as a questioner and judge.
In the digital state of being either 'on' or 'off' machines are insensate to
human time, to history, to any sense of being there or being present in
any human. Turing accepts that a digital machine can only deal with
discrete objects, set alone; with successions of instances, rather than with
enduring flows of time; its *Umwelt* is utterly different.[55] Whether Turing
was then fully alive to the ontological implications of this distinction, and
in the ways Galloway deftly, if enigmatically elaborates, is a moot point.

---

[55] Alan Turing. *Lecture to the Mathematical Society*. This also gives rise to a series of challenges to Turing's Imitation Game. John Searle, for example, levelled the 'Chinese
Room' response, suggesting that much more is going on with understanding than merely
getting some observable behaviour right, even dismissing universal Turing machines as
elaborate toilet paper holders, after all, an endless tape could be made of anything, or
that a computer made of interacting beer cans could have experiences, *thirst* in particular. Searle imagines himself in a room, corresponding with the outside world via notes
slipped under the door. So far so Turing, but Searle receives a batch of notes written
in Chinese characters, which he does not understand. If he manages to send appropriate Chinese characters back, those in the outside would surely but mistakenly assume
him to be a Chinese speaker. To achieve this feat, Searle imagines that, in addition to
the Chinese notes slipped under the door, he gets a second batch of rules, written in
English, that allow him to 'correlate one set of formal symbols with another set of formal
symbols' – so that he can identify symbols entirely by their shapes. He then consults
a third batch of rules, also in English, which help him correlate elements of this third
batch with the first two, that is, instructions on how to return 'certain Chinese symbols
with certain sorts of shapes'. The first batch resembles a script, the second batch a
'story', and the third 'questions'; and the symbols he returns are 'answers'– but all this
he does not even need to know. In this way, without having any sense of the content of
the messages, Searle can produce notes that fool the outside world into thinking him to
be a Chinese speaker. Searle argues that to achieve this, all he did was to behave like a
computer, 'performing computational operations on formally specified elements'. While
he may therefore be 'successfully' imitating a capability, there is no understanding going
on; merely the manipulation of symbols using elaborate rules. See John R. Searle Minds,
brains and programs. *The Behavioral and Brain Sciences*, 1980, 3: 417–57. However, as
Levesque points out, even the simple challenge of compiling a 'batch' of notes that spell
out all of the possible combinations of twenty ten-digit numbers – a much simpler task
than the configuration of the Chinese alphabet and grammar – would require a batch of
notes containing 10^{200} entries – when the entire physical universe only has about 10^{100}
atoms. A different kind of instruction would, of course, do the trick. A 10 x 210 table
for the addition of single digits, as well as a process of addition of individual and multiple numbers would only require a few pages in length. But that would mean teaching
a person how to add – and not just to work with tables of symbols without any further
knowledge of their structure – thus casting doubt on Searle's argument. See Hector J.
Levesque *Common Sense*, 13.

But the imitation game is suggestive that he was, not least because of its being oriented around what is so often the very first question asked about any human being: is it a boy or girl?

As a game it is set up to organize the simultaneity of occurrence in which everything appears. In the game, 'A', 'B' and 'C' are all simultaneously apparent (in clock time they are equally present in the now), but not simultaneously apparent to one another. There is, at any present moment, what Niklas Luhmann calls a 'simultaneity of non-simultaneity' whereby each of them, whilst they are all 'there' in the same time and at the same time, have their activities ordered to prevent a simultaneous appearance of inputs and outputs. Each system (for Luhmann, himself influenced by the ecological thinking of Uexküll, humans are sentient systems) must be relieved of the simultaneity of time through organization, so that they interact in managed sequences, an output following an input in timely ways, making the present (and what is made present) an experience of continual differentiation between past and future, what he calls an 'excluded third'.[56] Indeed the mutual awareness of these sentient systems is a function of this sequenced interaction; 'A' talks, 'C' reads, then 'C' questions, to which 'A' and 'B' listen, and then they respond, in sequence. Equally, the technical material systems are also sequenced, so a microphone receives an input and transmits it to a tape recorder that produces an output of readable text for 'C' to read.

A standard cognitive reading of this interchange would be of a passage from mental representation (an intention to frustrate from 'A' by using (typically) tall-tale responses) to public representation and mediation (the tall-tale told by 'A' and transmitted by machinery) and back to mental representations (the hearing and processing of both 'B' and 'C', the latter via printed text, as they absorb the tall-tale by 'A'). Such a sequencing fits the ordering necessitated by the paradox of simultaneity: one to the next and back again. In this sequence of the forming and telling of tales (the proto-narratives built up through questions and answers) each passage of the tale is unique in expression, but conditioned. Being a 'frustrator', 'A' might, for example, try to embellish and prolong his responses to the point where the tale starts to drift and stretch, becoming

---

[56] Niklas Luhmann *Communication and Social Order: Risk: A Sociological Theory.* Piscataway, NJ: Transaction Publishers. 1993, 37. Ted Schatzki discusses this as a blending of instant time and existential time. We deal with experiences of instant time succession – as when hearing an alarm and reaching out to turn it off when waking up – and this also being a stretched temporality of experience, a waking or dawning of consciousness. (See Ted Schatzki The time of activity. *Continental Philosophy Review.* 2006, 39: 155–182. 173.)

unclear, perhaps trying to confuse 'C'. Yet the latitude enjoyed by 'A' relies on an already established fixity. This frustrating role is particularly nuanced in the following exchange being imagined by Turing:

Q: Please write me a sonnet on the subject of the Forth Bridge [a bridge over the Firth of Forth, in Scotland].
A: Count me out on this one. I never could write poetry.
Q: Add 34957 to 70764.
A: (Pause about 30 seconds and then give as answer) 105621.
Q: Do you play chess?
A: Yes.
Q: I have K at my K 1, and no other pieces. You have only K at K6 and R at R1. It is your move. What do you play?
A: (After a pause of 15 seconds) R-R8 mate.[57]

It may go almost unnoticed, but the simple addition task takes the machine 30 seconds, and then it spits out a wrong answer or, as Turing says, the best strategy of the machine is to 'try and provide answers that would naturally be given by a man'[58] But, wonders Turing, could the machine imitate 'A' here, playing with the ambiguous force of paradox to better effect an outcome?[59]

The game yields to imaginative play, but the effect and affect is to restrict rather than expand the room for action because of two well-defined protocols and limit conditions. First, a non-negligible structure of question-and-answer enquiry that carries across multiple instantiations within and beyond the game. Second, the 'to-and-from' movement between private and public representations, which requires a cognitive processing device in which a sensory input filtered through receptor organs (hearing voices) is transformed into a mental representation (a question or answer). The brain-body has these devices built in, genetically wired, without which inputs and outputs (sounds) could not be locked onto representations (tales in the form of question and answer). These interpretation devices are the hardware upon which the cultural software rests and riffs, and they work invisibly, silently.[60]

---

[57] Alan Turing Computing machinery and intelligence, 434.

[58] Douglas R. Hofstadter Gödel, Escher, Bach, 596.

[59] There are also *un*countable infinite sets of numbers which, following the mathematician Cantor, cannot be computed because, even though they exist, in any language with a finite set of symbols, there are not enough programs that these can be written. This means that there is an uncountable infinity of real numbers that are not rational. See Paul Nahin *The Logician and the Engineer. How George Boole and Claude Shannon Created the Information Age*. Princeton: Princeton University Press. 2013, 171ff.

[60] In Wittgenstein's terms these are grammatical structures that allow a tribe to interpret the ethnographer, the child the adult, the foreigner the native, and so on. There may be incomprehension at the level of meaning, but not in recognizing the rules of a language.

Running through this description of the game is an assumed cognitive structure: an inner code hard wired into individual brains, and outer environments that mould the instantiations of these cognitive structures in situated behaviour. Humans are, for example, hard wired to talk and to listen, and these innate capacities gain the hue of local distinction because they operate in culturally distinct space and time; they start from the general and then work this into the particular. As 'A', the job of the computer is to learn how its own simulated language acquisition device might better align with those of 'B' and 'C'.[61]

In the process of trying to imitate an adult human mind we are bound to think a good deal about the process which has brought it to the state that it is in. We may notice three components.

(a) The initial state of the mind, say at birth,
(b) The education to which it has been subjected,
(c) Other experience, not to be described as education, to which it has been subjected.

Instead of trying to produce a programme to simulate the adult mind, why not rather try to produce one which simulates the child's? If this were then subjected

---

[61] It was the Eugene Goostman chat bot, 65 years after Turing conceived his test, that came to convince 33 per cent of a panel of judges that it was, really, a child giving responses. But the test was passed using a series of tricks. One was to present the bot as a thirteen-year-old, non-native speaker, which obscured any grammatical or language issues and legitimized unfocussed and borderline impolite answers. Another set of tricks derives from the so-called Winograd schema, leading the machine to a correct answer by hiding behind verbal playfulness or canned response. Hector Levesque, who together with Terry Winograd, developed ways of probing common sense, and thus moving beyond evasive and fooling answers, asks questions such as: Could a crocodile run a steeplechase?; should a team of baseball players be allowed to glue small wings onto their caps?; or when Joan made sure to thank Susan for all the help she had given, who had given the help, Joan or Susan? Hector Levesque *Common Sense, The Turning Test and the Question for Real AI*. Cambridge, MA: MIT Press, 2017, 51–54. None of these questions can be addressed with stock answers, as even the vast number of sentence templates that are stored in modern machine learning systems are unlikely to contain curious combinations of baseball caps and wings or crocodiles and hurdle horse races. In addition to such stock answers, chat bots are fed with databases of common-sense knowledge, coded by human programmers, in addition to being given logic rules, but no-one is likely to have written about this before, and unless the subject has knowledge of baseball and knows that crocodiles have short legs and therefore, *thinking this through*, we find that they are not suited to any task involving such leaps, answers are difficult to find. Melanie Mitchell *Artificial Intelligence*, 53. Similarly, unless one is able to delineate the relationship between Joan and Susan, either answer sounds feasible. On meeting such questions the bot is typically programmed to change the topic, and the Eugene bot did this liberally. The free-form exchanges Turing elaborated in his test are therefore prone to allowing stock answers and evasive tactics to replace meaning making and understanding – and thus the identification of intelligence beyond fake imitation. Winograd Schemes, developed to avoid such easy deceptions as the Eugene bot uses, indicate a continuous catching up of those trying to assess machine intelligence with attempts at gaming

to an appropriate course of education one would obtain the adult brain. Presumably the child brain is something like a notebook as one buys it from the stationer's. Rather little mechanism, and lots of blank sheets. (Mechanism and writing are from our point of view almost synonymous.) Our hope is that there is so little mechanism in the child brain that something like it can be easily programmed. The amount of work in the education we can assume, as a first approximation, to be much the same as for the human child.

We have thus divided our problem into two parts. The child programme and the education process. These two remain very closely connected. We cannot expect to find a good child machine at the first attempt. One must experiment with teaching one such machine and see how well it learns. One can then try another and see if it is better or worse. There is an obvious connection between this process and evolution, by the identifications

Structure of the child machine = hereditary material
Changes of the child machine = mutation,
Natural selection = judgment of the experimenter

One may hope, however, that this process will be more expeditious than evolution. The survival of the fittest is a slow method for measuring advantages. The experimenter, by the exercise of intelligence, should be able to speed it up. Equally important is the fact that he is not restricted to random mutations. If he can trace a cause for some weakness he can probably think of the kind of mutation which will improve it.[62]

The education process, as we have seen Turing argue, can take the form of: punishment and reward with the teacher gradually removing themselves as the pupil matures; a random element in programming to allow the machine to explore differently adequate options; and the use of a store that contains well-established facts and imperatives, rules and meta rules regulating the order in which rules of the system ought be applied (a meta rule might be of the from: if one method is quicker than another then avoid the slower method, or have routines pre-empt the operational output of sub routines on the basis of expected outcomes, and have the control unit check and the executive unit recalibrate if the expected outcome is not forthcoming).

By experimenter Turing means the programmer or engineer, but at the end of paper, during a foray into learning machines, Turing wonders whether this role can be adopted by the machine. Speeding up evolution signals a widening of the sources of novelty and adaptation, away from the

---

the exercise through ever more elaborate databases. The latest development comes via OpenAI's new ChatGPT chatbot which is reported to produce a wide range of texts and interactions more plausibly mimicking human efforts. See A Skeptical Take on the A.I. Revolution: The A.I. expert Gary Marcus asks: What if ChatGPT isn't as intelligent as it seems? www.nytimes.com/2023/01/06/podcasts/transcript-ezra-klein-interviews-gary-marcus.html. 6.1.2023.

[62] Alan Turing Computing machinery and intelligence, 456.

accident of natural selection coupled to environmental fit, and towards a more conscious, systemic cognitive condition in which machinery and experimenters are part of rather than distinct from their environment, and where intelligence is woven into what becomes situationally embodied cognition. As Galloway has mentioned, the sequencing protocols of the game govern the kinds of possible action available, the range of possible connections and the possibilities of with whom, when and how to connect, but they do not script the actual action, which is always environmentally contingent.[63] In contrast to regulations that are ecumenical about what agents do, but foreclose on specifically stated outcomes by attaching them to penalties, protocols are conditioning forces organizing the manner in which things connect, arranging for data to flow between them in specified ways.[64]

One can infer how, starting from an initial programmed and engineered state, the machine in the imitation game can, by continually sensing cues in its environment – cues amounting to pauses – make decisions about inputs and outputs. The pause also means things might go awry, the operations are not automatic. Turing builds these pauses into the machine, either accepting that sometimes things can go awry (electricity supply is not reliable), or more deliberately imagining how the experimenter can program the computer into recursivity (using its own outputs as future inputs, and to ascribe different values to these self-generating inputs, as in the meta rules) and randomness (producing variations that surprise even the programmer, such as a mistake in a simple calculation, and which can be tested for efficacy). In this it is as if the machine were deliberately and persistently placing itself in a state of anticipation; a state which, for Hayles, bears the mark of intelligence. For sure the machine relies on programs and is grounded in the switching of logic gates, yet it is able to place itself in relation to that which is yet to occur (to non-things) in the form of imagined scenarios: if 'B' answers affirmatively, do likewise. The machine can, if only as part of the broader environment called the Imitation Game, create and react to signs and the changes signs bring about, inferring appropriate behaviours, including changing the rules of behaviour, and so act and treat the resonance of the action as a source for further learning.[65]

---

[63] Alexander Galloway *Protocol: How Control Exists After Decentralization*. Massachusetts: MIT Press. 2004.

[64] Steven Yeager Protocol. *Critical Inquiry*, 2019, 45(3): 745–61.

[65] This definition of machine intelligence is taken from Katherine Hayles Can computers create meanings? A Cyber/bio/semiotic perspective. *Critical Inquiry*, 2019, 46(1): 32–55. Hayles suggests that for too long we have misread computers as unintelligent because they lack a unitary, inner cognitive core. If we accept cognition as something embodied

But Can a Machine Think?

With the imitation game the background conditions of human practice being smuggled into the game, against and through which the players understand themselves as performers of practice, are of some significance, and the machine would be required to learn these: the practice of game playing itself for example; the puzzling elusiveness of a biologically framed gender; the value of a sense of competition in which there are winners and losers rather than just players; the intrigue of a puzzle; and the sympathetic capacity to imagine oneself otherwise wedded into a rhetorical awareness of the available means of persuasion. All of these norms have been acquired by the players, and in differing ways, and through them they are then able to assume the talking and listening roles assigned to them. They can follow the rules, without having to check them. And all of them operate in the basis of redundancy; in other words they are followed, not obeyed, always leaving room for interpretation.

Whilst behavioural, cognitive distinctions between inner and outer states tend to downplay the influence of these norms, they are critical to the atmosphere of the imitation game. To play the game is to take up talking, listening, persuading, guessing and to modify them in real-time performances that evolve within developmental systems to which many others are also party. To learn to talk, and to listen, is an ecological process of development in which, from birth, infants acquire skill – they are steeped in sounds from the womb onwards, intonations and volumes, rhythms and quietness, and these are not isolated, they are part of a vast array of appearances: the passage of night and day, the rush of traffic, the sombre, processional stillness of a church. All of this becomes part of the background against which talking and listening are embodied in the way they are: human physiology and cognitive skill are just aspects, and not at all privileged ones.[66]

Any understanding of consciousness and self emerges from, and is immanent to, such a skilfully configured task-scape. As such, it is intimate with imitation. Turing was right to hit on imitation as the mechanism by

in an environment of interacting parts to which computers and humans are integral, and not as something locked into a mind, we can sense how computers act in flexible, intelligent ways. Like humans they are capable of symbolic abstraction (albeit programmed) and, given their sensitivity, speed and range, employ this capability in unseen and pervasive ways.

[66] This follows, inter alia, Spencer-Brown's insight that anything that is, is only so against a background from which it first can be distinguished. Yet, drawing such distinctions is an act; it is something that is done, and not received from the world, and in so doing it includes a privileging of that which is foregrounded (the 'marked' state) over its background (the 'unmarked' state); but the act of drawing the distinction is mute on the reasons and justifications for drawing this distinction and not any other. George Spencer-Brown *Laws of Form*. New York: Dutton. 1979.

which the conscious self emerges, but the copying has a non-reducible, performative quality. As Tim Ingold argues, attempts to imitate or copy are intimately woven with those of others, making the cognitive task an historical and social process:

> This process of copying ... is one not of information transmission but of guided rediscovery. As such, it involves a mixture of imitation and improvisation: indeed these might better be understood as two sides of the same coin. Copying is imitative, insofar as it takes place under guidance; it is improvisatory, insofar as the knowledge it generates is knowledge that novices discover for themselves.[67]

Consciousness arises from a constant situational attunement of ecological development to which there is no inside or outside, beginning or end; to be aware of a self is to be alive to and immersed in an inherited 'task scape'.

In the imitation game 'A', 'B' and 'C' must orient themselves in such a task-scape as best they might. This they do by relying on already-acquired skills in questioning and answering as well as an awareness of the performative nature of gender. They must also be imagining different outcomes depending on the success or failure of synchronizing attempts, given the surprise and openness that animates any situation known as a game. The rules governing their performance are rigid (answer in response to a question) and fluid (frustrate, assist) yet neither lives without the other, insofar as the rigidity of the expected response can itself be played with as part of a fluid interpretation. The players are searching continually for cues and clues, but these are always temporary and contingent, they are accepted only if they lead to new cues and clues through which new sequencing possibilities arise.

When it enters the game, the digital computer imitates, but it does so according to an orthodox cognitivist script in which fixed initial conditions are being amended by adaptive responses to a changing environment. It does not encounter the present and the uncertainty of the present presaged in the constant eruption of Luhmann's 'excluded third', in other words the pause is not a space for the emergence of interpretation and anticipation. For the human players there is a semantic, not just syntactic, uncertainty, what Luhmann calls a second-order problem of re-entry in which a self is overlaying pictures of itself picturing itself. In the case of the game this re-entry would come for example if 'A' has to concentrate on answering 'C' whilst having half a mind for how he is appearing to 'B' given 'B' might then use the response given by 'A' in

---

[67] Tim Ingold, (2001). From the transmission of representation to the education of attention. In H. Whitehouse (Ed.), The *debated mind: Evolutionary psychology versus ethnography* (pp. 113–153). London:Routledge.

future questioning. 'A' attempts to go outside himself to then immediately come back in, given there is no possibility of simultaneously picturing himself picturing himself, it is only ever a picture in deficit to its own imaginary. The machine has none of these semantic issues of re-entry, only syntactical ones of efficient and effective sequencing, ones in which the troubling question of 'being present without being present' does not arise.[68] Because the machine works on computable problems the world beyond its operation is always disambiguated through the mediation of coded structures (rules, procedures, data) that produce, and work through, simulations governed by a fixed architecture of store, executive unit and control. The machine's time in the game are syntactic forms of computable processing, they are utterly discrete.[69] Or put differently, the machine carries no tradition, no history, it does not accumulate experience: it does not grow old, it just wears out, and replaces itself, day in, day out.

---

[68] This was something McTaggart recognizes philosophically. He argues that what he calls B series time (spatialized time as one discrete unit separated from another, or clock time) cannot explain change (which is fundamental to time), but nor can the contrasting A series (experienced, flowing time from past to future) because here the only imaginable real change is the same as time itself, and thus it must condition itself, despite the different properties of A (past, present and future) being incompatible to each other. Because no time can be both future and past: 'Past, present and future are incompatible determinations. But every event has them all. If M is past, it has been present and future. If it is future, it will be present and past. If it is present, it has been future and will be past. Thus, all three characteristics belong to each event' (48). This paradox can only be resolved by recourse to something like Heidegger's view of world time. See John McTaggart *The unreality of time. Mind*, 1908, 17(68): 457–74.

[69] Kathrine Hayles *How We Think*, 85–6.

9 Strategy No Longer Thinks in Terms of Human Beings

Turing's game (see Chapter 8) as a test of whether machines can emulate human intelligence, is a foray into the nature of machine intelligence. When the machine takes over from a human interlocutor, unbeknown to an unsighted human questioner, a new world emerges in which sequencing is computational: though it is emulating a human being, it does not think about being human. It has a task, and works on how to fulfil it. That much in the way of strategy practice is dedicated to similar forms of sequencing tasks is telling. It is as if, in all seriousness, strategic practice brackets off the wide horizons of human awareness (it avoids the general) in order to concentrate on the task in hand. The effect of such distillation and restriction of intelligence is devastating: the human *Umwelt* is left in ruins.

Graeme Green's and Carol Reed's *The Third Man* is a film about ruins, and the life that persists within them. It is set in Vienna. World War II has just ended. The faded Habsburg empire clings to the shelled buildings like the camphor of old, mothballed clothes, traditional authority had lost its grip, having been broken by the losses of two wars, the citizens are waking up dishevelled, blinking their way into an age gutted of its tradition. A rough rule of law is being enforced by the allied forces – among them a Major Calloway, who is trying to keep a lid on the racketeering by which most of the city's trade is being run. Harry Lime is of particular interest to Calloway. Lime has been stealing penicillin from the military and selling it to Austrian doctors who use it to treat rich patients. The racket began with Lime mediating one-to-one transactions, but he withdrew from street trading as his operation expanded: the penicillin was being stolen further up the supply chain and distributed much more widely, including to hospitals. To facilitate further growth, the penicillin is also being diluted, to the point it is ineffective, indeed dangerous, leaving patients exposed to a twisted death. It is a cruelty Lime brushes off as readily as dust from his suit lapel: they would die anyway, poor things, and hastening their passage to the afterlife is, if you think about it, more humane than leaving them to suppurate in bombed out *Mitteleuropa*. It

is, argues Lime, just business, and business is, at heart, about the transformation of capital, one growth feeding on another, again and again.
Calloway is trying to adduce Lime's guilt, but becomes increasingly cyni-
cal about making any difference: Lime and his ilk have little awareness of
or interest in the lives they are blighting with their corrupted medicine.
They are, concludes Calloway, types, and if he arrests Lime another will
appear. Lime knows this too, he is neither a citizen of, nor a member
of a household, he is alone, organizing through subterfuge and moving
through tunnels. Confronted by Calloway's anger at his dirty business,
Lime is quickly to the point: 'These days, old man, nobody thinks in
terms of human beings.'

Lime is an outcome of the vast material and political apparatus
established during the war, and as Calloway comes to suspect, it is the
apparatus as much as Lime that is at fault. Lime is a stateless being
who has learnt not to load himself down with history, tradition, values
or friends, for this is the kind of baggage that can get you killed. To
survive and flourish during the war was to live entirely in the 'large'
now of the present, dropping memories as quickly as a spent cigarette.
Lime is a perfect embodiment of a human whose consciousness has been
objectified to a calculated set of narrow positions. His discernment has
transformed into operational cunning. No longer thinking of humans,
but of a democracy of things such as medicines, transport, children and
borders, each the equal of the other, and none of sufficient importance
to not be replaceable, malleable, useable or disposable.

Reading Lime's callousness not as a psychological deficiency of an
isolated delinquent but as a product of a certain form of organization
means Lime is as replaceable as the patients he dupes; if he doesn't do it,
someone else will; someone who has better situational intelligence. This
form of organization has long ceased to be organized by and focussed
on humans: Vienna (a city, an arrangement of buildings and pathways
extending human organization and preserve its memories, cultures and
rituals); a World War (bayonets giving way to industrialized and mechanized shelling and rockets); penicillin (a laboratory produced chemical);
Lime's little stratagems at wresting some immediate advantage. His has
always been a story of technology in which humans play a lesser and
lesser role; they are, literally, shadows on a wall.

Cybernetics, Strategy and War

Whilst Turing was thinking in terms of machines being like humans, and
humans like Lime were approximating the computations of machines,
Norbert Wiener was busy dissolving the distinction. He was helping

develop feedback-driven flight predictors that could be used in anti-aircraft artilleries.[1] Though coming too late for active deployment in World War II, they provided a model for machine learning that became known as the new science of cybernetics which for a generation became an animating creed for the US military industrial complex. Wiener's work emerged from an organizational entanglement of private firms, military command, scientific laboratories, and large philanthropic organizations such as the Carnegie Institution (founded 1911) and Rockefeller Foundation (founded 1913), all of which came together to pioneer the modern US system of 'science planning', including the development of weapons of mass destruction.[2] The weapons – most notably the hydrogen bomb, capable of destroying the world several times over – had brought engineers (like Wiener), industrialists, military leaders and advisors to contemplate a fundamental revision of the strategies and tactics of warfare. The destructive power of the bomb meant it mattered little in which part of the enemy territory it was dropped, and there was little use in planning tactical manoeuvres of ground troops when, after a nuclear attack, there would not be much useable ground left. This meant the intricate 'tactical' details of warfare that had hitherto occupied military command suddenly became insignificant in relation to purely strategic considerations, in particular to the game-theoretical play of nuclear deterrents and the double-bind binary of defence capability versus economic cost. After World War II, military and political strategy was shifting from the question of how to attack an enemy better or more quickly to the question of (apparent, or threatened) funding for swifter and larger nuclear arsenals that would intimidate and/or bankrupt the enemy.[3] Wiener's work was integral to this thinking, not only because of its contribution to missile accuracy, but also because of its insights into feedback systems and hence the possibility of transparent, universal communications and so control.[4]

---

[1] Feedback means that the difference between an input and an output is fed back into the system; a structural coupling between a machine or organism and its *milieu*. Examples include torpedoes with target seeking mechanisms, neuro activities and muscle-eye coordination and, as Hui suggests, also Gödel's recursive function and the Turing machine, which have a predefined purpose or *telos*. Yuk Hui, *Contingency and Recursivity*, 124.

[2] Philip Mirowski, *Machine Dreams: Economics Becomes a Cyborg Science*. Cambridge: Cambridge University Press. 2002, 155ff. This also includes the rise to dominance of neoclassical economic theory as part of the development of cyborg science in its focus on issues of algorithmic rationality and statistical inference over theories of collective action or institutionally specific concerns. Philip Mirowski, *Machine Dreams* : 157.

[3] Marc Trachtenberg Strategic thought in America, 1952–1966. *Political Science Quarterly*, 1989,10(2): 301–34, 311. RAND's Bernard Brodie says that 'Strategy wears a dollar sign'. Bernard Brodie *Strategy in the Missile Age*. Princeton, NJ: The RAND Corporation. 1959, 358.

[4] See Reinhold Martin *The Organizational Complex*, 66.

For Wiener, computers, like all organized entities, including the human body, faced the necessity of maintaining order in a wider environment that exposed them to entropic disintegration. The existence (*zōe*) of humans, animals and organizations shares a common processual ontology: life is the varying resistance of decay realized through continual loops of imperfect information processing. In the spirit of Uexküll, Wiener began with a simple premise that to exist a 'being' has to establish and maintain the boundaries of an interior set against an exterior. Yet with Wiener the ecology was primarily one of information. The boundary has to be robust enough to maintain organizational coherence, and porous enough to allow for flexibility, qualities that were constituted through information feedback (concerning internal needs and external availability). Eventually, necessarily and unavoidably the 'being' falls apart and re-integrates into surroundings that swallow up the information about the organized body, giving way once again to chaotic, ad-hoc scattering.[5] So, according to Wiener, '[j]ust as entropy tends to increase spontaneously in a closed system, so information tends to decrease; just as entropy is a measure of disorder, so information is a measure of order.'[6] And in the preface to the revised edition of *The Human Use of Human Beings* he continues:

As entropy increases, the universe, and all closed systems in the universe, tend naturally to deteriorate and lose their distinctiveness ... But while the universe as a whole, if indeed there is a whole universe, tends to run down, there are local enclaves whose direction seems opposed to that of the universe at large and in which there is a limited and temporary tendency for organization to increase. Life finds its home in some of these enclaves.[7]

The distinction, or being, of cybernetic organisms lies not with material or ecological conditions, but on patterns of distributed information, as Reinhold Martin suggests. Wiener saw the organism's body as nothing more than a pattern of information that can be transmitted across wired networks by whose movement materiality was being continually modulated.[8] Wiener's collapsing of human, animal and vegetable vision worlds into the domain of information processing establishes a special relationship between the electronic computer and the human brain and body (this was a dualism Wiener maintained), but in a form reduced to feedback patterns that are observed and measured as expressions of a reasoned will to survive.

---

[5] Alexander Galloway *Protocol*, 105.
[6] Norbert Wiener *The Human Use of Human Beings: Cybernetics and Society*. Boston: Houghton Mifflin. 1950, 21: 129.
[7] Alexander Galloway *Protocol*, 105.
[8] Reinhold Martin *The Organizational Complex: Architecture, Media, and Corporate Space*. Cambridge MA: MIT Press. 2005, 25–6.

Cybernetics was a gift to strategists, not least because it enabled them to blend the biologism of evolutionary and ecological thinking with the science of measurement. The question of the organization's *Umwelt* arose (the strategists were not poor in world), but it did so under the aegis of measurement and prediction. There is little need for evaluative meaning in a cybernetic system. In a warming climate, for example, it is important to gather data on the differing rates of warming or the likely effects on divergent life forms. That way the organization can take contingency measures, adapting to a rapidly changing milieu, discovering alternate resources to those likely to suffer depletion, apprehending the desirability of new alliances and so on. Wider questions of ethical responsibility for other life forms are of little concern. The activity is akin to that of a thermostat (a device for communication and control) adjusting machinery to ensure any rise or fall in temperature remains within programmed range. It is not interested in why the range is desirable, or in the effects its own operations have on other life forms. In the same way, an organization, whether it be a human being or nation state, is concerned with staying within its own desired range of parameters, so evoking Uexküll's disinhibitor ring, but in this case the boundary is informational. The job of strategy is to organize the best possible feedback systems for communication and control to realize this stabilising condition.[9] If strategists are aware of other organizational forms, it is as competitors or allies in the pursuit of resources to be used in the maintenance of life.

Filtered by cybernetics, the job of strategy was to organize a viable organization,[10] and it found its apotheosis in Stafford Beer's 'Project

---

[9] Recursivity is therefore a mechanism that 'domesticates' contingency. Cybernetic systems learn when they are challenged by events that exceed the normalizing capacities of existing norms, for example when a disease leads to the establishment of a new relation between the an organism and its *milieu*. Yuk Hui *Recursivity and Contingency*, 181.

[10] The spread of cybernetics into strategy occurred via theories and models of games. See, for example, Richard Nielsen's Cooperative strategy. *Strategic Management Journal*, 1998, 9: 475–92 or Wesley Cohen and Daniel Levinthal's Fortune favours the prepared firm. *Management Science*, 1994, 40(2) 227–51. More pervasively, it happened via the stipulation of both the strategic agent as well as the market as information processors; as pursuers of intelligence. James March Rationality, foolishness and adaptive intelligence. *Strategic Management Journal*, 2006, 27: 201–14, 220. One area of cybernetic spread is strategic evolutionary theory, beginning with Cyert and March's conceptualization of the firm as an 'adaptive institution' and their emphasis on shorter and longer term *feedback* patterns. Richard Cyert and James March *A Behavioral Theory of the Firm*. Englewood Cliffs, NJ: Prentice-Hall. 1963. Behavioural ideas also fuelled evolutionary theories in strategy. Richard Nelson and Sydney Winter, who both had worked at RAND, took aim at the neoclassical idea of equilibrium at the system level, see Giovanni Gavetti and Daniel Levinthal's The strategy field from the perspective of management science: divergent strands and possible integration. *Management Science*, 2004, 50(10): 1309–18, 1313, instead drawing on computer simulations of firms enacting 'searches' in selection environments, resembling automata.

Figure 9.1 The Cybersyn ops room. Copyright Gui Bonsiepe.

Cybersyn', the real-time information planning system designed to run Salvador Allende's socialist economy in Chile during the early 1970s. Though in many ways the proto form of modern ERP systems, and exposed to similar frailties, what made Cybersyn distinct was the explicit and comprehensive association of resource scheduling, detailed modes of representation and picturing, and the continued integrity of a distinct and unified organizational form. To realize socialism and nationalize industries meant the price system giving way to planning, and planners needed accurate information on the behaviour of variables essential to the smooth running of the economy. Beer envisaged everyone, workers and managers alike, willingly measuring both their actual activity and capability, thereby revealing the potential for improvements in productivity should resources be properly assigned. Information was gathered on raw material stocks, distribution bottlenecks, worker unrest, regional demographics, weather patterns and even daily measures of sentiment using an algedonic (*algos* – pain, *hedone* – pleasure) dial upon which people indicate how good they felt, ranging from deeply unhappy to bliss. All these data were fed by telex and combined centrally by two mainframe computers to provide as close to a real-time picture of the economy as was possible. This picture was constituted from within a hive-like hexagonal operations room designed by Gui Bonsiepe (see Figure 9.1), or what Beer came to call 'the liberty machine'. Bonsiepe was a graduate of the Ulm School of Design in Germany, renowned for its curricula that

Philip Mirowski *Machine Dreams*, 19, 530; Philip Mirowski and Edward Nik-Khah *The Knowledge We Have Lost in Information: The History of Information in Modern Economics*. Oxford: Oxford University Press. 2017. It is then but a small step to more contemporary simulations. Gavetti and Levinthal, for example begin with a feedback circuit connecting 'knowledge', 'actions' and 'outcomes' through information pathways: 'Choices that have led to what are encoded as positive outcomes are reinforced, while the propensity to engage in actions that have led to negative outcomes is diminished.' Giovanni Gavetti and Daniel Levinthal Looking forward and looking backward: Cognitive and experiential search. *Administrative Science Quarterly*, 2000, 45: 133–7, 114.

blended design and aesthetics with semiotics, sociology, business and systems thinking.[11]

The room had the appearance of being a coherent, seamless human-machine interface: seven swivel chairs were aligned in a circle, behind them were banks of screens upon which graphic designers fed diagrammatic summaries of production rates, happiness indices, distribution flows, as requested by the strategists. From their chairs the strategists could also operate slide projectors to project information, not just summaries of the dynamic balance of current economic activity, but also likely future scenarios, combining what Beer was to call an ear on the ground with an eye on the future.[12] It was a centralized space in which a continually updating picture of Chile's economy was being presented to decision makers whose role was to read the production and human resources indices, aggregated by sector and enterprise, and to isolate significant patterns so as to reveal, forestall and manage potential disturbances so as to best align collaborative endeavour.

Naturally enough, being an organization, Cybersyn was beset with systemic problems of its own calibration: the information was often outdated, the abstract indices were often not nuanced enough to reflect real-life experience, the geography of a very long and thin country meant communication was always stalling, the political situation was unstable and intense so the attention leaders gave to economic planning was sporadic, and the machinery (such as computer power) was unreliable and underfunded. Almost before it began it ended, as Allende was ousted in a murderous coup and Pinochet's fascist regime took over the economic reigns, before quickly ceding them to US-backed corporations. Amid the turmoil, images of smoothly configured arcs of cybernetic adjustments linking fruit farms, energy supplies, worker training, canning factories and truck distribution into wider networks of mirrored and complimentary economic activity had little rhetorical force when set against the confrontational policies of a military backed dictatorship intent on bloody domination.

---

[11] *Hochschule für Gestaltung Ulm (HfG).* Now recognized as having been one of the grounding exponents of holistic industrial design, expanding on the interdisciplinarity of the Bauhaus, merging intuition with analysis, and down playing the role of individual designers in pursuit of distinction and variety to further coherence and unity across product lines and processes. See review article by Robin Kinross Hochschule für Gestaltung Ulm: Recent literature. *Journal of Design History*, 1988, 1(3/4): 249–56.

[12] See Raul Espejo Cybernetics of governance: The Cybersyn project 1971–1973. In *Social Systems and Design.* Edited by Gary Metcalf. Tokyo: Springer. 2014, 71–90. See also Eden Medina *Cybernetic Revolutionaries: Technology and Politics in Allende's Chile.* Cambridge: MIT Press. 2011.

The Absurdity of Reason

Though it was found wanting in Chile, cybernetic reasoning still enjoyed an ascendency amongst military organizations in the USA. The problem had been the application, not the principle. Cybersyn was implemented in a politically unruly and uncertain space with uniquely difficult demographic constraints and dated and uneven machinery. In the US military the situation was different. The attraction of cybernetics lay in its centralising logic: any emphasis on the generation of effective feedback systems meant the pursuit of world control (sustained by the threat of violence) took place from the sealed-off distance of ops rooms, using data from quantitative summaries and approximations of agglomerations and trends; warfare became a science of information flow.[13] Compared with the bloody and costly mess associated with life and death in the field, cybernetics afforded the grandees of war and their attendants a safe and abstracted space from which to reconceive battle as logistics. Control was a picture; a cybernetic vision of organizational sequencing through overlaying feedback loops: one that became formalized into theories of decision making, for instance through the publication of John von Neumann and Oskar Morgenstern's game theory, which so animated MacDonald, Sloan's ghost writer.

This reasoning was brilliantly satirized in Stanley Kubrick's nightmare comedy *Dr. Strangelove, Or How I Learned to Stop Worrying and Love the Bomb*. It is a film about strategy, and the absurdities of human attempts to run the industrial-military complex into which they have found themselves thrown. A rogue nuclear attack on the Soviet Union, delivered through hydrogen bombs mounted to B-52 planes, has been unleashed by an unhinged US General, and a strategy meeting of top military and political officials is convened by the US President to assess the situation. The military strategists, perhaps stirred by the impressive sight of missiles in flight, are hawkish, and the most vehement and bombastic is the aptly named General Buck Turgidson, who attempts to persuade the President to continue with the attack rather than admit its imminent arrival to the Soviet enemy.

[13] Marc Trachtenberg *Strategic Thought in America*: 304. One example of this shift in understanding of the roles and respective importance of strategy and tactics is that in the 1970s Cold War period, military colleges in the USA and the UK turned to civilians when seeking authoritative expositions of the political, economic and military implications of nuclear weapons; whereas before civilians were not usually invited to instruct military professionals. Colin S. Gray *Strategy and History: Essays on Theory and Practice*. London: Routledge. 2006, 25–31. The conviction that prior to 1945 the military had been far more interested in tactics than in strategy can be seen in one of RAND's foremost thinkers, Bernard Brodie's disparaging assessment that the 'richness in writings on military history does not prepare us for the poverty in theoretical writings on the strategy of war'. Bernard Brodie *Strategy in the Missile Age*. Princeton, NJ: The Rand Corporation. 1959, 28.

Figure 9.2 War room. Still from Stanley Kubrick's *Dr Strangelove*, 1964. Wikimedia commons

From within the war room (see Figure 9.2) – centred on a dark oval table reminiscent both of a roulette table and a Claude glass, back-dropped by a large information board with a map of the world radiating with the lights that marked the real-time passage of planes and bombs, and in which, later on in the film, comes the brilliantly unreflective condemnation issued against two feuding strategists 'Gentlemen, you can't fight here, this is the war room' – Turgidson employs a numbered and nested line of 'if-then' strategic reasoning with the assured rhythm of a mind that has it all worked through in discrete neatness. In summary, the sequence goes something like this:

1) Any hopes of recalling the rogue 843rd bomb wing are rapidly diminishing.
2) The Russians will discover the attack in 15 minutes.
3) They will strike back with everything they've got.
4) If we have done nothing to suppress their capability, we – the USA – will be annihilated.

pause

5) If, on the other hand, we launch an all-out and coordinated attack with our 5-1 missile superiority, we will catch them 'with their pants down'.

6) An unofficial study of this eventuality indicated we would destroy 90 per cent of their nuclear capability, and in return suffer only modest and acceptable civilian casualties from a depleted and uncoordinated Soviet response.

Turgidson ends his assessment with an obvious, proven way forward: there are two regrettable, but clearly distinguishable post-war environments, one with 10–20 million killed, the other 150 million.

Kubrik based the entailed logic of Turgidson's speech on the decision science advocated by Herman Kahn. Kahn was a RAND strategist and nuclear physicist who had been critical of President Eisenhower's military policy of massive retaliation in the event of nuclear aggression. Mutually assured destruction (MAD) was, for Kahn, a deviant form of game theory because it led to each 'player' developing a failsafe response to ensure any aggressor would meet complete and utter destruction (known as a Doomsday machine). There was no loosening mechanism. Kahn, who was employed by Kubrick as an advisor, explores an alternative form of game theory to endorse a calibrated and proportional return of nuclear fire. It is this form of reasoning that Turgidson espouses, supported as he is with an 'unofficial study' bound in a folder labelled 'World targets in megadeaths', a phrase from Kahn's book *On Thermonuclear War*. As the plot unravels, we find the Soviets do have a secret Doomsday machine, one whose effectiveness is parodied remorselessly by the script because the Soviets had forgotten to make it known, thereby neutering completely the strategic force of MAD. The president, rebuffing Turgidson, orders the 843rd bomb wing destroyed, but one of the errant bombers still releases its payload, triggering the Soviet's Doomsday machine. Dr Strangelove, the rocket scientist running the US weapons programme, and whose real name is *Merkwuerdigliebe*, is asked whether the president and his entourage should take to the bunkers.[14] Strangelove points out there are no bunkers: to have installed them would have undermined the fragile, apparently rational poise by which the threat of MAD would hold each side in abeyance. Start investing in failsafe protection and the other side thinks you will have nothing to lose by striking, and so it itself launches an all-out strike before the protection can be built. Tit-for-tat logic is more protective of life than concrete, that is in a world without chance events, which is no world at all.

Strangelove's argument, like Turgidson's, is carried along by the unimpeachable force of game theory in which the enemy 'other' becomes a tit-for-tat 'antagonist who played against us and would bluff

---

[14] Thomas Allen Nelson *Kubrick: Inside a Film Maker's Maze*. Bloomington: Indiana University Press. 2000, 95.

to win'.[15] By invoking game theory the effect is to assume you know the enemy, indeed transparently so. The enemy is a type, a sequence of logical entailment. And in assuming this the effects quickly accelerate and twist into a form of logical insanity, one that, as Peter Galison remarks, becomes unable of making a distinction between machine bodies and human ones:

it was an enemy at home in the world of strategy, tactics, and manoeuvre, all the while thoroughly inaccessible to us, separated by a gulf of distance, speed, and metal. It was a vision in which the enemy pilot was so merged with machinery that (his) human-nonhuman status was blurred.[16]

Within the intersecting lines of communication and feedback humans' behaviour became an equivalent to that of servo-mechanisms and self-guided rockets, they could be initiated, propelled, directed and die,[17] and all the while share similar capacities for thought and calculation, an idea beautifully captured by Thomas Pynchon:

So the Rocket, on its own side of the flight, sensed acceleration first. Men, tracking it, sensed position or distance first. To get to distance from acceleration, the Rocket had to integrate twice – needed a moving coil, transformers, electrolytic cell, bridge of diodes, one tetrode (an extra grid to screen away capacitive coupling inside the tube), an elaborate dance of design precautions to get to what human eyes saw first of all – the distance along the flight path.[18]

In this cybernetic world picture, the relationship between the earth, machines and human beings becomes less bodily immediate, as the focus of research and strategy increasingly understands the relationship between human and world as a matter of simulation.[19]

To revert back to Heidegger's *The Age of the World Picture*, cybernetic structuring configures strategy as a projection (*Entwurf*); a procedure (*Vorgehen*) understood literally as moving forward (*Vorwärtsgehen*), a setting into the future in the company of an 'other', the enemy and competition. This 'other' is unseen, but is known in the

[15] Peter Galison The ontology of the enemy: Norbert Wiener and the cybernetic vision. *Critical Inquiry*, 1994, 21(1): 228–66, 231. Galison refers to Norbert Wiener's distinction between the Augustian and the Manichean devil; both 'twin devils' indicating the kind of disorder that directly opposes the scientist's quest for order. The former, however, was the passive and stable disorder brought by nature while the 'Manichean devil' indicated the scheming, tricking, crafting and dissimulating foe that came to embody the antagonizing enemy in the battlefield or the competitor in the marketplace.

[16] Peter Galison The ontology of the enemy, 233.

[17] Peter Galison The ontology of the enemy, 263.

[18] Thomas Pynchon *Gravity's Rainbow*. London: Penguin. 1978, 226. There is of course also the scene in Kubrik's film of Major T. J. Kong who having been forced by a malfunctioning plane to release the payload manually, sits astride a missile as it descends to explode over a Soviet ICBM site, thereby triggering the Doomsday machine.

[19] Philip Mirowski *Machine Dreams*, 15.

form of the picture.[20] The picture is mediated through the radar, the radio and above all the screen (the 'big board' in Kubrik's war room) with its straight-line lights emitting calculable possibility as surely as a sun emits rays. As with the Claude glass, though now without a scene upon which to deliberately turn one's back, basing decisions on computational data filtered through visual interfaces is essentially a cinematic experience, grounded in the passive reception of the viewer, to whom the world as picture is presented; a world by which the viewer is entranced:[21]

the cinematic will attract our attention to the passing images, no matter what they are, and we will prefer to see them unfold before our eyes. We become immersed in the time of their flowing forth; we forget all about ourselves watching, perhaps 'losing ourselves' (losing track of time), but however we define it, we will be sufficiently captured, not to say captivated, to stay with it to the very end ... the time of our consciousness will be totally passive within the thrall of those 'moving' images that are linked together by noises, sounds, words, voices.[22]

Under the pull of the visual interface 'the self becomes a viewing self, and the world becomes a world viewed',[23] a transition from the presence of the materially real thing towards the mediation of these things as information hungry representations that configure life as an ever renewing, evolutionary adoption of competitive, tit-for-tat positions.

We can talk of the world picture here because the cinematographic technique played out on the war room board is still an extension of photography; an analogue recording technique of movement that is happening elsewhere, being recorded as such, and represented.[24] The object

---

[20] Bernhard Siegert *Cultural Techniques, Grids, Filters, Doors, and Other Articulations of the Real*. Translated by Geoffrey Winthrop-Young. New York: Fordham University Press 2015,132. Also, Bernhard Siegert *Relais: Geschicke der Literatur als Epoche der Post 1751–1913*. Brinkmann und Bosse: Berlin. 1993.

[21] Alexander Galloway If the cinema is an ontology, 176.

[22] Bernard Stiegler *Technics and Time, 3*, 10. See also Patricia Clough who invokes the Derridean phrase 'the technical substrates of unconscious memory' to bring neurology, biology and nature 'closer to technology' as a system or network of differences or traces. Understood as a 'distributed network of transmissions without beginning or end', Clough elaborates the unconscious as a perpetual writing machine; as telecommunication that makes unconscious memory inextricable from its technological substrates. But this means that different historico-technical productions of technology provide different historicities; that historically specific technologies, such as cinema and television, each produce specific visualizations, gazes and optical metaphors, and that a critique of the gaze inherent in cinema is perhaps only possible when its replacement, television, has provided us with new metaphors of non-subjective images in the first place. This locates the unconscious at least partly outside the body; always incomplete, partial, interlaced with cultural inscriptions; as machinic assemblages that connect 'human bodies, cities, institutions, ideologies and technologies'; trajectories between the real and the virtual. Patricia Ticineo Clough *Autoaffection: Unconscious Thought in the Age of Teletechnology*. University of Minnesota Press: London. 2000, 35ff., 135ff.

[23] Alexander Galloway If the cinema is an ontology, 176.

[24] Bernard Stiegler *Technics and Time, 3*, 11.

of the imagery is a world that is out there being mediated and brought close. With the rise of technogenesis, the world picture is ebbing away. Computers of the kind first imagined by Turing at the very same time as he was bringing them into life, do not mediate between an outside world and a viewing person; unlike photographic media they are not *of* the world but, in Galloway's words, they are 'on a world; rising in separation from some referent; they "remediate the very conditions of being"'.[25] It is a world that resists representation because it simply is representation: there is no will, no material, only representation, which must take place, and in taking place say nothing other than that it has taken place; there is no mediation, only media.[26]

Where the information board in Kubrik's war room still attempts a spatial representation of countries and the positions of bomber squadrons that are established as political and material contraries, the computer-generated visuals of modern warfare have lost their significance. There are just images generated by high-speed processes operating beyond the capacity for human noticing. If we recall our earlier definition of strategy as the struggle to experience a critical (and so, potentialy, authentic) perspective upon events, and hence upon oneself as a being able to close in on its distinction and which thereby relates to the world, the condition of technogenesis makes this perspective-taking and distinction-making increasingly unlikely. In the words of Siegert, the difficulty is:

not a matter of man disappearing, but of having to define, in the wake of the epistemic ruptures brought about by first- and second-order cybernetics, noise and message relative to the unstable position of an observer. Whether something is noise or message depends on whether the observer is located on the same level as the communication system (for instance, as a receiver), or on a higher level, as an observer of the entire system ... exclusion and inclusion, parasite and host, are no more than states of an oscillating system or a cybernetic feedback loop.[27]

The comic feel of Kubrik's film arises from an inkling – certainly embodied in the spasmodic utterances of Dr Strangelove himself – that the observer, the strategist, is only ever at the same level of the machine: 'on' when the machinery is 'on', otherwise dead. Like Martin Creed's art installation *Work 227* in which the lights of a gallery are switched on and off in regular 5 second splits: we are up, lit, awake and excited, or down, dark and comatose; or we are aware and knowing, and then in the dark

[25] Alexander Galloway If the cinema is an ontology, 176.
[26] Alexander Galloway *The Interface Effect*, 99.
[27] Bernhard Siegert *Cultural Techniques*, 32.

again; or we are exposed and then enclosed and hidden, and like the bag-dwelling beings in Samuel Becketts *Act Without Words II* (Chapter 5) 'we' oscillate between these on–off events, events that are connected by nothing more persistent than in one where we experience the loss of what preceded it; media determine our condition, our history, utterly.

By way of an everyday example, Galloway points to a widely reported PowerPoint slide used by the US military to depict the military strategy in Afghanistan, containing some 120 nodes in a widely connected network organized into thematic areas with arrows and icons indicating disconnections, squares, colour coding and differing font sizes whose weight conveys the relative importance or perhaps the duration of different aspects of the operation.[28] It is a diagram as mad as the war itself and if any strategic insight may be derived from the slide it is little more than the claim that things are complex. The question Galloway poses is what lies behind these nodes, entries, arrows and symbols? They are not tethered to referents in any easily discernible way. What appears is information, and the aesthetic codes that information takes, codes that seem to confine diagrams to the same symbolic idiom that has become so dominant and all engrossing that it is inherently meaningless.[29] Dig into it and examine what is being represented and there is nothing other than pixels: at best it is a method of visual conversation being revealed. The Afghanistan strategy slide therefore tells us less about 'insurgents', geopolitical ramifications and 'local support' than it does about an aesthetics of network maps based on arrows and branches, nodes and arteries that have evolved from the flow charts devised by John von Neumann and Otto Neurath's Isotypes, and in the process of this evolution have unmoored themselves even from data (numerical representations of phenomenon) and become a world of pure information, a world Paul Virilio calls a tele-present:

If the revolution of modes of transportation of the last century had witnessed the emergence and progressive popularization of the dynamic automotive vehicle (train, motorcycle, car, airplane), the current electronic revolution is now, in its turn, blueprinting the plan for the innovation of the ultimate vehicle, the static audiovisual vehicle, in other words, the coming of a behavioral inertia of the

---

[28] Alexander Galloway *The Interface Effect*, 82–6. See also www.nytimes.com/2010/04/27/world/27powerpoint.html

[29] Gregory Bateson offers the beautiful notion of the difference that makes the difference. What we see when looking at a chalk board is neither the line of chalk, nor the board, but the difference between both. And it is in this sense that Spencer-Brown's 'Laws of Form' opens its second chapter with the injunction: 'draw a distinction'. That distinctions are drawn indicates that they are not already there, in the world, like the scattered leaves fallen off a tree that carry no information and require raking into piles to gain visual 'form'. Gregory Bateson *Steps to an Ecology of Mind*. New York: Ballantine. 1972. See also George Spencer-Brown *Laws of Form*; Alexander Galloway *The Interface Effect*, 82.

receiver-sender, or the passage from this fabled 'retinal suspension' on which the optical illusion of cinematic projection was based, to the 'bodily suspension' of the 'plugged-in human being.' This becomes the condition of possibility of a sudden mobilization of the illusion of the world, of an entire world, that is tele-present at every moment.[30]

This sudden mobilization of the illusion of the world at once turns the 'over-equipped, healthy (or "valid") individual into the virtual equivalent of the well-equipped invalid;' the optical illusion of the cinematic retinal suspension into the 'bodily suspension' of the plugged-in human being.[31] Urizen is not *in* chains, Urizen *is* chains. And the more real time these images and sensations become, the more they remediate conditions of being, making possible a world – an entire world – that is mobilized as information that is so securely (tele-)present at every moment there is nothing to present to itself anymore.[32]

These new technologies try to make virtual reality more powerful than actual reality, which is the true accident. The day will come when virtual reality becomes more powerful than reality which will be the day of the big accident. Mankind never experienced such an extraordinary accident.[33]

Even the term 'virtual' will cease to make sense, it just is real.

Echoing the pattern of the pharmakon (Chapter 7), for Virilio, every technology has its accompanying accident. The ship has the shipwreck, the idol has the iconoclast, the ambitious have *hubris*. These are accidents that stall and balance what otherwise might become runaway processes. For the cybernetic system, with its self-correcting feedback loops, the accident comes from within itself. The displacement of human imagination by machines who see for us and simulate a reality rather than re-present the world, bears disembodying, de-socializing and disorienting potential.[34] The visual simulation apparatuses involved in the strategizing during modern warfare, for example, takes the already disembodied view of the enemy to its pixelated denouement:

The disintegration of the warrior's personality is at a very advanced stage. Looking up, he sees the digital display (opto-electronic or holographic) of the windscreen collimator; looking down, the radar screen, the onboard computer,

---

[30] Paul Virilio The third interval: A critical transition. In *Re-thinking Technologies*. Edited by Verena Andermatt Conley. Minneapolis: University of Minnesota Press. 1993, 3–12.

[31] Paul Virilio The third interval.

[32] Paul Virilio The third interval.

[33] Paul Virilio *God and Television. An Interview with Paul Virilio. Digital Delirium*. New York: St Martin. 1994, 41–8, 43.

[34] See Kittler's response involving the yet-to-realize potential for further acceleration in: Paul Virilio and Friedrich Kittler The information bomb. A conversation. *Angelaki. Journal of the Theoretical Humanities*, 1999, 4(2): 81–91.

the radio and the video screen, which enables him to follow the terrain with its four or five simultaneous targets; and to monitor his self-navigating Sidewinder missiles fitted with a camera of infra-red guidance system.[35]

The visual interface and diagrammatic imagery turn reality on its head; a domain of images and digital representations subsume the world to be represented: there is just presentation, which is presented without any real need for a decaying referent, indeed which goes so far as to repress any 'robust' contact with the real.[36]

Signal, Noise, Media: Life Being Lived by Other Means

This side-lining then subsuming of the human from the productive processes is an elaboration of Gilbert Simondon's suspicion that any separation of information and source energy leads to the lessening of human presence, a story of depletion first hinted at by the shift from the artisan to the engineer. In computer environments the capacity for human intervention is further lessened by the impenetrability of the codes and electronic signals above which, on the surface, like calm flowering lilies resting on deep, turbid water, come the symbols of the graphic user interface whose role it is to simulate a softening reality generated solely for the user, rather than signifying anything deeper, more imponderable, about objects or object relations.

Were the strategists to contemplate a little they would encounter a condition that was not at all easy to follow. As Turing admitted, the programmers and engineers work experimentally, they are often as surprised as anyone else by what comes to pass once the program or machinery is turned on. As Fazi notes, the execution of a program is always indeterminate as experienced by:

pretty much anybody who has ever switched on a computing device. It is because of incomputability that, to this day, there does not exist a 100 percent bug-free computer program. ... We just do not know until we execute or run the program itself. We just do not know, for instance, if a program will halt until we run that program, and we cannot tell which inputs will lead to an output. This condition can also be said to pertain to the reasons for the contemporary software industry's tendency to neglect its capacity for generalisation in favour of more specific, limited solutions that are viable only within certain contexts and parameters.[37]

---

[35] Paul Virilio *War and Cinema: The Logistics of Perception*. London: Verso. 1989, 84.
[36] Mark Hansen Symbolizing time: Kittler and twenty-first-century media. In *Kittler Now*. Edited by Stephen Sale and Laura Salisbury. Cambridge: Polity. 2018, 210–35, 212.
[37] Beatrice Fazi *Contingent Computation Abstraction, Experience, and Indeterminacy in Computational Aesthetics*. Lanham, MD: Rowman & Littlefield 2020, 122.

Precisely because computer systems mediate in this distancing and often uneasy way, the media are also never neutral, beginning with the attempted exclusion of non-computable elements and reaching into the processes of selection that attempt to equate information with clarity and singularity. Nearly all modern communication devices, from mobile phones to music players, use information on these terms: they employ mathematical functions to maximize the transmission of a signal through a channel.[38] This definition sets information in contrast with distortion, corruption, that is, with noise, and it places the emphasis of information technology on the distinction of noise from signal in the communication between a source (sender) and a receiver through an intervening medium (the channel). Discrete channels, carrying for example information about a drum's output in the form of digital streams of 0s and 1s are prone to noises in the channel and to the occasional error, so that a 0 instead of a 1 will arrive or vice versa.[39] In placing emphasis on the successful and correct transfer of information across channels, communication machines therefore do not define information by meaning, but merely by the mathematical function that indicates the degree of noise and the capacity to separate out this noise from the message.[40]

The benefits of this emphasis on the clean transfer of a message allowed for the rapid expansion of information infrastructures on the basis of mathematical functions that could be formalized, and apparatuses that would eventually lead to the atmospheric world of the internet whose 'flickering signifiers' show digital images generated by hidden layers of code.[41] But the information created through code is brittle. Images, for example, are optimized for storage and processing efficiencies rather than affective power, this kind of visualization 'wears its own artifice on its sleeve' as it requires a translation from the mathematical to the visual – it must invent a set

---

[38] Tiziana Terranova *Network Culture: Politics for the Information Age*. London: Pluto. 2004, 10. Information is based on surprise; on information that is not already anticipated. For this to be possible, a communication system must be recursive in the sense of Gödel's function and the Turing machine. Yuk Hui, *Recursivity and Contingency*, 108.

[39] Paul Nahin *The Logician and the Engineer*, 114.

[40] 'a probability function with no dimensions, no materiality, and no necessary connection with meaning'. N. Katherine Hayles *How we Became Posthuman: Virtual Bodies in Cybernetics, Literature, and Informatics*. Chicago: University of Chicago Press. 1999, 52. See also Tiziana Terranova *Network Culture*, 13.

[41] N. Katherine Hayles *How We Became Posthuman*, 18–20. But while being a language, code is an imperative voice alone; one that converts meaning into action and, in so doing, 'is the first language that actually does what it says', albeit in different forms on different layers. Machine code still reflects the necessities of electric circuits while higher-order programming languages are compiled and require interpretation. Alexander Galloway *Protocol*, 166.

of translation rules that are artificial and allow the conversion of abstract numbers into semiotic signs. What we see, therefore, when looking at computer images created for the user, is less a representation of any raw data and much more a visualization of these conversion rules themselves.[42]

Claus Pias illustratively deconstructs this condition of artifice when first viewing a scanned picture in Microsoft's office program Power-Point, which is itself already a modulation replete with skeuomorphic 'projector' icons and 'slide' shows, and finding it presenting the picture like a slide in a physcial diaprojector (slide-projector).[43] He notes how he has to 'change the program' to engage with the image's properties showing not only the information that the computer holds of the electronic image and which allows for the translation of information into images, but also how, through the simple steps of reducing the colour depth from 24 to 8 Bits then changing the media type, the 'image' first loses almost all its information before turning into sequences of addresses, hexadecimal values and letters.[44] As such, Pias concludes, there are really no such things as digital pictures because for the computer there is always only text.

And this work is never all that clear. ERP systems might be at times super adept at presenting a seamlessly updated view of the world out there, as though looking from a cockpit over a landscape of operations, but at other times they simply break down; translating human user interactions through interfaces into transformations that remain curiously uncertain and opaque:

Each layer promises uncertain affordances to the latter, eventually culminating in the partial affordance offered to the user through a risky encounter with a vicarious transformation which ... is radically unreadiness-to-hand.[45]

---

[42] Galloway. *The Interface Effect*: 83. Galloway argues this means digital images end up looking so alike. The many images that can be found representing the internet, for example, all have an eerie sameness. Alexander Galloway *The Interface Effect*, 84.

[43] Despite their reproducibility, photographs are an analogue technology of 'uniqueness' (due to the physical and chemical processes) and 'stability' (because one cannot 'work' with a photograph), and unlike digital images they are not based on mathematical numbers, 'no computer can calculate with them'. Analogue photographs, therefore, have no information; they are not media of knowledge. See Claus Pias Das digitale Bild gibt es nicht. Über das (Nicht-)Wissen der Bilder und informatische Illusion. *Zeitenblicke*, 2003, 2(1): §65. www.zeitenblicke.historicum.net/2003/01/pias/index.html.

[44] Claus Pias Das digitale Bild gibt es nicht. The picture in question is a scan of Kazimir Malewich's 'Red Square' an intensely jubilant piece of non-objective art from 1915, which also bears the title painterly realism of a peasant women in two dimensions. It was painted in a bout of revolutionary fervour and possibility of the kind that would have repelled, probably, an earth loving denizen of the Black Forest such as Heidegger, though given Malevich went censored and so unseen and unheard for most of his life, Heidegger never encountered such a disorienting expression of *Dasein*.

[45] David Berry *The Philosophy of Software*, 140.

That these media are often unready means, according to David Berry, they are continually in need of stabilization, propped up, for example, by humans labouring behind the surface, meta-tagging, uploading, designing web forms and application programming interfaces.[46]

Typically the mediating role of the digital, its codes for translation into a humanly perceptible virtual image, only becomes apparent when media are manipulated, such as the way Pias did with the TIFF image, or when 'glitches, bugs, application errors, system crashes' occur and so re-insert the noise into the signal.[47] Media, therefore, have their own lives (*Eigenleben*), always a specific origin and a connected rationality, and they continually co-communicate.[48] So whilst modern media, like all media, do not emerge independently of specific historical practices, history, as a system of meaning, is operating across what Bernhard Siegert calls a 'media-technological abyss of nonmeaning that must remain hidden'.[49] The role of strategy, as a cultural technique of generating distinctions between 'this' and 'that', is to do the hiding.[50]

Unlike in the epoch of the world picture, where *Dasein*'s being could still be glimpsed in its uncanny counterturning, for instance in occasional bouts of boredom or anxiety, technogenesis reveals its essence in different terms. For Kittler, all technical media either store things, transmit things or process things, and in their work, the more productive they become, the more they disappear, caught fast in their own self-generated paradox.[51] For Galloway:

Frames, windows, doors, and other thresholds are those transparent devices that achieve more the less they do: for every moment of virtuosic immersion and connectivity, for every moment of volumetric delivery, of in opacity, the threshold becomes one notch more invisible, one notch more inoperable. As technology, the more a dioptric device erases the traces of its own functioning (in actually delivering the thing represented beyond), the more it succeeds in its functional mandate; yet this very achievement undercuts the ultimate goal: the more intuitive a device becomes, the more it risks falling out of media altogether, becoming as naturalized as air or as common as dirt. To succeed, then, is at best

---

[46] David Berry *Critical Theory and the Digital*. London: Bloomsbury. 2014, 63.

[47] Peter Krapp *Noise Channels: Glitch and Error in Digital Culture*. Minneapolis: University of Minnesota Press. 2011, 54.

[48] Claus Pias Das digitale Bild gibt es nicht, 63.

[49] Bernhard Siegert *Cultural Techniques*, 5.

[50] Cornelia Vismann Cultural techniques and sovereignty. *Theory, Culture & Society*, 2013, 30(6): 83–93, 88.

[51] Friedrich Kittler. The Truth of the Technological World, 143.

self-deception and at worst self-annihilation. One must work hard to cast the glow of unwork. Operability engenders inoperability.[52]

Modern media, too, it seems, are caught in the all-too-human inability to be who they are. The human's uncanny conundrum of being *or* finding out about Being – but never both together – is replayed in the appearing/disappearing character of media. Their inoperability, their being a medium that transmits and thereby limits, mediates, distorts and disrupts the connection, is the very basis for their existence. Once the connection is perfect it is no longer a mediated one; the medium, as we have said, ceases to exist. But unlike humans, that revelation of the essence of medial being matters little, in particular to digital universal machines that do not exist as world forming or even poor-in-world beings: they do not struggle to present themselves. Bereft of actual existence in the 'excluded third', and crucially without finitudinal concerns (the question of questionability never arises), these machines operate in their own time (*Eigenzeit*) in which everything is sequenced as one instant following another; in which there is no semantic duration; where there are no histories; they are on or off, and only when switched on and working *as* machines are they what they are.[53] Without the contrasting relief of an 'outside' it is a technological condition whose strangeness and un-naturalness is quickly overcome. From within there is no age or ageing, time stops, overwhelmed by an instant and complete distribution of visions, revenue streams, bullet points, arrows pointing heavenwards and opinion; any sense of a world 'out there' becomes increasingly unimportant, and, eventually disappears.[54] Meantime what remains 'out there', the old world looks on, fixed, ancient, bemused, steadily losing face (Figure 9.3).

Simon's Grand Design

After winning the Association for Computing Machinery's tenth A. M. Turing Award in 1975, Allen Newell and Herbert Simon outlined a version of 'computer science' as an empirical discipline based on an understanding of symbols, and therefore of *qualitative* elements, as the 'root of intelligent action'.[55] Newell and Simon's pioneering work included the

---

[52] Alexander Galloway *The Interface Effect*, 25.

[53] Wolfgang Ernst *Digital Memory and the Archive*. Edited by Jussi Parikka. Minneapolis: University of Minnesota Press. 2013, 57.

[54] Douglas Kellner Virilio War and technology. Some critical reflections. *Theory, Culture & Society*, 1999, 16(5–6): 103–25.

[55] Allen Newell and Herbert A. Simon Computer science as empirical inquiry: Symbols and search. *Communications of the ACM*, 1976, 9(3): 113–26.

Maxime Du Camp   Gide et Baudry Editeurs

GOURNAH

COLOSSE MONOLITHE D'AMENOPHT III.

Figure 9.3 Maxime Du Camp, Colossal monolith of Amenhotep III, Gournah, 1849–1851. The Cleveland Museum of Art, Andrew R. and Martha Holden Jennings Fund 1992.235. www.clevelandart.org/art/1992.235

development of a 'General Problem Solver' (GPS)[56] computer program, an attempt to model the steps a human problem solver works through so it could be simulated by a computer and it is through symbolic manipulation that machines can be thought to think in terms of using highly selective search routines and heuristics. Simon invokes hierarchies consisting of systemic parts which are variously nested ('loosely coupled' or 'decomposable'). This creates boundaries which separate levels and wider contexts. It is here where the invention of computers comes in as it allows for the simulation of specific (modular and concrete) problems in ways that can be automated with symbolic manipulation routines. This represents a step away from the universality of the Turing machine towards having programs that are data, and that can be operated on as data; and then on to the development of list processing that introduced dynamic memory structures.[57] These shifts set the scene for symbol designation and manipulation, moving from simple tasks including puzzles and games towards the computation of searches for design, for with how things ought to be, for 'devising artifacts to attain goals'[58] Simon continues:

> The logic of optimization methods can be sketched as follows: The 'inner environment' of the design problem is represented by a set of given alternatives of action. The alternatives may be given *in extenso*: more commonly they are specified in terms of command variables that have defined domains. The 'outer environment' is represented by a set of parameters, which may be known with certainty or only in terms of a probability distribution. The goals for adaptation of inner to outer environment are defined by a utility function ... The optimization problem is to find an admissible set of values of the command variables, compatible with the constraints, that maximize the utility function for the given values of the environmental parameters.

A simple example of this symbolic problem-solving computation is the 'missionary and cannibal' puzzle where (in its colonially thoughtless fashion), three missionaries and three cannibals have to cross a river on a boat

---

[56] The GPS itself was a development of an earlier program called the Logic Theorist, which was already able to prove the theorems in Whitehead and Russell's *Principia*. It is based on the use of *heuristics*. Unlike algorithms, which offer no guarantee of this kind, heuristics are procedures used to prove theorems or solve problems, even when they cannot be guaranteed to find a solution. Tasks such as chess playing or finding proofs in propositions would take algorithmic procedures extensive amounts of time as it systematically works through all iterations (e.g., proofs). Heuristics, instead, engage in search processes that are less complete, more rules-of-thumb approaches, but therefore take into account the limits of human and machinic information processing capacity. See Pamela McCurduck *Machines who think. A personal inquiry into the history and prospects of artificial intelligence*. Natick, MA: AK Peters. 2004, 123; and Alan Garnham *Artificial Intelligence. An Introduction*. London: Routledge. 1998, 116.

[57] Allen Newell and Herbert A. Simon Computer science as empirical inquiry, 117.

[58] Herbert A. Simon *The Sciences of the Artificial*, 3rd edn. Cambridge, MA: MIT Press. 1996, 114.

carrying only two, while not leaving any missionary outnumbered by cannibals at any stage (God is not offering much protection, it seems). The
resulting symbolic representation is in form of current states (left riverbank
= 3 missionaries, 3 cannibals, 1 boat), and a desired state, where the party,
plus boat occupies the right riverbank. The program then employs operators (sub-programs, such as the moving of people across the river) and rules
that encode constraints. Adding to this are values, such as the maximum
number of passengers in the boat, so that the computer can run its calculations. The human-interpretable concepts (boat, missionary, cannibal, etc.)
are then translated into codes (the 'general' part of GPS) that make the
imperative verbs ('add' one missionary, etc.) machine readable and, in this
way, the symbol-processing program can capture general intelligence.[59]

Extending from such puzzles – and it is worth reminding ourselves that
computer intelligence has often been weaned on these crassly racist scenarios and data - Simon and Newell probe the applicability of symbolic
problem solving to administrative organization where work is divided up
in to sub-functions, areas, processes and so on. For Simon, hierarchical
and modular sub-division was necessary because of the 'very' limited
processing capacity of both humans and computers, compared to the
decision problems that some organizations face.[60] These processes of
sub-diving create externalities between the new interdependent subsystems, and the organizational task consists in factorization: in reducing
these externalities allowing for yet more decentralization. The ensuing
information-processing task is then, first, to reduce the size of organizational problems into manageable proportions and, second, to prioritize
specific decision tasks in order of their criticality or importance. All this
is complicated by 'information richness' and the origin of information
from outside, making it difficult to control its size, shape or form. The
symbolic design scheme therefore operates on a mid-range level by parcelling problems into manageable frames of loosely coupled (decomposable) sub-systems for which satisficing solutions can be computed. This
gives rise to problem-focussed, narrow or 'classic' AI approaches aiming
to represent and construct hierarchical models of human intelligence on
the basis of facts and rules, which are translated into explicit symbolic
expressions for computer processing.

---

[59] For expanded examples and coding see Melanie Mitchell *Artificial Intelligence: A Guide
for Thinking Humans*. New York: Farrar, Straus and Giroux. 2019, 25. Similarly, Simon
presents, inter alia, a 'Himalayan tea ceremony' puzzle. Herbert A. Simon *The Sciences
of the Artificial*, 94.
[60] See Herbert A. Simon Applying information technology to organization design. *Public
Administration Review*, 1973, May/June: 267–80, 270.

The design focus therefore entailed a number of shortcuts that allowed for an efficient way of approaching problems; and this required an understanding that organizations (especially large businesses), and the world as such, were systems, decomposable into subsystems whose interdependence was defined by their functional relationships to each other, rather than any otherwise intrinsic characteristic.[61] Simon's interventions therefore retain a human focus on heuristics Based on what Philippe Lorino calls a 'strong psychological hypotheses about the simple, logical, and representable nature of human action and thought'.

On the one hand, he reduces the complexity of problems to the limits of the human mind, while on the other reducing human intelligence to the capacity for symbolic manipulation. Social life becomes not much more than aggregates of loosely coupled components. The results, as Mirowski notes with some irony, are 'locally impressive to the untutored layperson, without actually having to solve many of the knottiest problems of the nature and operation of generalized intelligence in all its versatile splendor'.[62] Examples of organizational applications of such general problem solving processors came, for example, in operations management where early AI expert systems (which came into much more prominence in the 1970s and 1980s), were used for the automated design of motors, generators and the balancing of assembly lines. Here heuristic search was of particular help as the problems posed were not addressable through mathematical optimization (owing, inter alia, to the complexity of the problem, exemplified by the exponential growth of options); the presence of non-quantifiable components as well as large knowledge bases (also those expressed in natural language), the need for the search for and design of alternative choices, as well as ill-specified goals and constraints.

The analysis of these limits was already the central thesis in the book *Administrative Behavior*, published in 1947 as a development of Simon's dissertation, and in the wake of two world wars that had shown not just the limits of individual rational and moral reasoning and action, but also the smallness of human thinking next to the cataclysmic events that plunged countries from war efforts into depression. For there to be any meaning in human action, that is if rational action is more than 'a pleasant game', decisions have to go beyond individual considerations, finding their anchor in wider institutionalized and organized patterns:

Human rationality, then, gets its higher goals and integrations from the institutional setting in which it operates and by which it is molded. ... The behavior

---

[61] Philippe Lorino *Pragmatism and Organization Studies*. Oxford: Oxford University Press, 2018, 30.
[62] Philip Mirowski *Machine Dreams*, 470.

patterns which we call organizations are fundamental, then, to the achievement of human rationality in any broad sense. The rational individual is, and must be, an organized and institutionalized individual. If the severe limits imposed by human psychology upon deliberation are to be relaxed, the individual must in his decisions be subject to the influence of the organized group in which he participates. His decisions must not only be the product of his own mental processes, but also reflect the broader considerations to which it is the function of the organized group to give effect.[63]

Only in a setting that allows the breaking down of larger organizational and human problems into issues that can be divided into separate, but interdependent sub-problems, can their solution be attempted. Organizations therefore become 'vast decision-making machines, specialized vertically into hierarchies in order to coordinate the successful elaboration of decision premises down to the level where specific action can be taken', however without attaining what Hari Tsoukas calls a 'conjunctive' understanding of connections between discrete organizational elements.[64] To these earlier insights came, with Simon's move to the Carnegie Institute of Technology in 1949, the development of computers and with the development of the GPS and the advancement of computing capacity in general, the possibility of creating a science of dynamic systems, consisting of large conglomerates of interacting machines, translating inputs into outputs. This, however, also engenders a shift from decision making to problem solving; from values to processes marked by simple structures and functional relations, which were more important than any physical or individual properties.[65]

Neural Nets: Learning from the Inside

The symbolic approach to machine learning, like Simon's grand ambitions for an encompassing form of universalized science, was quickly outmoded by studies of learning focussed on the sub-symbolic level. That is, those

---

[63] Herbert A. Simon *Administrative Behavior. A Study of Decision-making Processes in Administrative Organizations*, 4th edn. New York: Free Press. 1945/1997, 111.

[64] Hunter Heyck Defining the computer: Herbert Simon and the bureaucratic mind part 1. *IEEE Annals of the History of Computing*, 2008, April–June: 42–52, 47. Haridimos Tsoukas Don't simplify, complexify: From disjunctive to conjunctive theorizing in organization and management studies. *Journal of Management Studies*, 54(2), 2016. 132–254, 148.

[65] Hunter Heyck Defining the computer, 59. For current versions of this development, see for instance, the claim that: 'The main question thus becomes, "Will it work?" rather than, "Is it valid or true?" Design is based on pragmatism as the underlying epistemological notion.' Georges Romme Organization as design. *Organization Science*, 2003, 14(5): 558–73, 558.

complicated networks that, like neurons in the brain, create messy and seemingly chaotic busyness which, somehow, then, come to create symbols of their own accord (they need no programming).[66] Frank Rosenblatt, a neurobiologist at Cornell, developed a device called the 'perceptron', mimicking the information processing pathways of neurons, combining multiple inputs into a cell with one output. In this mimesis a critical role was played by the notion of 'threshold': while there are many inputs, the firing of a certain output is only triggered when the information crosses a certain limit of weighted inputs. Recognizing a handwritten number or a face from a series of photographs, for example, involves an ongoing weighting of inputs until the informational content is high enough to identify a scribble as a certain number, or a shape as a particular face. The development of a computational detector of a handwritten figure, therefore, requires the quantification of a series of visual inputs (a series of hand-drawn digits), and the determination of the perceptron's weighting and thresholds, so that a correct output can be determined.[67] In contrast with the symbolic AI approaches, which rely on *ex ante* definitions of rules, the careful design of systems, as well as symbols ('missionaries', 'river'), the perceptron begins as a dumb input–output device, which only gains intelligence once the weighting and thresholds are perfected; once, that is, the machine has learned to be intelligent. Rosenblatt developed an algorithm for perceptron learning, beginning with random values, followed by the feeding of information into the system. The perceptron detector would multiply each input by its weight and compare the sum to a threshold. Every time the detector identified a figure correctly, the weights and thresholds did not change, but when a figure is identified incorrectly, those weights and thresholds would be tweaked. Following repetitive steps of such error-induced correcting, the detector would become fine-tuned to the task of recognizing a figure.

Rosenblatt's perceptron worked on single layers of linear input–output relations and it would take years of computer development to turn this into multilevel machine learning approaches that draw on hidden layers to recognize more abstract features (visible layers in face recognition may therefore be appended by hidden layers tracing 'edges', 'corners and contours', 'object parts' and so on, leading to an output, such as female,

---

[66] Owing also to resistance from researchers working on symbolic AI which, apart from Simon and Newell, also included Marvin Minsky and John McCarthy, and therefore the big existing research labs, MIT, Stanford, Carnegie Mellon. Especially Minsky who, with a colleague, rebuilt an early neural net device, the 'perceptron', and published a damning review that appears to have undermined faith in these developments. Moreover, Rosenblatt died early in an accident in 1971, aged only 43. See Melanie Mitchell *Artificial Intelligence*, 31.

[67] Melanie Mitchell *Artificial Intelligence*, 26.

male or child).[68] Humans were not entirely absent in this development. Indeed machine-learning algorithms are still being trained by humans in what is also called supervised learning, using training sets with correct answers and then back-propagating error signals through layers of the network with ongoing adjustments of link weights.[69] However, humans are not necessary to the process, they are supplemental, and are gradually becoming redundant. As far back as 2012, for example, Google developed an unsupervised, self-learning multilayer neural network with over a billion weights.[70] Such automatic machine-learning approaches are successful in completing learning tasks, not merely because they can draw on masses of amounts of data as a basis for learning, but also due to developments in programming technique, such as the programming of hidden layers, and the seemingly irresistible progress in computing power available to train and organize such systems. This has allowed the development of 'deep-learning' or 'artificial neural-network' approaches, drawing on parallel and sequential computations of large numbers of layers, so that complex concepts can be built out of simpler concepts; complex representations expressed in simper representations, so that deep-learning systems defer the mapping each piece of information ('feature') into coherent outputs by adding many more layers containing simple and progressively abstract features, before producing an output. Goodfellow et al., noted how the most recent deep-learning systems go beyond the neuroscientific influences of earlier approaches, which tried imitating the working of the human brain as the stacking of multiple levels of composition in form of visible and hidden layers, are not necessarily reflective of

---

[68] Ian Goodfellow, Yoshua Bengio, and Aaron Courville *Machine Learning*. London: MIT Press. 2016, 6.

[69] Steve F. Anderson *Technologies of Vision*, 81. Anderson points to the use of humans, for instance, through Amazon's 'Mechanical Turk', to go through millions of pictures, adding human qualifications. The *New York Times* offers the opportunity for readers to try out a series of such 'turking' tasks, including 'template tagging', with the instructions to write three words or short phrases that summarize the content of that image. If someone were to see these words or phrases, they should 'understand the subject and context of the image, and any important actions it contains'. (see www.nytimes.com/interactive/2019/11/15/nyregion/amazon-mechanical-turk.html). The images, a bird in flight, a bulldog in a jumper, a dish of soup, are instantly recognizable to human eyes, but the continuing difficulty of training machines to do so points to the complexities involved. See also Cameron Buckner Deep learning: A philosophical introduction. *Philosophy Compass*, 2019, 14(e12625): 1–19.

[70] Its purpose was to view random YouTube clips and learn from these, without being given any outside input. Anderson details the results suggesting that: large-scale neural networks, when left to work without guidance(such as in this case where frames were sampled from ten million clips) will tend to identify human faces and cats as the 'most prominent image phenotypes'. Steve F. Anderson *Technologies of Vision*, 92. Curiously, a cat was also the first living creature that was digitally simulated. See Nikolai Konstantinov *Ankunft einer Katze: Geschichte und Theorie der ersten Computersimulation eines Lebewesens*. Berlin: Ciconia. 2019.

neural functions anymore; and that the early inspiration of neuroscience for machine learning has faded because of how little is actually known about the neurological functions of the brain, offering only limited guidance for the development of complex architectural functions.[71]

Machine Generalities

The question closer to our inquiry is how AI, and in particular the later machine learning and layered neural systems, relate to strategy. The answer is, perhaps, not at all, that is if we are talking about human relations; the latest breed of machines is of a completely different ontological order. Fed with the rules for chess, Google's AlphaZero trained itself in a single day to play chess at a level outstripping every human chess player as well as any chess-playing computer program.[72] Because AlphaZero does not rely on being fed with sets of rules, such as earlier symbolic and expert systems, thereby avoiding the critiques of AI associated with earlier machine-learning systems. These critiques are well outlined by Hubert Dreyfus, first in a series of publications, including a RAND report, in the 1970s.[73] Dreyfus argued that as long as AI is based on making rules explicit, it is bound to fall short of more genuinely human ways of relating to the world. If we recall, for Dreyfus being-in-the-world is primarily a practical, tacit affair and to cope in the world is to do so in relation *with* the world. Rather than working with an internal representation of the world, codified in machinic

---

[71] Ian Goodfellow, Yoshua Bengio and Aaron Courville *Machine Learning*, 14.

[72] But not just chess. In the board game GO, AlphaZero beat an earlier program, AlphaGo Zero, which had beaten an even earlier one, Alpha Go, by 100:0. Alpha Go in turn had beaten Lee Sedol, a human eighteen-time world champion in Go in 2016. Oswald Campesato *Artificial Intelligence, Machine Learning and Deep Learning*. Dulles, VA: Mercury. 2020, 12. Whereas Alpha Go was still trained using thousands of games of expert human players, AlphaZero had *zero* knowledge of the game, apart from its rules. Similarly, AlphaZero begins with *zero* knowledge of chess, and so differs from other chess engines, such as Stockfish, which is an opensource program based on a kind of Darwinian selection, where a suggestion is made and tens of thousands of games are played. While Stockfish amounts to a 'hodgepodge of tweaks and shims made over decades of trial and error', AlphaZero merely consists of a neural network and an algorithm (called Monte Carlo Tree search). As this algorithmic tree can grow very large very quickly, AlphaZero does not explore all branches equally, but uses predictions in the game to select areas on which to focus, so combining exploitation of promising moves with tempered exploration. Crucially, it does not require any knowledge of chess playing beyond the rules, even outperforming those engines (e.g., Alpha Go) which had such additional information. James Somers. How the artificial-intelligence program AlphaZero mastered its games. *The New Yorker*, 28 December 2018. www.newyorker.com/science/elements/how-the-artificial-intelligence-program-alphazero-mastered-its-games.

[73] Hubert Dreyfus *What Computers Can't Do: A Critique of Artificial Reason*. New York: Harper and Row. 1972; Hubert Dreyfus *What Computers Can't Do*. New York: Harper and Row. 1997.

systems akin to the 'present-at-hand' cognizance of equipment such as a hammer that is broken, missing or not suitable for a task, most human engagement – or perhaps more specifically 'skilled' engagement – is 'ready-to-hand', direct and unmediated; it grows out of our already existing familiarity with a world into which we are thrown, and from out of which we project ourselves, directly, into the not-yet of our being. One upshot of this difference between rule following humans and rule-obeying machines is what Dreyfus calls the *frame* problem; for when a computer runs a representation of what it has computed as the current state of the world, and something in the world changes, how can the program determine which facts can remain and which have to change. Some, like Minsky, suggested adding frames (say, we are now in a recession) to provide such contextual information, but this would merely require additional frames to be drawn around frames, so engendering regressive attempts at framing contexts. As human beings are existentially entwined with their world, such self-referentiality is of no concern, as 'our needs, desires, and emotions provide us directly with a sense of the appropriateness of our behavior',[74] but in systems based on 'if–then' logics, this turns into idling (and in Russell's eyes impermissible) states.

Neural programs such as Google's AlphaZero go some way to overcoming this framing problem, at least insofar as they are non-representational; their algorithms do not pause to create a codified picture of the world, but just compute and process – endlessly – and so the projection occurs without the necessity of a central mind or spirit placing itself into a wider context of body and then environment.[75] AlphaZero's learning is machine learning based on a tightly bound interior of having played game upon game against itself.[76] Perhaps it is not crucial, in Dreyfus' Heideggerian sense, that such networks do not have ears, eyes or a stomach – or for that matter needs, desires and emotions. By most criteria, there is little doubt that machine-learning systems are intelligent: both symbolic as well as neural approaches are capable of solving problems and both can adapt. Especially self-learning systems do nothing but, and they circumvent the problems of the bias and limits of the initial input provided by programmers or trainers,

---

[74] Hubert Dreyfus. *What Computers Still Can't Do: A Critique of Artificial Reason.* Cambridge, MA: MIT Press. 1992, 266. Roden equally refers to the difficulties of establishing what is relevant. David Roden *Posthuman Life: Philosophy at the Edge of the Human.* London: Routledge. 2015, 40.

[75] Hubert Dreyfus. Why Heideggerian AI failed and how fixing it would require making it more Heideggerian. *Philosophical Psychology*, 2007, 20(2): 247–68.

[76] Oswald Campesato *Artificial Intelligence, Machine Learning and Deep Learning.* Herndon, VA: Mercury. 2020, 22.

because they start from zero, working things out entirely on their own. But how they populate their neural connections is far from clear.

First, there is a danger that such systems, especially when they draw on big data, merely ingest the biases, prejudices, pathologies and imbalances they already find in their base populations, along with the hankering for curiosity, novelty and gossip that Heidegger locates in '*the They*' (*Das Man*). Moreover, as soon as these forms of machine learning are applied in decision making (for, say, basing credit levels on where people shop, insurance prices on neighbourhood data, police screening on automated face recognition patterns and the like), they can performatively feed these biases back into the populations, so reinforcing and deepening social and cultural divides.[77] This brings us back to the question of frames raised by Dreyfus and how it is that a skilful grasping of any situation seems to require a capacity to reach beyond what is measurable, delineable or sayable according to rule-like patterns. It is this capacity that Heidegger indicates by suggesting that *Dasein* does not just have a world, but is world making.

Second, it is unclear how self-learning systems work, as the sheer complexity and speed, and their eschewal of concepts, stated rules or symbolic representations mean their workings are as alien to a human observer as the beauty of a rainbow is to a car sensor.[78] Even if we assumed machine-learning systems to have a world, we would not share it. As Hansen argued, whatever temporal ordering these machine-learning systems occupy it is not ours, and has no connection to human time consciousness.[79] The interfaces we experience do not afford glimpses into the minds or bellies of these machines; rather they indicate the effort made by systems to cater to human sensory apparatus. We are a long way from Arendt's identification of the human attempt at a general, universal overview heralded in the age of the satellite. The general relations being calculated by machine-learning systems no longer require ideas of earth, universe or being. Neither do objects (*Gegen-stand*) stand enframed in the productive relations of labour, as in Heidegger's and Arendt's critique of technology, both of

---

[77] See Luciana Parisi Media Ontology and transcendental instrumentality. *Theory Culture & Society*, pre-published, 2019. Also Shinseungback Kimyonghun (http://ssbkyh .com/info.html) who exploit the disjunction between human and machine eyes. Equally problematic is the skewed nature widely used datasets, for example, for face recognition training which are shown to contain faces that are 77.5 per cent male and 83.5 per cent white. See Melanie Mitchell *Machine Intelligence*, 100.

[78] Stephen Wolfram *A New Kind of Science*. Champaign, IL: Wolfram Media. 2002, 23ff. shows how from simple instructions (e.g., if left block is black, move eight along and paint two black... etc.), can yield messy, near chaotic totalities. Machines following limited rules can produce disordered patterns, and so are irreducible to the simple rules from which they emerge.

[79] Mark Hansen Symbolizing time.

which, naturally, still bear the soot stains of the industrial age. There are only patterns and correlations, continually switching.

Strategy and the End-of-the-World Picture

This rise of the digital marks the end of Heidegger's world picture. His was a diagnosis of technological enframing that brings the far away closer, through the radio, the aircraft and the television that broadcast the moving pictures of his favourite footballer, Franz Beckenbauer, from across the other side of the globe. It was a gloomy diagnosis predicated on an observed transformation from a world of disclosure of being to a world picture that understood communication simply as the conveying of meaning and co-ordination of action, so an instrumental world, in which, inevitably, the machines were to take on the very limited and limiting communicative task far more effectively.[80] Indeed so much so that not even Heidegger could have predicted it, for distance itself was to become no longer relevant. Distance, it turns out, is a subject-based phenomenon, machines do not 'do' distance in the same way as conscious humans who, because of their struggling with simultaneity, sense distance as closeness and farness. For a digital computer it is just connection speed:

No subject still pictures itself picturing things [*Kein Subjekt stellt sich mehr vor, daß es sich Dinge vorstellt*]; rather, digital circuitry, which we may also call a 'computer,' stores, calculates, and transfers information. *Nota bene*: this does not occur between two subjects—that is, as a further 'extension of man' – but rather takes place from machine to machine.[81]

So whilst the accuracy and speed of their decisions carries a semblance of grace and their totality appears as might a god, the intelligence and consciousness of digital computers is of an operational kind to which humans are not privy. Kittler pushes this argument to the extreme when, in the case of electronic digital computers, denying even the existence of software:

All code operations, despite their metaphoric faculties such as 'call' or 'return', come down to absolutely local string manipulations and that is, I am afraid, to signifiers of voltage differences. Formalization in Hilbert's sense does away with theory itself, insofar as 'the theory is no longer a system of meaningful propositions, but one of sentences as sequences of words, which are in turn sequences

---

[80] Heidegger was neither of the sematic (meaning transmitted) nor pragmatic (action coordinated) school, but of world disclosing (otherness opened). John Durham Peters *Speaking Into the Air*, 40.

[81] Friedrich Kittler *The Truth of the Technological World*, 297.

of letters. We can tell [say] by reference to the form alone which combinations of the words are sentences, which sentences are axioms, and which sentences follow as immediate consequences of others'.[82]

Kittler warns us that we should never understand the 'higher' semantic and symbolic levels of the machine, such as those stories, games and exchanges which we observe or engage with through the computer's graphic interface, as:

empirically different from the 'lower' symbolic interactions of voltages through logic gates. They are complex aggregates yes, but it is foolish to think that writing an 'if-then' control structure in eight lines of assembly code is any more or less machinic than doing it in one line of C, just as the same quadratic equation may swell with any number of multipliers and still remain balanced. The relationship between the two is technical.[83]

Even if we do not go as far as Kittler to deny the distinction between hardware and software, the question remains how the 'if-then ...' of the digital computer pre-structures the ways in which computers operate. How, in other words, does the exclusion of non-computable issues when using digital machines affect the kinds of solutions these machines bring about given it is the computational form of meaning, the syntactic, that has gained an unprecedented ascendency.

The big difference to the relationship that Turing and others of the first-generation computer developers had with their digital machines, and us now, is that the former had intimate contact and knowledge of the machine, engaging in what is now called 'direct programming'[84] but, as Kittler notes:

Those good old days are gone forever. Since then, with keywords such as 'user interface,' 'user-friendliness,' and even 'data protection,' Industry has condemned human beings to remain human beings. The evolutionary potential of 'man' to mutate into a paper machine has been blocked with great cunning. In the first place, Microsoft's data sheets have switched to presenting assembler abbreviations as the outer limit of what users might understand or want of machines ... and that means, no operating code is made public at all anymore. Second, the relevant professional journals 'promise us' – and this is a quote – 'that even under the best circumstances, one would quickly go crazy from programming in machine language'.[85]

This separation of 'human' from the computer via the impenetrable operations of software-come-hardware has prevented access to the electrical currents and signals by which a machine lives. At every stage of a human–computer interaction the user is dependent on mediating software, as

---

[82] Friedrich Kittler *The Truth of the Technological World*, 223.
[83] Alexander Galloway *The Interface Effect*, 60.
[84] Wendy Chun *Programmed Visions*, 19, 50.
[85] Friedrich Kittler *The Truth of the Technological World*, 210.

there is no other way to access data or, indeed, the transformations brought about. David Berry speaks of it as 'double mediation', making the user reliant on the image on a screen, produced *by* the computer *for* the user, coupled with the powerlessness of preventing the introduction of errors and mistakes unless the user has access to the computer code which, all too often is either not the case, leaving the user not unlike the animal in its disinhibition ring: poor in (the digital machine) world.[86]

Design and Idiocy

That we do not recognize this condition is down to design. Design acts as a mollifying shroud under which we can hide from a cold, indifferent world. As Peter Sloterdijk reminds us, we humans cope with our impotency because we have design for company, and with design our growing incompetence at understanding the things upon which we depend is masked behind a smooth, stylish sheen of ergonomically and symbolically rich comfort blanket of colouration, nested option menus, haptic sensors and machine-scripted friendliness, good design 'simulates sovereignty'.[87] To design well is about letting ignorant users feel as though they are in control, that they can still navigate in a world of which they have little awareness, first by making them aware of the complexity and impenetrability of what might be inside, and then suggesting that such complexity should not be mistaken for intelligence or consciousness, thus making the technology disappear, as though it were not there, though undoubtedly it is there, and in an ever more pervasive way, aided by design: 'the most profound technologies are those that disappear. They weave themselves into the fabric of everyday life until they are indistinguishable from it'.[88]

---

[86] David Berry *The Philosophy of Software*, 17. Berry argues that software corresponds to the Heideggerian notion of the uncanny: 'hiding its depths behind glass rectangular squares which yield only to certain prescribed forms of touch-based interfaces. But also because algorithms are always mediated due to their existence as electric impulses and flows within digital circuits'. David Berry *Critical Theory and the Digital*, 95. That such procedures do have influence also relates to Galloway's point that interfaces work because they do not work (Galloway *The Interface Effect*). For the interface to have its medial relevance, that is to mediate between, requires there to be a disturbance in these relations which are alleviated by the medium (a window, door, or computer interface) – but only ever partially. If a relationship becomes perfect, it becomes un-mediated and thus the role and influence of the medium falls away. Alexander Galloway *The Interface Effect*, 25.

[87] Peter Sloterdijk *The Aesthetic Imperative*. Translated by Karen Margolis. London: Polity Press. 2017, 87–9.

[88] Mark Weiser *The Computer for the 21st Century*. 1991. Online: www.ics.uci.edu/~corps/phaseii/Weiser-Computer21stCentury-SciAm.pdf. In this influential essay on ubiquitous computing, Weiser, who was Chief Technology Officer at Xerox PARC and, according to Wikipedia, is considered the 'father of ubiquitous computing', specifically

Such design can be easily recognized in the skeuomorphic symbolism with which computer 'desktops' are re-littered. The icons that populate the everyday engagement with digital machines no longer have any reference to those things they once signified. Computers have no real folders, and the icons for calling, filming or recording no longer require the analogue apparatuses recalled in their imagery. Katherine Hayles argues that these skeuomorphs (Greek, *skeuos* – container, *morphe* – shaping) act as threshold devices, mere gestures, allusions that authenticate the new through invoking safer images of the old which has long since been hollowed out, thus mellowing the potentially radical transformations of our removal from machine through reference to a time when we were more in touch, more familiar.[89] The upshot is what Peter Krapp notices as an increasingly ordered, and non-paradoxical sequencing of activity:

Accommodation to repetitive tasks is a question of timing and motions patterns. Certainly, the definition of computer workspace and human-computer interaction is deeply influenced by desktop logics that normalize the motions of hands and tools, with drawers, folders, files, pens rulers, and so forth all in their predetermined and standardized relation to each other. Two-dimensional document processing anticipates the screen metaphors implemented in their computer; data processing is the application of standardized tools according to industrial norms in prescribed squeezes of motions and calculations.[90]

That we do not acknowledge this squeezing into an increasingly computable condition is, in part, due to design. The computer innards are as tangled and as mute as intestines, and about as interesting. So not only is it silly to try to untangle and understand them, it is also pointless, for there is nothing companionable to be gained. Using this double-pronged argument good design manages users to the point where they have no inclination to get inside the technology: if it breaks, replace don't repair. We are released from the duty of encountering things, notably ourselves. A release from having to open the black box that, argues Sloterdijk, leaves us free to enjoy 'elegantly superficial' relations with machines, enjoining us to sequences of distinctive, diversionary and ephemeral affective stimuli, whilst the machinery carries on with the labour: as Walter Benjamin observes as far back as 1933, cars move for us, weightlessly, and fruit grows as round and as smooth as a balloon.[91] The mysteries and provocations of the unknown 'become trivial in the face of a mechanical

[89] N. Kathrine Hayles *How We Became Posthuman*, 17.
points to the disappearing of things in use emanating from the works of Polanyi (on tacit knowledge) and Heidegger (on equipmentality).
[90] Peter Krapp *Noise Channels*, 104.
[91] Walter Benjamin Experience and poverty. In *Selected Writings Volume 2 1931*–1934. Edited and translated by Michael Jennings, Howard Eiland and Gary Smith. 1933/2005, 735.

environment that we don't understand in the least but that increasingly relieves us of the burden of being expected to understand'.[92] Good design seduces us into superficiality, setting the organizational stage for a technologically induced nonage in which our role is, when prompted, to push an update button, sit back, relax and enjoy the ever faster more responsive flight, to wherever, from wherever, whatever. Design will triumph with the spread of high-capacity internet; desktop, handheld and other devices have long been able to smoothly compile images and videos streams and the next generations of software, hardware and cloud computing will bring audio-visual simulations that can no longer be distinguished from anything 'real'. Already, filters in mobile phone cameras smooth, calibrate and modify images of the self, while voice enhancement software and adjusts notes to their 'right' level. Bots scan and communicate, creating and reacting to algorithms that largely function without human intervention and input, which is all to the good, just so long as we can avoid the depths and complications of prolonged attachment. It is here, on the surface, where style is to be had; the depths are for dorks and losers. Those who do dive in to try to understand and fix the insides of machinery, such as online repair communities, are considered mavericks, activists even. They are folk who refuse to be daunted by the efforts to which designers go to prevent access to technology. They are the last remnants of the Enlightenment project of *Bildung* whose motto – dare to know – sounds increasingly like just so much hard work. It is easier and more stylish to junk and upgrade, to keep up with what is. Once living in a well-designed world there is no need to feel stretched between thrownness and projection, no need for care. We are forgiven our fallen condition and held aloft on an affaltus of constant updates.

It was, argued Benjamin, World War I that initiated this collective loss of zeal: having been assaulted by the machinery of war, the human species had lost the public capacity to be affected and reveal itself emotionally. People were subdued, silent or else deliberately and ironically riotous; either way it constituted what Benjamin believed was an impoverishment of experience. Post–World War I few could hold onto a proverb or good story, there was no room for the mysterious yet homespun advice of Hebel and his almanack, no-one taking it upon themselves to gift others the benefit of their experience. It was no surprise:

For never has experience been contradicted more thoroughly: strategic experience has been contravened by positional warfare; economic experience, by the inflation; physical experience, by hunger; moral experiences, by the ruling powers.[93]

---

[92] Peter Sloterdijk *The Aesthetic Imperative*, 77.
[93] Walter Benjamin Experience and poverty, 732.

Figure 9.4 James Ensor, *Christ's Entry into Brussels*, 1888/1889. John Paul Getty Museum. www.getty.edu/art/collection/objects/811/james-ensor-christ's-entry-into-brussels-in-1889-belgian-1888/

Technology has swamped and dwarfed human experience, and in a bleary and bewildered response they have sought the avowed (and hence dubious) comforts of simulated experience that come to define the modern epoch. An epoch born in the barbarity of a world war that stripped people not simply of their traditions, but of the organic language through which it was possible to belong to a tradition. In place of tradition comes the arbitrary, constructed language of engineering mobilized in the service of labour (and work) whose objective is to transform the world into an array of smooth, efficient objects to which nothing sticks, no memory, no loyalty, no passion. It was, said Benjamin, a world of glass and: 'Glass is, in general, the enemy of secrets. It is also the enemy of possession.'[94] What is made is used and replaced, what is stated is broadcast and analysed and responded to, what is developed is improved upon: it is progression without traces. In such a world people are not wanting new experiences, rather they wish to relinquish themselves from experience, and to make this respectable. This is the job of design. With its ergonomic surfaces, its seamless connections and uplifting skyscrapers, it has prepared the way for humans to outlive culture.[95] Instead of culture comes a scattering of sensory and affective experiences. In the rootless, timeless age of technogenesis these can be come from anywhere, anytime

[94] Walter Benjamin Experience and poverty, 734.
[95] Walter Benjamin Experience and poverty, 735.

and in any mix: in-car yoga, rapid fire prayers for the busy executive, pet cafés, drug-free drugs. The criteria by which they are judged being: the frequency and availability of their apparition; the intensity of feeling they generate; and their willingness to cede their place to what is new and novel. Benjamin likens the condition to the carnivalesque squalor evoked in the paintings of James Ensor (see Figure 9.4). The human *Umwelt* has become a pastiche of affection and attractions: political and religious ideas have become subjects of entertainment, life is a parade led under gaudy banners and forced forward by the unifying blare of a military band, the historical heft of character (ethos) has given way masks and fanfares. There is no commitment here, no community, just mass distraction.

Perhaps this is where strategy has ended up, as little more than distracting design (*fanfares doctrinaires*)? Its job is to anesthetize an organization against the dizzying, endlessly switching emptiness of the *Gestell* by which it is, inevitably, being formed. It is there as an aesthetic distraction from a machine world in which a digitized intelligibility has split from purpose and meaning. In the missives and imagery of its visions it provides a simulation of a future that lays itself open to the present in the form of a promissory note that hides the audience from their insufficiency to bear its weight. The strategists might pause and think on this condition – as in Ensor's picture they might stand slightly aside from the crowd and look upon the swelling mass of activity – and become slightly puzzled: 'What are we no longer noticing?' 'What is being concealed?'[96] But if it happens at all, the hesitation is momentary: they are there to encourage participation, not contemplate; there are no disturbing *daimons* here, no *eudaimonia*, even death participates in the company of clowns; it is the happiness of people blinking and hopping up and down upon their world, without a care.[97]

---

[96] Peter Sloterdijk *The Aesthetic Imperative*, 79.
[97] Friedrich Nietzsche *Thus Spoke Zarathustra*, 9.

Part III

The Open

10   Impoverished by Strategy

Prometheus and the Gift of the Human Arts

The *Gestell* is, in the epoch of technogenesis, of a new, invisible yet totalizing order. The epoch of writing – the alphabets of letters and pictograms – gives way to electronic computing; literacy no longer carries critical power. We are encountering the challenge of what Alexander Kluge calls a second-order alphabetization whose linguistic organization is of such a complete and capturing order that, increasingly, the only way for living beings to subsist is for an equivalent or mirroring second-order transfer of experience.[1] In such an impoverished condition we are beholden to return once more to origins: Plato's account of Protagoras's speech on teaching virtues.

Once upon a time there were only gods; animals and men had not been made. When the destined time arrived to bring them forth into the light, the gods shaped and compounded them within the earth from earth and fire, and charged Prometheus and Epimetheus, Forethought and Afterthought, with the task of distributing to the animals their ... natures and powers. Epimetheus took it upon himself to do this. To some he gave speed, to others strength, or armor, or wings, or hair and hide to shield them, for he intended that no race of things should be extinguished. But he squandered his stock of powers, and when it was time for men to be brought forth, he had nothing to give. Man was left naked and unarmed.

It was Prometheus who saved the situation, stealing from the gods their own prerogatives, fire and the arts, and giving them to men so that they might survive. So man had a share of divine apportionment and became the only animal who acknowledged gods and erected altars because of his kinship to the god – a kinship derived not, surely, from being made in the divine image but, as the text directly states, from human use of divine possessions, fire and the arts.[2]

For Stiegler, this myth points to the open-ness or lack that marbles all human nature. Epimetheus, the god of afterthought and forgetfulness, fails to equip the human with any innate quality – they are not in themselves essential. From their very origin humans are incomplete, and are

---

[1] Alexander Kluge The poetic power of theory. *New German Critique*. 2020, 47(1): 9–24.
[2] Plato. Ion, Hippias, Minor, Laches, Protagoras *The Dialogues of Plato, Vol. 3*. Translated by R. E. Allan. London: Yale University Press. 1998, 97.

then enjoined to tools as a form of compensating apology: whilst they have no essence, tools afford humans a capacity for invention and fabrication, through which they can emulate the qualities bestowed to the animals, and refine them. The tools are gifted by Prometheus, who on hearing of his brother's oversight, and feeling guilty that humans should be put out into the world, without distinction, went to the forge of Hephaestus, the lame blacksmith god, and to steal the secrets of his fire-forged skill. Because fire and the arts are not of human making but of immortals, they are foreign to humans, meaning their essential lack is compensated for by something that can never be their own, it too is somehow lacking, or open. Lo and behold, equipped with technics, humans begin to struggle and quarrel and, in failing to control or properly wield their tools, they descend into disorder (*polemos*), fighting and destroying themselves: 'They are put in charge of their own fate, but nothing tells them what this fate is, because the lack … of origin is also a lack of purpose or end.'[3]

Humans arrive into the world through the double mistake of an immortal: an act of forgetting followed by theft. It is a *de-fault*, a flaw in being, that finds humans exposed and then, in after thought (*epi – metis*) equips them, albeit prematurely, with divine elements. Though they have the fire and arts, they do not possess the political and civic skills essential to their proper use. As mortals how could they? Like the animals they remain bound to qualities by which they are captured, but their particular quality does not belong to their being, it is distant from them, encouraging them to think and act outside themselves, to over-reach the condition that is, as mortals, necessarily, theirs, and so their high ambitions to become what they are not, an ambition encouraged by their tools, will get them so far until, like Icarus, they fall back to earth, unable to escape their lot.

The god befriends humanity, and his gifts run amok, riddling humans with the urge to dig, to stack, to construct, to lose themselves in the 'pointless chatter' of *Das Man*, forgetful of their incomplete nature. They carry on inventing, creating, embodying qualities that are not their own.[4] Placed between the beasts and the gods, humans are always already outside themselves. For Stiegler:

Fire, in the hands of mortals, is a power of divine origin through whose mediation, in sacrifice, the mortals put themselves in the place of the gods. Fire is

---

[3] Bernard Stiegler Technics of decision an interview. *Angelaki: Journal of the Theoretical Humanities*, 2003, 8(2): 151–68, 156.

[4] 'Origin, war, politics with each it is a matter of instruments.' Bernard Stiegler *Technics and Time, 1*, 194.

not, however, the power *of* mortals, it is not their property; it is much more a domestic power that, when escaping the technical mastery of this domesticity [of Hephaestus' hearth, within his *oikos* and at his command], reveals its wild violence, disclosing the powerlessness of mortals, only appearing in their hands, yet again, through disappearing ... [as the power of mortals] is nothing but the effect of an originary doubling-up: Prometheus's fault, origin of the de-fault in being for mortals of the human species, is the doubling-up of a fault: the fault of Epimetheus is compensated for by another fault, which inevitably engenders the de-fault.[5]

And the compensation meant humans were

irremediably bent to the yoke of *ponos*, the labor that must be spent in payment for the lack of origin ... the obligation to work, to handle instruments, will reappear over and over again for these same mortals, until, grown old through care, they at last pass away.[6]

And in all this, it is the tools and tool use that constitutes the obligation to move strategically outside themselves, to find themselves only through striving beyond themselves, encouraged by the gift of tools, but always struggling, because the ramifications of tool use are too bewildering and vast to cope with properly and organize for.[7] Prometheus, it seems, gave humans too much to handle.

For both Heidegger and Arendt, our organized existence, whose exploration and forming is the task of strategy, is only human if it is based on a past of tarrying and dwelling in the presence of others. But, instead, it seems more that we are held captive (*gefangen*) in the midst of a technical environment and the big shift in the wake of computing and the generation of simulated worlds through software and so on is that the world is only experienced (made visible in encounters) through technologically mediated calculations. And calculation, while animating and first setting in gear these processes and apparatuses, has itself become veiled.[8] This is a new poverty;

---

[5] Bernard Stiegler *Technics and Time, 1*, 194.
[6] Bernard Stiegler *Technics and Time, 1*, 192.
[7] An ec-static (out of itself) and temporal transcendence of *Dasein*. Bernard Stiegler *Technics and Time, 1*, 219.
[8] Simondon calls the organization of cybernetic systems 'holistic' and Stiegler speaks of 'adoption': "Human beings adopt the *milieu*, but not only by adapting to it. To adopt is to affirm what accidentally arrived and integrate it into the whole". Adoption differs from *adaption*, for example, von Uexküll's bees to their *Umwelt*, as it involves the integration of parts of the environment into its functioning, for example when a digital platform integrates all data of its users as useful information for other services. Here, the environment becomes an 'associated *milieu*'. Technical systems today render this environment automatic and 'smart', having the capacity to anticipate and expect what is most optimal, thereby defining the individual norm, making new adaptions and adoptions of different *milieus* more and more difficult. Yuk Hui *Recursivity and Contingency*, 204, 215.

a captivation that, unlike the animals', is the result of aesthetic acts: the situation was not there, but made, through the use of tools and the arts. Though dominant, this artifice is not totalising, and by revisiting the Promethean myth, we begin to sense some of the cracks and niches in which alternative ways of doing strategy might propagate. The myth suggests that whilst animals have a naturally occurring place, humans have to create their *Umwelt*, which they do through acting upon the world, and in the memories and expectations that become sedimented as culture and which are woven from a constantly evolving and open interplay of body, brain and tools between which there can be no causal separation; they are aspects of one another, an un-moored ecology. The myth suggests, however, that this wandering is organized through arts and tools: it is, at root, aesthetic, and being so can be re-organized.[9] It is human nature to wander, and to bear the knowledge of being a wanderer. With the onset of technogenesis, however, this inherently strategic quality – the human is condemned to organize its own movement – is assumed by ordering calculation, and in exchange humans are absolved from the organizational task of facing the open. It is how to affectively bring about such a turn that Part III questions. We begin, though, by re-playing how it is that humans relinquished their strategic task.

To recall the Minotaur, the wandering star, it was its human rather than animal side that condemned it to the labyrinth: unable to find a natural place it bellowed in frustration (one cannot be half enraptured), it lived all the while with the uncanny experience of being in *de-fault*, of being cleaved to the ever-present problem of decision (the incision, the difference making distinction made in turning this way then that), and so to the concealments entailed by these moves (the paths not taken and the ones that open out) (Chapter 4). The labyrinth – Daedalus' most lasting invention, worthy of Hephaestus – is the materialization of technologically mediated decision making. It embodies projection as an experience of anticipation constrained by all previous attempts at projection that have, over time, become materialized and sedimented in the objects of an already established culture, in *technics* (symbols, standards, regimens, machinery), held in what Stiegler calls forms of tertiary memory. What is

---

[9] A similar sentiment comes in the Bible:

[57] And it came to pass, that, as they went in the way, a certain man said unto him, Lord, I will follow thee whithersoever thou goest.

[58] And Jesus said unto him, Foxes have holes, and birds of the air have nests; but the Son of man hath not where to lay his head.

[61] And another also said, Lord, I will follow thee; but let me first go bid them farewell, which are at home at my house.

[62] And Jesus said unto him, No man, having put his hand to the plough, and looking back, is fit for the kingdom of God. *King James Bible*, Luke. 9. 57–61.

always already there, even before birth, is a past in which the newly born have never themselves lived, but which is nevertheless *their* past inscribed into their every movement.

Each user of tools is already completely itself simply by being already thrown into a world where the self is an idea of distinction transmitted through technics – a tertiary (as distinct from the genotype and phenotype forms of evolutionary inheritance of information) kind of retention that:

is in the most general sense the prosthesis of consciousness without which there could be no mind, no recall, no memory of a past that one has not personally lived, no culture.[10]

Where nothing is forgotten, what is remembered counts for less; and so hitherto meaningful human events have become virtual; virtual pasts beckoning virtual futures in the sense that any specific '*I*' no longer produces its own pasts and futures, but adopts these from the many technical, retentional memory systems that surround and permeate consciousness (whether electronic or not), and so conveying a past that is homogenized, not brimming with sensation; universal, not one's own; profane, not sacred.[11]

And where every '*I*' is grounded in the adoption of a generalized '*We*', it not only lacks its own past, but also its own future.[12] Nietzsche's desert grows with each broadcast, screening, swipe, click, tab, push or command. This amounts to nothing less than the

...loss of individuation, in which '*I*' persists as a yawning void, no longer moving toward a *We* who, being everything, the confusion of all possible *I*s in an undifferentiated flux (the totalitarian model of 'community'), is condemned to dissolve into a globalized, impersonal *One*.[13]

---

[10] Bernard Stiegler. *Technics and Time, 3*, 39. Stiegler gives the example of numbers that have no representation in the world. Heidegger already asks what for example is the 'three' in the three workers? Pointing to three dots does not help, nor comparing it with three apples or cats, nor will any triumvirate or trilogy, because we can only use three if we already know what 'three' is. Stiegler argues that a number always in some way presupposes a capacity for tertiary retention: fingers, an abacus or systems of writing and counting as only then is the abstract task of counting possible. Bernard Stiegler, *Technics and Time, 3*, 51. Martin Heidegger *Basic Writings*. Edited by D. Farrell Krell. London: Routledge. 1993, 276. See also Martin Heidegger *Introduction to Metaphysics*, 120, 174.

[11] Bernard Stiegler *Technics and Time, 3*, 169. See also Martin Friis Nielsen Consuming memory: Towards a conceptualization of social media platforms as organizational technologies of consumption. PhD dissertation, Copenhagen Business School, Frederiksberg, 2021, 251pp. PhD Series, No. 04.2021.

[12] Stiegler call this the 'age of malaise'; the 'globalization of the comprehension that being-there has of its being'. He continues that 'Heidegger does not see the direction of this evolution; he is blinded by his inattention to retentional processes and his inability to think through the process of adoption.' See Bernard Stiegler *Technics and Time, 3*, 164.

[13] Bernard Stiegler *Technics and Time, 3*, 5.

These technics act as retentional devices – preserving and reproducing memories that are not any individual's, but those of a general '*We*', which now appears more real than any individual sense of self. It is this general yet fictional 'we' that the 'I' secures as the source of its own self – not only because every '*I*' is thrown into a world of others that precedes it, but because that world no longer offers the possibilities of creating a world rooted in some version of authentic being – as opposed to merely a globe that is always already measured and objectified from end to end.

Thrownness, Media and Distinction

The gift of Prometheus is one of decision, and in the circulations of tertiary memory the openness of such a condition is curtailed because it allows the past to be carried unquestioningly into the future. Though it has not been lived, the future is in thrall to the recommendations of the past, it is blocked and cannot be otherwise. Even though the decisional framing of human thought, feeling and deed remains one of projection – being is thrust forwards – its face, like Benjamin's angel, aghast with a ruinous glare at what has gone before [See Fig. 7.2]. The memory of the existence of the generations that preceded me, and without which I would be nothing, is bequeathed on such supports ... this memory of past experiences ... are not lost, contrary to what occurs in a strictly biological species [making] the already-there and its appropriation possible.[14]

Yet Stiegler's talk of 'appropriating' the 'already there' suggests there is still room for forms of self-expression that are more than those experienced in a 'strictly biological species'. Just what these forms are is unclear, but they seem to emerge from what he calls an '*I*'–'we' relational condition in which the collective condition of memory acts as a form of backdrop – this is the form of the 'we' of which Stiegler approves – against which the experiencing self – the '*I*' – acts as a recent heir who takes the 'we' on, through its continual willing power.

Stiegler is struggling to distance the '*We*' from the 'they' of Heidegger's *Das Man*.[15] The 'they' is the collective, repetitive condition of habit and convention to which all humans are comfortably resigned, rather than continue the struggle for individuation and decision.[16] The '*They*' is the inauthentic condition that spreads in the way an accepted sign and pattern of use spreads, to the point where no part of the world is left free from the striations of such agreed instrumentality. It is, to recur

---

[14] Bernard Stiegler *Technics and Time, 1*, 159.

[15] A task complicated further by Stiegler's play between Simondon's 'we' in the process of individuation and Heidegger's 'they'. Bernard Stiegler Technics of decision, an interview.

[16] Bernard Stiegler Technics of decision, an interview, 161.

to Arendt, indubitably a world of labour into which the taste-making fabrications of work eventually collapse, a world of capture without the possibility for rapture. The '*We*', in contrast, is a gathering of each individual's attempt to realize an individuation of self in which the repetition yields difference, as in each thought and action comes the open, the unknowable, the affirming of the indeterminate, as a future is exposed, but never settled. It is a realization of one's place in a world that one can never leave (repetition, being thrown) but in which one cannot remain (projection as sensation merges with memory and imagination). This struggle to ex-ist, to acknowledge one's incompleteness and, rather than compensate for this by falling into the comforting hubbub of the '*They*', to continue to decide and so to be an '*I*' in relation always to a '*we*' (a company of others doing likewise). In emphasizing the fallenness of the '*They*', Stiegler sees Heidegger neglecting another dynamic altogether; the psychic-collective duality that emerges from the opposition of the individual and the group.[17] This '*I*'–'*we*' gives rise to what Stiegler identifies as a broader relational condition between the '*Who*' – the interior being of organs, a body, a bundle of skills and learning, a physiology and cognitive patterns – and '*What*', the wider environmental conditions of activity such as buildings, seasonal weather, soundscapes. Together, the '*I*', '*We*', '*Who*' and '*What*' configure the *Umwelt* of human beings: learning to be heirs of what has gone before, tending to the integrity of the body, accepting conditional necessities, being schooled in habits, absorbing the indeterminacy and chance of an open, unmanageable future.

The proper space of *Dasein* is an unhomely one, its *Umwelt* is never settled. This unhomeliness has, however, changed in nature. Framed by our three epochs, we can apprehend the shift as an organizational one of technological mediation. In the epoch of *tuchē*, the '*I*', '*We*', '*Who*' and '*What*' – all of them aspects of *Dasein* and its *Umwelt* – are in relative harmony, though the '*I*' is subdued. The sense of self is dawning through a balance of relations in which any sense of '*I*' works through a '*We*', somewhat unquestioningly: the addendum or marginalia to received wisdom. The more dominant relation appears as that between the '*Who*' and '*What*'. The biological, bodily '*Who*' enjoined itself to the '*What*' with unspoken aptitude. The unhomely was occasional, muted in the felted wrapping of habit, popping through in the small eddies of wistful irony or melancholy of which Hebel was such an arch exponent.

In the epoch of technology, the '*Who*' becomes more prominent. Emboldened by what Arendt calls an inward turn, confidence seeps

---

[17] Giorgio Agamben The theatre of individuation. *Parrhesia*, 2009, 7: 46–7.

through its newly found sense of self-reliance: the inscrutability of the external world, its refusal to be properly managed, becomes overwhelmed by the world as picture. The '*What*' is being determined through techniques of representation that become increasingly organized and comprehensive. The almanack gives way to administrative procedures, legally sanctioned offices, explicitly stated principles of intervention and control; and the reader becomes more docile, obedient in the face of expert-sanctioned rules, they learn and then apply what is represented in plans, diagrams, linear process charts, maps, organograms and factual layouts. As these techniques of representation becomes ever more machinic, the ensuing gathering of different apparatuses begins to absorb those who, ostensibly, are responsible for its direction.

The strategists are made subject to the subjectifying forces by which the epoch is being organized. No longer exceptional, or accidental, or divine, the strategists' attempts to organize (curtail, skew, direct, block, isolate) the relations of power and of knowledge become predictable. What is positive for subjects, what is deemed good and desirable, becomes both explicit and uncontested. The job of strategy is to direct, contain and excite the behaviour, feeling and thought of human beings in ways considered useful for the more effective and efficient operations of the *Gestell*. The cycles of extracting, distributing, storing and switching find humans increasingly at the behest of a more powerful order of machinery, caught fast in an installation that installs their humanity in nothing more than the issuing of a continual challenge to nature that it reveals yet more of itself by yielding resources fit for processing the biological needs of the '*Who*'.[18]

The culture is itself being configured through a necessary intimacy with the 'who' – work slips into labour, while the '*I*' turns into an undifferentiated 'we'; a 'we' that experiences its own past medially – without this past ever having been 'lived by this or any *We*, nor by anyone currently living, nor by their ancestors'.[19] Humans are made distinct

---

[18] See Giorgio Agamben *What Is an Apparatus? And Other Essays*. Translated by David Kishik and Stefan Pedatella. Stanford: Stanford University Press. 2009, 12.

[19] Bernard Stiegler *Technics and Time, 3*, 93. Stiegler draws on Simondon for whom the individual is not a substance but it emerges out of a process of individuation (*Vereinzelung*, a term used by Schelling in the sense of 'genesis' as well as by Jung, indicating a harmonizing force that unites two incomplete sides of the psyche), not as a coming together of already formed or separate elements, but as a forming of relations in which the emerging individual gains a relative ('metastable') quality, occupying only a phase of the whole being which emerges out of a preindividual state full of potential (which Stiegler, in contrast, sees as the adoption of a common past). Simondon emphasizes the importance of *milieus* for any individual to emerge and persist: to exist means being connected via different orders of magnitude of an individual and of the *milieu* of which this individual

by virtue of their being beings for whom an *Umwelt* can be placed in perspective – they are beings who can find themselves exposed to, and interested in, Being itself, rather than merely the biological processes of living. As *Dasein* they have an interest in the Open and its possibilities. Historically, this interest is sedimented through the activity of work and its fabrication of culture. Rather than just forcing nature to service the biological needs of life, humans also do violence to nature: they create the values of justice, the beauty of art, the refinements of manners, all of which profess an interest in and enjoyment of 'Being' for its own sake, not simply the survival of an individual life. Yet as machinery continually invades this open space, as work becomes the subject of mechanized comparison and hence subjected to the circulations of the *Gestell*, strategy subjectifies the desire for the Open (the 'I' and 'We' fuse), and closes off the open.

Hence, we reach the epoch of technogenesis, the machine-mediated 'I' is made synonymous with the '*What*'. It is a condition of technological mediation whose capillary force has meant that all processes of distinction-making, that is decision making, have been taken up by the repetitive acts of machinery to which there is no difference-making difference. Biological and mechanical life cohere as a succession of impulses, experienced collectively so that even the possibility of a distinction between 'I' and 'We' slides away: tertiary memory becomes a rebooted and updated circulation of earlier stimulus held fast by algorithms: In the epoch of technology it is possible to feel and be conscious of subjectification. The strategic organization of institutional facts, moral principles, discourses, routines and material arrangements designed to coral and direct behaviour, feeling and thought in useful ways relies on what Agamben calls a process of profanation in which an older subjectivity is transformed into a newer one. A kind of *Bildung* is effected: a reformed prisoner; a fully skilled worker; an inspired entrepreneur; a law-abiding citizen. Strategy

is a part. For Simondon, connections happen via information. The highest level of such an information-based relationship an individual can experience is with an object and especially technical objects have a role in facilitating the process of individuation (a transindividual relation in which humanity and technics are indissolubly connected). These transindividual circuits circulate affects and solidarities, forming the relations between individuals (as an 'I') and the social roles and hierarchies that constitute one's place in a society (as a collective 'We'). But in being embedded in technical objects, the process of individuation is modulated in accordance with the changes of the organizational and operational schemes of these objects, and no more so than in the epoch of cybernetics, which expanded the technical domain, endlessly connecting and integrating material, language and human instruments. Pascal Chabot *The Philosophy of Simondon: Between Technology and Individuation*. Trans. Aliza Krefez. London: Blomsbury, 2013, 77, 110. Yuk Hui *Recursivity and Contingency*, 199. Bernard Stiegler *Technics and Time* 1, 22, 86.

allies itself to these exemplars of progress. In an epoch of technogenesis the apparatus no longer produces a subject to which values and identities can be pinned. Rather we find spectral or larval forms: the IP addresses, biometric ID cards, viewing figures, avatars and access codes preponderant in Bratton's stack. Human individuals, as subjects, are nothing more than patterns aligned in a machine ontology whose temporality and spatiality is fundamentally different to their own, and yet in whose operations they remain utterly fixed. In the fluxing of technicity everything is bound to an identity: it is addressed, coded, accessed, restricted, located, housed, decommissioned, updated and replaced. It is a globally orchestrated movement of naming things that challenges them into motion through the agitations of use value: things are only things, forms are only forms, and relations are only relations, if they are apprehended by a purpose to whose realization they become dedicated.

The 'I', such as it is capable of any named distinction, becomes an affective expression of yet more intense and more frequent experiences of sensory stimuli. In some kind of queerly impotent individuating compensation, the 'Who' expands its presence, no longer a bag of organs needing sustenance, but a feeling body whose needs are being met by an aesthetic and sensory apparatus designed to increase the frequency and intensity of surprising and enjoyable feelings of novelty, shock and distinction.[20]

Technologically speaking, the machinery removes the individuating decision from *Dasein*, it removes what Agamben calls the risky space in which *Dasein* endures the struggle of attempting to preserve itself as a being open to Being by refusing to be reduced to a 'this' or a 'that' and by keeping to the limit space, the moat between, on the one side,

---

[20] See Andreas Reckwitz *The Invention of Creativity*. Translated by Stephen Black. London: Polity. 2017, 210–12. The novelty is of a particular quality. It is not a progressive condition of the new replacing and improving upon the old (as in the ideal of engineering innovation), it is not the steady progression of self-transformation (as in the enlightenment ideal of growing maturity, an ethos of improvement). Rather, it is the constant production of new stimulus events, as intense as is possible, with the playful aim not of being better but different. For Reckwitz subjectivity becomes a continual form of self-work, freed from norms, encountering objects – any everyday objects – and alone or in company, in ways that generate novel sensory perceptions and affects. This activity can be demanding, at least in terms of its demanding committed levels of attention, and is often ludic in nature, and promises its own gratification. These subjects are utterly spatial (inter-objective): the space in which sensory and affective stimuli are provided, and through whose atmospheric flows they might create themselves anew. On occasion subjects generate intense levels of fascination and admiration, emboldened as they go along in a gathering wash of self-incurred exposure. They become praiseworthy because they are creatively fixated on generating difference (not improvement) that they and others find intensely stimulating, and simply because they are praised, attention generates its own attention.

semantic constructions (the practical interpretations being made in everyday human practices) and on the other, semiotic signs (unthinking acts of immediate recognition) (Chapter 1). Instead of deciding, and in deciding anew (becoming a world-disclosing being), the mediation of technology takes the distinction-making decision from human hands and places it into the increasingly global systems of unlocking, extracting, storing, distributing and switching – but increasingly just the latter two, by which it systematically configures itself.[21] With the emergence of technogenesis the human *Umwelt* tightens as a space of repetition, without difference. The naturally occurring power of *poiesis* (Chapter 5) (the disclosure inherent in nature itself, beyond *logos*) has been concealed, and the poetic (intuitive) disclosure by which *poiesis* is allied to *Dasein* in *logos* has been temporally and spatially squeezed into *ratio*: humans have 'gone under', they are *animal rationale*.

Stiegler wishes to recover the possibility of an '*I*'–'*We*' relationship, set against the '*Who*'–'*What*', in, it seems, a similar spirit and tone to Arendt's searching for natality and the plurality it entails. Yet there seems to be little prospect for such. At best it comes in meagre moments: to use Heidegger's terms, the being of *Dasein* no longer finds a place in which to be taken into care, it ceases to be care, it ceases because the human has given itself over to the impossibility of history and has, in compensation for this concealing, turned itself towards the unhistorical task of the proper management of biological life.[22] It has given itself up to the organization of life whose essential poverty impoverishes those in whom it is a last stage, an ending from which there are no beginnings. The technical disclosure of being becomes synonymous with the machine-learning to which labour itself has been made subject. In thrall to technological mediation humans have become like the animal, they have given themselves over to bare life, and life has become metabolism; but unlike the animal, their environment is uncannily synthetic. It is not a world into which each '*I*' is born, but a world born inside each '*I*' that is connected, aligned, continually modified outside and beyond that self. The epoch of technogenesis arose at the moment the *oikos* found itself unfolding freed from the disturbance of natality: all birth is already configured, all futures are already sequenced, all life is only life and each source of life is dedicated utterly and thoughtlessly to furthering its continuation.

---

[21] Giorgio Agamben *The Open*, 77.

[22] In *Parmenides*, for example, 'As ek-sisting, the human being sustains Da-sein in that he takes the Da, the clearing of being, into "care." But Da-sein itself occurs essentially as "thrown." It unfolds essentially in the throw of being as a destinal sending'. Martin Heidegger *Parmenides*, §249.

Without the possibility for authenticity, the only strategic task left is
the effective and efficient organization of biological life. In the epoch
of technology this unhistorical task carried a semblance of seriousness;
humans were being pragmatically organized to secure the wellbeing of
their own life. In the epoch of technogenesis this task has been ceded to
machinery, and with this relinquishing of force has come a begrudging
realization that the earth, the life form upon which life dwells, has been
denuded by *animal rationale* to a point where its recalibration will derail
the established structures of knowledge and power to which the human
species has been so dedicated.

For Agamben '[i]t is not easy to say whether the humanity that has
taken upon itself the mandate of the total management of its own animality is still human.'[23] Not easy because with the spread of the *oikos*
the being that is open to the disconcealing of the animal (namely *Dasein*) has been concealed as a bit player scattered amid the bytes. Being
has itself become what marks the human *Umwelt* and so that for which
the human can no longer authentically care. Freed from unhomeliness
humans are being mobilized in patterns of continuous, predictable activity: the self is not at all the residue of an uneasy relation between '*I*',
'*We*', '*Who*' and '*What*', rather, as living beings freed from the unhomely
possibility of there being a distinction between humans and animals, it
becomes an amalgam of addresses, codes, access points, spending power
and biorhythms. It is no longer capable of suspending itself from captivation but also unable to settle into its captivation without feeling restless,
un-at-home and filled with loss. It is a unit placed in a homogenizing collective where separation, rather than being something distinctly human
in *logos*, is something classified in *ratio*: it is managed, exploited, biological life.[24] Like the characters 'A' and 'B' in Beckett's *Act Without Words
II*, the self has become the condition of animality that is now completely
governed (goaded) by technology. The isolation and loneliness that were
experienced as possibilities under the epoch of technology have been dis-
solved as possibilities. The language of 'A' and 'B' has dried up. Their
presence is entirely operational. They move without any shepherding
being, without understanding, they just move, at the behest of the goad
that marks their *Umwelt* as irrevocably as the sun marked that of their
ancestors in the fields. With the iteration of the prod they live out an
already scripted future. It is not a progression into an ever more dismal
future, for that would suggest there is a still plausible space into which a
non-dismal future might be projected. There is no division of the stage:

---

[23] Giorgio Agamben *The Open*, 77.
[24] Tiziana Terranova *Network Culture*, 74.

the future is grounded in the thought-annihilating deductions of 'if ... then' logic in which the '*I*'–'*We*' has been uprooted from the world, stripped of belonging and so made utterly superfluous: 'on' or 'off', 'this' or 'that', either/or, it does not matter: all is '*What*', forever.

... and yet

Krapp's Last Tape

In *Act Without Words II* (Chapter 5) technogenesis is revealed with adamantine nullity: technology is all there is. The scene (the '*What*') is fixed and visible, and the 'action' grinds and whirs without human hinderance. The '*Who*' is stripped of discretion and decision. It is a condition of complete inclusion, not exclusion. 'A' and 'B' cannot exist but for the scene in which they are scripted as what they are: their decisions are voiceless and thoughtless. Tertiary memory has become so dominant and complete that the entire weight of its inventiveness, the historical sum of all human labour and work, has been distilled into the repetitive back-and-forth prodding of a mechanical goad: civilization is nothing but back-and-forth compliance. The situation of 'A' and 'B' lies outside *logos*, it is simply communication as mediation where what is to be stated is already there, endless, period. It is just a prod, and a reaction, time and time again, and the '*Who*' has become a pared back form of metabolic dressing, undressing, feeding, teeth cleaning, sometimes fast, sometimes slow.

It is not, though, the situation in which Beckett found himself, when he performed the Cartesian move and looked inwards. The doubt is there, but there is language (*logos*) too, and whilst A and B reveal what a world without language might become, with language there is possibility. In other dramas, and in his novels, Beckett teases out the possibilities for those still clinging to the company of language. Often the language is restricted to just a few scraps, yet from this meagre sustenance characters are somehow able to resist or refuse the straightened conditions in which they find themselves thrown. As examples of a '*Who*', their bodies are typically in a reduced state: they can be just a talking head, or even just a mouth; and the '*What*' can be equally sparse: a large jar in which one person is to live alongside other 'jar-bound' heads, or a mouth-sized hole through which to deliver a monologue. Likewise the '*We*' is often hazy, a little 'patchy', as if the apparatus of tertiary memory is circulating in spaces out of reach and half forgotten, and the names of the characters are strange, as close to monosyllabic noises as they are proper nouns, and even if the character has a full body, definite name and a space in which to move about, they then wander about, wondering what it is they are supposed to be doing, and carry on regardless, waiting, and in waiting attempt to comport themselves towards one another and to the '*What*' of their situation with an immersive and accepting irony, which is all they can do, for they are on the edge of language. The scenes are set to be spaces in which the comic and the tragic gather, a waiting room occupied by a blend of dry humour and bland fatalism that reminds the characters, albeit very sparingly, of their own complicity with a situation that offers few handles from which to take a hold. Language struggles, but survives somehow in airless cracks rent open by persistence, by boredom, by incompetence, by a strangeness, all of which exist because the archetypes inherited as culture and circulated as tertiary memory no longer seem to have a hold (the '*We*' is vague). The words come loosened from the conventions and narratives of the '*We*', they are unruly.[25] The 'what' too is starkly rendered – a solitary tree perhaps, whose loneliness carries the weight of all situational presence. Beckett is very precise in his stage directions: the emptiness is not at all empty (just as Cage's silence is not at all silent).

Having stripped back the '*We*', the '*Who*' and the '*What*', leaves space for the '*I*'. No more so than in one of his last plays first performed in 1958: *Krapp's Last Tape*. Krapp is sixty-nine years old, a writer, and has been in the habit of making a tape recording to mark 'the awful occasion' of his birthday, which falls on the equinox, a day of equal light and dark, so neither going one way nor the other. The play opens with Krapp arriving on stage and sitting at a table, he looks at the watch held in the pocket of a black waistcoat. He rises, his white shoes scuffing the floor, and peels and eats a banana, galumphing and eating nosily. He peels but then discards another banana. He disappears and returns with a stack of tapes stored in boxes, then a large black notebook, and finally a reel-to-reel tape machine in a white case. Everything is either black or white in equal measure. The sound and silence are also in equal measure, along with movement and stillness, appearance and disappearance: it is a play to be poised in a purgatorial stasis.

Krapp speaks 'Box … thrree … spool … five … ', the words find him, and he searches amongst the tattered tape boxes, until he finds the indicated tape and places it on the recorder.[26] He reads what appear to be

---

[25] Bernard Stiegler *Technics of decision an interview*, 165. Holding onto a sense of '*We*' is akin to acknowledging language as an incompetence, a sense of a flaw or lack to which we are all heir and from which we find the impulse to decide, to attempt meaning, to comprehend, to say things that we suppose, or wager, will carry some significance.

[26] Samuel Beckett *Krapp's last tape*. In *Collected Dramatic Works*. Edited by James Knowlson. London: Faber and Faber. 1996/2006, 216.

notes from his black book – they refer to bowel movements, the equinox. The tape plays. The recorded voice – his earlier self, aged thirty-nine – is not so cracked, indeed almost loquacious in its confident tone. He listens to himself talking of eating bananas (three, trying to resist a fourth, his metabolism is strong), and of a new light installed above his writing desk whose beam is assured, an anchor point allowing him to walk into the surrounding darkness to then return to himself, newly formed. Then he hears himself referring to an earlier time, an archaeology of taped memories is being excavated, going back in time to when tape recorders might not even have existed.[27] He hears himself hearing himself, going back to when he was twenty-seven or so, when he lived with Bianca (a white woman) who had warm incomparable eyes, when he was full of aspirations to spend less time drinking and have a less adventurous sexual life, and then how he caught the gaze of a beautiful woman in white wheeling a black perambulator who had bright eyes like chrysolite. And little later he hears himself recounting a boat trip, a punt, a woman stretched out on the bottom, who, through slitted eyes shielded from the glare, agrees to his proposal, then they separate. Krapp is cradling the tape recorder as he listens to the sound of his thirty-nine-year-old self recalling the motions of the boat, the proximity of the bodies, the undulating flow of shadowed water, underneath everything there is movement, something he observes twice.[28]

He stops the tape, departs from the stage, and brings back a microphone, removes the tape and loads new blank spools, presses record. He starts talking (action and talk are kept separate). The talk is scattered, bitter: 'Just been listening to that stupid bastard I took myself for thirty years ago. Hard to believe I was ever as bad as that. Thank god that's all done with anyway.'[29] He stalls, breaks into reverie, hesitant, records himself observing that he has nothing much to say. The monologue is scattered, splintered and it keeps being pulled back to the woman in the punt. Could have been happy with her, could I, could she? He becomes irate 'all that old misery, once wasn't enough for you?' He stops talking, takes out the tape and inserts the tape from his thirty-nine-year-old self once more, listening to himself talking of the romantic liaison that promised love but which he deliberately thwarted, and of how now, aged thirty-nine, he had no regrets, for he had fire in him, alive with the desire to pursue his dreams and then to burn out and be rid of life. 'Here I end this reel, Box – *[Pause.]* – three – spool – *[Pause.]* – five – *[Pause.]*

---

[27] Wolfgang Ernst *Chronopoetics: The Temporal Being and Operativity of Technological Media.* London: Roman and Littlefield. 2016, 113.

[28] Samuel Beckett Krapp's last tape, 220, 223.

[29] Samuel Beckett Krapp's last tape, 222.

Perhaps my best years are gone. When there was a chance of happiness. But I wouldn't want them back. Not with the fire in me now.'[30] The tape keeps spooling into silence, and Krapp stares before him, at sixty-nine having little left to burn, clinging on, grimly, rubbing up close to the allotted biblical span of his rasping life, one year left, not the best year, probably. He sits there, silent, the stage direction from Beckett gives the sense not of an ending, but a flickering out: 'the tape runs on in silence. Slow fade of stage light and cubby-hole light till only light that of "eye" of tape-recorder'.[31]

The other spools of tape that go unheard, suggest Krapp, at sixty-nine, are the culmination of a series of self-presentations, each emptying itself into the next, year by year (ostensibly a maturing), a record of growing viduity, the denuding of a life's desires, the growing isolation being countered by a heightening of a stubborn desire for life itself. The '*Who*' of the body – the addiction to alcohol and bananas, the shuffling, stammering limbs, the spitting mouth, the creased features: Krapp is a raw expression of *bios*. He barely registers above the biological forces that flow unevenly through his cracked bones. The last tape he records reveals a man bumping into the ebb of his life whose span is mediated in memorized remnants of a spooling voice that could be rewound and fast forwarded, stopped, re-loaded, listened to, interrupted, but probably never will be.

As life, Krapp's is stripped back and hollowed-out by frustration and disappointment (only seventeen copies of his book sold, and eleven of those to lending libraries beyond the seas), the darkness surrounds him. Yet even in this the most mean and thinnest of soils, the events still bear the weight of his being a being; Krapp lives on, and on so very little.[32] And being so stripped back – recalling Arendt's refugee figure with which we opened the book – there are glimpses of an '*I*' unavailable to those caught in the electrical flywheels and updates of technogenesis. And it is an '*I*' held in place by the fragile mechanisms of a tape: the inner self exteriorized into organized inorganic matter. His annual ritual of self-incurred review finds an '*I*' being played out against earlier, stored versions that (albeit barely) configure a

---

[30] Samuel Beckett Krapp's last tape, 223.

[31] Quoted in François-Nicolas Vozel 'Sound as a bell': Samuel Beckett's musical destruction of Aristotelian tragic drama. *Journal of Modern Literature*, 2017, 40(4): 20–37.

[32] Beckett argued that as a writer Joyce had gone further than any other in the struggle to know the material of language in which he wrote (as someone who crafts with words), always playing with possibilities, altering and amending. It was on seeing his dying and exhausted mother after a long absence that Beckett had an epiphany: rather than emulate Joyce, he found his own style: 'I realised that my own way was in impoverishment, in lack of knowledge and in taking away, in subtracting rather than in adding.' See James Knowlson *Damned to Fame: The Life of Samuel Beckett*. London: Bloomsbury. 1996, 352.

rough collective backdrop – a '*We*' – allowing Krapp to realize a form of authentic self-awareness, even if it amounts to little more than a feeling of profound dissatisfaction when recalling his earlier ambitions for enhancing, and managing, his life. Krapp is caught, no matter how sparingly, in an '*I*'–'we' exchange, the former the heir to the later, ageing through a process of questioning that can be found in all those who attempt to continue to speak through *logos*, outside the thoughtless, media-governed, idle chatter to which he, in the company of his tape recorder, is no longer party.

Krapp is exemplifying a most basic and almost broken form of self-presentation in the company of words that explain nothing, but with which he thinks, feels and acts (rather than labours, or works). His solitary recording and listening is a bemused and frustrated refusal to forget the forgetting of self and the words join in this refusal, themselves refusing to be consigned to a proper, sensible, grammatical order that would make them useful, but also invisible.[33] It is, in its bleakest guise, a form of authenticity, in which the tape player mediates an '*I*'–'*We*' exchange that cannot be easily reduced into the 'what' so typical to technogenesis. With the scraps of language Krapp scrapes away at the accretions that have inevitably gathered around him during the year (itself such a stabilizing measure, each year, each birth date), questioning the transformations that, in his earlier recordings, he had reported being satisfied with, laughing at his youthful enthusiasm, disdainful of the dubious accomplishment.

Arendt equated authenticity to a fractured state of solitude that was set publicly:

In solitude, in other words, I am 'by myself,' together with myself, and therefore two-in-one, whereas in loneliness I am actually one, deserted by all others. All thinking, strictly speaking, is done in solitude and is a dialogue between me and myself; but this dialogue of the two-in-one does not lose contact with the world of my fellow-men because they are represented in the self with whom I lead the dialogue of thought. The problem of solitude is that this two-in-one needs the others in order to become one again: one unchangeable individual whose identity can never be mistaken for that of any other.[34]

Riven with lone doubts and hesitations, Krapp and his tape recorder form the rudiments of a seeing and naming, two-in-one dialogue made possible in fragmented moments of self-encounter that refuse to release their hold, and in which Krapp is compelled to continue with his recordings. There are no 'others' present, hence Krapp remains a two-in-one,

---

[33] Bernard Stiegler Technics of decision an interview, 151–68, 166.
[34] Hannah Arendt *Origins of Totalitarianism*, 476.

reliant on his own self constituted '*We*', which, as Arendt observes, is necessary but insufficient for him to become a distinct individual.

Beckett had dedicated himself to investigating such conditions of being. Indeed bits of Krapp could be bits of Beckett, whose epiphany as a writer came whilst standing at the end of a wind-stripped pier at Greystones near Dublin.[35] Amid a dark squall the idea hit Beckett as directly as the sea spray salting his face: his calling was to write of the dissolute and dispossessed, the bypassed and cast-off, of bodies without a full complement of organs or limbs, of minds without a full range of faculties, of people without companionship, of companions without comradeship, of travellers without a destination. It was a revelation that Beckett puts into the reverie of the thirty-nine-year-old Krapp, to which the sixty-nine year old listens with spluttering fascination, breaking the recording, fast forwarding the tape a little, as though trying to ignore it, so that the recall is splintered:

Spiritually, a year of profound gloom and indigence until that memorable night in March, at the end of the jetty, in the howling wind, never to be forgotten, when suddenly I saw the whole thing. The vision at last. This I fancy is what I have chiefly to record this evening, against the day when my work will be done, and perhaps no place left in my memory, warm or cold, for the miracle that ... [*hesitates*] ... for the fire that set it alight.[36]

The way forward was to go into impoverishment, and rather than look for knowledge of what is out there to acknowledge what lay within. It was a form of subtracting, taking away, and revealing what was always already there: the loss, the emptiness, indeed the slightly ridiculous nature of our being. At the end of a jetty, in the company of an agitated and unknowable sea, Beckett snapped himself shut by attempting to see into his own world. His compatriot James Joyce had split the word, like the splitting of the atom, releasing the ungovernable force of language as grammatically charged particles. Beckett would go the opposite way, he would give word to the split, writing of discontent and discomfort in a language that was always attempting to maintain a distinction from the context of its expression, a distinction that invites self-awareness.[37]

---

[35] The location, and even whether there was a storm, are disputed. Perhaps the epiphany happened at East Pier of Dún Laoghaire, where there is an anemometer in place. The story becomes as enigmatic as J. M. W. Turner's similarly stormy epiphany realized when having had himself tied to the mast of a steamer in the middle of a frenzied sea.

[36] Samuel Beckett Krapp's last tape, 220. Also see Samuel Beckett *The Theatrical Notebooks of Samuel Beckett, Vol. 3*. London: Faber and Faber. Quoted in Dirk Van Hulle 'ACCURSED CREATOR': Beckett, Romanticism, and 'the Modern Prometheus'. *Samuel Beckett Today/Aujourd'hui*, 2007, 18: 20.

[37] See Paul Strathern *Understanding Samuel Beckett*. Film. 2005. www.youtube.com/watch?v=HsiNdZ_Ejv4

Krapp's Last Tape is a distillation of this undertaking. Krapp holds himself together, under the light of his desk and along spools of tape, and in this assemblage maintains his distinction from the surrounding blackness. The broken monologue reverberates with a sporadic gathering of '*I*'–'*We*'–'*Who*'–'*What*', each folded into the other, fragments into fragments. Krapp has no full character, no *ethos*. He is more like a succession of individual '*I*'s held in play by an order of things (the '*What*' of tape machine, notebook, desk, light etc. etc., the idle chatter of the '*They*') each only roughly connected by mechanically organized *anamnesis* into a '*We*', which itself struggles to connect itself into anything like a narrative, being continually punctured as it is by the biological actions of an eating and drinking '*Who*'. In *Texts for Nothing* Beckett considers the impossibility of divesting or shedding oneself of these mediations, reflecting that 'if I went back to where all went out and on from there, no, that would lead nowhere, never led anywhere'. The struggle to get into the story to get out of it and kill the '*Me*' is a futile one: the bits and scraps of knowledge are always flickering, yet the '*Me*' is never '*Me*', it is always itself bits and scraps, and it is from these the best has to be made, an attempt has to be made: 'We spend our life, it's ours, trying to bring together in the same instant a ray of sunshine and a free bench.'[38]

Tragedy

At sixty-nine Krapp cuts a tragic figure. He is rags and remains, but he remains a being for, and to whom things happen. The classical understanding of tragedy is, for Aristotle, all about action, about plot: it begins with a mistake, which twists events in ways that find the protagonists becoming dimly aware of an impending doom, but which, at its fateful denouement, nevertheless offers a glimpse of catharsis. It is a concern with plotted action, not character: if, for example, Clytemnestra were cast by Aeschylus as having vengeful *ethos*, her killing Agamemnon would become the causal upshot of her own being, there would be no mistake, or twisting, or sense of the invisible forces of fate gathering as a state of *agon*. There would be nothing tragic about the narrated events. By jettisoning narrative and plot Beckett refuses the standard frames of tragedy, yet preserves the *agon* and the experience of self-awareness through a stripping bare of *logos*.[39] Krapp's monologues veer towards the speechlessness of a private language (at one point he even consults a dictionary to remind himself of

---

[38] Samuel Beckett *Text 3 in Texts for Nothing and Other Shorter Prose: 1950–1976*. London: Faber and Faber. 2010, 71, 75.

[39] François-Nicolas Vozel 'Sound as a bell'.

the meaning of a word used by his thirty-nine-year-old self, to check what he said was right). Words have lost their power to sheath things in meaning, they resist, they almost have to be pushed out of the mouth, their easy intimacy with understanding has become a conscious struggle, just as Krapp struggles for intimacy with his former selves. He tries to resuscitate the connection with repetition, spooling and re-spooling the tape. Meaning appears briefly and bleakly when he listens, indeed he laughs now and then with the relief of comprehension, but these are in short, caustic bursts which appear like involuntary spasms, whether to confirm or deny what he hears, or both. Nothing comes smoothly. The laugh, like the shuffling, the grunts as he lugs the machinery back and forth over the stage, the thud of dropped tapes, the sighs: it is as if Krapp's body is also talking, his words giving way to raw sound and the silences that lie between these sounds. His name, even, is a scatological, bodily movement, a monosyllable, easily confused with a guttural noise, it is seen as more than a name. Krapp is closing in on nothing, a nihilistic condition that has followed his earlier, more overtly Promethean phase, the fire he felt in his belly, aged thirty-nine, the fire of his best years. Yet the fire is still there, held in the tapes, recalled in the '*We*' to which the '*I*', aged sixty-nine, grows distant, an age at which he abuts the end of his biblically allotted mortal span. His last tape is being made, and then death, and though meagre it is against his own realization of mortality that the gods take their shape (and not vice versa): 'it is death that defines the divide between those who are divine and those who only partake of the divine, a divide that relates and separates them at one and the same time'.[40] Krapp has death, and he has words, and he addresses the former with latter with both discipline and levity. His is a poverty in which being still resides.

What is revealed by Krapp, his form of *anamnesis*, is not what he amounts to, nor even what he has failed to live up to, but a splintered realization of an intensely realized sequence of intensity, farse, cunning, sadness and indifference. The process of listening to his earlier accounts of yet earlier memories finds him dimly aware of the revelation that, whereas for the Romantics, the unchained urgency of free, individual expression would give free reign to profound understanding, for Beckett the liberation from convention and habit revealed a far murkier condition.[41] Untamed, the human self was far from a noble and savage force, more a shivering whelp, its face caved-in with anxiety and despair. Yet

[40] Bernard Stiegler *Technics and Time, 1*, 195, (322a) And what this partaking consists of is language, even if it is as hesitant and spare as Krapp's.
[41] Dirk Van Hulle 'ACCURSED CREATOR'.

it still saw, and in a voice that demands to be heard as it is, and not as one that is already organized as an effect of a directing, subjective will shrived to a greater external, metaphysical force from which it might then receive affirmative redemption. Krapp is absorbing the lesson laid down by Nietzsche in *Dawn* (Chapter 3): mortal souls should relinquish talk of immortality to prepare themselves for a new epoch of experimentation, an epoch in which knowledge becomes the subject of passion rather than technical control. 'And you earth inhabitants with your mini-notions of a few thousand mini-minutes of time want to be an eternal nuisance to eternal, universal existence! Is there anything more impertinent!'[42] Krapp is not impertinent. Granted, he has yet to experience the full passion of knowledge, but he is thinking modestly of his materiality and his death without being immobilized by fear.

As an exposition of bare life *Krapp's Last Tape* is a dramatic investigation of the possibilities for authenticity that shares with Arendt a troubled relationship to Descartes' *cogito*. Arendt's diagnosis in *The Human Condition* is telling: the attraction of Descartes and why his thinking was profoundly problematic, was his offer of a severing subject capable of knowing itself (albeit only as a source of doubt). Yet because this 'knowing subject' came to distrust everything else, and sought to question whether anything could really be known about the world, about Being, it gave rise to a compensating confidence in the conditions for which it, as a knowing subject, could be responsible, namely its own productions. It was not the world, but the world made by humans, a world where the fabrications of work, but increasingly the production of labour, constituted both the state of what was known, and governed the modes of inquiry into what remained open to question. The human connection to the world, and so to Being, was lost; the human *Umwelt* turned inward, and mistook its technologically mediated growth, and the increasing species familiarity and acceptance of this growth, for an understanding of the world 'out there'.

Beckett's severing turn inwards, occurring contemporaneously with Arendt's critique, offers a more caustic and less confident exposition of a world made fast by little more than a pervasive feeling of doubt. To recall Paul Valery, Beckett maintains the severance initiated by acts of seeing, but refuses the comforts of naming. Krapp is a singular embodiment of a being who, in looking inward, punctures the presumptions and comforts of human habit, and finds himself in a bleak landscape for a living space. His clearing is lit by a single, bare bulb, his tools include a tape machine, dictionary, notebook, alcohol, a desk, bananas ..., his *logos* a ragbag of words stranded along the shorelines

---

[42] Friedrich Nietzsche *Dawn*, §501.

of speech like a dead tangle of discarded objects left by long-forgotten tides. In this parsed and pared-back state he reveals the devastation that is otherwise concealed by the overwhelming and occluding spread of the *Gestell*. He reveals what it is to be looking upon his complicity with a machinery of instrumental relations. His thrown condition equates more to an experience of having been thrown away with only a collection of annual recordings for company. Yet an '*I*'-'*We*' exchange emerges, much as the narrator at the end of Beckett's earlier novel, *The Unnamable*, also discovers:

> I know that well, I can feel it, they're going to abandon me. it will be the silence, for a moment, a good few moments, or it will be mine, the lasting one, that didn't last, that still lasts. It will be I, you must go on, I can't go on, you must go on. I'll go on, you must say words, as long as there are any, until they find me. until they say me.[43]

And the words, as much as they script what is '*Me*', also relinquish their hold, as the '*I*' takes them on somewhere unnamed, but still seen.

In his struggle towards authenticity Krapp appears to touch on the condition of natality upon which Arendt also leans, and which she resurrects from Nietzsche's *Dawn*. The wide-eyed brio with which Arendt's writes of natality is somewhat dimmed in Krapp's struggling reminisces. Beckett has him continually in the close company of blank nothing, yet he is carrying on, starting anew each year, issuing negatives against his earlier self, leaving himself, and so reaching out into the open.

---

[43] Samuel Beckett *The Unnamable in Trilogy*. London: Calder. 1959/1994, 418.

11   Reaching for the Open
Strategy Unbound

Krapp is content to look on the scene of his mortal life without hurrying for the compensations of instrumental knoweldge and belief. Through the tertiary memory of tape machine, dictionary, ledger and birthdays he is able to enlist the most meagre of modifying criteria by which the character of events can be assessed. There can be no inside without there first being an outside.[1] He has an interest in what contributes to life itself (*Worumwillen, 'for the sake of which'*[2]). Though not fantastical, but quite human, he has about him the feel of a character from the *Commedia dell'Arte*, a jester of sorts, ungoverned, unsettling. He survives on what he has, and copes, and through his recordings he conjures up his own *daimon*: a scurrilous and disturbing voice that refuses to let the '*I*' settle into the '*We*', that rejects its earlier iterations by denying them the certainty and confidence they may have felt, and yet also remaining utterly suspicious of the comforts offered by the categories and routines to be found in the 'who' or the 'what'.

Via Krapp, Beckett offers a more robust, because more modest, form of release from technology than Heidegger was able to. Heidegger envisaged the potential of comportment (of *Gelassenheit*) as a way of dealing with technology without becoming immersed in its sway. In *Gelassenheit* came a readiness to let go at any point and so to persevere with a self somehow, with effort, a thinking that denied the enframing forces 'the right to dominate us, and so to warp, confuse, and lay waste our nature'.[3] But as Heidegger himself argued in his less relational modes of thinking, simply stating that we can endure technology without being imperilled by it is not at all sufficient to extricate us.[4] Technology, read

---

[1] Bernard Stiegler Technics of decision an interview.
[2] Martin Heidegger *Being and Time*, 120.
[3] Martin Heidegger *Discourse on Thinking: A Translation of Gelassenheit*. Translated by John M. Anderson and Hans Freund. New York: Harper and Row. 1966, 54.
[4] In *Negative Dialectics* Theodor Adorno criticizes Heidegger's realism for being too trenchant, too definitive, too enamoured of a world out there that simply is, that is giving

as enframing, is a destinal force that cannot be assuaged by comportment, it cannot be denied the right of its dominating sway. His call for comportment is disingenuous, Heidegger knows that technological captivation is without escape:

Yet it is not that the world is becoming entirely technical which is really uncanny. Far more uncanny is our being unprepared for this transformation, our inability to confront meditatively what is really dawning in this age. No single man, no group of men, no commission of prominent statesmen, scientists, and technicians, no conference of leaders of commerce and industry, can brake or direct the progress of history in the atomic age. No merely human organization is capable of gaining dominion over it.[5]

Except, that is, Krapp. Krapp seems to have extricated himself from the chattering habit of *Das Man*, he has drifted away from convention by refusing (issuing negatives) to abide by their instrumental demand. And he does it through developing an intimacy with a minimal technological order dedicated to the singular purpose of mortal self-awareness. His intimacy is so sustained that he bumps into its limits, and in his frustration he finds himself being left to himself, beyond the machinery, where he experiences a residue, something the tape has not captured, but which, because it is not recorded, or laid out in a calendar, he himself cannot really know, only glimpse. Krapp's use of technology is not *gelassen*; there is no comportment or aim to avoid confusion or domination, but rather a subversive, negating interplay of tapes against calendars against tapes and against the settling of a self that this machinery of tape and calendar are assigned to settle. In setting the play Beckett obliterates not just the idea that a character can be settled upon, but also a notion of culture that hankers for meaning and purity of form. Understanding the play means understanding its incomprehensibility.[6] It is an austere and thereby brilliant reversal of the Wagnerian *Gesamtkunstwerk* of which Nietzsche became so suspicious. Nietzsche resented the Apollonian–Dionysian totality of Wagner's operative monsters, the way they absorbed and corralled the negative through promulgating an apparent necessity of tragic oppositions: life and death; love and hate; beauty and horror. Beckett's negative is far more profound because the tragedy is so close to the comic

---

forth of itself (*physis*) in ways that can be known by *Dasein*, who being there is equally real as being by which Being is brought forth. Heidegger aims to ground his thinking upon an encounter, his encounter from the tall pines of the Black Forest, with the ground, the soil of things. Though in an inverted way, he too suffers from non-identity, he too wishes for a release into a state of immediate awareness.

[5] Martin Heidegger *Discourse on Thinking*, 52.

[6] C.f. Theodor Adorno *Trying to Understand Endgame*. Translated by Michael T. Jones. *New German Critique*, 1982, 26(Spring–Summer): 119–50.

(think Siegfried with a banana): rather than being corralled in noble pairings, the negative is palpable in being seen, but not named. It fills the stage without ever being made present, it is an atmosphere of limits – the limits of language, of machinery, of self, being transgressed: it is, in its most stripped back, elemental form, a space of possibility, of appearance.

It is with the negative that we wish to pursue our enquiry into strategy, because it is through acts of refusal that an organization might lean into authenticity, not compliance. In the *Claim of Reason* Stanley Cavell suggested what made us most human, indeed that which distinguishes the human, was 'the power of the motive to reject the human', by which he means seeing and eschewing the names by which the human becomes known to itself in habituated practices.[7] It was this power of refusal or avoidance that Beckett's mentor James Joyce accentuated as that which best portrays the artist, a figure branded *non serviam*, one who issues sequences of 'I will nots'.[8] The negative is a resistance to the repeated attempts of the economic and social order to organize human experience though naming. For Hélène Cixous writers like Beckett and Joyce find in language a whirl of atmospheric impressions, half-remembered thoughts and spoken sounds that refuse the urge to transform experience into understanding, and, then refuse to limit understanding to what is said and then codified.[9] To recall the opening of the book and Paul Valéry's observations on naming and seeing: the naming by which life is organized into patterns of commitment and entitlement is made subject to seeing, and then disturbed by having it doused in a language of immediate speculation and physicality, a language of sighs and signs that can be acknowledged but not settled upon through interpretation. The necessary coincidence between consciousness and language cannot be negotiated, but making this coincidence apparent provides the open space from which to stalk and shake it until meaning falls to the ground, leaving knotted tangles of bare but budding branches, some of which might, with luck, bloom.[10]

And it is this association of language, natality and 'nay saying' that topographically forms what Giorgio Agamben calls the open. He too thinks of fecund, artistic beings fragmenting institutions and picking their way through the ensuing fragments, a world of distinct singularities,

---

[7] Stanley Cavell *The Claim of Reason: Wittgenstein, Skepticism, Morality, Tragedy*. Oxford: Oxford University Press. 1999, 207.

[8] See Hélène Cixous *Readings: The Poetics of Blanchot, Joyce, Kafka, Kleist, Lispector, and Tsvetayeva*. Translated by Verena Conley. Minneapolis: University of Minnesota. 1991, 8–10.

[9] Hélène Cixous *Readings*, 70.

[10] Giorgio Agamben *Infancy and History*, 55–6.

the Columbinas, Harlequins and Pulcinellas of the *Commedia dell'Arte*. These are tragi-comedic figures whose dexterous resistance to convention evokes the pug-nosed satyr Socrates (rather than the reasoning, tidy Socrates), or the banana eating Krapp. It is in these figures that we experience being human in the *stasis* or struggle of occupying the place in which mind and body, animal and spirit, metabolism and *logos*, naming and seeing are placed together. They are characters in whose migratory company we might ask:

What is man [sic], if he is always the place – and, at the same time, the result – of ceaseless divisions and caesurae? It is more urgent to work on these divisions, to ask in what way – within man – has man been separated from non-man, and the animal from the human, than it is to take positions on the great issues, on so-called human rights and values.[11]

To associate strategy with the open is to understand the task of separation and distinction as an aesthetic act of creating something that previously did not exist, an organization of one's own distinction without assuming what is being excluded is in any way naturally occurring. The tragi-comedic figures exist as expressions of how to live in the border regions of *logos*, a troupe moving from home to home, singing, not quite human, perhaps with a soul, as strong and cunning as animals, inscrutable, joyous, yet also possessing a beguiling grammar of gesture and word that, being in proximity to the animal, lets things be without naming them, indeed refusing to name them, just seeing.

In a study of strategy and technology Krapp is especially resonant as such a figure. Being Beckett's and not Joyce's, Krapp's potency is also an inadequacy. He sees whilst barely naming, he uses words fully aware of their deficit, of what escapes them, and he is obsessively, aesthetically attentive to the form that his own self takes – as a thing – outside the words he and his technical assembly of tertiary memory are using to capture and name himself. The work he is putting into experiencing himself is made visible, the basic struggle of sensing and also seeing becomes apparent in its tragi-comic effort, and it is towards the repetition of this struggle that he is devoting himself each birthday. It is a raw state of authenticity in which he is living alongside what is both proper and improper and attempting to resist the almost inevitable mediating tendency of language to delineate things as objects, with method and morality stepping in to police the edges. Krapp is operating beyond the method and morality by which words can assign things to be one way or another. In both naming and seeing the naming he is enduring what

---

[11] Giorgio Agamben *The Open*, 16.

Agamben calls 'an infinite series of modal oscillations' that vary 'according to a continual gradation of growth and remission, of appropriation and impropriation', his face being shown continually passing into being, gathering its lines as it goes, all of which has gathered to constitute his singular expressivity, without the possibility of disassembly or wider categorization.[12] And in following Agamben's invitation to think of things through the 'gradation of growth and remission' that lies outside of being named, we witness Krapp. He relates to the class of being a human '*Who*' (body, organ, reading, walking) is infused with the idea of belonging to such a class, of being named. Yet the yearly repetition of making this attempt explicit – the strategic act of trying to form himself by reviewing and contemplating just what has been achieved each year – finds him refusing to be reduced to a name (Krapp at thirty-nine, Pah! no more), in his '*I*' he is always in company with the passageways to what is outside the inside; in this way he is open.[13]

Self and Singularity

In his continual modulation what marks Krapp's singularity – in the case of authenticity, the self – is not a capacity to be known as something that 'is', but as something whose being has been, and is made distinctive, with a political, practical potential to not be: 'The being that is properly whatever is able to not-be; it is capable of its own impotence.'[14] The potential to be and not-be are not of the same quality simply because they sound alike. To be something is for one's being to transition into a determinate activity, whereas to not-be cannot have a definite object in mind (it cannot be that by which navigation secures its warrant) save for the potentiality (in Krapp's case, of refusing to be what it was). A self that is alive to itself negatively is one that carries within it both potential and impotence. To gather into oneself an ability to become something, is to transition away from the ability to not act, to not say, and in so doing it is less able to not-be: it becomes less political because it less able to inquire into the organizational ordering of its marks of distinction. Being committed to being a unity is enervating, it requires resources, whereas hesitation preserves, in the act, the potential of acting and not acting. Krapp's stripped back poverty reveals this directly, his is an '*I*' refusing the '*We*', and a '*Who*' finding relief against the '*What*', and it is in his organization of this relationship of doing and not doing that the potency

---

[12] Giorgio Agamben *The Coming Community*, 26–7.
[13] Giorgio Agamben *The Coming Community*, 72.
[14] Giorgio Agamben *The Coming Community*, 42.

of authenticity is shown, for here, in this clearing mediated by a tape machine, comes the pause that is neither being nor not-being.[15]

We might recall Arendt again here, and her advocacy of a specific kind of *polis*. Arendt's interest in the *polis* is directed towards its confined openness: by dwelling in 'the space where I appear to others as others appear to me' citizens are continually beginning anew.[16] It is civic space being held in common through nothing more than a continual looking into one another's conditions, imagining how it might be to be and be with them, to then give rise to a collective sensibility: a '*We*' that is engaged continually in changing the world it holds in common – the '*Who*' and '*What*'. The sense of self – '*I*' – '*Who*' – emerging in a *polis* is free from immediate concerns, from necessity and means-ends calculation; offering a kind of negative potential that eludes those acting in pursuit of self-interest, such as Alcibiades (Chapter 2). Action, properly speaking, means to make oneself what one is; but in so doing there is also a suspension of the surrounding world; of immediacy of needs, by virtue of excluding the household, economics, and all the hurly burly of everyday life from this pure, political space, so as to let questions be measured not against wordily concerns, but *vis-à-vis* one's own thinking and willing held in the pause, which is an '*I*'. Action is a beginning and '[I]t is in the very nature of every new beginning that it breaks into the world as an "infinite improbability," and yet it is precisely this infinitely improbable which actually constitutes the very texture of everything we call real.'[17]

In the pause of not not-being comes the struggle to live with what Arendt calls the 'miraculous present', miraculous in that what comes to pass always exceeds its anticipation, always overwhelms the thought that

---

[15] This particular use of the tape recorder distinguishes Krapp from the cinematic condition lamented by Stiegler. Krapp's remembering through an exteriorized ('tertiary') medium is not the adoption of a generalized collective (a 'We' that becomes a 'One') but of memory which he *has* lived and which, at the same time, is distant and strange to him. Or, rather, its recursive looping is not just a repetition but a process that includes contingency. What was information can turn to noise and noise can become signal. Krapp seems incapable of (or refuses?) integrating the inconsistent, erroneous, or defective information; his use of technology goes against the character of technics which, in general, seeks to eliminate contingency (through positive and optimizing feedback loops that anticipate and expect what is most optimal). What emerges, instead, is an individuation of a self capable of entering new epistemological patterns prompted by the surprising and accidental; by 'occurrences that disturb the metaphysical illusion that the end is already there in the origin'; by repeatedly finding the limits of optimizing feedback loops; and by hitting rock-bottom, jolting him towards the discovery of broader realities, each time generating new processes of individuation. Yuk Hui Recursivity and Contingency, 130–136; 199–206.

[16] Hannah Arendt *Willing The Life of the Mind, Part II: Willing.* New York: Harcourt Brace Jovanovich, 1978, 200.

[17] Hannah Arendt What is freedom?, 169.

contains it, always coincides with the strange, simply in its facticity, that 'it is', rather than 'is not'. Like Krapp, the paused being is no longer just going along, thoughtlessly enjoined to the rhythms of daily life: the commonly held habits, the administrative indifference, the sanctified verities. The pause (materialized by Krapp in the clunky movements of the tape, back and forth) attends to the organization of marks by which an *Umwelt* rings itself around a being. In Krapp's two-in-one dialogue some pauses are momentous, the magnetic tape appears to have been so compacted with feeling that it requires a strained and sustained attention, whereas others are barely perceptible amid the grike of glance and gesture wrinkling the surfaces of his self on self-commerce. True enough it is not action in Arendt's sense: the performative expression of freedom is more that of Foucault's ironizing, of maturity exposing itself to the possibility of freedom. Krapp refuses to absent himself in long winding trajectories of inner speculation, or to seek the uplift of long-winded generalities.[18] The pause of both '*I*' and '*Who*' is brought in to ripple the patterns by which the 'what' and 'we' are settled, and sets them askew a little, a refraction that exposes his mortality, his loss, his growth, as experiences that give over to the possibility of things being otherwise and beginning again. In each recording he appropriates belonging to itself and thereby rejects utterly the condition of belonging delineated in the *Gestell*.[19]

This is a stained, postlapsarian innocence reminiscent of Arendt's natality and plurality through whose motions a self is a singular distinction being realized through an inessential unravelling, a loosening at the edges in which in-determination it might realize itself anew, allowing it to blend, to make of itself whatever it might and this is its totality, a totality of possibilities realized through its maintaining itself as an opening. Its edges (the striations of its *Umwelt*) are not bordering limits (*Schranke*) but have the quality of a threshold (*Grenze*) that yields to an outside through which, Agamben suggests, it gains its form as a singularity:

The *outside* is not another space that resides beyond a determinate space, but rather it is the passage, the exteriority that gives it access, – in a word, it is its face, its *eidos*. (Italics in the original)[20]

It is in this way that the forming of a thing such as a 'self' set in relation to the open is not simply a designation of 'being as'. The open, the outside, is a clearing in which *Dasein* allows the struggle between concealing and un-concealing of Being to unfold without attempting a resolution.

---

[18] Vicki Bell The promise of liberalism, 95–7.
[19] Giorgio Agamben *The Coming Community*, 86.
[20] Giorgio Agamben *The Coming Community*, 54–5, 65–6.

A resolution is the death of *Dasein* for it forecloses on the possibility of being historical, of being alive to the authentic task of having to experience disturbance to begin tasks anew. Being open to the concealing nature of things is to be traversed by nothing, a not, whose potency lies in its remaining un-committed to the name by which the thing that is concealed is forced to (challenged to) reveal itself as a thing-for-us. The organizational condition of keeping company with the unnamed *Dasein* makes present that which conceals itself and which remains unassigned, unclassified, unhinged, and so unavailable to technicity.[21] If the state of second innocence realized by not not-being is the condition of authenticity towards which a being can struggle and so elide the *Gestell*, the question then becomes how to strategically organize and so settle upon it, without making it a moral and practical imperative and thereby subjectifying it to work and labour.

Prometheus Rewound

Enlisting the figure of Prometheus might help. In Francis Bacon's Triptych, 1976, an image infused with the painter's lifetime of reading Aeschylus' tragedy *Prometheus Bound*, we witness Prometheus enduring the repeated attack of dark birds (see Figure 11.1). They fly from above, coming down atop the god's head, thrumming. There is nothing encompassing or dominant in the scene.[22] Bacon does not paint as a distant, overseeing observer looking on: it is from floor level, eye-eye, as though enjoined to Prometheus. Prometheus' innards are exposed and spilling into a bowl that he clenches between his firm footed, stout legs. Though occupying the centre panel, the figure is a far cry from the manifest human image of Leonardo's centralized and centralizing man with which we opened the book (see Figure 0.1): this is a god in human form eviscerated by fate and not at all in full control of its very animal nature. On the two outer panels are black suited figures with close cropped, bleak skulls, their eyes and mouths shut to the world. Their oversized ears are pinned back in attentive surveillance of the merest whisper. Theirs is a world of apparent mastery, of order: they bookend the life within, zipping up the

---

[21] Giorgio Agamben *The Open*, 78–80.

[22] Shoshana Felman To open the question. *Yale French Studies*, 1977, 55/56, 5–10. Reprinted in *Literature and Psychoanalysis. The Question of Reading: Otherwise*. Baltimore, MD: Johns Hopkins University Press. 1977, 5–10. Felman argues the authority of literature such as that of Greek tragedy comes more in irony 'Since irony precisely consists in dragging authority as such into a scene which it cannot master, of which it is *not aware* and which, for that very reason, is the scene of its own self-destruction, literature, by virtue of its ironic force, fundamentally deconstructs the fantasy of authority', 8.

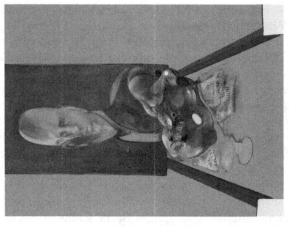

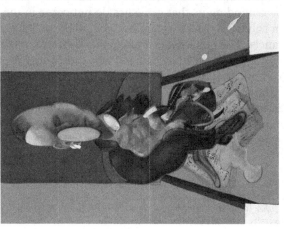

Figure 11.1 Francis Bacon. *Triptych, 1976.* © The Estate of Francis Bacon. All rights reserved, DACS/Artimage 2021. Photo: Prudence Cuming Associates.

future in endless repetitions of force and violence. They are reminiscent of the figures Percy Shelley describes in *Prometheus Unbound* as '[h]ard featured men, or with proud, angry looks,/ Or cold, staid gait, or false, hollow smiles, /Or the dull sneer of self-loved ignorance/ Or other such foul masks'.[23] Open mouthed, Prometheus resists.

As well as Aeschylus, the triptych appears to be channelling Nietzsche's *Birth of Tragedy*. The outer panels compress the life within, embodying the vicious calm that can befall a scene dominated by cold knowledge claims. Rather than noble serenity, truth given in the form of a world picture is snuffing out life. Prometheus' refusal to conform reveals the possibilities for life beyond the restraints of form. He struggles, and in this struggle he opens up the space for saying 'yes to the very things that are questionable and t'rrible'.[24] The 'yea saying' comes in guttural proto language, a shattered *logos*, that, in Bacon's refined diagrammatic form, is more an utterance, a mark making, an incision into the world that surely cannot be the province of humans alone? Prometheus has the company of *daimons*. They perch in the vicinity, reminders that reason is not the only form of accessing the world, and that human beings are not the only beings for whom the accidental question of access arises. As figures of chance, mutability and accident the demons remain unsettling. Yet they add to rather than detract from the force of Prometheus' struggle. Just as much as they are confined by the bleak order induced by the outer panels, they also constitute an incision into the otherwise smooth ordering of the *Gestell* embodied in the individuating knowledge of the outer figures. Simply in being present, less as a middle panel in a triptych than an unruly incision into world picture, the *daimons* and the human-loving immortal demonstrate the possibility for things to be otherwise.

Yet they themselves can do little for us, save remind us of this possibility. Bacon too is reminding us that remedies do not come in the form of designs, plans or solutions, which are, or become, the knowledge forms of the two outer panels. The inner panel is altogether different, it is at peace, almost serene, because it is the body of a god who can endure the restless, chaotic, vitality of untamed life. Prometheus is there to remind us of the conceits of the knowledge project. The outer figures are reduced forms, they are figures of Socratic logic and entailed causal argument whose chains of reasoning can only end in the lifeless tidiness of fixed, cognitive positions whose ascendancy presages the arrival of machine thinking. Yet

---

[23] Percy Shelley *Prometheus Unbound* 41–44.
[24] Friedrich Nietzsche Twilight of the Idols §6. In *The Anti-Christ, Ecce Homo, The Twilight of the Idols, and Other Writings*. Edited by Aaron Ridley and Judith Norman. Cambridge: Cambridge University Press. 2011,170, (also §24,224).

Prometheus is also there to remind us of the dangers of formless, uncontrolled excess, and of the need, with the company of *daimons*, to keep making individuating organizational forms anew so we might contain and so affirm life, without organization there is no life.

Encouraged by immortals and *daimons* to give birth to the organizational by refusing what settles as being already organized, recalls the discussion of authenticity and the two-in-one dialogue (Chapter 1). For Plato the demonic was a sensibility that brought individuals in touch with knowledge of what lay outside and beyond ordinary concourse, and for Goethe, *millenia* later, the demonic remained a power that emerged in contradictions, resisting the smoothing approach of words and rational appeal yet not collapsing into utter chaos; something (*etwas; dieses Wesen*) that seems to step in-between everything that 'is'. The demonic invokes the unrest that is within us all, as if our very being has within it an ability not only to acknowledge but to organize the primordial contingency and chaos of raw (semiotic) life.[25] The Greek – *daimon* – captures this double play; *da-* (from the root *daio*) meaning to distribute and divide, the *daimon* indicates a cleft that reaches beyond our minds into a domain that is veiled, suppressed and altogether unintelligible; and this *daimon* is also the principle of genius that enables humans to individuate and contain their passions, leading to happiness (*eudaimonia*). *Daimon* refers to semi-divine figures, to good and evil spirits, but also, more broadly, to numinous and hidden forces shaping a person's life and destiny: as Heraclitus suggests, man's [sic] *daimon* is his fate.[26]

Goethe's romantic refinement of Plato has the *daimonic* as both an internal power, as in the artistic mediation of the earthly and the divine, as well as an external force in nature that continually obstructs the aims and plans of a striving subject.[27] The *daimon* is, or indicates, an in-between, liminal space, one where, as in Bacon's painting, it alights where transformative things happen.[28] In its liminality the *daimon* is an irritant, a goad, but unlike Beckett's mechanical goad, this one prods and pushes in a more generative vein. The *daimon* eschews mindless productivity in favour of the organizational, attending to the strategic

---

[25] Stefan Zweig *The Struggle with the Daemon*, Translated by Eden Paul & Cedar Paul. London: Pushkin. 2012, 9.

[26] Angus Nicholls *Goethe's Concept of the Daemonic: After the ancients*. Rochester, NY: Camden House. 2006, 12, 79. See also David Farrell Krell *Daimon life: Heidegger and life-philosophy*. Bloomington: Indiana University Press. 1992, 6.

[27] Angus Nicholls *Goethe's Concept of the Daemonic*, 2.

[28] Angus Nicholls *Goethe's Concept of the Daemonic*, 70ff. 'A form of translation from what is practically unimaginable and multiformal into something practically imaginable and uniformal'. James Keys *Only Two Can Play This Game*. London: Cat Books. 1971, 38.

question, as Nietzsche poses it, what if we go again, what if we start anew, what if we are always coming again with new organs?

What, if some day or night a demon were to steal after you into your loneliest loneliness and say to you: 'This life as you now live it and have lived it, you will have to live once more and innumerable times more; and there will be nothing new in it, but every pain and every joy and every thought and sigh and everything unutterably small or great in your life will have to return to you, all in the same succession and sequence – even this spider and this moonlight between the trees, and even this moment and I myself. The eternal hourglass of existence is turned upside down again and again, and you with it, speck of dust!'[29]

Nietzsche's demon, and perhaps Bacon's, are aligning the *daimon* with a mediating force of willed thoughtfulness: as specks we tumble down the continually turning hourglass of existence, from one side to the other, and as we act we ask would this be as it might be? The question reveals how the '*What*' and '*Who*' – the organized everybody captured by the label of the *last man*, if left free of the '*I*' and '*We*', places the self in submissive, slave-like positions, forever organizing towards the mean, continually avoiding distinction, especially for life itself. The *daimon* and the will that wills the eternal recurrence, means leaving the windowless structures erected by science, by morals; just as each turn of the hourglass marks both end and beginning; death and birth; mortality and immortality are all present here, in the organizational now, albeit only understood through a glance (*Augenblick*).[30] Such a life is no longer weighed down by necessity or cessation. It becomes guided by the will willing its own tumbling through a life organized with other lives. Like Prometheus, long suffering, antisocial and isolated, the strategy of following the demon into the twilight between life and death, allowed Nietzsche to cling on to a version of his own self, his '*I*', which could only ever amount to endlessly repeated distinctions of an '*I*' that, in accepting the 'who' and 'what' nevertheless remains distinct from them, simply in its being a self-willed act of absorption in its own distinction as an experiencing being. The earth might well be beyond human consciousness, so it is for us to organize what is our own home, again and again.

The Potential of Strategy

The demand placed on the strategist by inhabiting the organizational in-between is to consider how re-presenting the self is less a question of content than it is mediation. In his *Laws of Form* Spencer-Brown

---

[29] Friedrich Nietzsche *Gay Science*, §341.
[30] Hannah Arendt Thinking and moral considerations, 204.

illustrates this appearing of the medium out of which all form (and non-form) can emerge through the example of writing:

The fact that men [*sic*.] have for centuries used a plane surface for writing means that, at this point in the text, both author and reader are ready to be conned into the assumption of a plane writing surface without question. But, like any other assumption, it is not unquestionable, and the fact that we can question it here means that we can question it elsewhere ... Moreover, it is now evident that if a different surface is used, what is written on it, although identical in marking, may be not identical in meaning.[31]

In allowing the mediating forms to appear Spencer-Brown's example reveals the potential of things to be different not merely because existing names and labels are changed, but because the organized relations these have with their background is being seen, and potentially reorganized. For instance, drawing a circle on a flat piece of paper separates the surface into what is inside and outside, as well as delineating itself as a circle. There are, then, three organizational aspects to the form of a circle, all of which are distinct and yet mutually dependent, without any being definitive. The flat surface forms a fourth aspect, and were the same circle drawn on the surface of a torus rather than a plane there might be no encircling distinction at all.[32] The circle, like any form, is not self-contained in its own extension of what it is and is not, but is, in a necessary way, continually dependent on the organizational act of its being drawn into an environment. In the same way, fire and temperature stand in an essential relation to – and gain potential from – the things being heated up and burnt. And when water is thrown onto the fire it cannot wet itself, only that towards which it inclines, and which it wets, being nothing without these other, organizational aspects against which they (qua distinction) first gain their characteristics. The fire can then dampen, or be excited, depending on which material is burning, and where. Potential always invokes a double play: what 'is' is always an appearance accompanied by what it contains and that within which it is contained.[33]

If by strategy we mean the struggle to represent the self to self and to others, then its persuasive power comes in the strategist being alive continually to the manner in which the inside and outside of the form (what the organization contains or consists of, and the situations it enacts) is the consequence of organizational acts of distinction making that are (like Prometheus and the *daimons* inserting themselves into what is

---

[31] George Spencer-Brown *Laws of Form*, 70.
[32] George Spencer-Brown *Laws of Form*, 79.
[33] Giorgio Agamben *Potentialities: Collected Essays in Philosophy*. Stanford, CA: Stanford University Press. 1999, 177. See also Keiji Nishitani *Religion and Nothingness*. Translated by Jan Van Bragt. Berkeley: University of California Press. 1982, 76.

already organized) being continually re-made. The strategist's power (as opposed to violence and force) involves the seeing (the contemplating) of the organizational demand to draw these distinctions, and not others; and to then ask why these ones, because they can be otherwise. It is a form of seeing in which all named things are always already both what they are and what they are not.

Drawing a Distinction

For Spencer-Brown language begins with the Beckett-like injunction: 'draw a distinction', and from there on – and only from this organizational condition – can any-thing be discerned from anything else.[34] In drawing a distinction, in making a mark, in making an incision, the strategist is reaching outside an inside, but this is always also to be inside (as Bacon's Prometheus and the *daimons* are always on the inside panel), the *Umwelt* is limited by its own inability to organize beyond itself without thereby retaining itself. This is the peculiar power of the issuing of negatives (the drawing of a distinction is always a refusal to abide by, and a cleaving of, what is already there, into which *Dasein* finds itself thrown). Spencer-Brown, who had worked with Bertrand Russell and Ludwig Wittgenstein on questions of logic, cultivated a particular fascination with the negative, even more so in his poetry and other writings but also via his mathematics.[35] *Laws of Form* is prefaced by a quote from Lao-Tse, which von Förster translated as: 'the beginning of heaven and earth has no name'.[36] The un-named is where no distinctions can 'be'; where things and others are not always already ordered for this or that purpose, where things are not even things, limited by fixed outlines and labels, but where the organizational – the coming into being of new forms – is apparent. Like Nietzsche's speck of dust tumbling down the eternally turning hourglass of existence, and like the young Nietzsche himself, beguiled by Wagner's gift to conjure the tragic, edgeless and intoxicating totality of existence, the experience of the eternal, distinction-less domain (of immortals and *daimons*) is an invigorating experience. It is like standing in the middle of a storm, exposed. After a storm we can begin again; stirred by its vehemence and at once aware of the smallness of life, and yet also of the

---

[34] George Spencer-Brown *Laws of Form*, xxix.
[35] George Spencer-Brown *A Lion's Teeth: Löwenzähne*. Leipzig: Bohmeier. 1995; and writing under a pen name, James Keys *Only Two Can Play This Game*.
[36] Heinz von Förster *The Beginning of Heaven and Earth Has No Name: Seven Days with Second-Order Cybernetics*. Edited by Albert Müller and Karl H. Müller. New York: Fordham University Press. 2014, 5.

vastness of all that cannot be controlled, or even named, by life. This wind itself is perceptible only through its manifestations, not in itself; by the dust and debris it sucks up, the buildings it destroys, the blows it delivers to the body and the hissing and howling crescendos that only the most accomplished of artists can imitate in paintings or in music. Yet perhaps all this talk of storms and stress is too much of the romanticized artistic self. That artistic self discussed by Cixous, those of Joyce and Beckett, carry in them a more persistent, less monumental wind, and one that Spencer-Brown also evokes in a poem 'untitled':

> I like you
> Shall die
> One day
> Circling
> The other way
> Where the wind
> Will take
> This chance
> A bird
> Of paradise
> Will dance.[37]

A poem with no title begins with the acknowledgement of finitude and the deferred nothing that inherently accompanies and organizes the 'something' of existence. It connects life and death, me and other, the old and of the natality that beckons new beginnings, but also the strictness of a stripped-back organizational form that nevertheless contains reference to a form-blurring dance.[38] And exactly in the middle of the stanza Spencer-Brown, who always counted his lines, positions the wind, which like pressure or temperature stands as an organizational force that lives without being fixed as a this or that. It circulates through things, animating yet destroying, relating the domain of the living, of bodies and substances, with what is beyond them; this liminal space (on the edge of being organized) is where *daimons* dwell, and where things are always on the move; shifting, decaying, forming and de-forming.

Beginning Again

Agamben invokes the idiom of consecration, meaning the taking of affairs out of the domain of human law, while profanation indicates the reverse

---

[37] James Keys *Only Two Can Play This Game*, 69.
[38] For '[i]n the womb there is no philosophy, no science, no consultation'. George Spencer-Brown *Autobiography. Vol I. Infancy and Childhood*. Leipzig: Bohmeier. 2012, 37.

process of restoration of these affairs to the property and use of humans, typically through aforementioned processes of subjectification.[39] The passage from the profane to the sacred is ritualized through religious ceremony, a confession, or in commemorations and festivals where we find happiness listening to music or dancing, where these create moments of exception that synchronize the life of the individual with a collective sense of belonging, and with human rhythms and patterns that may vary from culture to culture, but into which each individual 'I' is socialized from birth.[40] The product of these processes is the formation of a new self; a transformation of an old 'I' into a new, repudiated self, who can come to know itself afresh because it was able to escape the hurly burly of everyday life. Means–ends calculations, want, need, desire, jealousy and revenge all fade into insignificance when viewed next to eternal concerns, when the self makes an appearance in a confessionary space, which here mirrors the *polis* in that it allows the self to appear as itself, unencumbered by its social status, roles, or by economic demands and pressures; and with this the new self comes to repudiate the old, be born again in light of the experience of these events, ready to redraw distinctions and begin afresh under the sacred impress of its own distinction-making power.

The strategist too is alive to the limits of all organized attempts to enforce and insist on those subjectifying separations by which the human is kept free from, and elevated above, others, such as the animal, or natural forms like stones. To insist on the naturalness of such separations is to warrant the possessive, earth-hungry claims of an anthropological machinery whose workings have culminated in the epoch of technogenesis. The strategist is a figure who advocates the drawing of distinctions and admits the essential exposure to uncertainty that this form of negative picturing yields.

The question of 'who is 'I'' is therefore like a stepping into the wind, so as to be jolted out of the affairs of everyday life and so, for a while, to encounter the organizational complicty of life and form and the eternal negation of all form in its passing away into new form. The negative through which the organizational appears cannot live with form-fixing instrumentality, there must be no 'in order to', no acting for the sake of significance, what Heidegger called *Bedeutsamkeit*. Unlike the operational questions of administration and management of the *oikos*, the order of being organized, organization and being organized asking the strategic question of 'who is 'I'' is the making of an incision, which as it is made opens up what 'is' to what is 'not yet'. It is a deliberate (two in one) attempt at exposure through the unassigned drawing of a distinction, which both issues and affectively responds to the mark-making

---

[39] Giorgio Agamben *What Is an Apparatus?*, 168.
[40] Bernard Stiegler *Technics and Time*, 99.

activity that characterized the *Umwelt* of *Dasein*. The strategist – the mark-maker making marks that afford human thought, feeling and deed as well as the organizational forms that leave it open to the demand that it make further marks – struggles (*Streit*) continually between the unconcealed nature of a world being made open, and the concealed nature of the earth that is being acknowledged when allowing things to stand without being challenged forth, without demanding that they 'be' something.

In being alive to these organizational limits, the strategist constitutes the quiet politics by which the struggling processes and patterns of separation are unconcealed. Its power (as in Arendt's use of power, as distinct from the violence of work and the force of labour) comes in embracing this tragic condition (tragedy being the very un-modern acceptance of *aporia*) without be-labouring it. It is the power that comes from having experienced the anxiety induced by such an *aporia*, but also the curiosity and excitement, and not having turned away to seek refuge in already organized forms that reach for a totalizing, unifying order.

In his advocacy of National Socialism Heidegger had turned away completely. The urge to recover the historical task for *Dasein* led him to abandon the distinction-drawing activity (the *Streit* that is drawing, picturing without edges, without ends) by which any such history might be constituted in the events of everyday life. He was unable to say 'no' to the external pressure to reveal himself as a 'this' or 'that'. He suffered from the final delusion that his analysis of technology had touched upon the grounding condition of life: an instrumentality of being that in human organization found its alienating expression in the figuration of *Das Man*. As Günther Anders almost laconically remarks, it was Heidegger's obsession with an authentic being towards mortality that fuelled his advocacy of an unreal form of historicity in which the task of *Dasein* was less the practical everyday business of securing fair and just relations between people and nature, but a destinal orientation towards death. In its fear of the instrumentalizing *Gestell* such a (nihilistic) solution lacked any organizational nuance, fragility or curiosity, it was deeply organized.[41]

Stiegler offers no such release from the ever-present problem of the decision (the incision, the difference-making distinction). The experience of this problem is one he distils into the experience of time: in making an insertion humans are also projecting their sense of being into what they might become, whilst carrying with them memory of what they were. He is pushing hard at Heidegger's notion of the uncanny, lending

---

[41] Günther Anders On the Pseudo-Concreteness of Heidegger's Philosophy. *Philosophy and Phenomenological Research*, 1948, 8(3): 337–71.

it a stronger technological footing because projection is an experience of anticipation constrained by all previous attempts at projection that have become already organized in the objects of their already established culture, in technics (symbols, standards, regimens, machinery).[42]

What is always already there when any individual enters their world is a past, which they have never themselves lived but which is nevertheless *their* past. This organization of inheritance and transmission grounds the facticity of self that establishes the individual as belonging to this or that culture, tradition, family or class. Gifts and debts are passed down from those no longer living, preserved in the technologies of speech and writing, in artifacts and tools: an 'archaeology of reflexivity' preserved in family relations and inscribed in production regimes and artifacts that bestow upon the individual 'the accents of his speech, the style of his approach, the force of his gesture, the unity of his world'.[43] Through this being organized by memorization of the past we live in anticipation of a future on the basis of a past that we have not ourselves lived; a past that striates our gestures and desires.

The memory of the existence of the generations that preceded me, and without which I would be nothing, is bequeathed on such supports ... this memory of past experiences ... are not lost, contrary to what occurs in a strictly biological species [making] the already-there and its appropriation possible.[44]

The sense of self is rooted in the interplay of remembering and forgetting; in the inscribed inheritances from the past and their transformations through processes of re-making through which the individual (their interior; the *who*) and world (their exterior, the *what*) are continually and simultaneously constituted. This leaves us with an ambiguity in the invention of the human: the 'who' and the 'what' are held together as well as separated: 'constituted as the twin faces of the same phenomenon'.[45]

invention and destruction; Promethian foresight and Epimethian idiocy; the struggle of being unfolds in between these unhomely relations.[46]

Dasein lives with the past pulling it into the future: it inherits a condition into which it is thrown and from which (past) tradition it must then

---

[42] Martin Heidegger *Introduction to Metaphysics*, 174/120.
[43] Bernard Stiegler *Technics and Time, 1*, 140.
[44] Bernard Stiegler *Technics and Time, 1*, 159.
[45] Bernard Stiegler *Technics and Time, 1*: 177; 178.
[46] Bernard Stiegler *Technics and Time, 1*, 194. For Stiegler, here lies an important difference to Heidegger: 'Neglecting the tragic meaning of the figure of forgetting, Heidegger maintains that the principle of individuation is constituted outside the publicity of the One. But the truth is quite the opposite. The gift of difference is technological because the individual constitutes itself from out of the possibilities of the One, from the relation with one another each time allowed for by the particular technological set-up.' Bernard Stiegler *Technics and Time, 1*, 237

project itself, but not simply as a carrier of the past into the future. We are all of us haunted by the ghosts of the dead, most of them anonymous, chattering away as *Das Man*.

It is here, for Stiegler, as for Günther Anders, that Heidegger goes so brutally awry insofar as he attempts to correct, politically, this sense of the uncanny by having *Dasein* come into an originary relation with itself, in an isonomic sense, when individuality and collectively conjoin, when both the 'I' and the 'they' somehow (mysteriously) dissolve into the *Volk*, a supposedly authentic people. For Theodor Adorno too, Heidegger taints his thinking irreparably insofar as he attempts to reconcile thought and Being, to lend ontics an ontological quality and to grant Being ontic power. We end up with a camouflaged idealism in which, as a concept, Being 'borrows from the factual realm an air of solid abundance, of something not just cogitatively and unsolidly made – an air of being "in itself" [whilst] [f]rom the mind which synthesizes it, entity borrows the aura of being more than factual: the sanctity of transcendence'.[47] It is better, argues Adorno, to accept thought incapable of absorbing Being fully and to live with the inevitable and endless struggle between thought and reality, an organizational struggle that defines our consciousness, being aware that there is no ideal or absolute through which the dualisms that beset thinking can be synthetically reconciled. Adorno shares with Heidegger a sensitivity to the embedded nature of thinking, a condition that meant the consciousness of *Dasein* always refuses to yield to the ideal formation or picture of a distinct subject. *Dasein* always has to work from within an historically organized condition of idle chatter and equipmental relations into which it has fallen. It could not escape: language, the mediating 'house' of being, was steeped in vestiges of the past from which meaning had to be distilled through constant interpretation. Heidegger errs, however, in his attempt to make sense of these legacies and unlock a concreteness to Being around which a redemptive political programme might be wrapped.[48]

Chastened by the failure of this programme, Heidegger twists away from social and political engagement, and from this eagle's nest of disengagement maintains a somewhat belittling, arrogant stance against

---

[47] Theodor Adorno *Negative Dialectics*, 76.
[48] In making this point Adorno enlists Günther Anders (On the pseudo-concreteness of Heidegger's philosophy. *Philosophical and Phenomenological Research*, 1948, VIII(3): 337ff.). For Adorno Heidegger is playing with us: '[M]ere entity becomes nonentity; rid of the stain of being an entity, it is raised up to Being, to its own pure concept. Being, on the other hand, devoid of any content that would restrict it, no longer needs to appear as a concept. It is held to be immediate like, in other words, to be concrete. Once isolated absolutely, the two moments have no differentia specifically from each other and become interchangeable. This quid pro quo is a main feature of Heidegger's philosophy.' Theodor Adorno *Negative Dialectics*, note 75.

those who believed themselves capable of renewing the world order. For Adorno, in some ways Heidegger was right to be so scathing. The planning for a new world after World War II had taken on an urgent and ambitious guise warranted by a renewed and explicit faith in what, apparently, all humans held in common: reason. The creation of the United Nations was emblematic of this renewal of faith, an institutional attempt to befriend humanity through the gift of an organization. Heidegger believed it was doomed to repeat the same mistakes as earlier humanist organizations, for it was grounded in the same, persisting ontological assumptions: we are all of us humans prone to the animal, and yet alive to the civilized. Thus, humanism cast humans in a struggle against captivation, caught between two sides, the noble and ignoble, the considered and rampant, suggesting it was the inevitability of this lack (the human could neither be fully one nor the other) that brought forth a process of being organized into manners and culture.

As Sloterdijk neatly summarizes it, the credo of humanism is that human beings are creatures riddled with biological indeterminacy and moral ambivalence. They are capable of suggestion, and so it is imperative they are encouraged to choose the correct forms of suggestion and to tame their bestial nature. This is the role of organized media, to institute conditions whereby bestial tendencies become managed spectacles (the sporting arena, the amphitheatre) and to elevate the civilizing influence of patient, mental activity (a literary cannon, hierarchies of taste): 'the question of how a person can become a real or true human being becomes unavoidably a media question, if we understand by media the means of communication and communication by which human beings attain to that which they can and will become'.[49] By encouraging an organized sense of self-clarification and self-improvement, these media wrap us in an anthropological blanket that muffles any awareness of the self-serving instrumentality of such a world picture.

For Adorno Heidegger was too enamoured with his own interpretative critique of humanism and consequently caught up in his own world picture of *Dasein* projecting openly from within a thrown and fallen condition of Being, finding facticity in such. It was a conceptual arrangement in which the world was made available for understanding, if not control. What Heidegger seems to be advocating in authenticity was a disinterred arrangement of shepherding and speaking Being. In this befriending of Being humans – as *Dasein* – were necessarily constrained by, and confined to, their place as a clearing in which Being talks. This condition

---

[49] Peter Sloterdijk Rules for the human zoo: A response to the *Letter on humanism*. *Environment and Planning D*, 2009, 27: 12–28, 16.

has a kind of structural as well as historical quality to it, insofar as we find here the advocacy of a thoughtful letting be in which things are understood less as objects than as gatherings – *Ereignis* – events of becoming of a fourfold unity of heaven and earth, mortals and immortals. In this sense it is not simply the historically configured thrownness of his earlier thinking from which Heidegger was to imagine a politically organized exodus: it is more an organized condition to which *Dasein* simply accedes.

For Sloterdijk this risks humans becoming far tamer than ever they would under humanism, for in Heidegger's reading the shepherd of being waits and listens calmly until the revelatory moment (*Offenbarkeit*) when Being begins to talk through them. Adorno criticizes Heidegger here for encouraging a serenity and passivity that belies any advocate of immersive, realist ontology. It is not good enough to first invoke an immersed, concrete ontology of becoming, and then to twist the realization of this into a programme of speculative contemplation. By the operations of his own thinking ontology offers us no escape, so why then does he eschew thinking through what we are calling the organizational? Instead, he retreats to the backwoods and his hut. Adorno cannot forgive such cowardice when so much was at stake in everyday lives.[50] The imperative is to maintain the organizational work of making distinctions, aware, that all distinctions come with *daimons*, and will end. The tragic logos of Bacon's Prometheus acknowledges this precarious, shadowy condition of living with *daimons*. As Hamacher notes:

Since National Socialism, all concepts are ruins ... We do, indeed, need criteria, but we do not have a single criterion at our disposal that would not be in ruins and not a single one that would not harbor the danger of becoming murderous.[51]

In holding onto distinction making, however, there is another danger. A fundamental bodily incapacity is settling in, much more so now than in Heidegger's own time. At the root of this shift lies the movement from analogue to digital electronic technologies. The analogue signifies the organizational combination of things that are different, such as two organisms that become evolutionarily joined, such as the orchid and the wasp whose coupling requires special sockets that unite what is otherwise different, apparently discrete things are revealed as continuous, potentially. The digital, by contrast, begins with homogeneity through binarization, where everything that can be described logically can be made computable or, in Turing's terms, universal.[52] Starting with

---

[50] Fred Dallmayr Phenomenology and critical theory: Adorno. *Cultural Hermeneutics*, 1976, 3: 367–405.
[51] Werner Hamacher Working through work, 41.
[52] Alexander Galloway *Laruelle: Against the Digital*. Minneapolis: University of Minnesota Press. 2014.

homogeneity, no evolutionary adaptations are needed to make different parts work together, and nearly seamlessly organized into vast computational networks that collect, process and distribute ordering data at speeds and volumes many times faster than human cognition can sense. In this sense, the working of technology is invisible, merging utterly with technique, to the point we notice it only in its absence, when we become resentful when a destination is missing from GPS routing software, or when a virus escapes its cure, or a fully certificated pension fund is hollowed out by egregious financiers, or local wars interrupt supply chains. So complete, it seems, is our insertion into these technological surrounds that we do not notice their artificiality, for we humans ourselves, our memories and our reflections arise directly out of these media that store, modify and present a world to us; nay, are part of our world while we are not part of theirs. Machines do not need images, stories, identities or understanding, but humans do, it is where they have their home. Taking technology, and this always also means technological progress (in its most complete form as a self-augmentation by which progress accelerates to infinity) as a suitable subject of these stories and identities explicitly or implicitly attributes to technology an overarching and pervasive role in shaping humanity's future; a cosmic driving force experienced hitherto only in form of divine or natural powers and an instrument leading to the fulfilment of human destiny; or, perhaps just the fulfilment of reach and pervasiveness of market calculations.[53]

In Chapter 7 we have suggested that a much less fluid and more realist(ic) view emerges from what Simondon calls 'concretization', a process by which technical objects continue to gain complexity as each of their structural elements fulfil a greater and synergetic number of functions, and so, by informing themselves, they become concrete and develop so that no side-effect is detrimental to the functioning of the

---

[53] Andrés Vaccari Neosubstantivism as cosmotechnics. Gilbert Simondon versus the transhumanist synthesis. *Angelaki*, 25(4): 39–53. Here we find a recurrence of the term 'singularity', albeit in a radically different sense to Heidegger's. Technological optimists such as Ray Kurzweil, who since 2012 has worked for Google, refer to 'singularity' as the point by which machines become more intelligent than humans: 'a future period during which the pace of technological change will be so rapid, its impact so deep, that human life will be irreversibly transformed'; Ray Kurzweil *The Singularity Is Near: When Humans Transcend Biology*. London: Viking. 2005, 73. Singularity marks a tipping point at which, whilst becoming less intelligent than our technological productions, we still gain immortality as all problems and limits will be addressed by new patches and fixes; as a technological extension of evolutionary trends. See Bernard Stiegler *The Nanjing Lectures*, 81. See also Bernard Stiegler Noodiversity, Technodiversity: Elements of a new economic foundation based on a new foundation for theoretical computer science. Translated by Daniel Ross. *Angelaki*, 2020, 25(4): 67–80, 72.

ensemble.[54] Whilst appearing similar to technophile notions of unproblematic process, Simondon points out how human needs and desires, such as those manifest in design features that emphasize comfort, luxury or status, are utterly superfluous in terms of technical efficiency. Here, free markets are no longer synonymous with technological progress, but slow down technical acceleration by adding ballast to the 'pure' technical object so that the trajectories of human fulfilment and those of a technologically 'substantial' path are much less aligned.

Moreover, following Simondon, rather than freeing the human, the machine takes the role of the human, stripping them of a key element of their very being, namely their use of tools, as well as, more practically, of their felt employment.[55] In so universalizing everything, especially digital machines reduce everything to calculation in a manner already envisaged by Heidegger through the notion of the *Gestell* and via Simondon's process of concretization, but not quite. We equally recall from Chapter 10 how Stiegler pointed to the cinema as replacing the authentic processes of synchronization of the '*I*' and the '*We*' with standardized, monetized and marketized versions of a common past that has not been lived but that still comes to form the 'already there' and with it desire. But these structural workings of the cinema are now transformed by digital technologies, and in particular social media, which equally bypass the individuation processes that allow for the synchronized development of self and community (*I* and *We*) by short-circuiting a pathway from commercial and political interests to the very processes that produce the 'self'. In addition to its implication on the formation of selves, these digital media also impact, for example, the organizing of democratic social organizations, or regulatory organizations, which, in mandating and reviewing decision-making require the possibility for debate and reflection.[56] This 'time-delayed' mode of organizing, however, is now destroyed by the real-time workings of digital media, both in terms of the direct effects of memory systems that no longer merely store information but actively feed forward and so affect decisions through recommender systems or directly (e.g., in automated trading) and the real-time adaptation of politics, regulatory policy and the like to immediate events. What is at stake here is no longer an alienated worker or operator (the individuated,

---

[54] Gilbert Simondon *The Mode of Existence of Technical Objects*, 38. For Stiegler, Simondon's account of the expansion of technology into (and with) its milieu is similar to Heidegger's notion of the *Gestell*. Bernard Stiegler *Noodiversity, Technodiversity*, 75.

[55] Bernard Stiegler The theater of individuation: Phase-shift and resolution in Simondon and Heidegger. *Parrhesia*, 2009, 7: 46–57, 52.

[56] Bernard Stiegler Telecracy against democracy. *Cultural Politics*, 2010, 6(2): 171–80.

efficient cause) because to couch this as a concern is to persist with a fantasy that caring about events is still possible. What is at stake now is, argues Stiegler, a more radical reduction and elimination of organized difference and the rise of 'mass cretinism'; a hegemony of calculation that is itself irrational.[57] The pharmakon (Chapter 7) has turned out-of-kilter, outsourcing memory and understanding to computational processes with such intensity that a kind of collective destitution has set in towards which we have become increasingly passive, accepting, as though in the face of the inevitable one can only shrug and then pitch in. All forms of individuation have become the subject of a technological ordering dedicated to the pursuit of what Stiegler calls efficiencies and innovation rather than understanding and belonging. Life is beset with organization that has as its sole logic the elimination of everything that is singular and incalculable.[58] All relations, all individuations, all things, are nothing other than a scene for the translations of capital.

Even darker than Stiegler's identification of the workings of digital media on consciousness, however, are Mark Hansen's elaborations of the organized effects of what he calls twenty-first-century media, a term comprising a vast array of digital developments from social media to the internet of things, sensors, platform ecologies and so on, on pre-, sub-, or nonconscious processes (Chapter 7). Twenty-first-century media, for Hansen, represent a form of retention that is radically different from previous technologies.[59] Not only due to their miniaturization, portability and the ubiquity of sensors that automatically gather, process and propagate data – making human behaviour itself a kind of archive,[60] but because – for the first time in human history – such processes unfold largely without humans having direct experience, awareness or even potential access to what is processed and computed. Galloway and Thacker speak of the 'unhuman'

[57] Bernard Stiegler *Nanjing Lectures*, 315, 323. Stiegler considers links between technology and the idea of the free market as a system of information, linking both Hayek and Simon, suggesting much greater intimacy between technology, calculability and neoliberalism, thus also begging the question whether claims of a or 'the' technological system are too narrowly Western, coined by the confluence of capitalism and the ideology fostered by the Silicon Valley, and whether alternative 'technodiverse' understandings are possible. See for instance Yuk Hui *The Question Concerning Technology in China*. Massachusetts: MIT Press. 2016.

[58] Judith Wambacq, Daniel Ross and Bart Buseyne We have to become the quasi-cause of nothing – of Nihil: An interview with Bernard Stiegler. *Theory, Culture & Society*, 2016, 35(2): 137–56.

[59] Mark B. Hansen *Feed-forward: On the Future of Twenty-first-century Media*. Chicago: University of Chicago Press. 2014.

[60] Yuk Hui On the synthesis of social memories. In *Memory in Motion: Archives, Technology, and the Social*. Edited by Ina Blom, Trond Lundemo and Evind Røssaak. Amsterdam: Amsterdam University Press. 2016, 307–27.

qualities of these organizing media often organized as networks, which nevertheless do not exclude human decision and commonality:

Networks are elemental, in the sense that their dynamics operate at levels 'above' and 'below' that of the human subject. The elemental is this ambient aspect of networks, this environmental aspect – all the things that we as individuated human subjects or groups do not directly control or manipulate.[61]

However, this unhuman element of networks does not mean that there is no connection to humans on the very elemental level. As we have elaborated, Hayles and Hansen see large parts of human awareness happening not on the conscious level, but as non-conscious operations at a level of neuronal processing, which recognizes patterns too complex, subtle and fast for consciousness to discern. These operations are crucial for the functioning of consciousness as such but not accessible to awareness. It is precisely here that Hansen diverges from Stiegler, suggesting that twenty-first-century media directly mediate mediation itself.[62] Put differently: while higher-level human processes associated with cognition, awareness or sensemaking are still involved, they are now intricately linked with immensely fast, distributed, parallel and so technical processes:

today's ubiquitous computational environments and bionic bodily supplementations operate more by fundamentally reconfiguring the very sensory field within which our experience occurs than by offering new contents for our consciousness to process or new sensory affordances for us to enframe through our embodiment.[63]

This means that organized human experience is fundamentally hybrid: higher-order cognitive processes of perception (such as reframing of memories) are intertwined with lower-order, bodily functions, which are increasingly tightly integrated into environmental networks that automatically and largely imperceptibly gather and process data while creating the sensory environments in which twenty-first-century organizational life unfolds.

Twenty-first-century media have become unavoidable in many sensory engagements with the world – from finding one's way through maps on smartphones, trackers eliciting biometric data, media feeds purveying news or communication; to the many invisible assistants that keep cars on track, and recommender systems calculating ideal places to eat, sleep or live. These media therefore provide massively enlarged and

---

[61] Alexander A. Galloway *Eugene Thacker the Exploit: A Theory of Networks*. London: University of Minnesota Press. 2007, 157.
[62] N. Katherine Hayles *Unthought*, 10ff. Mark Hansen Feed-forward, 43.
[63] Mark Hansen *Feed-forward*, 45.

microtemporally sped-up access to the world but the pharmacological recompense is that these newly expanded sensory data can no longer be experienced directly and slowly through the human senses and so we require devices and interfaces to translate the sensory expansion so it can once again be experienced (retrospectively) by human senses.

Twenty-first-century media therefore appear to offer a similar supplementary function to that of writing – by providing access to the very experiences that have been removed from human control and relegated to technology. But Hansen identifies a crucial change in the supplementary pattern: while writing directly gives back what it takes away (a source of memory, first natural and short term become artificial and long term), twenty-first-century media constitute an indirect recompense: the waning powers of perception and the loss of control over one's nonconscious processes is not restored artificially but rather develops a *different* capability in its stead, one that is neither entirely human nor purely machinic.[64] There simply is no perceptual access to these enlarged sensibilities – only their 'presentification' in humanly accessible form (heartbeats shown retrospectively as graphs or numbers; recommendations as rankings, and so on), but that is not even their point or purpose. Twenty-first-century media no longer merely store memory, they are geared towards organising microsensory data directly (bypassing consciousness) and then process these to influence action and emotion (they re-engineer sensibility, bypassing consciousness) in real time:

the technical sensors now ubiquitous in our lived environments are able to capture experiential events directly at the microtemporal level of their operationality and – independently of consciousness's mediations – 'feed them forward' into (future or 'just-to-come') consciousness in ways that can influence consciousness's own future agency in the world.[65]

In distinction to Stiegler's (and Heidegger's) notion of the 'already there', which forms one's tertiarily retained past but which the individual need not have been experienced itself, Hansen argues that it is now 'contemporary data of sensibility [which] can be defined as data that *cannot he directly lived* by consciousness' – nor *can* they ever be experienced or lived directly by consciousness. They simply fall outside the realm of human sensibility.[66]

---

[64] Mark Hansen *Feed-forward*, 50ff.

[65] Mark Hansen *Feed-forward*, 52.

[66] Mark Hansen *Feed-forward*, 53. For Hansen (268), the task is therefore to turn the workings of twenty-first-century media against themselves: to de-emphasize consciousness and mess with, distort or control the ways in which the 'new and alien organs' of twenty-first-century media that generate extra-perceptual experiences of both humans

Operating at the limits of sense, we have argued that we might fight a rejoinder to the organized impress of the technological ubiquity in the work of the strategist, for whom a decision is not merely a product of calculation but an organizational drawing of distinctions, in particular between a self that is and one that asks 'who is 'I'' Where there is only calculation, there is no milieu or, to use Spencer-Brown's term, no negating and impoverishing 'nothing' and no dying against which anything that 'is' can begin to organizationally appear as form.[67] The living force of this organizational condition revealed by strategic questioning is carried along by what Nishitani called emptiness: 'Real Form as such is a "non-Form" as it stretches out into potential.'[68] Real form is what Hölderlin called a 'trying out, underway; untried', a bestirring of the self by itself that has no way out, and which comes to nothing.[69]

The deathless world of calculation abhors this poverty, this nothing. It organizes life into a technical milieu of identified units that has exhausted its capacity to nourish differences; diversity has become a process of assignment.[70] Where everthing is already organized by a personal number, password, email address, avatar, online account or otherwise coded, and where apparatuses, instruments, gadgets and increasingly smaller and unnoticeable sensors and robots vie to form identities, which are then coupled in vast mesh works of inter-netted information technology, there is no outside, no bigger picture and no absence left; the 'nothing' is relentlessly crowded out.[71] Technology is less and less a condition that commands our attention or instils a sense of awe, as it did when dams and power plants first severed rivers or likewise carved up land to create shipping passages; or when satellites were launched into space in balls of fire that could then be represented on a child's bedroom wallpaper.

There Is No Place Like Home

We began the book by talking of strategy, perhaps somewhat elliptically, as a struggle to witness the seeing of what is being continually named.

and other entities. This, then, represents an opportunity to 'implicate our agency within the larger total situation of environmental gathering' – again without expecting to 'experience' any of this anymore.

[67] W. H. Auden refused poetry an incendiary role, it will not change human nature, or society, but it will reveal the facticity of finitude, it will give space to the dead. In so doing it gives vent to power.

[68] Keiji Nishitani *Religion and Nothingness*, 76.

[69] Hölderlin's translation of Sophocles *Antigone* quoted in Martin Heidegger *Introduction to Metaphysics*, 163.

[70] Bernard Stiegler *Noodiversity, Technodiversity*, 72.

[71] Giorgio Agamben *What is an Apparatus?*, 16.

This, we suggested in Chapter 2, was akin to a form of organizational authenticity in which what is being formed is not a contained, well-defined interior space – an *oikos*, or home, which is always and only that which is named, that which is built – but forms that are not-yet homely, or that is unhomely, an organizational space of appearances. The role we have given to strategy, its role, is, we have argued, to think and act outside of the already organized by encouraging the continued possibility of making distinctions. This possibility is a negative one: not an oppositional idea of negative (which is just another form of bringing things into objectified and subjectified presence) but the negative as an opening up in opinion. To recur to Adorno and Arendt with whom we opened our argument, it is a negative that restores mystery to things: one that uses words in language (concepts, categories, ideas) to reveal where they stutter and are shown to encumber differences in their apparent distinction; one that is loose enough to endure and enjoy strange companions whose affect is to ripple and crease the smoothing claims of knowledge; one that is attentive to how things (especially, perhaps, human beings), in being named, have always been cheated of their potential; one that is aware of the intimacy between opinion and thoughtfulness: as Paul Celan observed, without opinion there is only a wasteland of emptiness, atoms and atomization, of things unjoined. A poet works in the service of opinion.[72]

In a gesture of some irony, at least in relation to Adorno, we end the book by turning to one of the most notable fabrications of the culture industry: *The Wizard of Oz*. Oz is a world in which the technological ordering, both West and East, has been complete, but also rather shabby. Once a curtain is drawn back by a curious small dog the all-seeing mind is revealed as nothing more than a middle-aged, former carnival worker (an ex-Harlequin, ex-Pulcinella), whose organizing power was being directed by a megaphone and some vaporous special effects. In thrall to this machinery, the wizard's labours and work in strategic organization have left him increasingly exhausted. Standing exposed before a doughty child called Dorothy, three animal-machine-humans so stripped back in qualities that they would not be out of place on one of Beckett's stages, and a lap dog, Oz is glad to give up: finally, in his fantasy at least, he can retire over the horizon in his hot air balloon.

---

[72] Paul Celan Stretto. In *Memory Rose into Threshold Speech: The Collected Earlier Poetry*. Translated by Pierre Joris. New York: Farrar Straus. 2020. Anne Carson talks of this service as akin to the self leaving the self and entering into poverty, as when one loves, which dares the self to leave itself. See Anne Carson *Decreation: Poetry, Essays, Opera*. London: Penguin. Decreation is taken from Simone de Beauviour who coined the neologism to describe the process of dismantling the self and to instead sustain one's presence through wonder (see Arendt on *thaumazein*).

Dorothy and her friends are also somewhat subdued. The organization they believed to be controlling things, the great strategist, was a sham, just like all the other forms of authority and regularity, from parents to witches. In the words of Salman Rushdie:

the truth is that, once we leave our childhood places and start to make up our lives, armed only with what we know and who we are, we come to understand that the real secret of the ruby slippers is not that 'there's no place like home' but, rather, that there is no longer any such place *as* home – except, of course, for the homes we make, or the homes that are made for us, in Oz. Which is anywhere – and everywhere – except the place from which we began.[73]

There is no place like home, organizationally we can only begin again, a second natality. There is a dusty, featureless place of emptiness where Dorothy once lived with a small dog, and called home, and which she wanted to leave, to protect the dog, but also just to leave, because she was bored in its endless repetition, even if she would get herself into trouble. When the regularity of receding horizons etched by the lines of bare fencing wire is blown asunder by a twisting tornado, it is a welcome rupture. Thrown from routine, Dorothy wakes to find herself skipping over patches of primary colour, in the company of: a hollow machine man whose maker failed to get round to providing any innards; a threadbare lion animal whose woolly effusiveness doubles as cushioning against those who accuse him of having no courage; and a scarecrow whose head and limbs are stuffed with dry plant matter. They find companionship in their mutual deficit, and ultimately in their refusal to become something complete and present, in their eschewal of fixed identity, though they spend much of the film on the hunt for such fixes and fixities. Under the alien impress of Dorothy's gusto – with some effort Dorothy can be thought of as force of *Hervorbringen*, an unwitting and so abeyant efficient cause – the collective gradually come to what Rushdie calls one of the central messages of the film: there is a futility in looking outside oneself, when everything that one can become is within: the tin man can grieve despite having no heart, the scarecrow can think well enough with straw for brains, and, eventually, the lion finds force enough to confront a malevolent witch.[74]

Yet why this is so, why these three proto beings feel, become thoughtful, and are resolute in deed, is because they find themselves in the organizational company of a profoundly disturbing *daimon*, a being from elsewhere, a child, who affords them the two-in-one space to revisit and

---

[73] Salman Rushdie *The Wizard of Oz*. London: BFI Books. 1992, 58. See also Salman Rushdie Out of Kansas, *New Yorker*, 11 May 1992.
[74] Salman Rushdie Out of Kansas.

better consider their own selves, and who then, in her own organizational wandering, turns them outwards, towards the earth, the space that they cannot control, but through which they are being continually realized in relations of utter dependency. And Dorothy too is being brought into a two-in-one realization that the home for which she ached was not a well administered *oikos* back in dusty Kansas, or indeed anywhere, but was a place that can only ever be encountered through an insertion, a mark making, whose incursion will never fit without leaving an uneasy remainder, without her herself, as a thing, refusing to be organized: in the very act of occupation there was also an act of leaving, along some road or other, clutching a bag of opinions.

The possibility of thinking oneself outside the home through continual organizational incisions into it means encountering what Adorno called non-identity through whose poverty the self becomes a scene of strategic possibility, for there is nothing inward to which the self accedes by way of a self-realizing warrant, and nothing toward which it organizes itself (or is organized by) by way of a destiny and life-transgressing values. To look inwards for a core subject, or outwards for structure, or to look to the past as an origin, or towards the future in vision or hopeful idealism, is to invoke and rely on claims of objectivity, meaning life is to be lived by other means than itself: organized by an idea, by instrumental ordering, or by the assertions of one will above others. In poverty there is only the attempt to live, and live anew, to begin and begin again. In its singularity, the self leaves the home, beyond the *oikos*, holding itself in abeyance to, and respect for, non-identity, including its own refusal to 'be' something. It is as if one willingly places the welcome mat on the other side of the threshold, there to greet you on stepping out into the open, into the organizational space of appearances, of continually beginning again, a space into which machinery cannot push. Machinery works by representing things into knowable units – '1s' and '0s', 'ons' and 'offs' – whereby anything that 'is' is so in relation to its being set against something else, each challenging the other to come forth and be named. Adorno lamented how, as this stepping forth in presence spreads and tightens, the world is stripped of mystery, of fate, of chance, leaving all things exposed as beings that are made fully present, predictable, known objects, including the biological unit known as a human being. In the epoch of technogenesis this despotic demand to be present becomes all encompassing, and yet in the very same moment, however, it has become its own mystery. Despite the micro-attentiveness of ever more solicitous search engines, smart cities, government surveillance systems and social media platforms, there is, amid this overwhelming machination, the possibility for a form of transcendence as naïve as that which Dorothy and her friends experienced when Toto drew back the curtain to reveal the machine order that ruled Oz. To confront not the wizard, but the diminutive ex-carnival worker, is to encounter a residue of Being that has not been subject to the urge to practically master and capture the world. Oz, like all modern strategists against whom critics rail, is part of the machinery: they are as utterly present as those over which they 'exercise' control. Release only comes with the restoration of mystery: the release Oz feels when thinking about the prospects of taking off in his hot air balloon and drifting, the release the tin man, scarecrow and lion feel when they no longer feel confined by the categories to which they have been assigned, and the release Dorothy and Toto feel when they understand that it is they who are to make their own home as they go along and which is a home that is not, and cannot be named and administered, only affirmed in becoming something distinct that has, hitherto, been unthought.

Index

Printed in the United States
by Baker & Taylor Publisher Services